BATTLES OF CONSCIENCE

Battles of Conscience

British Pacifists and
the Second World War

TOBIAS KELLY

Chatto & Windus
LONDON

1 3 5 7 9 10 8 6 4 2

Chatto & Windus, an imprint of Vintage, is part of the Penguin Random House group of companies whose addresses can be found at global.penguinrandomhouse.com

Copyright © Tobias Kelly 2022

Tobias Kelly has asserted his right to be identified as the author of this Work in accordance with the Copyright, Designs and Patents Act 1988

First published by Chatto & Windus in 2022

penguin.co.uk/vintage

A CIP catalogue record for this book is available from the British Library

ISBN 9781784743949

Extract on p. 250 from 'Bizerta' by George Campbell Hay, published in *Collected Poems and Songs of George Campbell Hay* (ed. Michel Byrne) by Edinburgh University Press. Reproduced with permission of the Licensor through PLSclear.

Typeset in 11/14pt Sabon LT Std by Jouve (UK), Milton Keynes
Printed and bound in Great Britain by Clays Ltd, Elcograf S.p.A.

The authorised representative in the EEA is Penguin Random House Ireland, Morrison Chambers, 32 Nassau Street, Dublin D02 YH68

Penguin Random House is committed to a sustainable future for our business, our readers and our planet. This book is made from Forest Stewardship Council® certified paper.

To Faye, Matilda and Sol

only good people are ever bothered by a bad conscience . . .

Hannah Arendt, 1971

Contents

INTRODUCTION

Just after dawn on a hot day in August 1944, Roy Ridgway waited in the hold of a ship that had carried him across the Mediterranean. As the vessel lay off the town of Fréjus on the southern coast of France – halfway between St Tropez and Cannes – Roy listened to the rhythm of the waves and rumble of explosions in the distance. For the past week more than 100,000 mainly French and American troops – backed by over 3,000 planes – had poured over the beaches up and down the Riviera, forcing the German military into retreat, as Operation Dragoon opened up a new front in south-western Europe. But the Germans were well dug in around Fréjus and their coastal guns were firing salvo after salvo, as the Allies called in their B24 bombers. Roy was part of a mobile medical unit attached to the First French Army, but as the Allied troops battled their way inland his supply truck was stuck deep inside the ship, and he was forced to stay on board as the temperature rose, anticipating incoming fire at any moment. He was one of the last men to reach French soil that day, eventually driving on to the sand with the smell of smoke and diesel hanging in the sea breeze.[1]

Over the following weeks, Roy and his ambulance unit made their way north through the Rhône valley and onwards into newly liberated France, greeted with smiling faces and glasses of wine nearly everywhere they stopped.[2] There was much to celebrate as the end of the war was in sight. It would be no simple victory march though, and there would still be several more months of fighting to come. A shortage of food in the villages meant the newly arrived troops often felt compelled to give away their supplies to hungry people.[3] In the medieval town of Dijon, near where the Wehrmacht had recently attempted to draw a defensive line, Roy was taken to a hospital morgue where a Frenchman proudly showed him six dead Germans, declaring 'I killed them myself, and tonight I am going to kill a woman who was a collaborator.'⁴ The bitter remnants of war were everywhere. For the next six months, Roy moved around France, as the last German pockets were captured or flushed out. The young man's uniform became a ragbag of bits and pieces picked up along the way: a German belt, an American jacket and British trousers, making it hard for other people to place him. What they would almost certainly not have guessed was that Roy Ridgway had started the war as a pacifist and conscientious objector.

How had this twenty-seven-year-old former clerk from Liverpool ended up working alongside the French army in the liberation of Europe? The answer is a story of deep convictions and doubts, taking us through love affairs, family arguments and time in prison, as well as fighting in Syria, Italy and France.

Battles of Conscience is the story of Roy and the other 60,000 British citizens who refused to take up arms during the Second World War. From 1939 to 1945, the people of Britain were mobilised to fight on a scale not seen before or since, as young and old, male and female, rich and poor, were expected to make sacrifices for God, King and country, as well as for friends, family and neighbours – if not for wider humanity. Alongside the millions in the armed forces, everything from mining to market gardening was organised around the needs of the war effort, as the nation faced up to the Nazi threat. But tens of thousands of people declined the call – influenced by a deep religious faith, hopes for socialist revolution or an intense objection to suffering. Although often profoundly opposed to Fascism and other forms of totalitarianism, they were convinced that force could never be the answer to violence. Some were unwilling to make any compromise and spent months behind bars, firm in their absolute convictions. Many more worked as farmers and foresters on the home front, or as ambulance crew and in bomb-disposal units near the front lines, as they tried to help others but stopped short of carrying guns. They could be found across the world: volunteering for medical experiments in Britain, driving supplies across the mountains in China, tending to the wounded in the Middle East or among the soldiers in the liberation of France. Although opposed to war, they went everywhere that battles were fought.

Popular memory seems to find it hard to place the people who

2

refused to fight in the 'good war' against Fascism, a war seen as not only just but necessary.[5] In contrast, the anti-war activists of the First World War occupy a significant position in public consciousness – often, if sometimes controversially, seen as brave individuals who opposed a needless, wasteful and cruel conflict.[6] Even for those who think that there were good reasons to start the First World War, the tragic gulf between the enthusiasm with which war was declared and the brutality that followed has ensured that the people who argued that the cost in blood was not worth it have been shown a grudging respect.[7] In contrast, although there were more than three times as many of them, those who refused to fight in Second World War Britain have largely slipped from view, condemned to being dismissed, ignored or misunderstood.

From the perspective of the twenty-first century, what might we make of these men and women? Even at the time they were hard to place. They were certainly stigmatised, ridiculed and harassed, condemned from the houses of parliament, church pulpits, parade grounds and saloon bars. Yet at the same time they were shown a grudging tolerance, if not respect. Figures from Winston Churchill to the Archbishop of Canterbury went on record supporting their rights, occasionally going so far as to suggest that the war was worth fighting only so long as conscience was protected.[8] If the Second World War was a war for freedom, conscience was an important part of the mix, and defending such freedoms seemed to stand in stark contrast to the totalitarian violence of Nazism.

Freedom of conscience is often seen as a key tenet of liberal democracies, something to be cherished and protected. Most of us also probably like to think that we have a conscience, that it helps us to tell right from wrong and that it acts as a force for good in the world. For centuries, poets, philosophers, politicians and many others have turned to conscience in moments of extreme crisis.[9] The heroes of our time are often men and women who stand by their convictions in the most difficult circumstances, turn from the path of least resistance or self-interest and refuse to buckle in the face of extraordinary pressure. We may disagree on who deserves a place in this pantheon of saints, but few would deny that conscience is a foundational – if fragile – source of moral guidance, going right to the heart of what it means to be human.

The meanings and virtue of conscience are not self-evident,

though.[10] Ideas about conscience have a diverse history; it has been thought to be located in the heart, the head, the soul or even the stomach. It has been understood as defining what makes us human or as politically and morally irrelevant. Its sources have ranged from a divine gift from God to a deeply personal intuition, to a form of public reason. The look, shape and significance of conscience have been as varied as the people who have laid claim to it. So how do we know when conscience is talking and why should we listen to it? What if it is misguided or mistaken? Even its staunchest advocates have worried that it can be a form of self-importance and vanity, hiding more base instincts. We do not need to look far to see that some very bad things have been done in the name of conscience, and demanding that conscience be respected can take us into uncomfortable places. All sorts of terrible people have claimed to act out of conscience and some very guilty men and women have said that their consciences are clear.[11]

It is in the middle of this conflicted history that we can find the people who refused to fight. Were the conscientious objectors of the Second World War principled or self-absorbed, brave or naive, or something else entirely? On the one hand, these were people who stood up for what they believed in, often at great personal cost, committed to principles that many people still find immensely attractive, such as peace and freedom. On the other, these very same people also refused to take up arms against the Nazis, while millions of others sacrificed almost everything at a time of national emergency, and millions more were being slaughtered around the world.

Responses to those who refused to fight in the Second World War are inevitably very personal. Although not a pacifist, I have always had a strong, if amorphous, sense that war, in almost all cases, is deeply wrong. Some of my own earliest memories are going on Babies Against the Bomb marches in a pushchair in the early 1980s. Decades later, I also marched against the Second Gulf War, standing on the Embankment with two million others, declaring the coming battles were not in our name. My mother's cousin, a Baptist minister who blessed my marriage, was also a conscientious objector in the 1950s in the last years of National Service. At the same time, like many people, I also have relatives who fought – and were injured – in war; one grandfather was a doctor on board

4

the ships of the Malta and Archangel Convoys in the early 1940s, and much more recently my brother-in-law and his wife did tours in Afghanistan and Iraq with the British army. Like many, I have also always thought of Fascism as being as close to evil as it is possible to be. To put it mildly, the objectors of the Second World War troubled my own conscience.

This book started life as an attempt to understand what we might make of the British people who refused to fight in 1939–45. I am trained as a social anthropologist rather than a historian, although the difference between the two disciplines can be overplayed, and I spend a large part of my professional life rummaging around in archives. The past, as the cliché suggests, can be another country. As an anthropologist, like many historians, I leave it to philosophers, theologians, psychologists to think about whether conscience is a universal attribute of all humans, or to establish how we might define it in an absolute sense.[12] And as an anthropologist, like many historians, one of the particular things I am taught to do is take other people's claims seriously, even if I find them uncomfortable. My training pushes me to try and understand what conscience has meant in a particular time and place.

At the same time, a central part of much anthropology is the attempt to make the apparently strange seem familiar and the familiar seem strange. This can have two linked implications. The first is that while it is important to understand how conscientious objection 'made sense', we should not lose track of how extra-ordinary it was, both to those who invoked it and to observers looking in from the side. The second is that in making the familiar strange, we can confront our own assumptions. This is not a form of relativism, but a type of moral and cultural reflection that is based in the things that people say, feel and do.

The lives, dilemmas and choices of conscientious objectors raise questions about the things for which we might fight, the sacrifices we might make and the conditions under which we would do so, getting to the heart of the tensions of war and many other things besides. This book then is a story about the moral obligations we owe ourselves and each other in times of need. In doing so, *Battles of Conscience* asks the reader to think about whether, and in what ways, the convictions and disappointments of the people described in this book resonate, to ponder how they might diverge from the

5

reader's own and to ask what we learn from the lives of people who confronted the most difficult questions of life and death, even, or especially, if we disagree with them.

In the pages that follow there are no simple heroes or villains, nor are there straightforward tales of redemption or dishonour. There are, however, many acts of both bravery and cowardice, hope and despair, often in places where you might not expect them. In describing the struggles of people opposed to violence in a world at war, this book can also be read as a story about the tensions between pessimism and optimism, between accepting a measure of violence as a tragic part of the human condition and the conviction that things might be otherwise. In other words, it is a story about the moral imagination, about the relationship between necessity and possibility, and the difficult space in between. But if it is a morality tale, it is one that is complex and fraught, with no straightforward answers. And ultimately it is a story about the very limits of morality when confronted with the question of how we might live together in difficult times.

The following pages focus on five key people and those closest to them, but draw on dozens more, tracing the arc of their lives as they first tried to prevent war and then decided how to live in a world immersed in violence, walking a path through conflicting demands and personal ties. In doing so, *Battles of Conscience* seeks to understand how claims of conscience both shaped and disrupted their hopes, commitments and relationships. It picks up their lives in the middle of the 1930s, in a period when anxiety about battles to come and plans to stop them were widespread, and the relationships, feelings and ideas formed in this period would affect responses when war arrived. Conscience did not, despite seeming to on occasion, spring from nowhere. It was forged out of the personal, cultural and social raw material of the preceding decades. The Second World War did not mark a complete break in social, political and moral lives, but saw some important continuities too. The book then follows the threads laid down in those earlier years through the turmoil of the war, before asking how the resulting battles and bloodshed, refusals and rejections, influenced the objectors' later lives as they emerged from the struggle, transformed in ways they probably had not imagined possible.

Although they all objected to the war and fighting, *Battles of Conscience* is concerned with a diverse and varied group of people. It is about people who tried to help others by making sacrifices without holding weapons – people such as Roy Ridgway and also Tom Burns, a teacher from east London who volunteered for an ambulance unit and was patching up the wounded in the snows of Finland in early 1940 while most British soldiers were stuck in their barracks during what was known as the phoney war. It is also about people like Stella St John, who trained as a vet against the wishes of her parents, fell in with more than one radical priest and ended up in jail after she concluded that she could not see 'how you could be a Christian and not be a pacifist'.[13] It is the story of people whose horizons stretched far beyond the shores of Britain, people like Ronald Duncan, a former public school boy with a German father, who visited Gandhi in his Indian ashram, set up a collective farm on the coast of south-west England and was visited several times by the Special Branch under suspicion of subversion. And it is also the story of people like Fred Urquhart, a working-class Scottish socialist and writer with a growing literary reputation, who in the absence of a revolution hoped the war would leave him alone so he could see out the hostilities with a pen, not a gun, in hand.[14]

Along the way we shall encounter dozens of other characters who argued and fought, loved and cared for one another, as they faced up to the question of what people who are committed to peace should do when the world tips into war. These are young men like Michael Tippett, who moved from radical socialism to a mystical form of pacifism, and Benjamin Britten, who sailed to the US in 1939, deeply worried about what was happening to Europe, soon returned to England to register as a conscientious objector. Both men would go on to write some of the most startling music of the twentieth century. Some of the wider cast of characters were not conscientious objectors, being too old to be conscripted, but nevertheless played important parts in the social, cultural and political lives of those who refused to fight. These include John Middleton Murry, a literary critic and one-time revolutionary socialist who turned to Christianity and became a leading pacifist; Vera Brittain, the writer who lost the two people she loved most in the First World War and dedicated the rest of her life to exposing what she saw as the cruelty of battle; and Muriel Lester, who set up a commune in the East End of London and was detained in Trinidad while on a world tour campaigning for an end to the hostilities.

Conscience is always very personal, and there is no single story that can be told about such a self-consciously individual group of men and women; they certainly never thought of themselves as a group in any simple sense. They had strong and various forms of religious faith, socialist conviction and humanitarian sentiment, and often a mixture of all of these. But for all of them questions of conscience were never simply abstract issues of principle, philosophy or theology – although they could be that too – but are also deeply intimate. If conscience speaks to our most deeply held beliefs, it runs through our relationships too, and conscientious objectors did not just confront questions of personal conviction and principle, but had to grapple with the wishes and disappointments of those close to them as well.

Roy Ridgway, Ronald Duncan, Stella St John, Tom Burns, Fred Urquhart were all just on the brink of adulthood or making their ways in the world when war was declared, their lives stretching out before them with all the aspirations and confusions that can imply. When the whole country was mobilised, with war penetrating deep into people's most intimate lives, so too was the refusal to fight. Conscience was threaded through ties with mothers, fathers and siblings, as well as nation, class and religion. Roy Ridgway's family life was marked by blazing rows, as one brother joined the army on the eve of the war, and Roy was deeply worried about the effect his pacifism might have on his mother. Stella St John was estranged from her brother, while Fred Urquhart fell out with his father and his best friend over his refusal to take up the battle against Fascism. New relationships were also forged through pacifist convictions, Roy later recalling that the 'people I got to know during the war are friends for life'.[15] If what one ate, what one wore, where one worked and what one talked about was all part of the war effort, pacifism could never simply be reduced to a refusal to bear arms, but became a constant issue in everyday encounters, embedded in the ordinary as much as the profound. It is in responses to the obligations and misunderstandings produced by living alongside others that consciences and moral lives took shape.

Battles of Conscience tells the stories of conscientious objectors and those close to them through their own words. Fred Urquhart, once described as Scotland's 'greatest short-story writer', created prose full of his hatred of war.[16] Ronald Duncan wrote poems, plays and several memoirs about his war years and Tom Burns produced numerous poems and short stories. Others produced paintings, prose and music, putting an otherwise intangible set of beliefs into concrete form and leaving behind a rich artistic legacy. But it is in letters and diaries that we can see the often torn presence of conscience most clearly. Through the late 1930s and on most days during the war, Roy Ridgway recorded his thoughts, experiences, triumphs and failures, and throughout his years as an ambulance worker Tom Burns wrote to his close friend Cathy Bunting – a fellow teacher who was several years older than Tom – giving a detailed account of his hopes, fears and exasperations. Fred Urquhart and Stella St John kept similarly moving and personal journals.

This rich archive should, of course, be read with a critical eye. It favours the literary and articulate. Many things were still left unsaid or unwritten. And while letters and journals give us an insight into people's most intimate thoughts and relationships, they are always partial, idiosyncratic and one-sided. What is more, there are large holes in the record of individual lives, as people were too busy to write, mislaid their diaries or deliberately destroyed them, and as a result some of the characters in this story will fade in and out of view. Only the letters Tom Burns wrote after 1939 survive, for example. We are left to put together the details of what happened before from family memory and the few scraps of paper he left behind from this period, and this book therefore picks up the details of Tom's story later than those of the other four main characters. There are more systematic gaps in the archival record too, particularly in relation to women, and the traces left behind are either incomplete or partially erased. Finally, all memoirs and interviews produced after the war have to be read in the light of hindsight and shifting ideas about the war. Yet, having said all this, we should not interpret everything written by conscientious objectors as an attempt at camouflage or self-justification. There is much honesty and realism in these pages too. Although we can never get inside their heads, we can try to understand the diverse ways in which conscientious objectors debated with themselves and others, and in doing so gave meaning to their lives and sought to give their convictions a tangible shape.

*

As well as being about an intriguing and extra-ordinary, if sometimes difficult, group of people, this book is also about the history of Britain in the middle of the twentieth century. The story of the country in the Second World War is usually told through tales of bravery in battle or stoicism on the home front, as the British public stood together against apparently insurmountable odds.[17] The Second World War has a particular hold on the British public imagination, leaving powerful traces in memory, myth and metaphor, offering firm and simple moral lessons and standing as an example of both virtue and absolute vice. How though does the story look when seen through the eyes of people like Roy Ridgway and Stella St John? What does it do to the version of the war in which the country was all in it together, pulling in the same direction, making heroic sacrifices and standing up for freedom, when we focus on people who tried, in their own ways, to go against the flow? The answers to these questions reveal a country that had both more in common and more that held it apart than it sometimes liked to think.[18]

It is perhaps tempting to dismiss the conscientious objectors of the Second World War as a small, inconsequential and even cranky fringe group, who at their peak numbered less than 2 per cent of people being conscripted. But we should not mistake numerical size for significance. To do so ignores the wider cultural, moral and political importance of the conflicts that these seemingly marginal people went through. The ethical and social tensions of society are often played out most intensely through lives lived on the edges, and it is through such people that assumptions which are otherwise taken for granted are refracted and come to the surface. Although they were small in number, conscientious objectors tell us a great deal about the relationship between freedom and obligation, war and peace, conviction and faith in the middle of the twentieth century.

Crucially, pacifists had no monopoly on conscience and were not alone in hating war. Those who advocated the use of military force could be driven by conscience too, in the shape of their desire to defeat Fascism. They could also be deeply worried – for example, in the wake of the firestorms created by the carpet bombing of German cities – about whether the ends justified the means, and just where to draw the line in judging how much violence was acceptable to defeat the enemy. Soldiers can loathe battle as much as, if not more than, anyone else. What is more, being a conscientious objector did not necessarily make you a pacifist in the sense of being opposed to all wars in all times and places. It was possible to be a conscientious objector and oppose only some wars – those that are ungodly, capitalist, imperialist or simply unnecessary. There are just as many ways of opposing war as there are of living with a conscience. In some ways, this is the whole point: those who refused to take up arms, and those around them, had to grapple with the different things that conscience seemed to be telling them to do.

Britain has no monopoly on conscience – far from it. Across the globe, there are multiple culturally embedded ways of talking about conscience, drawing on diverse religious, moral and political traditions for inspiration, where conscience is seen as a matter of following the heart, scripture or clergy, or even as morally insignificant.[19] There are histories of conscience, conviction and pacifism that can be told about other places too. But claims of conscience have played out in very particular ways in British history and have been seen to have very specific implications and inflections, rooted in time and place. There is a long – if somewhat problematic – tradition of thinking that the rights of conscience are a uniquely important part of Britain's 'providential' role in the world, central to its particular traditions of liberty.[20] This is also a history in which dissenting Christianity has played an important, if often contested, role, where socialist commitments, although widespread, have never quite reached the revolutionary intensity of other parts of the world, but also where a public commitment to particular forms of freedom and toleration have been central.

There are different ways to tell the cultural and political history of conscience in Britain, but most accounts go through the bitter conflicts that marked the Reformation and Counter-Reformation of the sixteenth and seventeenth centuries.[21] In this period the idea that conscience lies somewhere within the individual and is a source of deep and very personal moral guidance came to prominence. This differed from other ways of talking about conscience that, for example, looked to the Bible or the commands of the church for guidance. The post-Reformation conscience was asked to do a great deal of work: to hold the moral and political world together and provide the foundation of a tolerant political order.[22] Without people following their conscience, so the argument went, tyranny, and perhaps even evil, would take hold. This form of conscience did not stand still in terms of the way it was understood. At the start of the Reformation, to talk of conscience was to rebel and disrupt, to challenge the state and the church hierarchy. It was anarchic, unruly and disruptive. In the decades and centuries that followed, conscience was often tamed, walking within an ever narrower and more respectable path.[23] As the institutions of state, church, law and parliament began to speak in the name of conscience, it lost at least some of its radical edge. This would have important implications in the years to come.

If freedom of conscience is part of the British self-image as a nation that values freedom, this has not always been straightforward. When the point of respecting freedom of conscience is that it allows space for people to believe things we do not agree with, it can also give them space to do things we find uncomfortable or unacceptable. In practice, there have been difficult questions about where we draw the line, and just how much freedom we give to conscience.

Culturally, the intense convictions of conscience have seldom stood easily alongside a self-consciously British sense of decorum, as public life has been marked by a detached irony, where, until recently, deep commitments are mistrusted and downplayed in favour of steady practical judgements. This is a context in which, as one writer has memorably described it, 'people are expected to be painfully self-conscious, clammy in their own skin, and alert to their own folly and deceptions, lest they be spotted first by others'.[24] If conscience is seen as a particularly British virtue, appearing to act conscientiously also risks appearing too fervent, too committed and somehow unBritish. The expressions of conscience from people like Tom Burns, Fred Urquhart and Stella St John therefore had peculiarly British tones, often painfully restrained, tempered and controlled, playing out on a muted scale, but also deeply principled and committed.

The limits of freedom – conscientious or otherwise – were, and continue to be, political as much as cultural, and not all claims to liberty and not all claims to conscience have been listened to with the same care and attention. The Second World War, after all, was being waged in the name of freedom, but large parts of the world still remained under British colonial control. British freedom had its limits at home too, in a manner that would shape the lives of many conscientious objectors: homosexuality was illegal, gender inequality was entrenched and class remained a determining factor in many people's lives. This would make a real difference to the ways in which conscience was treated and acknowledged. In short, not all consciences were created equal.

While the tale of conscientious objectors told in this book might also be a story about Britain, it is also a story that cannot be constrained by national borders, as conscientious objectors drew on ideas and relationships from around the world. In Japan and Germany there was deep, if often fragile, political and religious resistance to militarism.[25] In the US and Scandinavia, there were active Christian pacifist movements.[26] In many countries, socialists mobilised against capitalist and imperialist wars.[27] And the colonised people of the world struggled with the question of how to confront far more powerful foes without weapons. These ideals and movements, as well as the friendships that they helped to forge, stretched around the globe, inspiring and consoling those in Britain who opposed war. Ronald Duncan was not alone in his pilgrimage to visit Gandhi in India, hoping that non-violence could both defeat Fascism and show that peace was possible. Other conscientious objectors had bonds of solidarity that reached beyond their country, and Fred Urquhart felt deeply tied to the German and Soviet working class. In the first half of the twentieth century, relationships had formed through international organisations such as the Women's International League for Peace and Freedom, the International Fellowship of Reconciliation, and War Resisters' International, bringing together German, French, American, Chinese and Japanese activists.[28] For these people, if war was seen as a global phenomenon, with consequences that spread far and wide, so too were the solutions.

Battles of Conscience then is a particularly British war story of heroism, fortitude and sacrifice, and not a little patriotism, but one that is also full of tensions and differences, in which Britain is not simply an island nation, standing alone, but is caught up in currents swirling around the world. Although the country might have been standing up for freedom, this was freedom of a very particular type, where sacrifices were not equally distributed and the people were not all in it together in the same way.

*

Finally, this is not only a book about a particular set of people in a particular place. It is also a wider story about war and conviction. In moments of crisis people have asked what it means to fight both for other people and for your own beliefs. They have also questioned just how much violence can be condoned in the face of injustice, asking whether bloodshed is an inherent part of life and what forms of optimism, naivety or cynicism might lie in the way of a better future.

As I write this book, there are frequent claims that the first part of the twenty-first century has similarities to the tense atmosphere of the 1930s and the decade that followed, perhaps part of a British obsession with seeing every crisis through the lens of very particular myths about the Second World War. We need to be careful with analogies, as they can produce blind spots as much as insights, and the differences between the two periods are often just as striking as the similarities, but a violent undercurrent in political life, an escalating anxiety about what the future might hold and conflicts between individual freedom and mutual responsibility give, at the very least, pause for thought.

Looking back some eighty years on, conscientious objectors might appear naive or even utopian. There is an important sense in which they lost the argument: they failed to prevent the war, and it was military might rather than non-violence that defeated Fascism. But the period before and after the Second World War also saw large numbers of people, conscientious objectors among them, asking how they might live differently in the years to come. In a time when the normal way of doing things was up in the air, there was a strong sense of the possibility of radical change, for good and bad. Conscientious objectors, and others too, faced up to questions about the relationships between personal fears and the obligations that we owe to one another, the sacrifices we might make and the limits of violence in solving our problems. These are vitally important questions in the twenty-first century, as they were eight decades ago.

Just as the traces of the Second World War have continued to rumble through our social, cultural and political lives – the globe shaped by the divisions, solidarities and ideas that the war helped to forge – the significance of conscientious objectors likewise did not end in 1945, or even with the abolition of conscription over a decade later. For one thing, they left a rich legacy in prose, poetry and music, and their commitments continued to resonate for decades to come, even if in often indirect ways. Many of their convictions emerged intact from the ashes of the war, as bodies like the UN asked similar questions about preventing war, even if they came up with different answers. Conscientious objectors were not just part of a peace movement, they were also caught up in new struggles, taking the call of conscience with them as they went, and playing an important role in the growth of human rights and humanitarianism in the second half of the twentieth century.[29] They have therefore had deep, and perhaps disproportionate, cultural and moral impacts. As the traditions and principles they helped forge now appear to be fraying at the edges, or being taken in new, unpredictable directions, it becomes all the more important to ask what was at stake in their commitments, both personally and beyond. Conscientious objectors are interesting not because they offer easy answers, but precisely because they do not.

CHAPTER 1

War, Fear and Hope

On New Year's Eve 1936, Fred Urquhart, like many twenty-four-year-old Scots, celebrated late into the night. As the Hogmanay crowds filled the streets of Edinburgh's Old Town, Fred and his friends made their way from pub to pub, going out into the cold air only when the mixture of drink and overheated rooms became too much.[1] Swept up in the mood of the evening, Fred's companions tried to kiss as many girls as possible while avoiding getting into fights with the boyfriends. The atmosphere was one of boisterous celebration as people wished each other well for the coming year, but Fred had his eyes on someone in particular and ended the evening disappointed. He eventually made his way home, the worse for wear after all the drink, past the austere splendour of the Georgian New Town and on towards the northern suburb of tenements and cramped terraces where he lived with his parents, before collapsing into bed.

The mid-1930s was a period when many young men and women were thinking of making more of themselves, as the future seemed ripe with possibility. Fred's diaries are full of places he hoped to go to, the things he wanted to see and love affairs he dreamed of having. Edwardian attitudes to sex were slowly falling away, and popular culture was light-hearted. If – and this was a big if – you had a job and some money, there were more films to watch, more holidays to take, more objects to buy than ever before. Fred had been awarded a scholarship at school, but left at fifteen with few qualifications, and during the day worked filling envelopes for a bookshop. This was not where Fred wanted to spend the rest of his days. He was writing a novel and had aspirations to become a 'great and famous writer', escaping the family home near the shores of the

Firth of Forth. He had already had some success, and a number of fashionable periodicals had published his stories; although he was not yet making much money from his efforts, there were signs of promise. It was a considerable achievement for a working-class young man without connections. Fred was part of a generation that looked forward with what the novelist Elizabeth Bowen called 'candid expectancy', and there was considerable room for personal optimism.[2]

But for Fred, and for many other men and women, as 1936 turned into 1937 hopeful expectation was set against an increasingly gloomy atmosphere, as war seemed to be just beyond the horizon. When Fred looked to his future, violence hung in the background, threatening everything he hoped to achieve in life.[3] As the young man walked home that New Year's morning, the Spanish Civil War was about to enter its sixth month, a conflict that was seen as a struggle between dictatorship and democracy, revolution and counter-revolution, optimism and fear. In Africa, Italian forces had invaded Ethiopia in October 1935, using mustard gas in aerial bombardments and killing hundreds of thousands of soldiers and civilians. In March 1936 German troops had re-entered the Rhineland, in direct contravention of the treaty marking the end of the First World War. On the other side of the world, the Japanese military was entrenching its position in north-west China, preparing for a full invasion and the massacres that would mark the following year. The international order was falling apart, violence becoming the default mode of politics between nations. In the years to come, things would only get worse.

As the world seemed to be crumbling again, public culture was shot through with the residues of past wars and premonitions of battles to come. Although it had ended two decades before, physical reminders of the First World War were everywhere, in memorials, wounded veterans and absent fathers, as books, films and radio broadcasts laid bare the horrors of violence. Although there was much laughter and music, as political tensions heated up across the world a return to the carnage of battle seemed a real possibility. Just when Fred was starting to make his way in the world, the world was on the verge of exploding, and he noted in his diary his visions of being 'blown to bits' in the trenches.[4] In late 1930s Britain, as people went to work, fell in love or made plans for the future, the possibility of war was everywhere. Dreams about sex, happiness, money or fame could easily tip into nightmares about the violence to come, feeding into 'the nervous irritability' of the time.[5] Imagining the best and the worst that humanity could do to itself, and the particular mix of hope and anxiety – both personal and collective – would be of crucial importance to the forms of opposition to war that emerged through the decade.

Photos of the time show Fred with a thin face, sharply parted fair hair and a self-conscious smile. He lived by the sea with his mother and father in a house where residential streets gave way to small-scale industrial decay. It was a close-knit family and he visited his nearby grandparents almost every day.[6] The Urquharts were part of the 'respectable' working class, and Fred's father had been a chauffeur for a succession of wealthy Scots, including the Marquess of Breadalbane. Fred also had two younger brothers, and would be the best man at both of their weddings, although they barely feature in his diary. The novel Fred was working on in early 1937, which was eventually given the title *Time Will Knit*, tells the story of a working-class family living in a small Scottish fishing port, and was partly based on the experiences of Fred's own family.[7] It portrays a tightly bound, if poor, community, not without its warmth, but also marked by conflicts and petty rivalries.

Fred's relationship with his father was a tense one, with Fred feeling that he was not taken seriously. His father teased him that he would never make money out of writing, and family rows would come and go – often over nothing particularly significant, but ending several times with his father threatening to throw Fred out of the house.[8] When Fred returned drunk one night, father and son had an especially ferocious argument, Fred writing that 'ever since I can remember he has always picked on me. I guess he does not like me . . . I wouldn't be broken hearted if I never saw him again.'[9] He was being dramatic, partly perhaps as a result of nursing a hangover, but the words nevertheless expressed the underlying tensions. Despite these conflicts, his parents were proud of their son's achievements, even if they did not always know what to make of them. When Fred received an offer for the novel – complete with an advance of £25 – Mum, Dad and the siblings were excited about how he might spend the money. His grandparents greeted the news by asking him not to put any swearing into his writing.[10]

Fred's cultural horizons spread far, and he was deeply immersed in the books, plays and films of the era. He was a particularly avid theatre- and cinemagoer, some weeks sitting almost every night in the cheap seats at King's Theatre in Edinburgh or at the Royal Lyceum a few streets away. His diary contains lengthy lists of everything he read that year, with a focus on Scottish classics and political tracts, which he pored over during long afternoons in the late-Victorian splendour of Edinburgh Central Library. Fred read so much that it is hard to imagine how he found time to write, but his first story had been published in 1936 by the *Adelphi*, a literary magazine edited by the critic and sometime pacifist John Middleton Murry which featured regular reviews by George Orwell, as well as short stories by D. H. Lawrence and Dylan Thomas. Fred's own writing was not a quick path to riches, and to earn a living he worked in various jobs, including the bookshop and a stint in the General Post Office in the centre of town – where he took great pride in his ability to throw parcels long distances. He hated the work, feeling it destroyed his creativity.[11]

There was still time for fun, alongside all the writing, reading and work. Although Fred could sometimes be awkward, he had lots of friends and enjoyed drinking with them. What only a few of his closest friends knew at the time was that he was gay and desperate to fall in love.[12] Outwardly conservative and Presbyterian, Edinburgh was not without its potential for romance, as long as Fred could get over his bashfulness. The writer, poet and translator Edwin Muir, who later became a friend, described the city's crowded street life in the inter-war years as 'filled with unsatisfied desire'.[13] Fred wrote in his diary how, on walking down a suburban street on an autumnal day, he passed a man in a green tie, and for a moment the two men looked at each other and smiled, before looking away. That evening, Fred chastised himself: 'I shouldn't be afraid. I should tell myself that six rebuffs would be worth it if I succeed in finding what I like for the seventh time. I must not look away.'[14] Fred was drawn to a line in *White-Maa's Saga*, a novel by fellow Edinburgh writer Eric Linklater: 'Mentally I am free thinking, promiscuous, free loving, but physically I am a Victorian.'[15] Later, after another failed sexual encounter, Fred asked himself, 'Why the hell am I so afraid to embark on adventure?'[16] This was not the last time Fred would chastise himself for his lack of bravery.

It was more than a brief encounter that Fred was after.[17] He had strong, unrequited feelings for his friend Willie, but their busy social lives meant that they never seemed to be alone.[18] When Willie left Edinburgh, not telling anyone where he was going or what he planned to do, and the two young men lost contact, Fred began to wonder if he would ever be able to find love in Scotland and thought of moving south. There are large gaps in the diary during this period, as several pages are crudely torn out. Sixty years later, Fred added a short note, explaining that the missing leaves described his 'homosexual activities', and he had been scared the details might have been read by the police at a time when homosexuality was illegal and criminal prosecutions were increasing. Fear of the forces of British law and order would be another theme in the years to come.

Although worried about the law, Fred was also determined not to be ashamed of his desires, chafing at public hypocrisy.[19] After reading the prison memoir of a British Communist jailed for espionage, he wrote: 'it says quite a lot of hard things about a country whose harsh anti-sexual laws make homosexuality a penal crime outside prison, but winks at homosexuality in prison'.[20] According to Fred, such attitudes could have severe social consequences, and he speculated that Fascism was the result of repressed sexuality, writing that the Nazi regime was full of 'narcissists' and 'masochists'.[21]

For all the setbacks, the close but claustrophobic family, the unfulfilled desires and the anger at public double standards, it was war that most worried Fred. Indeed, it was hard to separate out a fear of war from his concerns about love or literature, as a new conflict threatened to put it all at risk. Fred's stories acquired a distinct antimilitarist theme, and *Time Will Knit* contains several characters who refuse to take up arms to fight 'oppressed people' in the South African and First World Wars, as well as a grieving mother who wishes that 'the men who started the war' were 'burning in hellfire'.[22] For a short time, desperate for work, Fred had managed to get a job in the NAAFI, the organisation that provided canteens for soldiers on their downtime, and drew on this experience in his writing. He was posted to Fort George, a stone fortress jutting out into the waters of the Moray Firth in north-east Scotland and worked in the shop, restaurant and bar. This was the first time the young man had encountered military life up close, and it was not a happy experience. Surrounded by rough and ready soldiers, he quickly learned to keep quiet, sensing that this was not the place to express his opinions, and he recorded in his diary that he was 'keeping my mouth shut and my eyes open'.[23] Shortly afterwards he wrote a story that described the life of a soldier increasingly alienated from the army. It ends with the lines 'I eat, sleep and drill. I'm a soldier – but am I a man?' For Fred, military life was profoundly dehumanising.

Wider public culture provided ample scope for reflection on the horrors of military life and its consequences. If late twentieth-century Britain looked to the Second World War for many of its moral lessons, in the 1930s it was the First World War that set the ethical scene. Over much of the previous decade, books, radio and films had been full of talk of the battlefield and its tragedies. The British public were at this time the most avid cinemagoers in the world, and going to see a film was a central part of the social life of many young people.[24] In the new grand film houses being built around the country, young men and women were watching dramas that helped stir their imaginations. More often than not these films were romances or adventures, but sometimes they also contained a message about war and peace. Fred watched many films in the art deco splendour of the Ritz cinema, on the edge of Edinburgh's New Town, but one film in particular stands out in his diaries, and he went to see it at least twice. *The Spanish Earth*, written by Ernest Hemingway and narrated by Orson Welles, was a propaganda piece for the Spanish Republicans, showing armed loyalists driving off the Fascists from a village in southern Spain. But it was not politics in the sense of nations and parties that Fred took away from the film. What struck him most was how ready people were to kill one another, and the casual way they developed skills in 'blowing people to bits'.[25] He came away thinking that humans could turn to bloodshed far too easily.

Even more than films, books shaped the way in which Fred imagined the world, and he was immersed in anti-war literature. In the late 1920s and early 1930s there was first a stream and then a flood of writing on the misery of the First World War. It had taken more than a decade for it to become possible for the full terror of the battles of 1914–18 to enter into public consciousness, but when it did, it did so with a vengeance. As the literary critic Valentine Cunningham has argued, the literature of the early 1930s was obsessed with 'violence – its images, its tone, its horrors, its pleasures'.[26] It sometimes seemed as if all that serious people could write about was war. Robert Graves's *Goodbye to All That* came out in 1929, the English translation of Erich Maria Remarque's *All Quiet on the Western Front* appeared in the same year, Siegfried Sassoon's memoirs in the early 1930s and Vera Brittain's *Testament of Youth* in 1933. Brittain's memoir in particular was both an impassioned howl of grief for the loss of so many people she had loved – her brother, her fiancé and many of their friends – and a careful argument about the waste, indignity and burdens of war, combining feminism, internationalism and a broad left-wing politics with a semblance of Christian faith in a powerful condemnation of the needless slaughter of the young. The book, which described the heartache of those left behind and the agony of what she saw when she volunteered as a nurse and cared for wounded German prisoners, was a bestseller on both sides of the Atlantic.

Anti-war sentiment was widespread in British political and cultural life through the 1930s, bringing together people from across the political spectrum and social classes. When the Oxford Union in 1933 famously passed the motion that 'This House will under no circumstances fight for its King and country' it was controversial precisely because it seemed to reflect wider currents.[27] However, while Brittain's, Sassoon's and Graves's books brought to life the destruction on the battlefield, they were not necessarily pacifist texts. It was possible to read them, be saddened by the great suffering depicted in them and still, perhaps, think that there was something noble in the loss. There was even a little pleasure to be had in stories of battle.[28] Although war was much feared through the early and mid-1930s, the lessons that people took from past violence were far from self-evident. The literary historian Paul Fussell argued that after the Somme it was no longer possible to take the honour of war for granted.[29] But the sense that the First World War had resulted in immense suffering did not necessarily lead to absolute anti-war attitudes.[30] It was relatively easy to tell people of the horrors of violence, but quite another thing to persuade them that war did no good and had no glory. Fred, though, was already convinced, and chafed at any suggestion that there was honour in battle.

Away from books and films, the physical landscape of Britain was full of monuments to the 'glorious dead' of war, and Fred railed against what he saw as their hypocrisy, describing war memorials as 'lumps of granite and stone in place of the millions of men and ladies who had been killed for something they knew nothing about'.[31] On the day he put the finishing touches to his novel, 11 November 1937, Armistice Day, a nervous-looking King George VI stood to attention before the Cenotaph in central London. As the assembled crowds marked the two-minute silence, a man tried to break through, heading for the monarch and angrily shouting, 'Hypocrisy . . . you are deliberately preparing for war,' before being wrestled to the ground and carried away. It was an uncomfortable interruption, and a reminder that the traumatic aftermath of war was still very present among the living. Press reports later named the protester as Stanley Storey, a middle-aged veteran of the First World War who had escaped from a private psychiatric hospital. The Cenotaph had been built seventeen years before, and every year thereafter the great and the good had come to pay their respect to the 'glorious dead'. But glory was not the first word that came to everyone's lips when they saw the monument.[32] Fred thought that Storey was 'by no means so mad'.[33] As he finished his book, he must have felt a mixture of personal satisfaction and deep concern at the state of the world into which he hoped to send his work.

A stone's throw from where Fred lived, there was another memorial to the dead. This monument was somewhat different, marking the death of hundreds of soldiers, nearly all from Edinburgh, who had never made it into battle. On 22 May 1915, over 400 volunteers of the 1/7th (Leith) Battalion of the Royal Scots boarded a train heading south to Liverpool, bound ultimately for Gallipoli, but on reaching the English border, disaster struck. The train carrying the troops collided with a stationary locomotive, and minutes later a sleeper train heading north ploughed into the wreckage. A gas leak caused a fireball to rage through the splintered carriages. The bodies were so badly burned that many could not be separated from the charred remains of the train, and a precise death toll was never established. Many years later, a veteran of the Royal Scots would claim that some of the trapped men had been shot in an act of mercy.[34] The dead soldiers were buried in a mass grave, their coffins laid three deep. The public were not allowed to attend the funeral.

You did not have to look to official war memorials for reminders of war. Fred had been born two years before the start of hostilities, and virtually every street in the part of Edinburgh where he lived had lost someone in Flanders, northern France or the Leith Battalion train disaster. By the mid-1930s, the losses of war were still all too visible, not least in those who were injured. From 1914 to 1918, three-quarters of a million British subjects had been killed and more than one and a half million seriously wounded, and families and childhoods were forever defined by absent fathers, brothers and uncles.[35] Nearly every family had a gaping hole left by a loved one who had been killed or remained missing. In 1918 there were 750,000 permanently disabled soldiers in Britain; twenty years later 1.6 million men were in receipt of a war pension.[36] Widowed wives and mothers also had to find new ways of earning a living and supporting their families. Old soldiers were a common sight on the streets of Edinburgh and of most towns and cities across Britain, and their misery could offer a sharp rebuke. As one writer put it, there were 'ex-servicemen at every street corner, turning the handles of automatic pianos, blowing hard into trombones, and eliciting a scraping whine from one-stringed fiddles, reproaching the social order with arrays of old medals and the cards – Disabled, no pension, three children.'[37] The legacies of war were hard to ignore.

To make matters worse, by the 1930s people feared that any resumption of hostilities would dwarf the violence of the last war. New technology had taken the art of killing to new levels. With the use of aircraft in particular, it was possible to kill on a scale never seen before.[38] As in the nuclear age that followed, the belief grew that both soldiers and civilians were defenceless against new and ever more powerful weapons. Since the first Zeppelin raids on British cities in 1915, the Royal Flying Corps (and later the Royal Air Force) had used aircraft to deadly effect in putting down anti-colonial rebellions in the Middle East, Africa and south Asia. In 1932, Stanley Baldwin, the leader of the Conservative Party, had told the House of Commons that 'the bomber will always get through . . . The only defence is in offence, which means that you have to kill more women and children more quickly than the enemy if you want to save yourselves.'[39] This new way of war was terrifying. Beverley Nichols, one of Fred's favourite authors at the time, produced a short book, *Cry Havoc!*, that described the ways in which another war 'might destroy all life, human and animal, over a large surface of the globe'.[40] Vera Brittain similarly wrote of a future London destroyed by mass bombing, with gas seeping into homes and panic-stricken hordes filling the streets.[41]

Fred Urquhart's response was to imagine that in the coming battles 'those who don't get killed by bomb or gas will find when the war ends that they are slaves under an absolute Fascist dictatorship . . . in a way the picture of the future seems so terrible that one would perhaps be better to be killed'.[42] For Fred it was almost too much to bear that, twenty years after the so-called 'war to end all wars', another war looked inevitable. He felt the world had 'gone mad'.[43] As he often did, he turned to literature to try and work through how he felt, noting down the well-known lines from W. B Yeats: 'Things fall apart; the centre cannot hold: / Mere anarchy is loosed upon the world, / The blood-dimmed tide is loosed, and everywhere, / The Ceremony of innocence is drowned . . .' Yeats's allegorical poem of the apocalypse spoke directly to the young Scot. He wrote in his diary, 'I hate war, but like everyone else I see it coming and can do nothing about it.'[44]

Fred was not alone in his despair. There was a widespread sense that war was inevitable. And this sense of inevitability was rooted in a resignation about the condition of fallen humanity, which seemed to contain within itself the seeds of its own destruction. John Middleton Murry, who had published some of Fred's stories, wrote that the 'catastrophe of humanity which so many . . . have dreaded and struggled to prevent has overtaken us . . . the struggle will involve so vast a degradation of mankind as may be irrecoverable . . . whoever wins will lose'.[45] Middleton Murry went on to warn that war risked the 'invasion of men's souls by moral savagery'.[46] As W. H. Auden, perhaps the most influential poet of the 1930s – both politically and stylistically – and another favourite of Fred's, wrote in his poem 'Herman Melville' at the end of the decade: 'Evil is unspectacular and always human, / And shares our bed and eats at our own table . . .' For an increasing number of people, violence seemed to be a depressing and irredeemable part of the human condition.

Historians have debated the extent to which pessimism marked the years between the world wars. For Richard Overy this was a 'morbid age' full of anxiety about the future.[47] For others, the pessimists of the 1930s were largely marginal intellectuals – people like Fred perhaps – whose predilections did not match the general light-hearted mood of the times.[48] It is certainly true that the 1920s and 1930s saw a boom in the joys of leisure and consumption, shot through with a sense not only of fun, but also of optimism – that a better life was possible. Elements of such hope run through Fred's diaries, as he enjoys the cinema, goes drinking and falls in and out of love. But the distinction between pessimism and hope, fear and optimism can be overdrawn. For young men like Fred, war was feared not so much despite the general sense of fun and optimism about a life well lived, but precisely because of it. It was because life was full of potential, of experiences yet to come and aspirations to be fulfilled, that war seemed so ominous, putting at risk everyone and everything of value.

We can look at this the other way around too: hope always contains the knowledge that we might be disappointed and is always tinged with uncertainty. It was in this particular mixture of hope and anxiety that pacifism flourished. As the historian Martin Ceadel has argued, pacifism combined a pessimism about war and an optimism about human progress.[49] This expressed the conviction that war is terrible, but that it can be overcome and, equally importantly, that it is worth overcoming. Indeed, the more overwhelming the foretaste of war, the stronger the belief that people should and could live a life at peace. Amid the despair, this was also a time of great enthusiasms rather cynicism; there was a feeling that life did not have to be this way. Although Fred thought he could see war coming, along with thousands of others he clung to the belief that war was not an inherent part of the wider human condition, and that it could, just maybe, still be avoided this time around. It is to these sources of hope that the book will now turn, as personal dreams for the future were harnessed to visions of more collective redemption.

CHAPTER 2

Pledging Peace

Down in London, Roy Ridgway had spent the last evening of 1936 watching the crowds in Piccadilly Circus.[1] Earlier that night he had attended a service at St Martin-in-the-Fields on the edge of Trafalgar Square, before meeting up with his brother to join in the more secular festivities. People were wearing paper hats and waving balloons as they danced and sang into the night, though Roy was slightly too shy to throw himself fully into the mix. As a boy in Liverpool he had run a small magazine and after leaving school had moved to London, drawn by hopes of a job in Fleet Street. Soon he was living off a diet of cigarettes, fried eggs and toast as he tried hard to be a vegetarian. The capital was new and exciting, if a little intimidating, and Roy's first New Year in London must have seemed full of promise. He too, though, was haunted by the fear of war, later writing in his diary that the battles to come 'might bring the end of civilization'.[2] But he thought he had found a solution to violence and conflict: a simple act of individual refusal. If enough people stood out and said no, war would simply be impossible. First, he would have to overcome his nerves.

Roy Ridgway was a serious young man with literary ambitions, one of four children born into a lower-middle-class family. Determined, thoughtful and principled, he was also conventional and self-conscious. He would later remember his childhood as a happy time, with chickens in the back garden and toy soldiers to play with in the house. His father kept a *Times* history of the war, and the schoolboy Roy used to pore over its 'pictures of generals on horses, maps, ruined buildings'.[3] Images of war and its aftermath resonated through his early life. He was born during the First

World War and many years later recalled, as a five-year-old, seeing a man shaking his head and looking up at the sky in bewilderment, only to be told that it was 'shell shock'. Roy's father had been a clerk on the railways and so was exempted from military service, but one particularly 'gentle' uncle fought at Gallipoli, where, family stories had it, he had stuck a bayonet into a Turkish soldier's belly and been so horrified that he 'ran like hell', hating himself ever after.[4]

The young Roy soaked up ideas from outside the family home, and while a teenager went to services at the recently consecrated Liverpool Cathedral, where a controversial dean was experimenting with new forms of service. Roy saw Alfred Einstein and General Jan Smuts – the once and future Prime Minister of South Africa – speak from the pulpit. One particular speech stuck in his mind: Charles Raven, Regius Professor of Divinity at Cambridge, telling the congregation that 'love and not force is the ultimate power in the universe'. It was an idea that Roy would carry with him in the years to come, and an idea that would be severely tested.

Roy's cultural influences were broad, and he was as likely to read anti-imperialist pamphlets, Japanese poetry or Aldous Huxley as the Bible, but he later recalled that his anti-war sentiments really began to firm up after seeing the documentary film *Forgotten Men: The War as It Was*.[5] The film, released in 1934, with an introduction from General Ian Hamilton, the Commander of the expeditionary force in Gallipoli, shows interviews with veterans and starts with a clipping from a newspaper headline: 'Youth Must be Told of the Horrors'. In the tones typical of senior army officers, Hamilton describes the Western Front as a 'species of war with humanity abstracted out'. One shot of a man writhing on the ground after being shot in the stomach would long stand out in Roy's memory.[6] For him, the response was at once emotional and intellectual.

The move to London had partly been an attempt to escape his family, but Roy's parents, brothers and sister soon joined him, eventually settling into a house in the fast-expanding London suburb of Hendon, where, for not too much money, you could find a semi-detached house with a patch of grass. Roy did not stay annoyed by their arrival for too long, as there was a comfort being back in the family home. The siblings – Roy, Alfred, Derricke and

Joy – were also very close, and spent many evenings talking about the state of the world or playing cards in front of the open fire, with the radio on in the background bringing in news of mounting crises around the world. Roy's brothers and sister shared many of his developing pacifist sentiments, but his father was deeply sceptical, while his mother remained silent.

A youth from the provinces, Roy lacked the connections to find a job as a journalist in Fleet Street and ended up working as a clerk for a finance company. It was a position he did not hold for long, evidently finding it hard to hide his lack of enthusiasm from his employer. Days were then spent walking around London's parks, visiting its grander churches and meeting his mother and brothers for a cup of tea in a café. Once a week he had to sign on at the employment bureau, and one time on the train home sat next to a drunken old soldier loudly 'moaning about the war'.[7] We can imagine the shy young man trying to avoid the eye of the older passenger, who was shouting at no one in particular: 'Have you ever been gassed? Well, I have and you will one of these days.' Roy noted in his diary that, on leaving the train, the man gave everyone a salute, saying 'I'll see you in the next war.'

A few years earlier, in the first half of 1930s, an earnest young man like Roy, opposed to war and looking for solutions, would probably have been drawn to the League of Nations. After the end of the First World War, Britain, France and the other victorious powers had thought that, by developing new international norms around the idea of collective security, states could move beyond the era of great-power politics that had led to the disaster of the First World War. The League of Nations, based in a former hotel on the shores of Lake Geneva, was the institution that they hoped would herald a new era of international law and order, and in Britain the League of Nations Union was established to support the new body. At its peak the Union had over 400,000 members and was a firmly established part of British middle-ground opinion; enthusiasm for it was felt across the political spectrum, from conservatives to socialists, but was particularly strong among liberals and on the left.[8] Sympathisers were found among teachers, clerks, lawyers and civil servants, but also among peers of the realm, bishops, retired generals and philanthropic ladies of the upper-middle class, as well as among writers, poets and more radical agitators.[9]

There was a lively circuit of speakers who toured the country, moving from church hall to church hall, from club house to club house, explaining the merits of the League's vision of global order.[10] These were high hopes for an organisation that employed just over 700 civil servants, smaller than the staff of many British provincial town councils. Nevertheless, in the minds of its supporters, war was a problem that could be fixed in its wood-panelled committee rooms. The League was armed with the power of negotiation, arbitration and international agreements, backed by the threat of sanctions. For its advocates, international order and collective security would be based in collectively agreed norms. Support for the League represented a very particular form of optimism. This was a faith that war could be avoided so long as the correct legal and bureaucratic framework was put in place; conflict can be overcome through rational compromise and technical skill. It was a belief that would not last long this time around, but would later find echoes in the institutions of the United Nations and the European Union that rose out of the debris of the war to come.

In late 1934 and into early 1935 the League of Nations Union had decided to test public opinion and carried out a voluntary referendum, eventually canvassing nearly twelve million Britons.[11] Over nine and half million people said they were in favour of the abolition of military aircraft. Even higher numbers supported banning the sale of arms for profit. But over 58 per cent of respondents also said they were willing to support military measures 'if a nation insists on attacking another'. For the majority of people who answered, armed force was therefore resolutely not off the table. The implications of the ballot have been debated ever since, but either way it represented a high-water mark for the League of Nations Union.

In the face of the mounting crises of the mid-1930s, the League was toothless, or at least unwilling to bare such teeth as it had. The United States was never a member, and the colonised half of the world was never even asked to join. Japan had left in 1932, and Germany had withdrawn in 1933. Ultimately, the League's principles had to be enforced, and its members were unwilling or unable to do so. The League did next to nothing about Japanese violence in China or about the war in Spain, and although it declared Italy the aggressor in Ethiopia, it imposed only very limited sanctions.[12]

In the face of military invasion, the League was powerless if it was not willing to back up its rules with action. As such, the League was always an awkward place for those who were absolutely opposed to war, because it ultimately relied on the threat of force to prevent another war. And without using that threat, the optimism that it had once inspired in many people withered on the vine.

Roy was drawn elsewhere as he looked for a way to prevent war, and to the alluring figure of Dick Sheppard in particular. Sheppard was a radio personality, an Anglican priest and in many ways a deeply establishment figure, a Conservative Party supporter born in Windsor Castle where his father worked as a clergyman for the royal family. Before being appointed Canon of St Paul's Cathedral and then Vicar of St Martin-in-the-Fields, two of the most fashionable positions in the Church of England, he had served as a chaplain in the First World War.[13] Radio broadcasts from his evening services at St Martin's meant that he was a household name, described by one admirer as 'the most loved priest in all England'.[14] He was one of many charismatic preachers in the anti-war movement, but was probably the most charismatic of all.

In 1934 the Rev. Dick Sheppard launched a newspaper appeal inviting any man to send him a postcard with the simple pledge 'I renounce war, and never again, directly or indirectly, will I support another.'[15] This was a different vision of peace from the collective security and international norms of the League of Nations. Instead, it was based on individual moral fortitude and a very personal call to renounce war. A similar form of individual action would much later be seen in the consumer boycotts of the second half of the twentieth century and early years of the twenty-first, rooted in the assumption that if enough people expressed their own personal refusal you could turn things around. In 1934, the initial trickle of cards sent to Sheppard became a flood, and over the next year well over 100,000 people would post their pledge. Roy was just one of the thousands who signed his name. Sheppard's own pacifism was a moral response to the mass suffering he saw in the trenches, and it was this moral vision that brought thousands of people to listen to his message.[16] Following his initial invitation, a Peace Pledge Union was formally established in 1936 and that same year women were also invited to sign the pledge.[17] Before that it had been assumed that war, and opposition to war, was a matter for men only, despite the crucial role many women had played in the peace movement over the previous decades. In October 1936 there were a reported 183 local PPU groups.[18] Three months later there were over 3,000. At its height the PPU employed more than forty people, its newspaper was found in 40,000 libraries across the country and its *Peace Service Handbook* sold 165,000 copies within weeks of publication.

For a while at least the PPU brought hundreds of thousands of people together through Sheppard's inspiring message, in a way that no dedicated peace movement in Britain has done before or since. One member from Essex recalled that the people he saw at meetings were members of the Labour Party, the Esperanto Association and the International Friendship League, as well as Quakers, Anglicans and Methodists.[19] Leading members included the religious leaders Donald Soper and Maude Royden, the writers Aldous Huxley, A. A. Milne, Siegfried Sassoon and John Middleton Murry, the politicians Fenner Brockway and George Lansbury and the academics Bertrand Russell and Cyril Joad. Many, like Vera Brittain, had moved away from the League of Nations, turned off by what they saw as its stale hypocrisies, and attracted by Sheppard's less equivocal approach. The PPU was formally a secular organisation, but could often have a distinctly Christian atmosphere. Sheppard and many of the senior members who followed him were clergy, and even if others did not hold formal religious positions, they could have a distinctly pious tone.[20] Indeed, the movement was often described as a 'crusade'.[21] Although there were sometimes tensions between the PPU and more explicitly religious peace bodies, the membership reflected the broad religiosity of the leadership. Socialists, anarchists and humanists certainly joined the Union, but they were outnumbered by the Quakers, Methodists and other assorted Christians.

There was plenty of room, perhaps a little too much room, under the broad roof of the PPU. You can get a sense of how wide a movement the PPU became when you consider that one of the early leaders was Brigadier General Frank Crozier. Crozier had tried to join the British army during the South African War, but was rejected on medical grounds and effectively became a mercenary. With the outbreak of the First World War, he served as an officer at the Somme, winning medals for bravery and ending hostilities as a brigadier general, but he later admitted that he had ordered the shooting of sentries who had fallen asleep on the job. By the mid-1930s he was ready to declare that he could not serve in another war 'without ratting on myself and the people of England whom I love'.[22] Despite his new-found pacifism, Crozier retained his distinct military style throughout; at one PPU camp in rural Derbyshire, he is supposed to have stood, sword in hand, declaring that if his audience did not sign the peace pledge he would chop off their heads.[23]

Although Roy signed the pledge to renounce war early on, it took him a while to summon the courage to attend his first PPU gathering. Signing a piece of paper was one thing, going out in public was quite another. Shortly before he turned twenty-two he showed up at his first meeting in suburban Hendon, later admitting that he had hoped to 'make an impression' on the PPU branch, but his confidence left him and he was too afraid to speak.[24] Instead Mr Anderson, a Scot and a Fleet Street journalist with the 'gift of the gab', did most of the talking. Roy noticed that the rest of the group seemed to be socialists of various persuasions. A few weeks later he was invited to a PPU demonstration, but was unsure whether he would go.[25] Even so, over the coming months Roy spent an increasing number of evenings with his new acquaintances.

A chain-smoking asthmatic, Sheppard was found slumped over his desk, dead from a heart attack in October 1937, just two months after his fifty-seventh birthday. Others were determined to continue Sheppard's legacy. From the mid-1930s, it was common to see PPU volunteers selling the weekly *Peace News*, holding up posters and giving out pamphlets on many high streets. The PPU could be pacifist camaraderie at its most intense. Members busied themselves with leafleting, holding regular meetings and forming discussion groups. In this way, the PPU fitted into a wider pattern of joining clubs and associations that marked life for many, especially in the middle classes, in 1930s Britain.[26] The PPU groups became centres of social life, and some even formed theatre and singing offshoots to spread the pacifist message. Many members had previously never met another pacifist and had been ploughing a rather lonely furrow, so all this activity could be exciting. Numerous lifelong friendships and not a few marriages were launched during these encounters. Roy seems sometimes to have found this intense sociability hard to take, hesitant as he was to come forward among a group of people who were confident in their own opinions and had a great deal to say. He did manage to hand out pamphlets in front of the Classic Cinema in Hendon; the crowds seemed benign if not entirely supportive, and one night, much to his pleasure, he managed to get rid of over 100 pamphlets in less than an hour.[27] He was gradually growing in confidence.

Roy's determination would be sorely tested in the years to come. The message of the PPU was simple: in the face of war all that was needed was for each and every individual simply to say no. But then what? Signing a postcard was simple, but it did not tell you very much about the depth of a person's commitment when the going got tough. Being against war was one thing, but a negative injunction, a refusal to participate, needed to be turned into a positive statement, or it risked becoming hollow and empty.

CHAPTER 3

Socialist Futures

By 1937 Fred Urquhart was regularly arguing with his family about politics over the dinner table. Although Fred's father was a Labour Party voter, he was well to the right of his son. The older man had worked for years driving for some of Scotland's wealthy families, and familiarity with the rich and privileged had bred a measure of contempt in his son. Edinburgh, then as now, was a socially divided city with steep gradations in wealth; and Fred was particularly frustrated by his parents' respect for the aristocracy who owned much of the land around the family home and left much of the housing to rot and decay. When Fred had found a publisher for his first novel, his father's response was to try and work out the editor's relationship with the Marquess of Bute, with whom he shared a surname.[1] Later, Fred wrote in his diary that he would be happier as a poor writer than in some dreary job with a 'bourgeoise existence' like his father.[2]

Although Edinburgh's left-wing political scene was less intense than its equivalent in the industrial West of Scotland, there was still plenty going on and lots of ideas floating in the air.[3] While never an enthusiastic joiner of groups, Fred was a keen member of the Left Book Club, established by the publisher Victor Gollancz to help 'the struggle for world peace' by educating the British public through its distinctive red paperbacks. The Club played a major role in Fred's intellectual and social life, as he attended its monthly meetings, met new friends and extended his horizons, while excitedly discussing events in Soviet Russia, the evils of the arms industry or the way to socialism. Most importantly for him, socialism not only offered an exciting alternative to dreary office work and a constricting family life, but also promised a world without war.

In the first decades after the First World, socialism and anti-war politics often went hand in hand, as left-wing ideology provided a rich vocabulary for talking about war, peace and injustice. Resentment of the generals and politicians who had sent working-class men to their slaughter combined with intermittent economic misery and recession to fuel class-based anti-war attitudes. The attraction of socialism was not simply that it condemned capitalist wars and offered a diagnosis of what was wrong with the world. It was also profoundly optimistic about human nature. In many of its variants, humans were seen as inherently and ultimately perfectible, promising a brighter and better future, a life where war was not inevitable and humanity not condemned to fight tooth and nail. In 1930s Britain, in the long wake of the Russian Revolution of 1917, many believed that it was possible to transform the world fundamentally. Although revolution never did arrive in mainland Britain, there were still significant pockets of radicalism, not least in Scotland.[4] For the committed, change was not some vague abstraction over the far horizon, but was concrete, real and coming into view. A world without war and exploitation was something that could be achieved with just the right amount of blood, sweat and tears. For pacifists of a socialist persuasion, though, the blood bit could be a problem.

Socialist commitments and anti-war politics were not without their frictions. There was certainly a strong absolute pacifist line that ran through the political left – in the sense of a total opposition to all war in all and every circumstance – and this was a line that was stronger in Britain than in any other place in the world.[5] But the rhetoric of the barricades was also an important part of the socialist tradition. Revolution, after all, was usually very violent. Fred and thousands of others of the political left therefore had to grapple with the tension between an objection to war on the one hand and a politics often forged in violence on the other, as they debated whether war was the midwife or the executioner of their hopes for a better world.

Sitting at his typewriter in his small room, Fred saw his writing as the best way to work for socialism: he was willing to 'starve at home' so that he could fight with 'my pen'.[6] After watching a western at the local cinema, he had an idea for a comedy about a collective ranch called the 'Cowboy Communist'.[7] Thankfully perhaps, the show seems never to have been written, one of many unfinished projects. Fred also mulled over a play telling the story of civil war between Fascists and Communists, in which two lovers found themselves on opposite sides.[8] Nevertheless, some of his ideas did come to fruition, and his novel *Time Will Knit* put his political beliefs firmly on display. Alongside its pacifist elements, the novel is also clearly left-wing in sentiment; in the book, Wattie Gillespie's tumbledown family home by the sea is condemned as unfit for human habitation and the family is eventually forced out by the landlord. Wattie is full of anger, but his socialist credentials are constantly compromised by the need to feed his loved ones. The strain caused by trying to reconcile personal convictions with wider responsibilities would become an important issue for Fred too.

Fred was ultimately left dissatisfied by his political writing, frustrated that he felt unable to express his convictions fully on the page: 'It is bad enough sometimes when I am talking I stutter and wave my hands about helplessly looking for a word, but it is awful when I can't explain what I mean in writing.'[9] He quickly came to see his self-consciously socialist writing as 'childish' and decided that he found 'character studies' easier.[10] He needed other political outlets.

As Fred looked around for inspiration, Scotland was not short of radical role models, and he was, for a time, drawn to the figure of the Glaswegian James Maxton.[11] Maxton was a teacher before the First World War, but after the introduction of conscription in 1916 and his conscientious objection, he worked on barges on the Clyde, from where he organised strikes. He would become a legendary figure on the British left, particularly famed for his oratorical skills and his willingness to take a stand, particularly against war.[12] During the First World War, many on the political left across Europe had eventually come out in support of hostilities – national loyalty trumping international solidarity – but small pockets of socialists, along with feminists, led the campaign against the killing.[13] In Britain, although most on the left had ended up favouring war too, it was socialists who helped to put war resistance on the political agenda.[14]

Maxton was a central figure in the Independent Labour Party, or ILP, and later became one of its MPs in Glasgow. Anti-war

attitudes ran through the bones of the party. Many of its later leaders, or at least those who were young enough to be enlisted during
the First World War, refused conscription and were sent to jail. The
police also repeatedly raided their offices and by the end of the war
many of the most senior members had been detained.[15] Maxton
was himself imprisoned for sedition in 1916, emerging from jail
after a year both exhausted and emaciated.[16] Fenner Brockway,
another ILP leader – who also went on to become an MP and
party Chair – led a strike in Liverpool's Walton jail after being
sentenced to a term for refusing military service. Born to British
missionaries in Calcutta, Brockway was a lifelong anti-imperialist
and vegetarian. In 1914, he had issued an open letter inviting anyone not prepared to 'render military service under conscription' to
enrol their names on his list, and shortly afterwards he helped to
establish the No-Conscription Fellowship, or NCF – probably the
most influential movement of its type at the time.[17] At its peak, the
organisation had around 10,000 members, and most were also
members of the ILP; Maxton became the leader in Scotland.[18]
Importantly, the NCF declared that 'We yield to no one in our
admiration of the self-sacrifice, the courage and the unflagging
devotion of our fellow countrymen who have felt it their duty to
take up arms.'[19] Although against war, the NCF did not want to
condemn those who were asked to fight. This was an organisation
that was self-consciously loyal, determined not to put itself beyond
the pale, and this was a pattern that many of those opposed to war
would try to follow in the decades to come, sometimes with great
difficulty.

The ILP's anti-war attitudes rested on four pillars, of differing
strength. First up was internationalism, which provided a strong
sense that the working classes of different countries had more in
common with each other than they did with their rulers. Going to
war with another country was therefore going to war against
brothers and comrades.[20] Linked to this was an anti-militarist tradition.[21] This was an opposition to the expansive role of the military
in economic, political and social life, based on the argument that a
coalition between the arms industry and the armed forces drove
countries to fight and stoked antagonism between nations in capitalist and imperialist wars.[22] On top of this, conscription was seen
as a form of undemocratic forced labour, eroding employment

protections that had only recently been won. The ILP believed that enlisting people to fight was a step away from slavery, a conviction that involved breaking with a mainland European socialist tradition which promoted citizen armies.[23] Finally, there was a much more absolutist pacifist line, albeit of varying strength, that opposed all war and violence. Whilst, internationalism, anti-militarism and opposition to conscription did not rule out all wars, so long as the cause was just, for some in the ILP there was a feeling that war was always wrong. The NCF 'statement of faith' declared human life to be 'sacred', and similar combinations of political and religious language ran through much left-wing opposition to war.[24] War was objected to not just because it was capitalist or imperialist, but because it involved killing other people.

By no means all of the political left was pacifist or even anti-militarist. The broader Labour Party, of which the ILP was but a part – until it disaffiliated in 1932 – remained especially split. Labour was always both less socialist and less pacifist than the ILP, but for a brief while after 1932 it was led by George Lansbury, the Christian socialist, campaigner for women's suffrage and absolute pacifist.[25] When he was elected leader, Lansbury sent a message to his constituents declaring, 'I would close every recruiting station, disband the Army and disarm the Air Force. I would abolish the whole dreadful equipment of war and say to the world: "Do your worst." '[26] Although never without his critics, Lansbury was far from an isolated figure.[27] Ramsay MacDonald, who had campaigned against the First World War, became the first Labour Prime Minister in 1924, and although Lansbury had himself been too old, the party had several MPs, ministers and shadow ministers throughout the 1920s and 1930s who had been conscientious objectors in the First World War.

The early 1930s was the high point of Labour Party pacifism. At the 1935 party conference Lansbury was deposed as leader, with an exasperated Ernest Bevin, a trade unionist who later became Minister of Labour, accusing him of taking his 'conscience round from body to body asking to be told what to do with it'.[28] The pragmatic and straight-talking Bevin saw all this talk of conviction and belief as a form of hand-wringing moral self-indulgence. Such divisions between those absolutely and ethically opposed to war and those who were willing, under the right circumstances, to countenance a resort to arms would return to haunt the Labour Party in the decades after the Second World War, running through debates over nuclear disarmament in the 1980s and into the twenty-first century in splits over the invasion of Iraq.

In the late 1930s, the Civil War in Spain brought tensions within socialism over the virtues and vices of war closer to the surface. After General Franco's military coup of 1936 had been supported by Fascist Italy and Nazi Germany, the left strongly identified with the Spanish Republican cause, and the war became a rallying call for many socialists around the world. In the spring of 1938 Fred began to read *Spanish Testament*, Arthur Koestler's account (published by the Left Book Club) of his time as a prisoner of Franco's Nationalists, just as Nationalist forces reached the Mediterranean fishing harbour of Vinaròs, fatally splitting Republican-held territory in two. Fred wrote in his diary that he wished that someone would 'push' Franco into the sea.[29] He joined a group of Scottish authors in writing to the press pleading for help for the Catalans and Basques, who were particular targets of Francoist violence.[30] It was an emotional as much as a political issue for Fred. He particularly upset by the failure of the British government to intervene on the Republican side and was on the verge of despair, finding it hard to find the words to express his feelings about a war he thought would 'never end'. And yet, amid all this anxiety, he noted that 'life goes on as usual' as he spent his days in a series of mundane jobs, while democracy was 'tortured slowly'.[31] The ripples of war were still, for now at least, far from Fred's life.

As the Spanish Republican government faced defeat, a large number of socialists saw the turn to arms as the only viable political, moral and practical response. Even the ILP sent its own contingent to fight on the front line in Aragon, where they were joined by George Orwell. Fred's own hope for intervention implied supporting violence if the cause was right. Maxton, by now the Chair of the ILP, remained absolute in his opposition to war and militarism, but Brockway later reflected in his autobiography that the Spanish Civil War had made it clear to him that 'I could no longer justify pacifism when there was a Fascist threat.'[32] Brockway reluctantly came to see force as the only option, recalling that 'emotionally and spiritually I remained a pacifist. I've never held a weapon in my life. I think I can quite honestly say I would rather be killed than kill anyone. And yet intellectually I recognise that war can have progressive purposes.'[33]

By the end of the 1930s, Fred was spending an increasing amount of time with a new friend, Mary Litchfield, and over the next few years she would become very important to him, both personally and politically. Mary would also pull his loyalty in different directions. She was a surprisingly glamorous former teacher living in the Fife market town of Cupar; ill-health had forced her to stop work, and Fred had got to know her when she wrote him a letter saying how much she liked his published work. To begin with Fred was not sure what to make of Mary, although he found her intriguing, writing that 'she is about forty with dark hair . . . She evidently regards herself as a vamp . . . a scarlet woman!'[34] Their relationship quickly grew warm. After one night spent talking until the early hours before going to bed at dawn, Fred noted that 'I found her on closer acquaintance to be even more delightful than I had thought already,' adding that 'she is the first woman with whom I have discussed my homosexuality and I will always remember her gratefully for her sympathy and understanding'.[35] Fred would frequently make the journey north by rail over the Forth Bridge, as Mary's hospitality provided an escape from the strained atmosphere in the family home. It is also surely no coincidence that the person he felt most comfortable talking to about his desires would also turn out to be one of his greatest political influences. From the glimpses we get of Mary from Fred's diary and letters, she appears serious and committed, but also deeply caring towards Fred.

Above all, Mary was Fred's great introduction to a wider Scottish literary and political scene. She was rumoured to have been engaged to the writer Edwin Muir and to have had an affair with John Laurie, at that time a Shakespearean actor but much later best remembered for his role as the deeply pessimistic Private Frazer in the TV sitcom Dad's Army. Mary was also friends with the poets Hugh MacDiarmid and Douglas Young, who were both socialists and important figures in Scottish public life. Young was an imposing figure, standing at over six foot seven inches. He was also a Scottish nationalist. Later, for a brief period during the Second World War, he would become leader of the Scottish National Party, spending time in jail for refusing military conscription. MacDiarmid – a pen name for Christopher Grieve – had attended the same Edinburgh school as Fred nearly a generation before, and was a deeply controversial personality, described as an 'eccentric and maddening genius' capable of writing that haunted 'the mind and memory'.[36] In the course of his life, according to his daughter-in-law, MacDiarmid 'entertained almost every ideal it was possible to entertain at one point or another', including briefly expressing sympathy for some forms of Fascism.[37] He was also, like Young, a Scottish nationalist, and wrote much of his poetry in Scots vernacular, to much acclaim north of the border but largely to incomprehension further south. Mary's home, despite being in a small provincial town, must have been an exciting refuge for Fred.

Fred and Mary do not seem to have shared the nationalist sympathies of Young or MacDiarmid, but both Mary and Hugh MacDiarmid were members of the Communist Party, although MacDiarmid was repeatedly expelled for 'national deviation'. Fred had strong Communist sympathies, and sometimes dreamed of moving to Russia, but he never seemed to have joined the party, or any other party for that matter, preferring to remain a fellow-traveller. Although always small on a national scale, the Communist Party of Great Britain had a particular pocket of support in central Scotland.[38] In Fife, where Mary lived, the industrial west of the county had elected the Communist Willie Gallacher as its MP in 1935.[39] Gallacher was a veteran trade unionist who been jailed for his anti-military activities and once led a strike in Glasgow that was put down by the British army. Of all the varied groups on the political left, the Communist Party was probably the most awkward home for someone opposed to war. The Russian revolution had after all been shot through with acts of brutal violence, and the Red Army was a formidable fighting force. The Communist Party of Great Britain would flip-flop several times during the late 1930s, predominantly following the line set by Moscow, as it supported or opposed the resort to arms against Fascism, seeing war sometimes as imperialist, sometimes as a matter of defending the revolution. Fred's always slightly loose party loyalty would be put under severe strain by the sudden shifts in the USSR's approach to war over the coming years.

Either way, if it followed that the best way to prevent war was socialism, Fred Urquhart was still pinning his hopes on revolution. The question was how to bring this about. Violence stalked Fred's dreams of a socialist future, both as a way forward and as an obstacle, a source of both optimism and dread. In many ways the issue came down to the relationship between means and ends – whether socialist ends could only be achieved through violent means, or whether there was a non-violent way forward.

Some would-be British revolutionaries saw violence in itself as a cleansing force, necessary for the eradication of capitalism and the capitalist classes, pulling on a much wider tradition that ran through both the European left and right. For a brief time in the early 1930s, the critic and editor Middleton Murry was a member of the ILP and embraced violence as an 'opportunity for radical action'.[40] He argued that any socialist who claimed to be an absolute pacifist was not really a socialist at all.[41] But within a few years of declaring his support for violence he began to feel that resistance to war rather than support for revolution was the best way to defeat capitalism. In a letter to James Maxton, he argued that the 'long-view policy of Revolutionary Socialism in the proximate future is to organise resistance against war'.[42] In a reversal of his previous logic, Murry was arguing that, rather than socialism preventing war, the shortest path to socialism lay in the abolition of war.

Unless pacifist socialists could show there was a non-violent route to the socialist future, they risked being seen as an obstacle rather than a central part of the socialist project.[43] As the historian Martin Ceadel has argued, there was a rift between those who saw socialism as a struggle for economic and political power and were therefore opposed only to capitalist and imperialist wars, and those who saw socialism as a more personal moral transformation.[44] When push came to shove, most socialists found it easier to give up an anti-war politics than to abandon socialism, concluding that it was not possible to defend the working class, let alone bring about revolution, without at some point resorting to arms.

What remained? Fred would try to cling on to both his socialism and his pacifism, putting his personal relationships under heavy strain. Others would fall back on a form of socialism rooted in the cultivation of personal virtues – a moral rather than political commitment – as the line between socialist and religious conviction had always been hard to draw. Fred was hostile to all forms of religion, but for some on the left socialism had always been a practical expression of Christianity, seeing the Bible as a radical tract with its message of love for the poor. For others, socialist convictions played a role in their lives very similar to religious faith, or what the poet Cecil Day Lewis described as plugging the 'hollow in the breast' where God might otherwise be.[45] Middleton Murry eventually abandoned his socialism altogether, turning to a mystical form of Christian pacifism, rooted in what he saw as the 'willing suspension of disbelief for the moment which constitutes poetic faith'.[46] More broadly, as the second part of the 1930s wore on, the pacifist movement would become less and less concerned with social transformation and more focused on the cultivation of character, turning away from political revolution. Pacifism became an increasingly personal faith.

CHAPTER 4

Christian Faith

The King's Weigh House is an unusual red-brick building, shaped like a giant gothic saucepan, sitting on a side street in fashionable Mayfair. It is not the obvious place for a very nonconforming Protestant church, but through the 1920s and 1930s the church attracted a diverse congregation. In the wake of the destruction of the First World War, the Weigh House played a central role in the development of a distinct stream of Christian pacifism. In 1917, its minister had led his flock through the streets of the West End to Trafalgar Square, where he stood on a plinth under Nelson's Column and preached on the need for peace. By the early 1930s, the quietly determined Stella St John had found her way to the church.[1] Both her parents were dead, and her relationship with her only brother was strained. Although there was a strong military tradition in her family, she had become a convinced pacifist, moving into a room in the run-down parsonage attached to the church, given over as a hostel for members of the congregation. For a time, she felt right at home.

Stella was a long way from the rather staid and conservative Anglican environment of her suburban childhood. Life in the hostel must have been all-consuming, as the residents shared meals and worship. W. E. Orchard, the minister, was a magnetic personality, famed for both his intellectual abilities and his emotional power, and had honed his preaching skills on the streets of east London. He was also fiercely committed to the idea that no Christian could justify the taking of another person's life, and called for an end to what he called the gospel of 'force, blood and iron'.[2] Orchard had served as a chaplain to conscientious objectors imprisoned in Wormwood Scrubs during the First World War, and in the years since his pacifist sermons had filled the church, inspiring great loyalty among his congregation.

For much of the nineteenth and early twentieth century, pacifism in Britain had a distinctively Christian flavour. While socialism held centre stage during the First World War, throughout the 1920s and 1930s various forms of Christian pacifism rose to prominence again as the political left grappled with the implications of anti-Fascism. For these Christians, the destruction of the First World War had not been grounds for abandoning faith, but a reason to reinvent it. They had seen the bloodshed of battle and come away newly energised by the conviction that Christianity had to be a religion of peace or it was nothing at all.

But the relationship between pacifism and Christianity was troubled.[3] In previous centuries, the violent excesses of the Inquisition and imperial expansion had been justified in the name of Christ, and during the First World War the pulpits of the Church of England had seen the delivery of numerous sermons fervently supporting the fight against Germany. Anti-war activists could quote numerous verses from the Bible supporting their position, and frequently did so: 'Thou shall not kill' and 'love your neighbour' seemed powerful and straightforward. However, non-pacifist Christians could cite back many other passages in support of their position, and the Old Testament in particular is not exactly a call for non-violence. Non-pacifists also pointed out that whatever the pieties of the Sermon on the Mount – with its impassioned calls for love – it was hardly a blueprint for modern life. This is not to say that Christianity is necessarily a bloodthirsty faith, but simply to point out that the cross and the sword had often been held by the same hands.

By the fourth decade of the twentieth century, Christianity within British public life was as much a loose but pervasive sensibility as it was a doctrinal force.[4] As George Orwell put it, the British 'retained a deep tinge of Christian feeling, while almost forgetting the name of Christ'.[5] People may not have gone to church regularly, nor even have prayed, but the Church still held an important institutional position, with well over two-thirds of babies baptised, most people marrying in a church and the vast majority of funerals being formally religious.[6] Christianity, and Protestant Christianity in particular, set the broad moral tone within which people lived their lives, and offered a rich basis against which you could argue about both war and peace.

Within the many strands of British Christianity, it was the non-conformist Protestant conscience – the convictions of Quakers, Methodists, Baptists and others – that came to dominate Christian pacifism, with Quakers particularly to the fore. Theirs was a conscience that was personal, idiosyncratic and convinced, not just found in the teachings of the Church, but coming from deep within the individual believer. It was the conscience of the 'here I stand and can do no other' variety, a type of conscience that can require people to stick resolutely to their principles, sometimes at great personal cost. It was a type of conscience that could be energising, but it could also be alienating and difficult. Above all, intense moralism can sometimes be lonely. 'Me against the world' can easily become 'me alone'.

For Stella St John there was comfort in religious faith, but it could be hard to find a way through competing theological interpretations, religious schisms, family allegiances and personal animosities, as she sought to live a life marked by the love of Christ in a world seemingly more focused on hellfire and brimstone. When she confronted the question of what it meant to love your neighbour, she would make some surprising and difficult decisions which would shape the rest of her life.

Stella was born seven years before the First World War began, growing up in a seventeen-room house with servants at the point where the expanding London suburbs finally gave way to rural Kent. She has left few traces in the archives, apart from the occasional letter, a journal she kept during one remarkable month of her life and an extended interview given to the Imperial War Museum in the early 1970s. From the little she left behind, she comes across as modest but resolute. Despite the relative lack of archival fragments, commonly the case among many women of the time, pacifists or otherwise, Stella's life, hopes and fears have touched on the key moments in the often fraught history of Christian pacifism in the twentieth century.

One grandfather was a colonel in the 30th Regiment of the Madras Native Infantry of the Imperial Indian Army and Stella's father was a civilian surgeon; the St Johns were a firmly established part of the English upper-middle class, with vague aristocratic roots and a conservative outlook. The young Stella dreamed of becoming a doctor, but her father would not countenance it. She then tried to persuade him to let her study to be a vet, but again he refused, and Stella ended up training to be a horticulturalist, eventually finding employment at the medieval Dartington Hall in south Devon. Home to a slice of early twentieth-century English bohemia, Dartington was an unusual place for a daughter of the conservative suburbs. Stella's father might have been scandalised by the idea of her becoming a doctor, but she had now ended up in a place full of the sort of people George Orwell called fruit-juice-drinking, nudist sandal-wearers.[7] By the time she arrived at the Hall, Stella's father was dead, but he must have turned in his grave.

The Hall was home to a school and charity set up by the philanthropists and social activists Leonard and Dorothy Elmhirst.[8] Dorothy was one of the richest women in America and founder of the 'progressive' *New Republic* magazine; Leonard was the former secretary to the Indian Nobel Prize-winning writer Rabindranath Tagore. Tagore had established an ashram in Bengal, complete with experimental school, garden and an Institute for Rural Reconstruction, and the Elmhirsts had been inspired to set up their own version in England. Dartington Hall was to be both a school and a community, where the classroom was to be the farm, gardens and workshops, where students and staff were to be treated as equals and where education was to be an end in itself and not simply a means to qualifications. Sigmund Freud's grandchildren – Clement and Lucian – started at the school in 1933, and adult visitors included the artists Ben Nicholson and Barbara Hepworth, as well as the publisher Victor Gollancz. This was the sort of place where children ran free; it was decidedly not the sort of place where young women would be told they could not aspire to do whatever they wanted to do. It must have been a relief to Stella.

Stella worked outside, experimenting with new scientific growing techniques and cultivating fruit and vegetables in the beautiful walled garden. She seems to have been a relatively marginal figure – appearing nowhere in the histories of Dartington – but we can imagine that she soaked it all up. As with so many other self-consciously progressive organisations of the period, the ethos was distinctly pacifist and left-wing, and Stella appeared to find this deeply attractive. While her family were 'true-blue Tories', at Dartington she began gradually to see the 'socialist point of view' and canvassed for the local Labour candidate in the 1929 general election. However, although the Hall was resolutely progressive, the village and countryside around were not, and the campaign was unsuccessful.

For Stella, growing fruit and vegetables was just a brief interlude. Following the death of her mother, and after inheriting enough money to pay the fees, she finally entered veterinary college in London at the age of twenty-four, able to follow her dream at last, or at least get part of the way there. She still wanted to be a surgeon but could not afford medical school.

Studies were not the only thing on Stella's mind; she had initially 'given up on religion' when her mother died but was slowly making her way back to a very particular form of faith. The church at King's Weigh House was Congregationalist, a Protestant denomination notable for making up most of the members of the New Model Army of the English Civil War. The 300 years since had been rather less tumultuous and members were now largely drawn from the suburbs. The church building had been designed by Alfred Waterhouse, the man behind those other monoliths to Victorian ambition, Strangeways Prison and the Natural History Museum, giving it a solid gothic aspect. In the Second World War, a bomb would fall near the altar during a communion service, killing a new minister's wife. Many years after that the building became a Ukrainian Catholic cathedral. In Stella's time, the atmosphere at the church was very different from Dartington Hall, with moral seriousness rather than free-spirited and experimental frivolity the order of the day, but both Dartington and the King's Weigh House were concerned with their own type of ethical uplift.

Sermons at the Weigh House were unusual.[9] W. E. Orchard had left school at twelve and went to work on the railways in Euston, but he had been drawn to preaching, where he could be inspirational, 'intense and compelling'.[10] He abandoned the railways and took up a lay position at a Presbyterian church on the Isle of Dogs, before training to be a minister at Cambridge University. In the summer of 1914, at the age of thirty-seven, by now married and with a son, Orchard had started at the King's Weigh House. At the time, the church was in trouble, with the congregation slipping below fifty souls, but Orchard soon began to draw the crowds. Many, like Stella over a decade and a half later, were attracted by his anti-war attitudes. For Orchard, the declaration of war in 1914 had resulted in a radical re-evaluation of his faith, and he later wrote that 'the war was, for me, simply the starting point from which Christianity had to be explored afresh'.[11] He became a vocal opponent of the war, condemning what he saw as the too easy equation of the redemptive suffering of Christ with the misery of the soldiers in battle.

Orchard stood out in other ways too, and this would sow the seed of his eventual split with Stella. Although trained in the austere Presbyterian tradition, he was increasingly drawn to Catholic ritual and the mystical side of Christianity, trying to bring new forms of liturgical practice into his services and rather unusually combining confession and plainsong with evangelical preaching. The whiff of incense must have been familiar to Stella from her High Anglican childhood. Orchard's ultimate ambition was for the King's Weigh House to be some kind of 'bridge church' to other Christian groups, but this unity was elusive, and in 1932 he resigned his ministry and joined the Catholic Church, much to Stella's regret. Stella continued to correspond with him, but their relationship was never the same again. As she recalled many years later, on moving to the Roman Catholic Church he 'seemed to change'. Not the least of the problems he faced was that the Catholic hierarchy had little time for pacifism.

Stella slowly began to acquire a wider circle of pacifist friends. She was firmly convinced by now that the only way to be a Christian was to be a pacifist, later saying that 'if I wasn't a pacifist I would not have any use for Christianity'.[12] Stella thought that pacifism and Christianity were deeply entwined, so much so as to be indistinguishable, and as she threw herself fully into the pacifist cause she began to feel it was best to spend time 'with people with the same train of thought'.[13] The pacifism of the time was often marked by an intense sociability, with frequent marches, meetings, lectures and discussion groups, and these activities soon filled her days. It was an exciting but somewhat serious-minded existence, with Stella recalling that there 'was never entertainment, there wasn't time'.[14]

After finishing vet school in 1935, Stella began work in a small clinic among the railway yards of Chalk Farm in north London, but it was the Fellowship of Reconciliation (FoR) that would soon take up most of her time. The Fellowship was dedicated to the idea that the love of Christ could stop violence, and every morning Stella worked in the office at 17 Red Lion Square in Holborn, tending to her sick animals in the afternoon. Her time at the Fellowship was spent keeping the membership files up to date. Popular legend had it that the headless body of Oliver Cromwell was buried in the square outside the office, a not so subtle reminder of what could happen to dissenting Christians. The work was not glamorous, and the pay was low, but Stella and her co-workers thought that from such seemingly mundane tasks the cause of peace could be built. The others in the office were mainly women in their twenties and thirties, and a blurry photograph taken forty years later shows the women reunited on a summer day. Stella is standing on the far right of the group in a cotton frock, with her fair hair over her ears and looking shyly at the floor. Her dog, a Pekinese, that she was apparently never without, sits in another woman's lap at the front.[15]

Founded in 1915 as a non-denominational Christian organisation, the Fellowship declared that Christians were 'forbidden to wage war, and that our loyalty to our country, to humanity, to the Church Universal, and to Jesus Christ our Lord and Master, calls us instead to a life-service for the enthronement of Love in personal, commercial and national life'.[16] For members of the Fellowship, Christian love – as seen in the figure of Jesus on the cross – provided a moral and practical vision of how to live. Between the wars it was the most significant specifically religious pacifist organisation in Britain, and W. E. Orchard had long played a leading role. Other figures included Maude Royden, a prominent campaigner for women's suffrage, the first woman in England to be given a full-time preaching role – in another Congregationalist church – and the person who described the Church of England as the 'Conservative Party at prayer'.[17] Alongside Royden were more conventional people like Canon Charles Raven, Regius Professor of Divinity at Cambridge and an army chaplain in the First World War, whom (as we have seen) Roy Ridgway saw preach in Liverpool as a child.

The Fellowship of Reconciliation tried to bring together Quakers, Methodists, Anglicans, Baptists and others in opposition to war. For much of the 1920s and early 1930s, anti-war sentiments, if not quite absolute pacifist commitments, ran through large parts of British Christianity – much as they did socialism – reflecting attitudes prevalent throughout British society. Both the archbishops of Canterbury and York urged Christians to work towards international collaboration and peace, and in 1930 Anglican bishops from across the world had gathered for the Lambeth conference, declaring that 'war, as a method of settling international disputes, is incompatible with the teaching and example of our Lord Jesus Christ'.[18]

The idea for the Fellowship came from a meeting of international Christian pacifists near the German border with Switzerland, just as the First World War was being declared. The organisation that grew out of this meeting was self-consciously ecumenical, hoping to draw together the diverse parts of the Christian faith. The First World War initially made it difficult to travel between countries, but by the early 1930s a wider International Fellowship was fully in operation, trying to overcome the narrow parochialism of nation, class and to a slightly lesser extent creed. Branches would eventually open across Europe, the Americas, Japan, China, India and parts of Africa, and this ecumenical internationalism was a central part of FoR goals and ambitions. Conferences were held throughout the 1920s and 1930s, and a Youth Crusade was organised across Europe, with 50,000 Protestants and Catholics marching on Geneva calling for 'total disarmament amongst nations'.[19] The Fellowship had its own flavour and dynamics in each country, but it was the British and American groups that boasted the greatest organisational and numerical strength. The American branch was particularly active and drew in some remarkable figures, including the theologian Reinhold Niebuhr, John Nevin Sayre – a wealthy and well-connected Episcopal priest – and A. J. Muste, a pastor and labour organiser. It differed from the British version in that it had a stronger left-wing element, with many of its leaders cutting their teeth in labour activism.[20] These roots in protest would have important implications in later years when members of the American Fellowship also became leading figures in the American civil rights movement, inspiring its approach to non-violent protest.

Wide as the membership of the Fellowship of Reconciliation

was, there were also important streams of Christianity that lay outside its reach. Groups like the Christadelphians, Jehovah's Witnesses and Plymouth Brethren all refused to fight during the First World War, but were definitely not part of the mainstream British anti-war movement. Jehovah's Witnesses, for example, are not pacifist in the narrow sense of the word, as it is not fighting in all wars that they object too, only ungodly wars.[21] The pacifists of the FoR often did not quite know what to make of such people.

At the Fellowship, Stella worked with a young woman called Doris Steynor. Doris came from nonconformist Christian and working-class East Ham, and the two women were drawn together. Although Doris also had two pacifist brothers, she later recalled that she felt her parents must have been a little 'ashamed' of her pacifism.[22] She had wanted to be a teacher, but cruelly had been told by her headmaster that her harelip ruled this out. As it was for Stella, the Christian peace movement became the centre of Doris's life, and she would later marry a man she met there, who had come to the Fellowship office seeking advice after feeling that no one else in his church understood his pacifism. Bernard Nicholls worked for a printing firm and came from a conservative, evangelical and Anglican family, spending his childhood moving around the small towns just north of London.[23] His meeting with Doris and her pacifist commitments changed his life. Many years later Stella would also remember being impressed by Doris's firm 'convictions'.[24]

Doris and Stella set up what they called 'peace shops', taking over empty shopfronts to display posters, hand out leaflets and try to engage with passers-by.[25] Doris found this last bit particularly uncomfortable. We can imagine that Stella must have too. For Doris her pacifism was the 'inevitable consequence of belief in our Lord' and she therefore found it difficult to explain to people who did not share her faith.[26] However, Doris noticed that although many people did not take her work altogether seriously there was little antagonism towards them.[27] People might have disagreed and thought they were 'crazy', but they were not aggressive, and the women came across enough Christian pacifists to feel succoured and supported. By the late 1930s, according to the lists meticulously kept by Stella, there were over a hundred Fellowship of Reconciliation groups in the London area alone, although their size varied considerably. This was more than enough to keep Doris and Stella busy.

Stella had been partly drawn to the Fellowship by Donald Soper, who was also a leading figure in the PPU and a Methodist preacher with a striking physical presence. Many years later, Soper would be the only person who visited Stella in Holloway prison. He revelled in controversy, later famously saying there was good in everyone, even Hitler, and he could be swept away by his own enthusiasm as he held an audience rapt. Standing out in the open, rain or shine, Soper made his name preaching just a short distance from the Tower of London, honing his own particular brand of pacifist and socialist Christianity as he saw off hecklers.[28] In 1936, he was appointed superintendent of the West London Methodist Mission, based in the seven-storey Kingsway Hall near the Fellowship office in Holborn. Kingsway Hall was more like an assembly room than a church, with classrooms, a youth club and a chamber with red velvet tip-up seats that could hold 2,000 people. Soper's oratory frequently drew full houses, but he could sometimes be a difficult person to get along with. According to his biographer, he had a tendency to 'high-handedness', relished his own status and seldom changed his mind.[29] He would not be the first person whose sense of principle could sometimes merge into vanity.

Many Christian pacifists stood in the broad middle ground between Christianity and socialism. For Stella, her pacifism 'came through the church, and socialism came with it through the church'.[30] Similarly, Soper thought that Christianity and socialism were inevitably linked and argued that 'capitalism depends on violence for its ultimate authority and sanction'.[31] Later in life, Soper caused consternation in some right-wing circles when he said that Thatcherism was incompatible with Christianity. Vera Brittain, whose opposition to war had always arisen through a mixture of feminism and socialism, more and more looked to her Christian faith. For her, Christianity was now the only 'condition of survival'.[32] She was an Anglican, but had little time for organised religion, and under the influence of the Quaker and First World War conscientious objector Corder Catchpool briefly flirted with the idea of joining the Society of Friends.[33] In her memoir she described her new approach to pacifism as being motivated by the 'prophetic challenge of an inner compulsion, for which Christ died, in the ultimate transcendence of love over power'.[34] If Vera was not formally a Quaker, she could certainly write like one. Across the spectrum, in the late 1930s, as the political left grappled with the relationship between opposition to war and opposition to Fascism, many who were both Christian and socialist increasingly stressed their faith in Christ alongside or even above their political commitments.

It is important to keep Christian pacifism in perspective. Despite its relative prominence, the Fellowship of Reconciliation only ever attracted around 8,000 members. Absolute pacifism, as opposed to a broad but somewhat non-specific opposition to war, was always a marginal presence within mainstream British Christianity. For centuries Catholic theologians had been developing the doctrine of the 'just war' – by which, along with other conditions, violence was justified if it was for a good cause – and the Pope after all had his very own army in the shape of the Swiss Guard. The Church of England too was definitely not a pacifist organisation. William Temple, the Archbishop of York who later became the Archbishop of Canterbury, went so far in 1935 as to call pacifism a 'heresy'.[35] For Temple, a left-wing Christian and former member of the Labour Party, to ask 'nations to act by love only, when justice is insecure', would produce no result.[36] As Temple saw it, Christians should not forget the violence of the Old Testament. Although the Methodist Peace Fellowship, with Soper leading the way, was the largest group in the Fellowship of Reconciliation, in 1937 the Methodist Conference decided not to take a formal position in relation to war.[37] Even Quaker pacifism was often far from absolute. The Quaker focus on individual conscience meant that holding a firm line on any issue was difficult. In the First World War, over a third of Quaker men of eligible age served in the military in some way.[38]

If Christian pacifism was only a minority concern in Britain, it was even more marginal in most of mainland Europe. In France and Germany, pacifism was only ever a very fringe concern for the Protestant and Catholic churches.[39] With some notable and lively exceptions, French pacifism between the wars was largely political and humanitarian. German Christian pacifism similarly had some significant figures, but was always a very small and fragile movement.

Mainstream Protestant Christian theology in the 1930s moved

strongly against pacifism, as theologians such as the American Reinhold Niebuhr and the Swiss Karl Barth – who became a leading figure in Christian opposition to the Nazis – emphasised the sinfulness of man.[40] Niebuhr, once a leading figure in the American branch of the Fellowship of Reconciliation, had by the mid-1930s turned his back on peace activism. For him, perhaps the most influential American theologian of the century, 'the dream of perpetual peace and brotherhood for human society is one which will never be fully realised'.[41] From Niebuhr's perspective, humanity was not capable of living harmoniously, and conflict and even war were inevitable. Individuals might have been capable of good, but this became corrupted when they lived together in society. He further argued that the absolute call for peace becomes hypocritical in the face of economic and racial injustice, a way simply to defend the status quo.[42] This was ultimately a pessimistic vision of humanity, one in which the only hope lay in the grace of God. This theological focus fitted in very much with the wider cultural mood of a 'morbid age' and gloom about the human condition.[43] Niebuhr and his brand of Christian realism were firmly part of the wider sombre atmosphere.

Against this background, it could be hard to be a Christian pacifist, even or especially among other Christians. After leaving the parsonage of the King's Weigh House Stella St John moved with other members of the church into rented rooms in Notting Hill, where the large houses were being broken up into cheap lodgings. Stella soon fell out with her housemates over her particularly ardent anti-war convictions and found a bunk in the more pacifist atmosphere of Soper's West London Mission, which was conveniently only a short walk from the Fellowship's office. Pacifists were often shunned by other Christians, and sometimes even asked to leave their congregations, especially in the Anglican Church. On discovering that Bernard Nicholls was a pacifist, his Anglican parish priest gave a sermon that turned into a direct and very personal condemnation of Bernard's position.[44] The extent of the sympathy or hostility towards pacifism often varied from congregation to congregation, and people often circulated between churches and congregations, like Stella and Bernard, until they found a form of worship and much more importantly a group of like-minded souls where they could feel at home.

The Christianity of pacifists was often deeply anti-institutional and anti-textual, in that it focused less on the meaning of biblical verses and more on the broader example of Jesus. Christian pacifists could also be profoundly disappointed by the Christian hierarchy, particularly in the Church of England, feeling it had 'gone astray' in its support for war.[45] John Middleton Murry, after leaving behind his socialist phase towards the end of the 1930s, saw pacifism as a way of renewing the Church, as a more authentic and intimate form of religion, and at one point he even described himself as a 'cleric without a church'.[46] Donald Soper understood pacifism as the 'practical interpretation of the way of Christ', later commenting that he thought the Bible was a 'very dangerous document'. For him the Bible allowed you 'to support any damn thing you want if you look diligently enough'.[47] For such Christian pacifists, moral questions such as whether or not to resort to violence were understood as being answerable simply by imagining 'what would Jesus do?'. The fact that Christ had chosen to die on the cross rather than impose the Kingdom of God was seen as a profound moral lesson.[48] In this vision, Christianity was a simple religion of love that had been made overly complex by theology and ritual.

In its focus on love, Christian pacifism was full of hope for redemption. Visions of possible human perfection ran especially strongly in Quakerism and some forms of Methodism, but could also be found elsewhere, stressing that although war and violence might have their origins in human lust it is possible to overcome these vices. Like socialism, this Christian pacifist tradition is based on the assumption that humans can be better, that sin and evil can be defeated and that eventually all people can live together in peace. But if socialism represented a faith that human beings can solve their own problems through revolution – through human sweat and tears – Christian pacifism resorted to more spiritual labour. This was not a grand vision of redemption brought about through dramatic divine intervention, but was small-scale and quietist, even if its ambitions were bold. Middleton Murry urged pacifists to lead exemplary lives, demonstrating the possibility of true peace. In doing so, he hoped to create the 'raw material for a new Christian church', a new Jerusalem amid the violent insanity of the world. The emphasis was on personal character and leading a life like Christ's. We can only assume that Stella St John took similar calls very seriously. By the start of the war, this upper-middle-class woman from the London fringes was serving soup to the homeless and sleeping in a flea-infested bed.

But imitating Jesus is not an easy task.

CHAPTER 5

Non-Violence, Gandhi and Beyond

At the end of January 1937, Ronald Duncan stood on the plains of central India, anxious to meet the man he hoped could teach him – and everyone else for that matter – how to step back from violence. Ronald was a twenty-two-year-old English pacifist whose German father had died after being interned as an 'enemy alien' in South Africa during the First World War. The young man grew up having very little to do with the paternal side of this family – who had Jewish and possibly aristocratic roots – as they disapproved of his mother, apparently fearing she might be an actress. Born in colonial Rhodesia, where his father was learning experimental agricultural techniques, Ronald spent his childhood in the London suburbs close to his English family. As a student at Cambridge he had flirted with socialism, before being put off by its abstractions and internal disputes. But he was still deeply concerned by the way the globe seemed to be turning, by what he saw as the world's moral decay, rampant forms of exploitation and cruel violence. And he thought that in rural South Asia he had found the answer to the world's problems. After a long journey, Ronald climbed off a small bullock cart and there in front of him, standing barefoot in the fields, was Mahatma Gandhi.[1] That same week in Berlin, Hitler called for Germany's withdrawal from the Treaty of Versailles and the return of its colonies in Africa. For Ronald Duncan, and many others, there was a lot riding on Gandhi's shoulders.

Gandhi seemed to offer pacifists hope. If war was a global phenomenon, so too were the solutions, and people like Ronald drew their inspiration from around the world, with India leading the way. Through the 1920s and 1930s Gandhi had led a campaign of non-violent resistance to British imperial rule, attracting popular support, a brutal response from the British authorities and international headlines.[2] The sight of masses of unarmed Indians, led by a thin man in a white loincloth, standing up to the might of the British Empire, gave people like Ronald confidence they had found not only an answer to violent aggression, but a path to moral uplift too. The lesson that many pacifists took from Gandhi was that through a rigorous programme of discipline, restraint and the cultivation of good character, where bodies were literally put on the line, it was possible to defeat a politics based on coercion, force and brutality. To pacifists Gandhi was an exemplary and inspiring figure, close to being a saint, who embodied all the ethical principles they hoped to defend, combining both realist politics and spiritual redemption. Sometimes the adoration for him could reach fever pitch. Wilfred Wellock, a Christian socialist MP who had been imprisoned as a conscientious objector in the First World War, wrote that Gandhi was the 'the greatest and most Christ-like figure in contemporary history'.[3] For his admirers Gandhi offered a promise that was both practical and principled.[4]

The trouble with moral saints is that they can be hard to follow – the standards they set can be too demanding, and they can disappoint us or seek to live in ways we find hard to copy. The Gandhi of the British progressive imagination – created from an unstable mix of anti-imperialist solidarity and exotic fantasies about the East – did not always match up with the Gandhi of flesh and blood, who could have ideas about the moral force of non-violence very different from those of many of the pacifists who sought him out. Above all, Gandhi's emphasis on an austere and chaste form of personal moral development was very attractive to some, but for people coming of age like Ronald Duncan it could also be extremely frustrating.

The unlikely meeting of a towering figure of the campaign for Indian independence and the young man from England came about after Ronald had sent Gandhi a copy of a short pamphlet he had written. Ronald's *The Complete Pacifist* was a diagnosis of the causes of war located in capitalist overproduction and the constant search for profit – partly inspired by his earlier undergraduate socialism – but the text also claimed to have found an answer to current inequities and suffering, arguing that 'the present economic system cannot exist without war, and if people refuse to fight in wars, then the system automatically must cease to exist'.[5] For Ronald, there was a way to end both war and exploitation.[6] He pointed to the example of industrial unrest in the Hungarian colliery of Pécs, where the miners had occupied the pit and gone on hunger strike before having their demands met. To test out his ideas, in 1936 he had briefly worked down a Derbyshire coalmine and had then headed to the South Wales pits, hoping to persuade some striking miners there to adopt his methods.[7] But he had left disenchanted after being chased out of town by a Communist trade union organiser.[8]

Despite the disappointments, Ronald did not give up hope. His pamphlet was picked up by the Peace Pledge Union and republished for its membership. Gandhi – or his secretary at least – responded to Ronald's letter, noting that the pamphlet was interesting although not without flaws. Blessed with the confidence of youth and class, Ronald wrote back suggesting the two men meet. In later life, Ronald described himself during this time as 'spiritually arrogant'.[9] He is perhaps being slightly unfair: one friend remarked of him that he was 'liable to see the worst about himself', and was both caring and 'in need of care'.[10] Self-assurance could hide a sensitivity. Either way, Ronald received an invitation to India, and the apparent affirmation must have been immensely exciting.

By the time the letter from India arrived in London, Gandhi's suggested date was just weeks away and Ronald set off almost immediately, taking along his new friend Ben Britten for the first part of the journey. Ronald and Ben – a recent graduate of the Royal College of Music and an up-and-coming composer – had bonded over their mutual interest in pacifism, music, poetry and sex (albeit with different people).[11] Ronald was particularly fond of what he described as Britten's 'schoolboyish' sense of humour.[12] They had been introduced by their mutual friend Nigel Spottiswoode, whom Ronald had met at Cambridge before Nigel was expelled for taking his experimental films too far.[13] Ben was working with Nigel at the Royal Mail Film Unit alongside W. H. Auden and was already a pacifist by the time he met Ronald. Together Ronald and Ben wrote a never to be performed piece called the *Pacifist March*. Ronald claims, in his not always entirely reliable memoir, that the music was either lost after been given to the PPU or locked away in a trunk somewhere. Either way, Ben never seems to have wanted his composition to be heard.[14]

Ronald and Ben made the most of a stopover in Paris, going to classical music concerts, buying a copy of James Joyce's novel *Ulysses* – banned in Britain at the time – and making a fumbling visit to a brothel before bashfully running out at the sight of naked women.[15] Ben, who was still coming to terms with his own sexuality, wrote in his diary that the 'nude females, fat, hairy and unprepossessing; smelling of vile cheap scent' left him feeling disgusted.[16]

After Paris, Ben ran out of money, so Ronald set off alone by train to Marseille, where he caught a steamer to Bombay. The ship was segregated along racial lines, and Ronald, who was placed at the Captain's table with the other white passengers, decided to sit with the Indian passengers, at which point many of the Europeans stopped talking to him.[17] The only white person who sought out his company was a Scotsman who insisted on sitting close to Ronald, puffing out great clouds of pipe smoke. From Bombay, Ronald took a train to Wardha, a small city that was a centre for the cotton trade and in the middle of the country. As the train made its way east, he found himself once again sitting next to the very same Scotsman, who revealed himself to be a police officer sent to see what Ronald was up to after the letters to Gandhi had been intercepted by the British Special Branch. The encounter appears more farcical than intimidating, as the detective complained that Ronald was travelling in too cheap and uncomfortable a compartment, but the two men 'exchanged cards' and spent the rest of the journey talking amiably.[18] Throughout the train journey, Ronald was bitten by mosquitoes, but was 'strangely happy' in anticipation of meeting the great man.[19] It was the dry season, and the temperature was thankfully cool, but Ronald took a cart the last few miles and finally arrived at his destination.

Gandhi had established his ashram in April 1936, less than a year before Ronald's visit, and had eventually given it the name Sevagram, meaning 'village of service'. Made up of one-storey mud buildings deliberately built in the common village style and surrounded by a bamboo stockade, the ashram was committed to some of the same principles of 'rural reconstruction' that lay behind the foundation of Dartington Hall in Devon, where Stella St John had been working. The humble buildings would later play a central role in the history of Indian independence – it was here that the Quit India Movement would hold its first meeting in 1942, demanding an end to British rule.

On his first evening in the ashram, Ronald sat by the well watching the villagers go by. Gandhi was taking a vow of silence the next day, as he did every Monday, but in the days that followed the two men walked through the fields together, Gandhi a few paces ahead, their conversations ranging over vegetarianism, chastity and self-control, as well as Spain and the League of Nations. It must have been quite a sight, a young English man with striking features, including a prominent nose and thick head of hair, following the elderly leader of the Indian independence struggle. Ronald noted in his journal that he found it hard to 'stay silent' even though he was eager to let the older man 'speak more'. He was particularly keen to talk about non-violence and the ideas raised in his pamphlet. As they walked through the village Ronald told Gandhi about his experiences in the mines and asked for advice on passive resistance, only to find that Gandhi disliked that term, as he thought it was too negative, and explained that there were no short cuts: the only way to true non-violence was self-abnegation and a rigorous form of self-denial.[20]

Gandhi's thoughts drew on an eclectic mix of Socrates, Thoreau and Tolstoy, as well as the Hindu *Bhagavad Gita* and Indian traditions of self-sacrifice. During his struggles in South Africa he had coined the term *satyagraha*, usually translated as truth, soul force or love force, pairing it with the idea of *ahimsa*, or non-violence. For Gandhi, this meant practising the virtues of humility and selflessness, seen most obviously in chastity, poverty and wearing homespun cloth.[21] This was a severe and moralistic vision of life. On one of their walks together, the two men saw four or five people defecating against a wall. Gandhi did not say anything, but proceeded to pick up the shit with his bare hands, and Ronald wrote that this incident taught him more about humility than any of their long discussions.[22] As well as sex, diets were restricted too, with Gandhi disapproving of all seasoning and spice, which he saw as aphrodisiacal.[23] Ronald was a heavy smoker and took to hiding among the sugarcanes for a cigarette. He tried to copy

Gandhi in other ways by abandoning his bedroll and sleeping out in the open, but woke up covered by a heavy dew, and with a severe chill and a stiff neck.

There were other challenges too. Ronald was shocked by the poverty around him, and felt distanced from the villagers, writing in his journal that he was seeing life 'through a screen'.[24] This was a very different place from the industrialised areas of England and Wales he had previously sought out. When not talking with Gandhi, he spent his days wandering through the nearby village and returned home at night to write of its 'terrible inhumane state', its people 'living on a handful of food and dirty water'. Above all, he blamed the British Empire for their plight and wrote that the 'BE' was responsible for 'mass murder'. Ronald had come to India to find peace, but was deeply disturbed by caste inequality and unsure how to respond. On one occasion he joined Gandhi on a visit to a meeting of bishops in Wardha, and the car was stopped on the way by the students from a girls' school. Gandhi 'smacked a few of their faces in fun' but Ronald's overall impression was that the people 'really worshipped him', and he worried that the man was being turned into a martyr by his followers.

Ronald Duncan was not the first European or North American to visit Gandhi and he would not be the last. The mahatma had become increasingly influential among the left, anti-imperialists, Christian pacifists and an assortment of others from across the globe who were searching for political or mystical fulfilment.[25] There was a constant train of visitors hoping that Gandhi could provide the answers to a wide spectrum of questions. Alongside thousands of Indians of all descriptions, British socialists, European feminists, African-American intellectuals, Polish professors, South African architects, Japanese politicians and German Nazis all came to sit on his floor.[26] One acquaintance from the time wrote that 'Gandhiji appealed to the imagination of the world as a little scrawny, half-starved, self-denying man in breach-clout – a wizened little monkey defying the terrible British lion ... '[27] We can probably assume that Gandhi was far more important to his European and American visitors than they were to him, but he still made time to see them and explain his principles of living, and sometimes saw them as useful allies in the cause of Indian independence.[28] In reality – and sometimes to the great disappointment of his followers – the mahatma was an astute and determined politician, but this did not stop many of his western visitors projecting their own visions on to him.

Not everyone who visited Gandhi was interested in politics, in the narrow sense of the word. Muriel Lester, a London Christian pacifist and preacher – dubbed the 'mother of world peace' by her biographer – visited Gandhi multiple times in order to try and understand what she called the 'Oriental point of view'.[29] In October 1926, she had first visited Gandhi's former ashram, Sabarmati, a compound of whitewashed huts surrounded by fields overlooking the factories of Ahmedabad.[30] Muriel clearly thought Christianity greatly superior to Hinduism, writing, 'I don't like Hinduism . . . I've never found anything in it to appeal to me,' but in the Gandhian ideas of *ahimsa* and *satyagraha* she saw clear echoes of her own slightly stark Christian belief.[31] This was important to her as she thought it showed her approach had a universal resonance. If a high-caste Indian could come to similar conclusions as an English Christian, perhaps a more general vision of human possibility was within reach. Muriel wrote to Sir Samuel Hoare, the Secretary of State for India, declaring that 'Mr Gandhi points to the same Way Out that Christ has always pointed to – the Cross, self-suffering, the way of God.'[32] Suffering was important to Muriel, and in Gandhi's sacrifices she saw a way to redemption.

Muriel was the daughter of a wealthy businessman who was president of the Essex Baptist Union. Together with her sister Doris, she had strong links with the suffragettes and had become a pacifist during the First World War, when she refused to pray for victory lest it be a 'vindictive' one.[33] She had also taken a vow of poverty – partly inspired by Gandhi – and following the death of her brother during the First World War had established Kingsley Hall in the East End of London in 1927, shortly after her first visit to the ashram. The hall was set in the slums of Bromley-by-Bow, designed to be a sort of 'teetotal pub' where the local residents could socialise and learn. As well as acting as a prayer hall, clinic, nursery and soup kitchen, it was a communal home for pacifists and other humanitarians carrying out good works.[34] Muriel was deeply sceptical of organised religion, and led worship at the hall for anyone who wanted to come. She ate her meals and prayed with a small group who had likewise taken a vow of poverty. She later described how 'ten volunteers give whole-time service and receive food, seven shillings a week and a cell on the flat roof as their portion; ignoring barriers of creed, class and nation, they serve in unity, cooking or organising, cleaning or teaching, scrubbing or praying'.[35] For Muriel at least poverty was the path to serenity, as she sought what she called the 'blessing, derived from intimate contact with the sorrows of the oppressed'.[36]

Muriel's plans for self-improvement among the slums of east London attracted many of the great and the good – or at least a very particular slice of them. George Lansbury, the Labour Party politician, Christian pacifist and fellow resident of the East End, had encouraged the Lester sisters to found Kingsley Hall in the first place. When a new building was erected, the people attending the bricklaying ceremony included the novelist John Galsworthy, who would later win the Nobel Prize in Literature; Sybil Thorndike, a Shakespearean actress and future Dame Commander of the Order of the British Empire; and Walford Davies, who would shortly become the King's Master of Music. Despite or perhaps even because of her vow of poverty, Lester was used to moving in influential circles.

When Muriel first arrived at Gandhi's ashram in 1926, he was busy with hundreds of visitors who had come for his fifty-seventh birthday celebrations.[37] Together with her eighteen-year-old nephew George Hogg, who had accompanied her on the trip, Muriel was allotted a 'small wooden shed' with two beds, a table and a chair.[38] On her first day the intense heat and lack of food were too much, and she was forced to retire to bed. When food did come – largely oranges, grapes and nuts – it was served on banana leaves tied together with thorns. Muriel settled into the rhythm of the place, with prayers at sunrise, then cleaning, cooking and laundry. She tried her hand at spinning, but with little success. Every evening there was a sunset walk, and every morning a swim in the fast-flowing river, but with all the people around Muriel was too shy to approach Gandhi directly. At one point Gandhi asked someone who this strange English woman was sitting alone in her room reading.[39] Muriel finally found the courage to strike up a conversation just a few days before her stay came to an end, and immediately blurted out an invitation for him to come to Britain. Surprisingly enough,

Gandhi accepted, but on condition that she persuaded the Lanca-
shire mill owners to stop exporting cotton to India. Lester thought
this was probably too large a task, so Gandhi instead requested that
she lobby for a change in British opium and alcohol policy in India.
She agreed. Not only did this seem more manageable, but it chimed
with her own ascetic sensibilities: Kingsley Hall had, after all, been
set up to promote teetotalism among the London working class.[40]
Muriel was a disciplined figure – although with a great capacity for
friendship – who freely admitted she could sometimes be a 'bit doc-
trinaire'.[41] She saw Gandhi as a kindred spirit.

British pacifists had first tried to put Gandhian ideas of non-
violence to the test in 1932, after Japanese troops rolled into
north-eastern China the previous year. A group of Christian pacifists called for the formation of an unarmed Peace Army of civilians
that would put itself between the warring parties.[42] Muriel Lester,
as well as Donald Soper, volunteered immediately.[43] Eight hundred
other people came forward too, and Muriel wrote that she hoped
to wield the 'tremendous spiritual weapon of active creative goodwill' against the assailants.[44] But the Peace Army never really got
off the ground, apart from marching to West India Docks in London, Muriel and Donald at the front, to protest about a boat
leaving for Japan full of arms, before they were turned away at the
gates by the police. One volunteer would later describe those who
came forward as a 'horde of elderly ladies, clergymen, earnest
authors, rampageous undergraduates'.[45] Even other pacifists wondered what such a group would do in the face of bombings from
the air, if they ever made it to East Asia.

The Peace Army was one of many attempts by pacifists throughout the 1930s to develop a theory and practice of non-violence
that they hoped could stop war in its tracks. Ronald Duncan was
particularly inspired by the work of an American lawyer, labour
activist and disciple of Gandhi named Richard Gregg. Gregg was
quiet and humble in person, but sought to develop a revolutionary
theory of non-violent action. Experience with the American railway unions and the violent repression of a series of strikes in 1922
led him to try and find techniques with which the relatively powerless could defeat those with far greater might. He thought time in
India could help develop his ideas, and spent four years on the

subcontinent, including four months with Gandhi at the Sabarmati ashram.[46] Like Ronald and Gandhi, Richard Gregg was alarmed by the evils of industrialisation as much as by war. And like Ronald and Muriel he had a slightly romantic vision of Gandhi and India.[47] Much later Gregg would be an important influence on Martin Luther King, who wrote a preface to the 1960 reissue of one of his books.

The central pillar of Gregg's thought was the idea that pacifists could make belligerents lay down their weapons through the moral power of example. In the face of an army of upright pacifists, it was imagined that any invading soldier would feel so ashamed of his actions that he would renounce war. Gregg claimed that through a form of 'moral jujitsu' pacifists could make opponents lose balance – both literally and metaphorically.[48] In order to develop the fortitude and strength to accomplish this, a programme of 'training for peace' inspired by Gandhian ideas of self-discipline was proposed. In this vision, war could be defeated through a tight regime of physical exercise and selflessness. Like Gandhi's, Gregg's idea of non-violence sought to merge means and ends, offering both a practical approach to preventing war and a commitment to absolute principles. What made this so exciting to people like Ronald and Muriel was that they did not have to compromise their pacifist principles to get things done in a violent world. The best way to get things done was to start with yourself. The author Aldous Huxley – who would later write *Brave New World* – was a great promoter of Gregg's ideas and saw pacifism as a matter of 'personal reform'.[49] Huxley believed that ordinary people could 'overcome evil ... turn aside anger and hatred' through the cultivation of moral character.[50] Such strength might take years of training to achieve, but it could be done. Huxley particularly endorsed a schedule of meditation, knitting, folk dancing and singing. This chimed with the emphasis on personal moral virtue that ran through Christian pacifism, and was one of the reasons why non-violence was so popular, even if folk dancing and knitting were not necessarily everyone's cup of tea.

Gregg's work brought to the surface a key tension; he saw non-violence as both spiritual and practical, and he was as much concerned with whether non-violence got the job done as with whether it was simply right in principle.[51] This opened up the question whether non-violence actually worked. It might feel personally virtuous, but would it make a practical difference? Was it too much about signalling moral purity and too little about preventing violence and suffering? Could self-discipline really prevent a tank from rolling into town? They would not be the first and nor would they be the last people of strong convictions to be potentially blinded by the light of their own goodness. George Orwell, the scourge of progressive pieties, wrote that 'If [pacifists] imagine that one can somehow "overcome" the German army by lying on one's back, let them go on imagining it...'[52] Non-violence, it was claimed, was all very well for student discussions and church sermons, but in the face of totalitarian violence it was at best naive and at worst complicit in suffering and destruction. It might work as a weapon against the British in India, but simply would not do against Hitler. William Temple, the Archbishop of York, told his pacifist nephew that non-violence would work only 'if the society itself is terribly civilised and has a good morality'.[53] Non-violence might have been effective, so the argument went, in an imperial Britain, with all its supposed moral sensitivities, but it was quite another thing in the face of the brute force of the Nazi boot. It is probably worth noting that the British Empire was also not always entirely averse to killing unarmed civilians, but that was not really the point.

Pacifists could also struggle with aspects of non-violence.[54] Gandhi never seems to have been a pacifist at all, at least in the sense understood by many of his European and American visitors. He had after all recruited Indian soldiers for the First World War, and while he would refuse to support British efforts in the Second World War – unless India was granted self-rule – he remained deeply ambiguous about the use of force. Some critics even felt that he was in fact perversely attracted to violence, or at least the suffering it caused, because he thought non-violence had to be tested against violence in order to prove its righteousness.[55] He told Muriel Lester that 'sorrow and suffering make for character if they are voluntarily borne'.[56] In the early years of the Second World War, Gandhi would controversially urge the Czechs, the Poles, the French and the British, as well as the Jews, not to resist the Nazis by arms, promising this would add 'several inches' to their moral stature.[57] Elsewhere, he argued that it was joyful to 'countenance ... thousands losing their life for *satyagraha*', on the grounds that 'it ennobles those who lose their lives'.[58] In this vision, suffering was not to be avoided but actively looked for. This icono-clasm could be frightening to many people opposed to war.

It was not just that suffering should be sought out but also that pleasure should be renounced. Back at the ashram, Ronald became troubled by some of Gandhi's attitudes. It was particularly difficult for the young man to come to terms with the mahatma's denial of sensual pleasure, which reminded him of the 'pettiness of English puritanism'.[59] Gandhi told him that renunciation was the way to 'find the truth' and that sensual delight was degrading of 'moral development'.[60] Ronald – who loved Schubert and Stravinsky, and was very fond of Ben Britten, was particularly upset to hear that Gandhi thought listening to music should be avoided, and that lik-ing Mozart might be a sin.[61] Gandhi also constantly asked Ronald to stop smoking – knowing all about his furtive trips into the canefields – and sent him boiled sweets as an alternative. Although he was touched, Ronald was not convinced. Gandhi told the still largely sexually inexperienced but hopeful Englishman that he had never forgiven himself for the sensualism that he had shown his wife in the early years of their marriage. The idea of abstinence clearly horrified Ronald, who exclaimed in his journal: 'to hell with this chastity poison . . . There is a divine function . . . in love.'[62]

After a few weeks with Gandhi, Ronald appears to have got bored, noting that he sometimes found it 'hard to concentrate on Gandhi's talk'.[63] He also increasingly felt that he could not be 'devotional', and that Gandhi's 'value is his moral strength' rather than his practical advice. Gandhi apparently agreed that Ronald's time was up, and wished him well, before urging him to take care of himself as his body was 'strained too much'. The young man collected his books and climbed back on the same bullock cart that had brought him into the village, heading off back to the train sta-tion in Wardha. He would never return.

For her part, Muriel Lester was attracted by this uncompromis-ing asceticism, writing that 'the new method Gandhi has introduced into politics is self-suffering; never to forget what it is to be hungry, being reminded of it every day by one's own hunger'.[64] She had after all taken a vow of poverty and was a teetotal vegetarian who never married, dedicating herself to her good works. She wrote that the 'business of the Church of Christ touches life at every point, and it is perhaps better not to join it than to come imagining that one can have a day off whenever one likes'.[65] In her memoirs, published in 1937, Muriel railed against the 'sex nastiness' of the cinema and called for the Christian Church to lead a campaign for decency.[66]

The all-encompassing perfectionism of Gandhian non-violence could be felt as a great personal burden – indeed for some adherents that was the whole point. For others, this could be distressing. The memoirs and recollections of many of Gandhi's companions are full of what his great-granddaughter described as the conflicting claims of happiness and moral virtue when trying to live up to 'Gandhi's extraordinary saintliness'.[67] All too often he could seem unconcerned by the burdens that such moral purity placed on others, and the sense of failure that could result. To put it bluntly, Gandhi appeared uncaring.[68] The demands of non-violence were uncompromising, denying many of the sources of pleasure that make life worth living. As George Orwell wrote: 'it's probable that some who achieve or aspire to sainthood have never felt much temptation to be human beings'.[69] If *satyagraha* was a form of love, it could look like an exclusive kind of love, bereft of romance, desire, joy and affection.

There was a significant wedge between non-violence and many pacifists, with many feeling deeply awkward about Richard Gregg's proposals in particular, not least because they risked playing up to a reputation for crankiness. One prominent pacifist called the activities that were supposed to promote self-discipline 'yogi-bogie exercises'.[70] We are firmly in George Orwell's territory of sandal-wearers and fruit-juice drinkers here.

With or without the yoga and singing, the emphasis on moral virtue was something that people like Ronald Duncan would sometimes struggle to live up to. It is hard, unattractive and even slightly inhumane to try and be a saint. But Ronald still ran with the idea that pacifists could live by the power of example and was looking for a place to put his plans into action.

Before that he would fall in love.

CHAPTER 6

Confronting War

The late 1930s saw international political crisis after political crisis pile up one upon the other. In March 1938 German troops marched into Austria and were greeted by cheering crowds; the *Anschluss* was just the latest stage in Hitler's dream of a Greater Germany, and the Austrian army was ordered not to resist as Hitler began a triumphal tour through the country, and any opposition was brutally suppressed. Within days Austria was annexed to the Third Reich, taking citizenship rights away from tens of thousands of Jews and Gypsies, with only the meekest protests from the League of Nations and the rest of the world. The international order set in place at the end of the First World War was unable or unwilling to right itself, as Nazi Germany sought to redraw the map of Europe and claim its own empire. Tensions rose, factories churned out more and more weapons and armies across the world grew, as Fascism became increasingly bellicose and confident. In Britain, air-raid sirens were tested in most cities and towns, gas masks were distributed and trenches dug in the city's parks. The country was being prepared for war, as families gathered most nights around the wireless listening to news of the gathering storm.

As the debates throughout the previous decade about the best way to avoid the horrors of war acquired a frightening urgency, pacifists were forced to decide exactly what it meant to stand up for peace. In doing so, the relationship between Christianity, socialism, non-violence and other commitments took on rough edges, with the space for compromise and ambiguity increasingly closed down. Some concluded that the brutal reality of Fascism meant that an anti-war stance had become practically and morally untenable. Others remained resolute in the belief that no evil could be worse than war. For millions of people around the world, pacifist and otherwise, in Britain and elsewhere, political and personal dilemmas were coming into ever sharper focus.

On his way home to Britain from Gandhi's ashram, Ronald Duncan had steamed north up the Red Sea. To the east, the Yemeni port of Aden had recently been declared a British colony. On reaching Cairo in the spring of 1937, Ronald picked up a letter from his friend from Cambridge days Nigel Spottiswoode, declaring that he was in love with a woman called Rose Marie and that he could not wait for Ronald to get to know her. Just days after arriving in London, as Neville Chamberlain became British Prime Minister, Ronald met Rose Marie for the first time, lunching at a vegetarian restaurant in Leicester Square. The young woman was a student at the Royal Academy of Music as well as an aspiring actress. Nigel was clearly besotted. And very quickly, so too was Ronald.

Naively perhaps, Nigel proposed that Rose Marie and Ronald both accompany him on a trip to Devon. Ronald later wrote in his memoir that on the long train ride to the south-west he was amazed by how easily Rose Marie seemed to believe 'all the lies' he told her about the trip to India, including that he had killed at least one man with a sword, surely an unlikely act for a self-declared pacifist.[1] Arriving in Devon during an unseasonably hot week over Easter, the trio stayed in a small cottage on the rugged coast, just a stone's throw from the Cornish border, where Ronald had sometimes holidayed as a child. There was only one bed, and the two men slept on the cold floor.

The visit seems to have been both awkward and chaste, but in the coming weeks Ronald and Rose Marie grew close, Nigel's affection for Rose Marie either forgotten or ignored. Over fifty years later Rose Marie remembered that first trip to Devon as deeply romantic; she recalled being impressed by Ronald's 'glamour', as well as the large number of letters he seemed to receive.[2] For his part, Ronald described the early stages of the romance as creating an almost religious sense of connection. Not only was Gandhian-style chastity and self-denial now firmly off the table, but Rose Marie also added a deeply personal dimension to Ronald's fears for the future. His poem, 'Down Tools', written at the time, contains the lines:

You don't care
Whether its gas or shrapnel
That kills Bill, and will
kick Rose Marie's womb out.[3]

Things were not straightforward though, because both Ronald's and Rose Marie's families initially disapproved of their relationship – his because she was an actress (repeating the response of the previous generation), hers because of his dark complexion. Rose Marie later recalled that when her mother first met Ronald, she made him hold out his hands, believing that by looking at his fingernails she could confirm her suspicions that he was an Indian.[4] Early in the relationship, Ronald was living in a 'respectable' boarding house with strict rules, while Rose Marie stayed in a flat with her brother, so it was not easy for the couple to spend time together. The answer was to return to the part of south-west England where they had fallen in love.[5]

The sweethearts eloped for the Cornish–Devon border at four in the morning. Ronald's family – his sister Bianca lived nearby in a house with their mother – soon embraced the couple after the rocky start. Ben Britten was most displeased, telling Ronald that he was an 'irresponsible devil'.[6] On reaching the coast, the couple struggled to find somewhere to live, as many of the locals disapproved of their unmarried 'illicit love'.[7] Ronald and Rose Marie eventually settled in West Mill, a three-room cottage with no lavatory or running water that, in Ronald's words, looked like a 'drunken charwoman', its rotten thatch slipping down over the walls.[8] Despite the dilapidation, the mill was just yards from a beautiful beach. It would remain their home for the rest of their lives.

For Ronald at least, the move to Devon was an opportunity to start a new life in more ways than one, given that the international situation was increasingly 'grim and serious'.[9] With little chance of avoiding war his faith in the power of non-violence was falling away. The pamphlet that Ronald had gone to India to discuss with Gandhi had provoked considerable controversy, bringing to a head a widespread unease about the 'crankiness' of non-violence, and in the face of criticism the PPU withdrew it, insisting that its proposals had never been official policy.[10] A small minority of pacifists, however, were still convinced that non-violence, as both a moral virtue and a practical technique, would work, even against Fascism. Donald Soper remained deeply committed to non-violence throughout his life, writing that 'perhaps the nation which renounced violence will suffer crucifixion, it is a possibility, though I think a small one'.[11] Others were less willing to take the risk. Suffering on the cross or on the end of the Nazi bayonet did not seem attractive options, and Ronald was already looking elsewhere for ways to live out his pacifist convictions.

For a brief while satire about the state of British and international politics seemed to be the only way to respond to the gap between aspirations for peace and a world on the brink of war. For Ronald, rather than simply weeping at the tragic turn of history, there was morbid humour to be found as the world lurched towards disaster. He started a small magazine – *The Townsman* – with the help of Rose Marie and his sister Bianca, and they printed a few hundred copies in a room at West Mill. Although its readership remained small in number, the magazine did get some attention for announcing the launch of a new movement dubbed the Rexist Party – which, apparently by accident, also happened to be the name of a far-right political party in Belgium. The satirical manifesto claimed that the biggest problem facing the country was working-class 'multiplication' and that the only way to prevent this was to shut down well-known spaces of temptation, such as Brighton Pier. The text was posted to every MP and member of the House of Lords, and although Ronald had meant it as a joke, other people took it seriously and he was soon inundated with requests to join.[12] Unperturbed, or perhaps emboldened, Ronald wrote another pamphlet, *Our Strategy in War*, which was again posted off to MPs and Lords. This new piece declared that there were 'no half-measures in war', and recommended poisoning the water supply and destroying the sewerage system, as well as dropping birth-control appliances all over the German countryside. The final punchline was that Fascists could be reduced to a state of moral apathy if the writers Stephen Spender and Edith Sitwell were parachuted into Berlin to a soundtrack provided by the music of Vaughan Williams. It is not entirely clear what Ronald had against these three members of the British artistic elite, but in one of his memoirs he claimed that the pamphlet resulted in a visit from two MI5 officers, who, focusing on the parachutists, wanted to know how he had come to hear about British plans to airdrop soldiers in Axis territory.[13]

In Scotland, Fred Urquhart's novel *Time Will Knit* was finally published in mid-May 1938 and he began to get nervous about its reception. Fred partly imagined himself resembling D. H. Lawrence, who was around the same age when his first novel was published, came from a similar working-class background and according to Fred was also close to his mother.[14] He did not want to be entirely like Lawrence though; Fred was determined to accept his homosexuality, and he did not want to die young. To his relief the book received critical praise, with the *New York Times* review being particularly effusive. Disappointingly however, sales were stubbornly low, and Fred, like many authors, was frustrated that the publisher seemed reluctant to push the book harder.[15]

There were plenty of other reasons for Fred to be anxious. On 14 August that same summer he went to the cinema to see the film *Captains Courageous,* an adventure on the high seas starring Mickey Rooney and an Oscar-winning Spencer Tracy. That day Prime Minister Neville Chamberlain stood up in the House of Commons and declared that there had been nothing his government could have done to prevent the German annexation of Austria in March unless they were prepared to use force.[16] The next evening Fred wrote in his diary that the 'whole of Europe is on the brink of war'.[17] He was particularly concerned that conscription was imminent, and that he would find himself in uniform with a gun over his shoulder. He was convinced that he would die if he got anywhere near the front lines, as it is 'always guys like me who get killed', and concluded that he would rather go to jail than throw away everything he loved and had worked so hard for.

Large numbers of pages from the summer and early autumn of 1938 were again ripped out of Fred's diary, as he feared blackmail or arrest. The next entry is in October and describes Fred's immense disappointment that his novel has sold only 254 copies in its first six months.[18] In the preceding month, the British Prime Minister had visited Hitler in Munich and agreed to the ceding of Czechoslovakia's Sudetenland to the Third Reich, returning to London to declare 'peace for our time'. We do not know what Fred thought of this particular event, as his fear of persecution in

Britain for his sexuality had erased from the record any thoughts he might have had.

For many pacifists, the appeasement of Munich seemed to be the only way to avoid war, and they embraced the relief it appeared to provide.[19] Ronald Duncan remembered Munich as a breathing space, allowing him to spend the summer trying to write a play and digging in his new garden. Ben Britten was blackberry-picking the day Chamberlain came home from Bavaria, and he told his friends, with evident relief, that he might even get to eat the jam the following year.[20] Donald Soper was particularly fulsome in his praise for Chamberlain. Referring to the Prime Minister's trademark accessory, he claimed that 'I am thoroughly in favour of umbrellas . . . for I think they have done more in the last few months than the battleships could have done.'[21]

It was not only pacifists who greeted Munich with relief. The poet Louis MacNeice described the general atmosphere of panic during the Munich crisis as being like the 'chattering terror of a beast in a forest fire', and noted the spontaneous and joyful crowds that greeted the Prime Minister on his way home from the airport.[22] Cosmo Lang, the Archbishop of Canterbury, who was a close friend of Chamberlain, declared that Britain was under no obligation to the Czechs and treated Chamberlain's return as a near-redemptive moment. The right-wing press similarly argued that Britain should stay out of events on the European mainland.[23] Large numbers of people agreed with Chamberlain that a small state in the middle of Europe was not worth going to war for.

Even if people did not fully support Chamberlain's policy, there was a widespread sense of confusion as to exactly what else to do. Many people were caught between the conviction that we should do all we could to avoid war and the fear that Hitler was ultimately unstoppable without the threat of weapons.[24] War was terrible, but Hitler was terrible too. For some of the population support for appeasement was in all likelihood prompted not simply by the fear of war, but also by the fear that if war was declared Britain might lose. At the very least people probably hoped that allowing German troops to annex the Sudetenland would buy some time.

Either way, Munich did not bring long-term relief. Even among pacifists the nagging doubt remained that Chamberlain had simply postponed war, and had sacrificed the Czechs to Fascism to save

Britain from immediate military action. As Louis MacNeice wrote, 'And we feel negotiation is not vain – / Save my skin and damn my conscience.'[25] Muriel Lester was in the East End of London when Chamberlain returned from Munich, and recalled in her autobiography that when a young neighbour shouted across the road asking whether it was good news, she could only smile hesitantly.[26] She then set off for Germany for a speaking tour with the International Fellowship of Reconciliation, on the very day Hitler annexed the Sudetenland. Starting in Stuttgart, she eventually arrived in Vienna, where she passed the blackened walls of the Cardinal's palace, burned by a Nazi mob who had also killed a young priest. Lester was told that 3,000 Jews had killed themselves in Vienna during the previous six months. In a letter home, she described the violation of synagogues and the ways in which worshippers were made to scrub the floors with sacred scrolls of scripture.[27] The onward train ride to Prague was blocked by the new German border, so Muriel had to fly. On landing, she found another city marked by fear. She later wrote that her time in the capital of what was left of Czechoslovakia was the 'sort of week one would like to blot out from memory', its people looking 'distressed' and 'sorrowful' as they searched for ways to escape.[28] Muriel was left deeply worried but slightly impressed by the devotion shown to Fascism by its adherents, and she compared this to the cynicism and apathy of many of its opponents, asking herself, 'how shall we combat Hitler's new sort of human being?'[29] It was an important question.

The sense that Britain had left central and eastern Europe to a terrible fate was hard to shake. Michael Rowntree, a Quaker and member of the family of chocolate makers, who spent large parts of the late 1930s trying to help Jewish refugees in central Europe, remembered that 'one's reaction to Munich was a relief that we hadn't been plunged into war coupled with the guilt anybody felt for what in a sense was sacrificing Czechoslovakia'.[30] The Methodist architect and pacifist Kenneth Wray later similarly recalled, 'I didn't think what Chamberlain did was the right thing, though one was grateful for it. But one didn't feel that he'd achieved peace. Then he came out with 1,000 million pounds for arms and we were horrified and thought, well, peace cannot be preserved if you are re-arming at that pace.'[31] Joyce Parkinson, a south London PPU activist and daughter of a Methodist minister, who had graduated from Oxford and went to work in social housing, like-wise remembered that after Munich she felt 'relief that war hadn't broken out but also a deep wonder of how long it could possibly last'.[32]

She was right to be worried. The Munich Agreement merely marked a new beginning. On the morning of 7 November 1938, the seventeen-year-old Herschel Grynszpan entered the German Embassy in Paris and shot Ernst vom Rath, the Third Secretary. Grynszpan was a Polish-Jewish refugee born in Germany and had just heard that his parents had been deported from the country of his birth.[33] Vom Rath died two days later. *Kristallnacht* began within hours. Across Germany, in an organised outburst of hatred, the armed thugs of the Nazi Brownshirts and Hitler Youth were sent out on to the streets. Scores of Jews were killed, 267 syna-gogues destroyed, 7,000 Jewish shops damaged and over 30,000 Jewish men arrested, nearly all eventually ending up in concentra-tion camps.[34] It was a foretaste of the violence to come, as Fascist anti-Semitism ratcheted up a gear. The composer and pacifist Michael Tippett later described the shot fired by Grynszpan as 'prophetic of the imminent gunfire of the war'.[35] He looked to music to try and understand what was going on, and the piece that emerged – *A Child of our Time* – dramatised the battle between light and dark, good and evil, starting with the ominous line 'The world turns on its dark side.'

On the northern edges of London, the atmosphere was grim. Roy Ridgway wrote in his diary, in a manner similar to Fred Urquhart, that as a pacifist he was sure he would be shot if war was declared.[36] He was determined not to give way to despair, criticising other pacifists for assuming that war was inevitable and writing that 'if there is only a shred of hope we must cling on to it'.[37] Among all the talk of global tensions, home life was fraught for the Ridgway family. Indeed, it was hard to separate international and domestic worries. Roy's brother Derricke had left the family home, declar-ing that he was going off to a monastery. Alfred, the other brother, said he was going to do the same after seeing the pacifist Maude Royden preach, and announced, presumably half tongue in cheek, that he now wanted to 'heal the sick and raise the dead'.[38] Three days later Derricke was sleeping in a church in rural Oxfordshire.

He returned to London, looking, according to Roy, 'brown as a berry', and stayed a few nights in the crypt of St Martin-in-the-Fields. Dick Sheppard's former church was a haven for London's destitute, who were allowed to bed down for the night and given a hot meal.[39] Derricke spent a few days there before returning to Hendon with Roy.

At home, Roy and his brothers were teased by their father, who saw their pacifism as naive and even mildly treacherous. One evening, as Roy was leaving for a pacifist meeting, his father gave him a mock Nazi salute and called out, 'Good luck.' At the meeting, the assembled pacifists discussed what they should do. Roy raised the question of whether they should expect to go before a firing squad if they refused to fight. One of the speakers, a former conscientious objector in the First World War, replied that this might be possible, but – echoing Gandhian forms of non-violence – that they should think 'of the effect it would have on the soldiers' who had to carry out the order.[40] This does not seem to have been comforting for Roy.

International events constantly featured in Roy's diary, punctuating his day-to-day life. More often than not he simply noted incidents, such as the German annexation of Austria or the Munich Agreement, without passing comment. By January 1939 his local branch of the PPU seems to have folded – members apparently left despondent by events – but a few weeks later he received a letter inviting him to a meeting to elect a new vice chair and secretary.[41] During a walk through Hyde Park he noticed that trenches were being dug.[42] Four days later he attended a PPU meeting on the Euston Road, where Donald Soper told the assembled pacifists that 'we must prepare not only for the worst, but for the best. The biggest evil today is the saturation of the whole of the community with the fear of war.'[43] Soper seemed to be telling his audience that they should not give into the pessimism that war was inevitable. But, if war was the worst, it was not entirely clear what the best might be.

The crises of the late 1930s saw a movement both in and out of the PPU, as old members left and new ones joined, some concluding that a supposedly inevitable war made pacifism irrelevant, and others feeling that it made pacifism all the more important. As George Orwell put it, those who were 'flabbily pacifist . . . promptly cooled off'.[44] The editor of the PPU's weekly newspaper commented that much of the previous support for the Union had been to 'prevent, or avoid or escape war', and everything changed when war seemed imminent. For many who had signed the pledge, when push came to shove war seemed the least bad option. As one activist later recalled, 'It's easy to sign a peace pledge in peacetime,' but those who signed up 'obviously found it difficult to adhere to when it came the time to prove their real beliefs'.[45] Many once-active PPU groups melted away.[46]

Support for appeasement also began to decrease among the wider population from late 1938 and into 1939, responding to developments in mainland Europe. After the annexation of the Sudetenland, a weakened Czechoslovakia was eyed hungrily by its neighbours on all sides. In March 1939, German troops marched further into what was left of the country, declaring a protectorate in Bohemia and Moravia, while Hungarian soldiers occupied the east of Czechoslovakia. Even Neville Chamberlain now felt obliged to declare, during a speech in Birmingham, that Hitler was attempting 'to dominate the world by force'.[47] Britain now became more concerned with preparation than prevention, and in early 1939 half a million people answered the call to join voluntary militias.[48] An opinion poll taken just one month after Munich showed that already 72 per cent of respondents now wanted the scale of weapons manufacturing increased.[49] In Parliament, all the main political parties supported a ramping up of rearmament. Kingsley Martin, the editor of the *New Statesman* and a First World War conscientious objector, wrote that pacifists were on the horns of a dilemma, a 'terrible mental conflict'.[50] They saw that Fascism meant a regression to an 'age of barbarism', but also understood that any war would be 'destructive of civilisation and likely to culminate in a way that can scarcely end until Europe is in ruins'.

Some of the leading members of the PPU came out in support of war. Maude Royden, who had previously told audiences that the territorial demands made by Hitler had to be taken seriously, retracted her previous support for peace at all costs.[51] Siegfried Sassoon, whose prose had done so much to highlight the folly of battle, came out in favour of the war too. A. A. Milne, Cyril Joad and Bertrand Russell all also eventually renounced their pacifism.

In truth, the broad anti-war alliance had always had a soft core.

Celebrating Munich, for example, did not mean that people had ruled out force as a last resort; the debate was over whether that last resort had been reached. As the swastika was raised over Prague, it seemed that day was getting closer and closer.

It is important to note here that very few people in Britain, if any, thought war was a good thing in itself. Most of those who enthusiastically supported rearmament believed that violence was something that should be avoided, saw war as a failure and recoiled from the idea of returning to the brutal fighting of the First World War. Where they disagreed with absolutist pacifists was over the question of whether war should or could be avoided at all costs. For years it had been possible to brush over these differences, but the cracks were growing larger and larger.

Those that still clung on were more steadfast in opposition to war than ever. Vera Brittain was overwhelmed by the number of speaking invitations from PPU branches.[52] There was a whirlwind of letter writing, leafleting, campaigning and public speaking. True believers held firm to the conviction that if enough people said no the seemingly inevitable could be prevented, and Roy's days were taken up with meeting after meeting.

At the end of April 1939 the British government announced that all young men aged twenty and twenty-one would be compelled to undertake six months' military training before joining a reserve. Although the call-up was relatively circumscribed, Roy was not pleased by what he saw as a 'departure from our traditions' and he marched through the West End with 500 others in protest.[53] The crowd, led by Soper and made up of students, ex-servicemen, clergy and members of the Women's Co-operative Guild, walked silently along Oxford Street, down Regent Street and through Piccadilly Circus. Pictures show them grey-suited and serious, with a marcher carrying a placard declaring 'Young Men Pay for Old Men's Folly'. Roy did not reply to the taunts of passers-by, one of whom shouted, 'If I had my way, I'd shoot the whole lot.' But not everyone was hostile, and Roy wrote in his diary that at the end of the march an ex-serviceman came up to him and said, 'I don't blame you.'[54]

In Roy's home life, the political turmoil was once more mirrored in personal conflict. His brother Alfred's drinking was getting worse and he threw a bottle of wine out of the window, where it smashed in the garden.[55] Roy was let go by his employers at an electricity company where he had only recently been given a job.[56] He could not bring himself to tell his father, complaining that he had come to London to get away from his dad, but the family continued to 'pester' him.[57] He went on to criticise his father for his obsession with material wealth, and mused that he might join the Church, although he did not say which one and in which capacity.

Within days of the reintroduction of compulsory military service for young men of a particular age, and although not yet liable himself, Derricke joined the army in a dramatic volte-face, informing the recruiting officer that he was motivated by 'insanity', but telling Roy that he was off to Aldershot to get away from the family.[58] We can only imagine the mixed motivations that led him to act in this way, but Derricke left home after refusing a cup of tea, muttering 'cheers' as he exited through the front door. His brothers were bitterly upset, and Alfred was almost in tears, writing to his newly signed-up sibling that 'your departure from Hendon has plunged me into the most bitter grief'. Roy tried to persuade Derricke to leave the army, but his brother refused, saying he was happy with a soldier's life.[59]

Within a month Derricke had changed his mind, explaining to his commanding officer that 'his principles did not conform with military life'.[60] Without much apparent fuss, Derricke was discharged, and Roy found him sitting at the kitchen table when he came home from a walk in St James's Park. It seems the army had decided it was not worth its time arguing with this particular young man.

By early July 1939 Roy was still unemployed and thinking about joining a pacifist commune.[61] It seemed the only way both to escape his home and to give some shape to his commitments. The other brothers were finding things difficult too. Derricke was now wondering what to do with his life, and Alfred was sent home from work drunk. The Nazis were demanding that the Free City of Danzig on the Baltic Sea – nominally under League of Nations protection and in a customs union with Poland, but with a large German-speaking population – be turned over to the Third Reich. In London, while on a trip to the cinema to see a film at the Golders Green Hippodrome, Roy told a friend that Germany should be given the city as 'the entire population was German'. His friend was furious, arguing that this would simply be the next step in more annexations, that pacifism simply would not work and, displaying either desperation, prejudice, an attempt at satirical irony or all of them at the same time, that 'even a little snivelling crawling beetle of a Pole has a right to live'.[62] Roy went home and asked his diary, 'why should we start a world war' over a small bit of land far away? Like thousands of others, he was being forced to question just how much he was willing to sacrifice for peace.

The desire to avoid war at all costs was pushing many pacifists into uncomfortable positions. For some this meant being willing to make concessions to Hitler, simply in the hope that the threat of war would go away. In the longing for peace, there was often a great deal of sympathy for the German position, as Nazi belligerence was widely understood to be a product of the unjust conditions imposed at the end of the First World War, the Treaty of Versailles being seen as malicious and vengeful.[63] Not only had Germany been forced to accept sole responsibility for the conflict, but it also had to pay massive reparations, and lost over 25,000 square miles of territory, as well as its colonies in Africa. For Vera Brittain, Fascism 'sprang from the colossal injustice' of this cruel peace.[64] Ronald Duncan's great friend Nigel Spottiswoode told a PPU audience that 'We forced the vindictive Versailles Treaty on Germany, and then ignored the hunger of her people, and the financial chaos that the enormous reparations caused.'[65] Peace News, the newspaper of the PPU, went so far as to describe the annexation of the Sudetenland as an 'act of justice', and the author of one PPU pamphlet argued that 'I see no reason why Germany should not have colonies and hegemony too ... we welcome the idea of a United States of Europe.'[66]

In one of those periodic reshufflings of the political cards that happened throughout the twentieth century – when old allegiances and animosities somehow no longer made the same sort of sense they once did – the build-up to war saw new, sometimes surprising and troublesome affinities formed, just as old ties were severed. For the pacifists who remained absolute in their convictions, their near-overwhelming desire for peace resulted in some strange bedfellows, including isolationists and Fascist sympathisers, for a short while at least. There was little evidence of pro-Nazi – as opposed to pro-German – sympathy among the vast majority of the pacifist movement at any point in the 1930s or 1940s, despite numerous accusations, but the common cause of stopping war against Nazi Germany nevertheless created embarrassing convergences. In the late 1930s *Peace News* published story after story implicitly downplaying Nazi actions. The paper suggested, for example, that stories of widespread looting during *Kristallnacht* were grossly exaggerated.[67]

There was a fine line between the outright denial of brutality and an at times blind faith in the innate goodness of human beings. Senior members of the PPU managed to find themselves signing petitions and letters alongside British Fascists. Donald Soper signed an open letter from a group calling itself the British Council for a Christian Settlement in Europe, which turned out to include several leading British Fascists.[68] Canon Stuart Morris, a former RAF chaplain who became head of the PPU after Sheppard's death, was for a very brief time a member of the Link, an organisation accused of being a Nazi cover. Morris seems to have joined in ignorance, and resigned as soon as its associations came to light.[69] The Duke of Bedford, a prominent peace campaigner who later joined the council of the PPU, was also patron for a short time of the anti-war but quasi-Fascist British People's Party, which called for an immediate end to hostilities and was led by former senior British Union of Fascist member John Beckett. The people left standing alongside pacifists in opposition to war could be an unattractive bunch.

One way to deal with all this anxiety, for those who could afford it, was to leave the country. Vera Brittain and her husband, the academic and aspiring Labour MP George Catlin, argued over whether to send their children Shirley and John to the US for safety. George was worried that, as he was an opponent of Fascism and Vera was a pacifist, both of them were particularly vulnerable in the event of an occupation and neither of them might survive the war.[70] The marriage was already strained, not least because George strongly disagreed with Vera's pacifism, and what to do with their children was another thing to disagree about. According to Vera's memoirs, her husband accused her of thinking only of herself.[71] Once the war had begun, they eventually decided to send their children to friends in Minnesota, about as far away from the war as one could get. Vera thought about joining them – deeply upset at the idea of being away from her children for so long – but eventually concluded that she had to stay in Britain and fight for peace.[72] The idea of moving semi-permanently to America in this period with the children never seems to have occurred to George, even though he spent various periods in the US for his work. Vera wrote to her friend Storm Jameson that 'it was the most terrible decision I have ever made'.[73] Shirley would flourish during their time in America, but John was deeply lonely and miserable, and he was somewhat ironically sent to a military school. His relationship with his mother would never really recover.[74]

Other people headed to America too. Ben Britten had written to a friend on 13 March 1939 that the international situation was giving him 'jitters'.[75] The day after Hitler invaded Bohemia and Moravia, he told his partner, the singer Peter Pears, that they should get away soon.[76] Ben and Peter sailed for North America in April, the same month the Spanish Civil War came to an end and Britain and Poland signed a military cooperation pact. The two men travelled first to Canada, and then on to New York, trying to persuade Ben's sister to join them. Ben hoped to do some work and what he described as 'intensive thinking'.[77] He would later recall that he thought Europe was 'more or less finished' and that he hoped to make a new future in America.[78]

Christopher Isherwood and Aldous Huxley, figures in the anti-war movement throughout the 1930s, had already gone even further west, finding shelter in the sunshine of California and settling into life as Hollywood scriptwriters.[79] Ben was also following his friend W. H. Auden, who had arrived on the east coast of the US a few months previously. Auden had left the UK partly to avoid his increasingly uncomfortable status as a public spokesperson for the left and partly out of a sense that Britain and Europe were sliding into the pits of hell.[80] The optimism that had once run through his poetry was falling completely away, and his work was becoming marked by a profound sense of the potential for evil in all human beings. Auden's poem 'September 1, 1939' originally contained the line 'We must love one another or die', and is often read as an expression of hope about the capacity of humans to live better lives.[81] However, when later faced with Fascist control of much of

Europe, Auden became uncomfortable with the poem's sentiments, seeing them as trite or even dishonest, and for some time he refused to have the poem published at all. He then rewrote the line to read: 'We must love one another and die.'[82] The replacement of 'or' by 'and', although apparently small, was significant; death was more than a fact, it was a destiny, and in particular Europe was done for. What future that was left lay in America.

There was desperate movement both ways across the Atlantic, and not just from Britain. In late August 1939, the thirty-three-year-old Lutheran theologian Dietrich Bonhoeffer left Germany for New York. A member of a well-connected family of doctors, scientists and lawyers, Dietrich was a leading figure in the Confessing Church that sought to oppose the Nazification of German Protestantism. He was also a pacifist of sorts, but his pacifism was always complex and far from absolute. In 1933, he had taken up a post as pastor of two German-speaking congregations in London, and while in Britain visited several Christian pacifist communes, coming away determined to set up a community that lived according to the Sermon on the Mount, even if such forms of monasticism were largely alien to the Lutheran tradition within which he worked. The next year, at an ecumenical conference on the windswept Danish island of Fanø, Dietrich told a Swedish delegate that in the event of war 'I pray that God will give me the strength then not to take up a weapon.'[83] He did not want to fight in a battle, but was not ruling it out entirely. At the same conference he made a speech asserting, 'there is no way to peace along the way of safety. For peace must be dared, it is itself a great venture and can never be safe.'[84] Dietrich had concluded that the Nazis could never be pacified. After his two-year stint in London, Dietrich had become director of the seminary for the Confessing Church in Germany, but it did not take long for the Nazis to catch up with him. The seminary was forced to go underground; Dietrich himself was arrested and held for a short period, and later deemed 'a pacifist and an enemy of the state'.[85]

Things came to a head in January 1939 when all Aryan men of Dietrich's age group in Germany were compelled to register for military service. A refusal to serve would not only have brought imprisonment and possible execution, but might also, Dietrich feared, undermine the Confessing Church; despite its opposition to the Nazis, the movement was still deeply patriotic and largely in favour of military service. He was out on a limb, torn between his own convictions and his loyalty to his fellow Christian opponents of Hitler. Although he thought it was 'conscientiously impossible to join in a war under the present circumstances', he was also anxious that other people should not see him as an example to follow.[86] It seemed the only way out of this bind was to leave Germany. In the early 1930s Dietrich had studied in New York under Reinhold Niebuhr and in the spring of 1939 he managed to activate his connections to secure a stay in Manhattan. But within days of arriving he was having second thoughts. He felt guilty about leaving others to their fate, writing in his journal, 'I haven't been able to stop thinking of Germany . . . the whole burden of self-reproach because of a wrong decision comes back again and somewhat overwhelms one.'[87] Concluding that he was obliged to suffer the consequences of the coming war alongside others, on 12 July 1939 Dietrich set off back to Germany, for an as yet unknown fate. He would not be the first person opposed to military violence to head into the fray.

Ronald Duncan's response to the march towards battle was to dedicate himself to a new rural life. It is not clear if Rose Marie initially shared Ronald's pacifist convictions, but she too threw herself into their new way of living. Although there was no electricity in West Mill, Ronald decided that, having once briefly worked in a mine himself, people should not use coal unless they were willing to go down the pit and get it for themselves.[88] It must have been very cold during the winter storms on the exposed Atlantic coast. He would also not allow any tinned food into the house, because he thought economic self-sufficiency was the only way to political freedom. The couple kept chickens, ducks, at least one horse and three Exmouth ponies. With help from Bianca Duncan, they set about clearing the garden and doing up the house, whitewashing the walls and making marmalade; in between Ronald wrote and Rose Marie painted. They all listened with 'morbid fascination' to Hitler on the radio and, as things got worse in mainland Europe, responded by growing more vegetables and filling dustbins with sugar to preserve their food for the days ahead.[89]

Beachcombing was one of Ronald's great passions and he would wake before dawn to make the short walk to Welcombe Mouth Beach and its rocky headland to see what the tide had brought in.

On one occasion he was arrested for 'stealing' a drum of petrol, only to be released after managing to assert his 'manorial rights' to the flotsam and jetsam washed up on the beach.[90] On good days Ronald traipsed back up the hill with a shipwrecked barrel of butter or burgundy.

Ronald decided that he wanted to build a community on the Devon coast based on his vision of mutual cooperation. If war could not be prevented, he wanted to show at least that it was possible to live in a better, more peaceful way, feeling as he did the need for an element of what he called 'monasticism'.[91] He found an abandoned farm at Gooseham, just inland from West Mill, and persuaded the siblings who owned it to sell. The smallholding consisted of a small tumbledown cottage where 'nettles lolled up against the walls like unemployed dockers', set in a steep overgrown valley overrun with rabbits and snakes.[92] The walls were rotting and a horrible musty smell pervaded the building.[93] The farmland itself consisted of four fields and a swamp. Ronald and Rose Marie were joined there by Nigel Spottiswoode, who had seemingly moved on from his previous declaration of love, and forgiven his friends, not least because he now had a new girlfriend. Bianca noted in her diary that Nigel now spent most days in a blue boiler suit and looked like 'a little boy off to bed'.[94] Ronald and Rose Marie continued to live in West Mill, as Nigel settled into the farmhouse at Gooseham. It was here that this unlikely group of young men and women hoped to build a new Jerusalem for when the tide of war finally went out.

They were not the only pacifists to step back and retreat to a self-made oasis. Realising that they had failed to offer a practical way to prevent the twin horrors of war and Fascism, John Middleton Murry wrote that he had 'relapsed into the non-politician'.[95] He went so far as to argue that the prevention of war was not the goal of pacifism, but that instead the 'pacifist cause will be won, if it is won, by those who have come to see that winning is a secondary affair. What matters is that men and women should bear their witness – and bear it, if need be, to the end.'[96] Middleton Murry now saw the goal of pacifist living as testifying to the possibility of peace. Pacifist witness might not be able to prevent war, but it could demonstrate that another way of life – one that shunned violence – was, just, possible.

From such a perspective, pacifism was not about getting things done, but simply about doing the right thing. Arguments about practical efficacy were long gone. It was all about moral necessity. Donald Soper now argued that 'the utilitarian argument for non-violence breaks down under the overwhelming pressure of brute fact'. His faith in pacifism was sustained only by a 'Christian faith which assures me that what is morally right carries with it the ulti-mate resources of the universe'.[97] The composer Michael Tippett had been a Trotskyist in the mid-1930s, trying to run a small revo-lutionary cell in north London, but, turned off by violence and attracted to pacifism and his music, he was by now firmly in quietist mode, writing to a friend that he was drawn much more to making a 'personal stand', having been impressed by those who argued that they wanted 'to live a human life as meant to by God'.[98] Vera Brit-tain too argued that pacifism could not simply 'derive its validity from political calculation' but must be based in the 'ultimate tran-scendence of love over power'.[99] For Brittain, as for Middleton Murry, this meant that she had to stand firm, bearing witness to the possibility of peace. She wrote to her husband that she thought it important 'that a few people ... are needed to hold up before humanity the, as yet, but not always, unobtainable ideal'.[100] This was one of the reasons why she stayed in Britain when her children were sent across the Atlantic.

There was a strong element of what Middleton Murry called the 'willing suspension of disbelief for the moment which constitutes poetic faith'.[101] One pacifist later wrote that he felt he had little choice but to 'hold one's breath and hurl prayers against the dark, windy unfortunate weather'.[102] From his new home in California, Aldous Huxley described his pacifism as 'the choice of the bolder hypothesis'.[103] Like most faiths, such pacifism seemed at its strong-est when facing apparent contradictions and challenges. For many pacifists, the personal and political difficulties of committing to peace strengthened their resolve. But if this was a pacifism based in faith, it was a faith in a relatively minor key. The hope of socialist revolution, at least of the pacifist sort, was firmly out of the run-ning, and, at least for most Christian pacifists, God was not about to return to earth to offer deliverance. The grounds for peace were instead to be found in the things that pacifists could do themselves, and existed on the cusp of ordinary human possibility. If there was any optimism left, it was that a few isolated souls could just hold on to a pacifist way of life as the war broke out all around them.

The summer of 1939 was hot, difficult and tense. In August, the Nazi–Soviet non-aggression pact shattered any pretence of a grand alliance against Fascism. In Britain, preparations for war intensified. In north London, Roy Ridgway was feeling increasingly lonely, writing in his diary that he had no friends.[104] His unemployment benefit had run out and, unable to get a job as a journalist, he answered an ad for a 'smart young man' to work as a credit clerk in a large bakery in East Finchley.

In Edinburgh, the summer of 1939 was full of disappointments for Fred Urquhart too. In June his publishers declined to publish his book of short stories.[105] The following month he told his diary, on his twenty-seventh birthday, that he was not 'as far forward' with his writing as he would like.[106] In August his grandfather died after a five-week illness. Numerous pages are again torn from his diary that month. On 31 August he reflected that the world was on the 'eve of war' and he did not know if he was going to be able to write any more.[107]

The next morning at 5.45 on 1 September, Germany invaded Poland. In Britain, a blackout was imposed, the first evacuation of children began from major towns and cities, and the army was mobilised.

In the London suburbs, Roy and his brothers spent the evening discussing what to do if and when they were called up. Late that night, Roy wrote that 'in 1937 I pledged never to support or sanction another war, and I will not go back on my word'.[108] The following day, presumably to take his mind off things, he went to a pub with his father, where everyone sang 'Land of Hope and Glory' well into the night. But Roy found it hard to stay cheerful – 'one cannot help being perturbed by the unimaginable horrors we will probably witness in the days to come'.[109]

Neville Chamberlain declared war on the morning of 3 September. It was a Sunday. Donald Soper was leading worship at Kingsway Hall when the howl of an air-raid siren broke through his sermon, and the congregation had to be led downstairs for shelter.[110]

Vera Brittain was staying in a cottage in the New Forest, enjoying walks in bright sunshine among the trees. A half-grown forest pony walked past their window, and the church bells rang out as Vera turned on the radio to hear Chamberlain declare the country at war. She later wrote that she was pleased her children could not see the 'pictures haunting' her mind of those who had been lost in the last war.[111]

As the Prime Minister made his announcement, Roy Ridgway went to collect his gas mask, only to be told the depot had run out. On the way home, he passed a woman crying on the street.[112]

Ronald Duncan was sitting by the radio as the news of the war in Europe was announced. He had spent four years talking about pacifism and now felt strangely exhilarated and bewildered at the same time.[113] Bianca wrote nothing in her diary throughout September. If Rose Marie kept a diary, nothing survives.

There is no record of what Stella St John was thinking on that same day.

Ben Britten was staying with a friend in Amityville in upstate New York. He wrote to his sister, 'God, what a mess man has made of things.'[114]

Two days after Germany invaded Poland, men aged between eighteen and forty-one were made liable for conscription in Britain. Fred Urquhart was twenty-seven, Roy Ridgway twenty-three and Ronald Duncan twenty-four years old. Women would not be called for another two and a half years, by which time Stella St John would be thirty-five, Bianca twenty-seven and Rose Marie twenty-six. The question of whether they would join the war effort, and what precisely this meant, was now deeply personal and profoundly political.

Their consciences were now on the line.

CHAPTER 7

War Arrives

Roy Ridgway spent the first night of the war crammed into an air-raid shelter, waiting for the all clear. The relative privacy of the family home was replaced by an awkward intimacy with people he had never met before. The young pacifist sat squeezed next to an elderly woman who reminisced about the previous wars she had seen, before asking him if he was looking forward to signing up. Roy's reply did not go down well.[1] In the following weeks Alfred Ridgway got into an argument on the street with a poppy seller after telling her that he was a pacifist. The woman shouted, 'What will you do if Hitler gets you?'[2]

The question for pacifists now was not how to prevent war, but how to live in the midst of it. Having lived for so long in anticipation of what was to come, the future had arrived and it was the one they had all feared. Initially at least, it was not the enemy in mainland Europe they were most worried about, but their fellow citizens, neighbours, friends and relations. Would a patriotic rush to war crush any form of dissent, as the country came together to fight a common foe? Popular memory of the treatment of conscientious objectors during the First World War was still strong. The social and political pressure felt by pacifists over twenty years before had been immense; white feathers were handed out to those who would not take up arms, newspapers referred to them as a 'fungus growth' or a 'deadly disease', over 6,000 anti-war activists were imprisoned, riots against conscientious objectors broke out in a handful of places, and some soldiers who refused to fight in the trenches were shot at dawn.[3] Shortly before the outbreak of war in 1939, Roy Ridgway and Fred Urquhart had both written in their diaries that they feared being executed by their own side if they objected to fighting. It is easy to dismiss these fears as the melodramatic writings of young men alone in their bedrooms at night, but they also show a very real and widespread apprehension about how pacifists would be treated once the country mobilised to fight its Fascist enemy, and not just by members of the public, but by those closest to them as well.

Within days of war being declared Ronald Duncan was called into a police station; but it was not his pacifism that had attracted attention. One of the first people to answer his call to build a new pacifist community had been a teenaged German called Horst, and Ronald was ordered to bring the youth in to register as an 'enemy alien'. Citizens and former citizens of enemy states were categorised according to the level of risk they were thought to pose to Britain, and to begin with a small minority of Germans, and then Italians, were detained.[4] Horst was brought before a tribunal and Ronald appeared as a witness on the young German's behalf, explaining that the teenager had fled mainland Europe due to his 'antipathy to Nazism, Jew-hating and violence'.[5] A police officer then gave evidence that Ronald could not possibly be a 'gentleman' or he would not have a German living with him, and was therefore not to be trusted. No one seems to have mentioned that Horst had, like many Germans his age, once been a member of the Hitler Youth. Ronald's own German father or Jewish heritage was not brought up either. Having had relatively little to do with the paternal side of his family, it was a topic that Ronald seldom seemed to raise himself. When the tribunal hearing had finished, both Horst and Ronald were allowed to go home. But this would not be the last of the matter.

Horst soon left the community – returning months later – after falling out with some of the other members. For the next couple of months few other ripples of war reached West Mill or Gooseham. Rose Marie wrote in her diary, half in disappointment and half in relief, that 'so far' the declaration of war had 'not affected us at all'.[6] All across the country, people were feeling something similar: a nervous anticipation as they waited for the other shoe to drop. After a short period of intense activity, the tensions of the summer of 1939 had given way to a pregnant pause. Poland had been overrun in a matter of weeks, with the Germans advancing from the west and the Soviets moving in from the east, but in western Europe nothing much happened, as the French and the British armies continued to build up their defensive positions. In mainland Britain, arms manufacturing was ramped up further and close to 160,000 British soldiers were sent to northern France as part of the British Expeditionary Force (BEF), but most of the new recruits saw out the autumn of 1939 on the training ground or in their barracks.[7] The British military might have been locked and almost ready to load, but scarcely a bullet had been fired in anger by the army. It surely could not last.

In Edinburgh, Fred Urquhart wrote in his diary that 'everybody is on edge. On the Western front "all is quiet" . . . [but] every man between the ages of 18 and 40 is waiting to be called up . . . Its maddening; it keeps you from settling down to anything.'[8] War was slowly beginning to creep up on Fred, as sandbags and soldiers in uniform filled the streets and train stations.[9] He had sent his new book to his publisher two weeks after the start of the war, but admitted that 'God knows if they will publish it.'[10] They never did. To celebrate finishing the manuscript, Fred visited Mary Litchfield in Fife for the weekend, determined to 'eat, drink and be merry'. There had been no air raids yet, but he noted in his diary that all the windows were painted black because of the newly imposed night-time restrictions. On the Saturday, Mary and Fred went into St Andrews for a party. Among the golfers and students of the small seaside town the sight of Mary wearing a long black satin ballgown and carrying a gas mask, as she went about shopping for black pudding for the morning after, seemed to be too much for some residents to take. Fred noticed that he and Mary 'caused quite a stir' as passers-by stopped at the side of the road to stare. Everyone was slowly having to readjust to what a country at war might look like.

At the end of October, Scotland experienced its first air raids as the Luftwaffe dropped bombs on the Royal Navy ships at Rosyth, not far from the towering splendour of the Forth Bridge.[11] In Edinburgh, several people, including a house painter from Fred's part of town, were wounded by shrapnel and stray bullets as the planes released more bombs on the way home. These were the first civilian casualties of the war in mainland Britain. There were more personal losses too. Fred's much loved granny passed away while he was visiting Mary in Fife, just weeks after his grandfather had died, and he wrote in his diary, 'Poor old soul, it's as well that both she and Grandpa are away now that this bloody war is here for God knows what will happen to us all . . . those who don't get killed or mutilated in the trenches or those who don't get killed by bombs or gas will find when the war ends that they are slaves under absolute Fascist dictatorship . . .'[12]

Despite the battlefields being far away, it did not take long for the tensions of war to make their presence felt for Ronald, Rose Marie and the others at West Mill and Gooseham. Two days into January 1940, a frost heavy on the ground, the police came to have a look around. As Rose Marie noted in her diary, there were 'rumours that a radio transmitter had been found in a nearby farm', which made her nervous.[13] Nigel Spottiswoode had enjoyed tinkering with technology since his days as a student film maker and had taken to collecting quantities of 'experimental wireless' equipment which could be seen lying all around West Mill. The police found nothing they thought obviously suspicious, but Rose Marie, presumably only half tongue in cheek, wrote, 'we shall all be shot as spies yet!' The next month, another police officer came down to West Mill, this time with a summons for Ronald. It must have been a relief when they discovered he was only wanted for a driving offence.[14] In the following weeks and months Ronald found a local 'busybody', Special Constable Jackson, a constant source of annoyance, as he led several further 'raids' on West Mill. This man was not only a voluntary police officer but a timber merchant, member of the County War Agricultural Executive Committee and an air-raid warden. In short, he had the power to be a real nuisance. Jackson had taken to visiting West Mill up to twice a day, wearing several different official hats, inspecting the ploughing or making sure the blackout curtains were up to scratch. Finally, after rummaging through the house and the barns, he pounced with glee on Nigel's collection of broken electronic equipment.[15] Yet another visit followed, this time led by a full-time police inspector; no arrests were made, but as the officers left they told Rose Marie that 'we shall be picking up' Ronald 'someday'. The sense of being under suspicion hung around West Mill and Gooseham for much of the next five years. Feeling the pressure, Ronald wrote a letter to the Home Secretary demanding, 'If I'm a spy, please deal with me as one.'[16] No reply was ever received.

The spring of 1940 was warm, and wild flowers covered the fields around West Mill and Gooseham. Things began to look up. Ronald returned from London with news that all the members of a 'revue' from London's West End might want to relocate to their community as air raids 'now seem quite a certainty'.[17] But in early April Denmark fell overnight to German forces. The Wehrmacht headed on to Norway, and the British, French and Polish government-in-exile rushed to send their forces to stop the advance. The Allied campaign in Scandinavia was a shambles; supplies were misplaced, the Germans quickly established air superiority and the different Allied armies in the field failed to coordinate effectively.[18] On 9 April, hearing of the Norway campaign, Bianca wrote that everything felt rather 'futile, with the news of further invasions'.[19] Ronald's concerns were more practical, as news of the Danish occupation prompted worries about the price of pigs, and he spent the next few days searching out a new sow. Bianca was persuaded to bring one over in her car, and during the journey home the animal urinated all over the seats.[20] Alongside the muck, there were literary endeavours too. Over the coming weeks Bianca, Ronald and Rose Marie concentrated on printing the *Townsman*, painstakingly putting together the stencils for inking.

On 2 May Nigel Spottiswoode came for dinner, as he often did with Rose Marie and Ronald, and the three of them listened to the wireless as Chamberlain announced the withdrawal of British troops from southern Norway. Bianca wrote, 'Now wondering whether all R's prophecies are going to come true so quickly.'[21] Nervous anticipation was giving way to outright fear, if not panic. It would quickly get much worse. On 10 May, with Germany invading the Low Countries and France and the retreat to Dunkirk beginning, the BBC announced that Churchill had become Prime Minister, Chamberlain finally being forced from office as his security policies lay in tatters. Rose Marie's diary in particular filled up with depressing news from Europe, and events on the farm were woven through worries about new Allied disasters in Belgium and France. On 27 May, she wrote, 'Belgium has capitulated, which means road to Dunkirk now open to Germans. This is very serious.' A handful of new volunteers arrived at their farm, raising spirits domestically, but four days later, on a fine sunny day, Rose Marie added, 'Heard that the BEF [are] evacuating . . . Poor devils.'[22] Within days Churchill had given a speech in the House of Commons saying '30,000 men killed'. For Rose Marie, it was 'really dreadful'.[23] The worst pacifist predictions of death and destruction were coming true.

On 6 June, the Wehrmacht broke through the French defensive line, and four days later Italy joined the war on the German side. In another week, as Rose Marie and Ronald worked in their barley fields, Rose Marie's diary declared, 'Paris is surrounded on two sides.'[24] Within days, the capital of France had fallen, the swastika was flying over Paris, most of the British Expeditionary Force had been evacuated across the Channel, and the French government was calling for an armistice. The British military had been humiliated and was now facing a rampant Wehrmacht. Britain, although by no means alone, was now the last country in western Europe fighting Nazi Germany. Rose Marie wrote, 'Britain . . . is going on with the war. Which will mean starvation. Or death. Or both. How cheerful.'[25] She was particularly worried about her parents in Sheffield as she felt it was sure to be bombed.[26] An invasion of Britain seemed imminent, as German planes became an increasingly common sight in the skies, and over the coming summer the dogfights of the Battle of Britain would buzz overhead.

Devon was slowly filling with a new wave of evacuees from London, Bristol, Birmingham and elsewhere, Bianca observing that the usual early summer-holiday crowd had been 'exchanged for grimy urchins'.[27] The road signs were all taken down in case of a German landing on the coast, so that the invaders would get lost in the winding country roads. At West Mill, early June was spent attempting to fix the waterwheel, tending to endless weeding and trying to hold back the bracken, which seemed to grow as fast as it was cut down. Rumours also began to intensify in the local community about what the people around Ronald and Rose Marie were up to.[28] A false story spread that Nigel had been arrested, and Bianca noticed that the papers were calling pacifists 'sissies'.[29] Ronald and Rose Marie heard through the grapevine that, according to the local gossip, they 'were plotting against the government'.[30] The police also started asking the neighbours to keep an eye on the group, and visited West Mill again, taking away what was left of

Nigel's electrical equipment.[31] Ronald and Rose Marie increasingly feared he would be arrested at any moment.[32]

Across the country, as the war went from bad to worse for the Allies, attitudes towards pacifists hardened. Membership of the PPU peaked in the early spring of 1940, but began to decline after the fall of France, dropping to a few thousand within a year. If anti-war sentiments had been a relatively respectable part of the national conversation in the run-up to 1939, they were very soon pushed to the margins, and the critical tone reserved for those who objected to war became markedly sharper.

The political left, so long a reliable source of support for pacifism, was now firmly in favour of war. As George Orwell put it: 'the Left intelligentsia made their swing-over from "war is hell" to "war is glorious" not only with no sense of incongruity but almost without any intervening stage'.[33] If Spain had begun to erode the alliance between pacifism and most socialists, the German invasion of Poland deepened the separation. Only part of the ILP and, at least for now, the Communist Party remained opposed to the war; the ILP's anti-militarism ran deep, and the Communist Party, with a few notable exceptions, was following orders from Moscow. The announcement of the Hitler–Stalin pact in the summer of 1939 meant that overnight the British Communists had gone from being pro-war as part of a broad anti-Fascist alliance to being officially against the war, although their position would change again in 1941 when Germany invaded the Soviet Union.

The overwhelming weight of the Christian establishment now backed military force too. When war broke out, William Temple, the Archbishop of York, argued that unless the Church thought a Nazi victory was God's will, then it had no choice but to pray for an Allied triumph. [34] The *Church Times* insisted that Britain was fighting for the 'independence of nations, the liberties of mankind, vital ideals of the Christian life'.[35] In Rome the Catholic Church was playing its cards close to its chest, but in Britain it came out strongly in favour of war. Cardinal Hinsley, the Archbishop of Westminster, argued that the turn to arms was part of the defence of our 'Christian civilisation . . . nourished and made by our Christian faith'.[36] Earlier, Hinsley had directly taken on those Christian pacifists who suggested that one should try and see the good in everyone, writing that 'I have been urged to receive the evil of the

Nazi regime into my own soul as a redemptive sacrifice, instead of resisting it. But no one has told me how I can do this.'[37] For Christian critics, pacifism had no answers to the very real evils of Fascism. Taking the fight to Nazi Germany was therefore part of Christian duty.

Yet not all Christians agreed that war against the Nazis and Fascists was the only way to walk with Christ. Muriel Lester was in the US on a lecture tour when war was declared, anxiously listening to the radio through sleepless nights and writing home that she 'felt ashamed to be so safe while the rest of you were in danger'.[38] For a while she thought about returning to London, but soon decided to stay in the US, at least for the time being. She was on the trip as part of her duties as a travelling secretary of the International Fellowship of Reconciliation, and two of the other secretaries, Henri Roser in France and Friedrich Siegmund-Schultze in Switzerland, were now effectively cut off by the war. Roser was a former lieutenant in the French army who had become a conscientious objector and set up an evangelical centre in a Parisian industrial suburb, working with disadvantaged youth and hoping to draw them away from the vice of alcohol. He was briefly imprisoned at the start of the Second World War by the French authorities for refusing a military order, but was released as the German army broke through the Maginot Line on the French border.[39] Siegmund-Schultze had been the pastor of the church in Potsdam where the Kaiser worshipped during the First World War, and after sending a letter to the Kaiser urging peace he had been arrested, interrogated, and condemned to death for high treason, although the sentence was later rescinded.[40] After Hitler's rise to power Siegmund-Schultze established an orphanage in Berlin, before being arrested and forced into exile in Zurich. By 1940, as the borders of Europe hardened at the point of a gun, Muriel was the only travelling secretary able actually to travel.

With her fellow Christian pacifists caught up in war-torn Europe, Muriel admitted that the 'responsibility of being apparently the only English pacifist in the US except the California group weighed on me'.[41] She was referring to the people around Aldous Huxley in Hollywood, whose temperaments were very different from Muriel's. As was often her way, her thoughts turned to Gandhi for inspiration, and she wrote that as 'in India in '26 . . . I found Mr Gandhi's technique of the "vow of truth" essential'.[42] She wrote immediately to the British Ambassador in Washington, Lord Lothian, whom she had met in London, and told him she could not support the government's war effort.

The Ambassador responded by inviting her for tea. Although anti-war attitudes were no longer part of the British mainstream, many of the ties and personal sympathies that had been created in the 1930s remained, meaning that individual pacifists were not beyond the pale. Lord Lothian, the son of a major general, was a former colonial official, politician and publisher, and had been present at the negotiations at the end of the First World War. He had also been a prominent supporter of appeasement, writing in 1935 that 'Germany does not want war and is prepared to renounce it absolutely . . . provided she is given real equality.'[43] Born a Catholic, he had converted to Christian Science under the influence of his friend Nancy Astor, the second woman to be elected to the House of Commons, and a controversial figure due to her reported anti-Semitic and pro-Fascist sympathies. Lothian was himself a man of eclectic interests, and had also spent time in Gandhi's ashram. He had been Ambassador in Washington for only a few weeks when war was declared, by which point he had, like many others, changed his views on the best way to stop Hitler's onward march. Even so, the meeting between the Ambassador of a country at war and the peace campaigner seems to have been very convivial, and Muriel wrote, 'What a grand thing it is to be English!'[44] This sense that respect for pacifist beliefs was somehow tied to British and, for Muriel at least, particularly English sentiments would be an enduring if controversial theme throughout the war.

Muriel was determined to keep the US out of the hostilities, and approached President Roosevelt, asking him to come to Europe to 'make peace'.[45] She toured the country, getting as far as California and Aldous Huxley's house, urging American Christians in churches and on campuses to bring the war in Europe to an end through the power of prayer, persuasion and negotiation. Muriel's message was warmly embraced by many in her audience. Although President Roosevelt was in favour of a more assertive foreign policy, Congress was largely non-interventionist, and the 1935 Neutrality Act, renewed in various forms for the next four years, prohibited the US from providing material support to any belligerents. As late as May

1940, after the Nazi occupation of France, opinion polls showed that only around 7 per cent of Americans thought the US should declare war on Germany.[46] There was a strong feeling that the US had been dragged into the First World War against its best interests, and that the conflict between France, Britain and Germany was simply a European concern. It was assumed, or at least hoped, that the Atlantic Ocean would keep a fratricidal war on another continent at bay.

The tide of anti-war opinion in the US only began to change from the summer of 1940. Events in East Asia were just as important in changing the mood as the situation in Europe, the Japanese imperial expansion coming dangerously close to the American-occupied Philippines. Vera Brittain's husband George Catlin was a firm advocate of an 'Atlantic Union', and spent much of the summer of 1940 touring the US as the foreign policy adviser to the Republican presidential candidate Wendell Willkie.[47] In contrast to Vera, George had been an opponent of appeasement from the start, and his goal was to try and persuade the US to enter the war, while his wife tried to do exactly the opposite.[48] The British government had similar goals to Catlin's, extensively lobbying the US and putting in place a secret propaganda mission – including false reports of a Nazi plan to take over South America – in an attempt to win over US public opinion.[49] In the November 1940 presidential election Roosevelt pledged to keep the US out of the war, but was already beginning to supply Britain with warships, and by March 1941 would put in place Lend-Lease legislation, which provided weapons to Britain.

As Muriel campaigned against the war, hecklers began to appear at her American talks, and there was some pushback in the US and UK press, accusing her of promoting Nazi propaganda.[50] In America, those still particularly opposed to US involvement included a mixture of pacifists, socialists, pro-German Fascists and American nationalists.[51] As in Britain, they made an unlikely and deeply uncomfortable group of allies. The America First Committee, with the anti-Semitic Charles Lindbergh as one of its key spokesmen, organised rallies across the country and had over 800,000 members at its peak. Muriel's work in America attracted the attention of the British authorities, as they were desperately trying to persuade the US to enter the war, and the British Ministry of

Information began to take an interest in what she was saying, monitoring her movements.

In the spring of 1941 Lester would make a trip from the US to South America, trying to persuade the nations of that continent to keep out of the war. On the way back to the US, Muriel's ship docked on the Caribbean island of Trinidad, and a British colonial official boarded, searched Muriel's cabin and told her to disembark. As she set foot on British-controlled territory for the first time since war was declared, she was promptly detained for a 'breach of colonial regulations'. She was initially allowed to stay in a hotel, the newly refurbished and gleaming white art-deco Queen's Park, but was soon moved to a detention camp. She noted in her diary that 'guards with fixed bayonets are stationed at ... each corner ... where towers and powerful searchlights are placed. Miles of barbed wire reinforce the three fences that surround us.'[52] This was evidently not a holiday.

For several weeks it was not at all clear why she had been held, apart from a vague rumour that it was for something she had said during one of her speaking engagements. Muriel's friends back in England began furiously to write letters and visit anyone they knew with any influential connections. In the US, Muriel had become close friends and a frequent correspondent with Nevin Sayre, one of the leaders of both the American and the International Fellowships of Reconciliation, often staying at his imposing family home in Pennsylvania. Sayre was a graduate of Princeton theological seminary and moved in high social circles. His brother Francis was married to the daughter of President Wilson and effectively became the Governor of the American-occupied Philippines in the first years of the Second World War. Nevin tried to find out what was going on with Muriel, pulling every string he could. Back in Britain, questions were being asked in the House of Commons as to why she was being detained, and the Colonial Office soon declared that the detention was designed to force her to return to the UK as her activities abroad were deemed 'damaging to the war effort'.[53] The Earl of Halifax, the Secretary of State for Foreign Affairs, who had known Muriel during his time as Viceroy of India, had previously warned her to be careful what she said in the Americas.[54] She apparently had not listened. Eventually it would come out that she stood accused of saying that Britain was responsible for the suffering of German children, that Britain should accept the German offer of peace and that Chinese blood spilled by the Japanese was also on British hands, all statements that it was claimed 'are liable to be, and have in fact already been, exploited by German propaganda'.[55]

Technically, Muriel had not been arrested, but had simply had her travel documents taken away. The same regulations would be used to prevent Vera Brittain from travelling abroad, a restriction she felt particularly keenly as it meant she could not visit her children in the US. The British Embassy in the US wrote to Muriel's American supporters explaining that 'Great Britain is at present engaged in a life and death struggle against a deadly and unscrupulous foe. While the struggle lasts the British people in general have agreed to the curtailment of the exercise of a certain number of civil liberties. The right of free speech, however, has not been suspended. It exists in full in Great Britain, subject to the necessity of preventing assistance to the enemy's war effort.'[56] This was a war for freedom, they were saying, but sometimes part of that freedom had to be curtailed slightly to allow the war to be won.

For her part, Muriel would be sanguine about her time in detention. We can imagine it appealed to her ascetic predisposition, because she was given an opportunity to move back into a hotel but preferred the internment camp, claiming that it was more 'convenient'.[57] She was housed in a special enclosure for 'Aryans' – Nazi Germany was not the only place that sought to divide the world by race – and given a small compartment with a canvas bed, cutlery, a blanket and a chair. Muriel quickly made friends with some of the other detainees, including an Irish labour activist and one of several interned German refugees. There were also 150 Jewish refugees from Europe, put in the camp as 'enemy aliens'. It rained incessantly in the tropical heat, and Muriel and one of the young Germans – a wood carver – got into a pattern of rising every day before sunrise to pray together. In the afternoons the camp warden imposed a two-hour period of silence, and Muriel told her sister that she had 'never known better circumstances for praying'.[58]

Finally, on 5 November 1941 Muriel would be allowed to leave Trinidad – but only if she returned right away to the UK – and she sailed back to Glasgow across an Atlantic swarming with U-boats. It was with some relief that, after two weeks at sea, she caught sight of the damp Scottish coastline. On land she was detained once again – apparently in error – and locked up in a cell furnished with flea-infested blankets, and from there she was taken by train to Holloway prison in London. Arriving at the jail, she was asked if she had venereal disease and her head was searched for lice. She was eventually released without facing any charges in late November, just two weeks before the Japanese attack on Pearl Harbor and the entry of the United States into the war.

Muriel Lester's detention and the police investigations into what was going on with Ronald Duncan at West Mill were not isolated incidents, but part of a tightening of the screw on pacifist activities. Early in the war, Roy's mother had told him she was 'proud of her boys'.[59] This was the first time she had ever said anything like this to any of her sons, and it clearly meant a great deal to Roy. He wrote, 'hitherto she has remained silent, and I had been wondering for a long time whether she would like her sons in uniform. Most mothers like to see their sons doing what other mothers' sons are doing.' But his mother's support would soon be put under pressure. In early July 1940, two weeks after France had surrendered, and with the evacuation of Allied troops from Dunkirk completed, two police officers had visited the Ridgway family home, much to the embarrassment of Roy's parents.[60] Roy himself returned from work to be greeted by his mother, her face deeply 'flushed', who told him there were 'two gentlemen' to see him. Roy at first assumed they were acquaintances from the PPU, but on entering the lounge found a police officer sitting comfortably in an armchair and another standing by the fireplace. The officer who was standing up flashed his police badge and asked, 'You are Heber Ridgway?', using Roy's rarely used given name, before explaining that Roy's brother Derricke, who had left two weeks previously to live in a commune in rural Suffolk run by a group of Christian pacifists, had been found in possession of two identity cards, and this had aroused suspicions. It seemed that Derricke had reported his card missing and received a new one, only to find the first one again, but, in breach of Defence Regulations, he never got around to turning it in. There followed a brief interrogation to establish why Roy and his brothers might object to the war. According to his diary, Roy responded with a classic line from Christian pacifism: 'I do not believe we can overcome evil with evil. The only way to overcome evil is with good.' A question followed as to what Roy would do if he was approached by a German parachutist, to which he replied, 'I would offer him a cup of tea.' There is no record in his diary of whether this was said with a straight face.

At this point, Roy's father, until then silent in a corner of the room, intervened, asking if the police officers were 'entitled to ask these questions', before adding, 'My sons are loyal subjects, but they object to war.' This expression of national and family fealty seems to have been enough for the detectives, who explained that they just had to make sure that people would not 'assist the enemy in the event of an invasion'. The police officers seemed particularly worried that the German parachutist might be shown the way to the nearby Hendon Aerodrome, but left apparently satisfied that Roy presented no threat, declaring that 'we are taking strong measures against people who are likely, wittingly or unwittingly, to assist the enemy'. The Ridgway brothers were safe for the moment.

As fears of invasion spread, Fascists, Communists and pacifists were all under surveillance as potential 'fifth columnists'. The PPU was calling for an immediate peace, and Ronald's *Townsman* included an article by the controversial anti-war campaigner the Duke of Bedford calling for negotiations. For many commentators, this was tantamount to collaboration.[61] In early May 1940, Regulation 18B of the Defence (General) Regulations had been extended to allow the detention of British citizens, not just 'enemy aliens', who were thought to be hostile to the war effort. Oswald Mosley and more than 700 other British Fascists were detained, but the aristocratic Mosley was allowed to live together with his wife and small child in a house in the grounds of Holloway prison. The internment of 'enemy aliens' also stepped up a gear, and nearly all German and Italian men between the ages of sixteen and seventy were detained. By July 1940 around 26,000 people, including large numbers of Jewish and anti-Fascist refugees, alongside Nazi sympathisers, had been forced into overcrowded and often insanitary camps, before being sent off to the Isle of Man, or Canada and Australia for those deemed the most 'dangerous'.[62]

In Glasgow, five anarchists were arrested and charged under the Defence Regulations for helping people to evade conscription.[63] Jehovah's Witnesses seemed to face a deliberate campaign of harassment too, with attempts made to close down their London headquarters and deport the American director.[64] Six members of the PPU were detained for encouraging soldiers to desert from the army after distributing a poster announcing, 'War will cease when men refuse to fight. What are YOU going to do about it?'[65] The six included the bespectacled figure of Canon Stuart Morris and Maurice Rowntree, a veteran conscientious objector from the First World War and another member of the well-known family of Quaker pacifists. To show how seriously the government was taking the case, the prosecution was led by the Attorney General, Sir Donald Somervell KC. At the hearing, however, the magistrate described the arrested men as 'reputable citizens', and the Attorney General evidently decided not to press the case so long as the defendants would agree to withdraw the offending poster, which they were more than happy to do.[66] In summing up, the magistrate declared that 'this a free country. We are fighting to keep it a free country, as I understand it, and these gentlemen fortunately for them . . . are living in a country where they can express their pacifism or their non-pacifism with perfect freedom.'[67] But printers refused to produce *Peace News*, and the weekly paper was instead printed on an old press donated by a controversial Catholic pacifist and artist called Eric Gill (who, it would later be revealed, was a serial abuser).[68] Meanwhile leading members of the PPU were taken off the airwaves. The voices of Soper, Charles Raven and Middleton Murry could no longer be heard on the BBC.[69] The screw was tightening gently.

Public attitudes towards pacifists were continuing to harden. The government's own Home Intelligence Reports, produced by the Ministry of Information on British morale, recorded in May 1940 that conscientious objectors were likely to be 'the object of public antagonism which may develop in ugly ways'.[70] A milkman who was also a conscientious objector was apparently chased by a 'crowd of angry women' near Birmingham.[71] The Mass Observation social survey, which tried to take the pulse of British attitudes, described how 'In addition to being scorned, mocked, derided, there are serious practical drawbacks to being a CO [conscientious objector]. Family pressure, from parents, wives, and girlfriends, which make private life difficult; economic pressure – COs being often fired or compelled to resign from their jobs . . . psychological pressure . . . The CO has to some extent become a social outcast.'[72] People opposed to war were beginning to stick out.

Alongside the legal and political pressure, most pacifists were as worried about what their family, friends and colleagues thought as what the police might do to them. Roy Ridgway's main concerns during the police visit to the family home was what his mum and dad were thinking, and the implications of his mother's 'flushed' face. Roy overheard a woman in the office where he worked say, 'So and so is a conscientious objector. I feel sorry for his poor mother.' If Roy's mother was ashamed, she did not tell Roy, or at least Roy did not record this in his diary. Roy's father's responses were generally between mild mockery and silence, and their relationship remained awkward at best. Although he had come to his sons' defence during the police visit, they would seldom see entirely eye to eye, even if relations did not break out into outright conflict. Many years later Roy described his father's attitude to his boys' pacifism as 'ambivalent' at best.[73]

Fred Urquhart's relations with his father had become more strained with the outbreak of war, and at one point Fred wrote that he had had 'another row with Dad about being what he calls pro-German!'[74] Fred's father accused him of not having a 'good word to say for your own country', adding, 'You wouldn't be so well off if you hadn't lived all your life here. Away you go to Russia or Germany and you'll soon see how well off you'd be there.' Fred did not argue back, telling his diary that there was no use, as his father would never appreciate 'that we have far more in common with the working people of Germany than we will ever have with the "aristocrats" who he admires so much'. The differences between father and son lingered.

Similar stories of family tensions and anxieties can be found in the diaries and letters of other pacifists. Vera Brittain and her husband George Catlin already had what they described as a 'semi-detached' marriage; he had spent much of the early 1930s teaching in the US, while Vera lived in London with her great friend Winifred Holtby.[75] Their different views on the war only intensified the emotional separation. George wrote that pacifism failed to confront 'the original sin of man without grace'.[76] For him humans were innately, if tragically, predisposed towards violence, and although violence could be reduced, it was naive, even dangerous, to think it could be eradicated entirely. Refusing to fight could let injustice run amok. It must have made for interesting dinner conversation in the family home. When war had started, George told Vera he could not support her pacifism, and was convinced in the decades afterwards that her public commitments had harmed his own largely thwarted political aspirations.[77] Vera also fell out with her closest friend, the writer Storm Jameson, over their diverging attitudes to the war.[78] Her relationship with Storm was particularly intense, part of a pattern of strong emotional and intellectual bonds with other women that contrasted with her sometimes distant relationship with her husband. Storm had been a sponsor of the PPU, but was always a hesitant pacifist, and had resigned, somewhat secretly and without telling Vera, in 1938. She later wrote that she had come to the conclusion that 'good is not stronger than evil' and that to profess pacifism would be dishonest cowardice.[79] When Vera found out she was deeply upset. Storm had been named as the legal guardian of Vera's two children, but Vera changed her mind and altered her will. The relationship had survived the outbreak of the war, but soon broke down completely, both sides feeling betrayed by the other.[80]

Families who had previously managed differing opinions now found it difficult. Corrado Ruffoni, a left-wing Londoner of Italian descent, argued bitterly with his girlfriend Pamela Moore over his pacifist convictions.[81] Pamela's worries about their relationship merged with her worries about the war. She wondered whether Corrado had enough in common with her; she was certainly against war, but she was not a convinced pacifist, advising Corrado that until pacifists were in the majority there was very little that could be done.[82] She wrote that she felt that Corrado was being unpatriotic and failed to recognise that 'England was not so bad', and later she accused him of having 'childish views on politics'.[83] Tony Parker, a Quaker pacifist living in Brighton, was forced to part from his girlfriend after she was told by her father that if he did not renounce his pacifism she would not be allowed to see him again. Parker replied he was not going to change his convictions, and his girlfriend said she had to do as her father told her, so they split up. Years later, Parker recalled, 'I've often thought back in the years since how strange it had been because I would probably have been married to her'.[84] Ken Shaw, a pacifist and a Methodist from south London, with a brother in the RAF, faced criticism from his father, who believed that it was 'everyone's duty' to serve in the military at a time of war.[85] Shaw's mother was upset by the whispers she felt she could hear from neighbours about her son's pacifism. Ronald Mallone, a socialist, pacifist and trainee teacher, was treated as a 'weird animal' by his relatives, and his aunt suggested he should have his hard-won college scholarship taken away.[86]

Friendship too could be put under strain. Leonard Bird was a Quaker PPU activist from Huddersfield, and a close friend, so close in fact that Bird's son was named after Leonard, refused to give him a job in his law firm until he 'got all this silly' pacifist business out of his head.[87] Alexander Bryan, a student teacher from York, gradually 'noticed a subtle change in attitudes towards me on the part of my closest friends at the hall of residence. Had they mocked me for my pacifist beliefs, I could have understood it – but they didn't. In some strange way, we suddenly seemed to have less in common.'[88] One friend, who was a scout, told him that 'pacifists and communists, but especially pacifists', were not welcome in the scouting movement. Tony Parker later recalled that 'about sixty percent of the neighbours, or around that, were antagonistic . . . I think one accused me of being a fifth columnist . . .'[89] Sometimes it could get violent, and he was once hit by a young boy in a swimming pool.[90]

It was at the workplace that life could be most difficult for those opposed to the war. After the start of the war, Fred Urquhart felt increasingly isolated at the bookshop, and found it hard to relate to his colleagues because they all had relatives in the armed forces; he believed the people he worked with were all too scared of each other to admit that they did not want the war.[91] He described his colleagues, and the working classes more generally, as 'fools who are quite content to be slaves, they just laugh at anyone like me'.[92]

Roy Ridgway's pacifism had begun to cause problems at the bakery where he had found work in the run-up to the war. At one point, he was called a 'sissie' by a girl in his office; he pretended not to hear, but admitted in his diary that he had been hurt.[93] During the First World War, conscientious objectors had been widely accused of being effeminate, limp-wristed half-men, and the stereotype still had some strength.[94] A typist had later come to Roy's desk and on seeing a PPU badge had blurted out, 'Oh no, Mr

Ridgway, don't be one of them.'[95] Then, at his work Christmas dinner in December 1939, a telephone operator had shouted out, so that everyone could hear, 'What is that badge you are wearing?' When Roy replied that it was from the Peace Pledge Union, the room went completely silent, or at least it felt that way to him. To his relief, attention was soon diverted when some of his co-workers started a food fight, rolls flying everywhere. Roy felt he could tell what everyone was thinking, even if they did not say it: 'coward, coward, coward . . . You're afraid to fight.'[96] This would be a worry that followed Roy all through the war and he felt that women in particular lacked sympathy for his stance. He was determined, like the former teacher and wartime ambulance worker Tom Burns, whom we shall turn to in later chapters, to show that refusing to fight did not mean he could not be brave – in fact precisely the opposite. A few months later, the company director took Roy to one side and told him that he 'admired' him, but did not agree with him.[97] Roy was too nervous to argue the pacifist case, as he was worried about losing his job.

The tolerance of Roy's boss did not last. Two weeks after Germany had invaded Belgium, Holland and Luxemburg, and on the day that British Union of Fascists leader Oswald Mosley was imprisoned, Roy found a small Nazi flag somewhere and put it in his pocket. It is not clear why, but Roy must have mentioned it at work, as the company cashier asked to see the flag and proceeded to march around the office, shouting, apparently in jest, 'Heil Hitler.'[98] That afternoon, Roy was called into the director's office and formally reprimanded for 'flourishing the Nazi flag' and previously making 'sneering remarks about the government's war efforts' and in support of the peace movement. The company secretary, who had been a conscientious objector in the First World War, was present but said nothing apart from agreeing that it was certainly 'indiscreet', as the director declared the PPU a 'dangerous' organisation and asked Roy to resign. Roy was determined to hold his ground and defend his position, arguing that the whole incident had been blown out of all proportion, and that if he really was a 'fifth columnist' he should be reported to the police. At this point Ridgway's colleagues rallied around, and that evening he wrote in his diary that one after another they had entered the director's office to tell him that they too would resign if Roy was forced out.

The director backed down, but asked Roy to be more tactful in future.

The criticisms faced by pacifists were real, but it is important not to overplay them. From the late spring of 1940, as the Allies experienced defeat after defeat, the screw may have been tightened on those who opposed going to war, but it was never forced all the way down. There remained considerable space for pacifists to carry out their campaigning and voice their opinions, and the Mass Observation claim that those who opposed the war were outcasts did not seem entirely to reflect the experience of many. Balancing pacifist commitments and familial relations could sometimes be hard, and could be shot through with misunderstandings, jealousies and personality clashes; but these same relationships could also be marked by sympathy and intense loyalty, often at the same time. Politicians and officials also maintained cordial relations with some of those who opposed the war. In July 1940, at one of the lowest points of the war, with a German invasion of Britain feared likely at any moment, the Home Secretary issued a memorandum declaring that 'in this country no person should be penalised for the mere holding of an opinion'.[99] The overall approach of the general public and the British state towards pacifists seemed to be 'we may disagree with them, but we respect their right to hold their beliefs'. As Mass Observation put it: 'Much commoner than active sympathy or admiration was the tolerant, fair play attitude. How far the fair play attitude is one of real tolerance, and how far of indifference, it is difficult to say.'[100] Such tolerance does not necessarily imply acceptance, but may suggest an often uneasy coexistence, with pacifists treated as something between an oddity, an irrelevance and a nuisance. Like all forms of tolerance, there were firm limits. It did not take much for tolerance to tip over into accusations of treachery or cowardice, and in the years to come the screw was going to get tighter and tighter, as the country ratcheted up its call on its young to take up arms, to risk life and limb for king and country in the fight against Fascism. To refuse to do so, while sons, brothers, friends and colleagues were placing themselves on the line, would cause ever greater unease and suspicion.

War brings questions of allegiance starkly to the surface. The boundaries of just who is thought to belong, often unstated for most people, are brought into sharp relief. In the first years of the war, the forms of dissent that were seen as acceptable grew ever more restricted. For those who opposed war, this was an uncomfortable place to be – under the watchful eyes of family, friends, lovers, police officers and bureaucrats. But it was the space in which Fred, Roy, Ronald, Stella, Rose Marie, Bianca and, as we will see, Tom Burns found themselves. They had arrived at this point partly by accident and partly by design, not necessarily as a result of some preordained or inevitable path, but through a combination of small-scale decisions and large-scale convictions, as circumstance, chance and commitments combined in unpredictable ways. Their deepest beliefs and relationships would now be put under severe strain, and in the face of such pressures some would change their minds, but others would become more resolute and determined, in ways that were hard to anticipate, and with unforeseen consequences. Above all they would be asked to justify and explain their refusal to fight. And this refusal would have to be given a name: conscience.

CHAPTER 8

Conscription and Conscience

At West Mill, the possibility of conscription weighed increasingly heavily on everyone's mind. By January 1940 all men between twenty and twenty-three years old had been required to register for military service, and Rose Marie wrote in her diary that she expected the next few age groups to be called up very soon.[1] Ronald and Nigel were twenty-five, but both men were determined not to be forced to carry weapons. Rose Marie and Ronald began to discuss what they would do if he was arrested, with Rose Marie finding it a most 'depressing conversation'.[2] Next month, the couple were visited by a friend who was fleeing military service and cycling around the country, trying to avoid jail.[3] It was assumed that women would soon be conscripted in some way too, and in late May 1940, with German forces penning in British troops at Dunkirk, Bianca had written in her diary that she stayed up late with Rose Marie and 'giggled nervously over the possibility of our future prison life when we refuse'.[4]

Across the country, military conscription had brought the war home. The whole of mainland Britain, in theory at least, was being asked to take part. Compulsory military service had an equalising effect – at least for those of the right age – that can be hard to grasp from the vantage point of the twenty-first century, where for most Europeans and North Americans at least, even in the middle of a war, the prospect of being forcibly sent into battle feels very remote. Conscription meant everyone, or nearly everyone, was being asked to face the possibly deadly sacrifices of war.

Conscription also had a twin in the shape of conscientious objection. Throughout the 1930s, those against war and fighting had used a variety of words to understand and explain their opposition:

love, solidarity, reason and faith. Conscience had been there too, swirling within a larger moral vocabulary of virtue and vice, but conscription gave it a firmer shape – in the form of the right to exemption. As they confronted the possible sacrifices of war, those who did not want to take up arms had to work out what conscience meant to them, and how it fitted into the other emotions and motivations that were churning around.

Historically, Britain had avoided compulsory military service for its citizens.[5] Whereas most of mainland Europe had conscripted its soldiers since the nineteenth century – both in and out of war – the British state argued that a voluntary army was both morally and practically superior. Even a year into the First World War, the Liberal MP G. N. Barnes had claimed, 'I refuse to believe that voluntaryism is going to fail us, because to believe that would be almost tantamount to believing in the moral bankruptcy of the nation.'[6] For MPs like this, forcing people to fight was somehow 'unBritish'. They had every confidence that enough men would be stirred by a love of King and Country to come forward. It took two years of mass carnage in the trenches and elsewhere for the politicians to change their minds, and compulsory military conscription for British citizens was introduced for the first time in 1916. When it came, it was partly the result of a shortage of soldiers, and partly an attempt to impose some order on those who came forward.

Conscription is one particular answer to the question of how a state at war decides who should be asked to kill and be killed in battle; it attempts not only to mobilise the labour needed to fight, but also to distribute its sacrifices across society, by calling eligible men, and sometimes women, to serve. But bumps and gaps remain. A state has to decide who is left at home to keep the factories running, food on the table and roofs over people's heads. For a liberal democracy – which purports to value freedom – forcing people into uniform also appears to go against the very principles it seems to uphold, even in a time of national emergency. On the one hand, we might ask how can a loyal citizen refuse a mutual obligation to help fellow citizens in need? On the other, how can those who act in the name of the people demand that some of those people kill or be killed against their will? In many countries around the world, the right to conscientious objection has played a key role in mediating these tensions between obligation and freedom. By exempting specific categories of people from compulsory conscription on the grounds of 'sincerely' held beliefs, the protection of conscience provides a compromise between the obligations to defend your country and the right to freedom of belief.

In Britain, the Military Service Act of 1916 allowed exemptions 'on the grounds of a conscientious objection to the undertaking of combatant service'. Away from military service, there was a much longer history of using such conscience clauses, for reasons of pragmatic compromise as much as principle. Nearly 230 years before, the Toleration Act of 1689 had established the right of Protestant dissenters to object to religious oaths, but was at least partly motivated by the Crown's eagerness to borrow money from the very same people and was therefore a way to bring dissenters back into the fold.[7] Two centuries later, in the late nineteenth century, a conscience clause was used in response to objections to mandatory smallpox vaccinations. It had been proving difficult to force parents to allow their children to be vaccinated and fines did not seem to be helping. It was also widely argued that those who objected were 'responsible' citizens and should not be criminalised.[8] A mechanism was therefore introduced to allow people to opt out, on the grounds of conscience.

The 1916 Military Service Act was similarly shaped by partly utilitarian and partly moral considerations.[9] When its conscience clause was first introduced, the Liberal Prime Minister went to great lengths to paint it as part of British traditions.[10] To gain support from socialists and atheist MPs, the right to conscientious objection was deliberately broad and undefined, potentially including both political and religious claims. At the same time, Ireland and the colonies were exempted from conscription altogether, partly out of fear that forced military service would lead to outright rebellion – although thousands did still sign up to fight. Women were exempted entirely as well. As such, the obligations of conscription and therefore the rights of conscientious objection were limited to those who were assumed to be the most committed and loyal citizens. In this process, a potentially contentious set of political and social conflicts was also partially defused by turning them into a question of tender moral scruples. The conflict was now about just what counted as conscience.

The legal right to conscientious objection came earlier and was wider in Britain than in almost any other country.[11] In the US, during the First World War, exemption due to conscientious objection was restricted to members of recognised 'peace churches' such as Quakers, Mennonites, Amish and Seventh Day Adventists. In the Second World War, expanded exemptions were introduced for those who objected to fighting due to 'religious training or belief'.[12] Only in 1965 did the US Supreme Court widen the right to include those who could show a 'sincere and meaningful belief which occupies in the life of its possessor a place parallel to that filled by the God of those admittedly qualified for the exemption'.[13] For the very first time, the American state had a secular conscience. In the Soviet Union, for a brief period after the Russian Revolution, religious minorities and Mennonites in particular were given the right to alternative forms of service, but the right was more formal than actual, and conscientious objectors were also widely classified as enemies of the people.[14] Germany did not introduce the right to conscientious objection until after the Second World War, when it was written into the 1949 constitution of the Federal Republic. France, with its strong republican tradition that emphasised the equal contribution of all citizens, and the parallel, if sometimes indirect, influence of Catholic thought that historically had downplayed personal freedom of conscience, did not introduce a right to individual conscientious objection until 1963. Elsewhere across the globe, it was only in the second half of the twentieth century that the right to conscientious objection to military service became enshrined in law.

In Britain after 1918, the British population remained generally hostile to the idea of conscription, a situation which should at least in part be seen in the context of the erosion of respect for military virtues. The historian Sonya Rose has argued that through the 1920s and 1930s there was a move – largely as a direct response to the war of the previous decade –towards a more 'tempered' form of masculinity.[15] Bravery came to be associated not simply with heroic deeds on the battlefield – although that was still an idea very much around – but also with smaller acts of kindness and more 'homely qualities' such as support for your family. This developed a particular patriotic tinge with the outbreak of the Second World War. If Nazis were imagined as cold-blooded and fanatical killers, British

'And Jesus said: suf-fer lit-tle chil . . .' An image of the destruction of war from Arthur Wragg's *Thy Kingdom Come*, published in 1939. Wragg was a pacifist and sponsor of the Peace Pledge Union (PPC) and many of his images were used in anti-war publications.

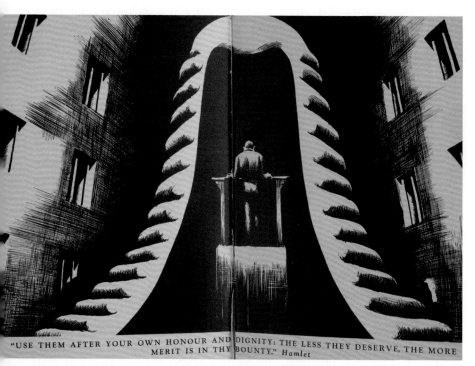

"USE THEM AFTER YOUR OWN HONOUR AND DIGNITY: THE LESS THEY DESERVE, THE MORE MERIT IS IN THY BOUNTY." *Hamlet*

A lone figure is judged before a tribunal in *Thy Kingdom Come*. Wragg himself was imprisoned as a conscientious objector during the war.

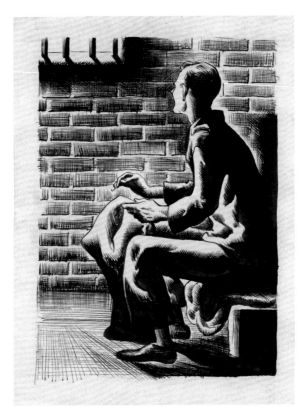

Wragg's image for the cover of the Central Board of Conscientious Objectors Report (April 1941–March 1942) showing an imprisoned objector sewing a mail bag.

A wartime sitting of the North Midlands tribunal for conscientious objectors. On the left are members of the tribunal. Before them sit an objector and his adviser, with supporters and other conscientious objectors looking on.

Conscientious objectors attending a course in mechanised agriculture in Essex under the Ministry of Agriculture's labour training scheme.

A sketch by an unknown artist (*c.* 1941–2) of a resident of the Hungerford Club, nicknamed Joad after the academic and former pacifist. The Hungerford Club was run by Christian pacifist volunteers for 'vagrants' not allowed into public bomb shelters.

Roy Ridgway in 1941, around the time he was sent to jail for refusing military orders.

Ridgway (middle) on the back of an army truck shortly after the Battle of Monte Cassino, Italy, in May 1944, while serving with the Hadfield-Spears Ambulance Unit.

Fred Urquhart, late 1930s, around the time that his first novel *Time Will Knit* was published to critical acclaim but poor sales.

MAXTON'S
GREAT ANTI-WAR SPEECH

THE speech of James Maxton, M.P., in the House of Commons on October 4th, has been widely quoted and commented on in the press but no paper has published the speech in full. Below

we give a verbatim report of the speech as reported in Hansard.

"I rise to say a few words on the matters before the House. I and those who sit with me made, more than a week ago, an unequivocal announcement to the country that if war took place we would be in opposition to that war and would take every step that lay within our power to bring it to a speedy end.

We did that with much heart-searching, knowing exactly what such a step meant, knowing how we should be derided and chased from pillar to post and misrepresented.

We did it because we believe that war is the one great over-riding evil that humanity has to face. We have every sympathy with Czechoslovakia as much as other people have. We have as much sympathy particularly for the working-class Czechs as other people.

We have the same sympathy for them as we had for the people of Belgium in 1914, but we did not see that as the issue.

We saw that the war in 1914 was fought for 4½ years as a war to end war; and it did not do that. It was fought as a war to make this land fit for heroes, and it did not do that. It was a war fought for democracy, and it did not do that, because to-day the big menace with which we are confronted arises from the fact that the aftermath of the last War was not the spread of democracy in Europe but the creation of more dictators.

10 MILLION LIVES LOST.

We saw our own country enter into that war as a democracy, and within a short time turned into a military dictatorship—of a necessity. An hon. Member opposite—I am not sure

DOUGLAS YOUNG

to the

Electors

of the

Kirkcaldy

Burghs,

1945

FREEDOM FOR THE SCOTTISH PEOPLE

to enjoy the life and wealth of Scotland—
That is the purpose of my campaign.

Douglas Young was the wartime leader of the Scottish National Party and was imprisoned several times for refusing conscription by the British state.

A studio portrait of Ronald Duncan as a young man, probably taken when in his early twenties and studying English at Cambridge, *c.* mid-1930s.

A portrait photograph of Rose Marie Hansom (later Duncan), *c.* 1930s. In the mid-1930s Rose Marie studied at the Royal College of Music, before moving to West Mill with Ronald in 1939.

Bianca Duncan, with cigarette in mouth, holding Ronald's horse, 1935.

A view of West Mill and the surrounding valley from above, *c.* 1930s. Rose Marie and Ronald lived in the house from 1939 while farming nearby at Gooseham.

Rose Marie and an unknown boy at Gooseham Farm, which was run as a pacifist community during the war.

The Duncan family at Welcombe Beach, *c.* 1940s. Left to right: Ronald, Mole (Ronald and Bianca's mother), Bianca and Rose Marie.

men were portrayed as compassionate, courteous and caring. For much of this time, and certainly for many of those in the ranks, joining the army was seen as somewhat desperate, 'between an embarrassment and a tragedy'.[16] There was little popular enthusiasm, at least in peacetime, for living a military life. As late as January 1938 Neville Chamberlain was telling parliament that there would be no peacetime conscription, claiming that it was 'not in accordance with the democratic system under which we live, or consistent with the tradition of freedom which we have always striven to maintain'.[17] Most people seemed to agree with him. An opinion poll taken in June that year suggested that 57 per cent of people were opposed to conscription.[18]

Attitudes began to change quickly after the Munich Agreement in September 1938. The government launched a voluntary National Service campaign at the start of 1939, and with pressure mounting to make a show of force, it legislated for a limited form of conscription in April of that year, amounting to military training for men aged twenty and twenty-one.[19] Opposition was muted, perhaps because the scope of compulsion was so narrow, and Roy Ridgway was one of only a few thousand who marched in protest. Trade unions were suspicious of what they saw as a form of forced labour – they argued for a conscription of wealth as well as labour – but were still strongly behind the preparation for war. The ILP was largely alone in standing resolutely against conscription, issuing a pamphlet declaring that 'If the rich want to defend themselves against the ruling class of other countries ... let them get into their uniforms and defend their interests. We will not follow them. We will encourage Youth to resist, even to the prison cell.'[20]

It was not until the day that war was declared that the National Service (Armed Forces) Act came into force, making all British men resident in mainland Britain aged between eighteen and forty-one liable for military service. Ireland was by now independent, but the North was still excluded from the obligations of conscription. In December 1941 conscription was changed to include all women between nineteen and thirty-one years old, although women were not given combatant roles and had the choice of other 'essential work' for the war effort.[21] In 1942 the law was extended to include Czech, Greek, Dutch, Polish and Yugoslav citizens on British soil.[22] In Imperial India, only the 'European races' were conscripted, although Indians did produce by far the largest volunteer army of the war.[23]

Exemptions on the grounds of conscience also came into legal effect with the National Service Act. These came in two types. The first was an unconditional exemption, which allowed the applicant to go off and do whatever they thought best, their conscience left free and untrammelled. The second was a conditional exemption, by which armed military service was replaced by a non-combatant role in the military or other work of national importance, a provision which sought to ensure that the people claiming conscience did not simply get an easy ride. The law however did not lay out any grounds for the tribunal to distinguish between the two, resulting in a gap that would be a source of controversy and conflict over the coming years.

The British military was desperate for soldiers, sailors and airmen. The size of the armed forces had been greatly reduced throughout the 1920s and early 1930s, falling to around 400,000 men in 1938; but between August and December 1939 alone over a million men joined up, a mixture of volunteers and conscripts.[24] Many of those who volunteered did so before they were formally called up, in the hope of getting into their favoured service or regiment, rather than conscripted into an undesirable position. Yet, despite this sudden growth, it was not as if all men were immediately sent to the front line. As already noted, for the first few months of the war there had been little fighting to do, and the first intake of conscripts did not occur until late October, with men called up by age group over the following months, with many having to wait until there was space to train and house them.

As men turned up at the Labour Exchange to register for military service, the general feeling was very different from that prevailing at the start of the First World War. Popular memory of the brutality and indignity of battle was still strong, and there was no sense of mass jubilation. An observer at the time reported that 'conscripts are joining up in a mixture of readiness and reluctance, relief and negative interest'.[25] The historian Alan Allport has described the general mood as being 'browned off'; it was not that recruits were not committed to the war – they were, and often deeply committed – but that there was very little sense of glory.[26]

Marching off to war was done with considerable ambivalence, the claims of mutual self-sacrifice were not always warmly or easily embraced, and the exhortations from politicians for everybody to come together were taken with a heavy pinch of salt.[27]

There was qualified support for the position of conscientious objectors right at the heart of the British state. In part, this was an aspect of the claim that Britain was a particularly freedom-loving nation, facing down fascist totalitarianism. Winston Churchill, no less, declared that 'the rights which have been granted in this war and the last to conscientious objectors are ... a definite part of British policy. Anything in the nature of persecution, victimization, or man-hunting is odious to the British people.'[28] William Beveridge, who later went on to be a key figure in the founding of the NHS, asserted in a radio broadcast that 'admission of the right of conscientious objection to serve in war is the extreme case of British freedom. Nor have I any doubt that it makes Britain stronger in war rather than weaker.'[29]

There was also more personal support. Some former conscientious objectors were now also senior politicians, with at least three serving in the wartime government, including the Home Secretary Herbert Morrison, who had spent much of the first war working in a market garden.[30]

Finally, the support for the rights of conscience was very practical. Taking lessons from the First World War, the British government and military were also reluctant to force people who did not want to fight to join up. As Neville Chamberlain put it, 'in the Great War . . . I think we found that it was both useless and an exasperating waste of time and effort to attempt to force such people to act in a manner which is contrary to their principles'.[31]

Importantly, conscientious objection was not the only way to avoid being sent into battle. If the issue was how the country distributed the responsibility to kill and be killed, many allowances were made for those who either did not want to fight or might be better placed doing something else. The language of 'all being in it together' that has marked so much public memory about the Second World War hides a wide variation in experience. As in any war, the majority of members of the armed forces were not front-line combatants, but were involved in logistics, administration, medical care or engineering, for example. Beyond the armed forces there were also reserved occupations, which at various times included miners, farm workers, accountants, tailors and dentists.[32] Among further exemptions were students, police officers, medical and prison workers and clergy. Others who objected to joining up emigrated, sought medical exemption or simply went on the run. Over the course of the war, 8 per cent of men under twenty and 35 per cent of those over thirty-six appearing before military medical boards were judged unfit for service.[33] One estimate has it that in 1943 alone more than 300,000 service personnel were discharged on medical grounds.[34] Other estimates have put the numbers who went AWOL over the course of the war at more than 100,000.[35] Alan Allport has suggested that many men in the armed forces viewed those who managed to avoid armed service with 'envy rather than indignation'.[36] Either way, only a very small minority of people would ever see action on the front line, and very few were raring to do so.

Ronald Duncan and Nigel Spottiswoode tried to register as conscientious objectors, but soon discovered, slightly to their disappointment but probably also with a sense of relief, that as farmers they were in a reserved occupation and already exempt from military service. For the first few years of the war, at least until women were made liable to conscription, Rose Marie, Bianca and Stella St John did not have to decide whether they would object. Fred and Roy, though, were both liable to be conscripted and had to choose whether they did so under the particular label of conscience or to seek another way.

In the first year of the war, Fred Urquhart had listened constantly to the wireless, expecting the announcement at any time that all men of his age group had to report to the nearest recruiting office, and fearing that this would eventually mean a near-certain and painful death on the battlefield.[37] Alongside a general hatred of war, his socialist commitments and his anxiety about his own safety, Fred's reluctance to join the forces was at least partly motivated by a belief that his fledgling career as an author should mark him out for protection: 'in a war like this it is imperative that people like me should be kept inviolable. We are part of a civilization that must be saved. A writer to be a great writer must suffer, but I do not see why he should suffer needlessly ... The degradation would kill anything creative in me.'[38] Like many artists, writers and composers from the time – Ben Britten, Michael Tippett and W. H. Auden among them – he believed that his art meant that he should be treated differently.[39] After Ben Britten had sailed to America on the eve of war, a supporter wrote to the papers asking 'Where would English music be today if those men who happened to survive the last war had shared the fate of their less fortunate colleagues?'[40] The implicit logic was that the freedom to create was one of the reasons the war was being fought and that this freedom should be preserved. There was no reserved occupation of artists and writers – although many did find employment through the War Artists Advisory Committee or the Ministry of Information – so those of a creative bent had to find another way.

Although he never articulated it in this way, the fact that Fred's most intimate desires were criminalised by the British state was probably not entirely irrelevant. It would be far too simplistic to draw a straight line between Fred's sexuality and his anti-war attitudes, but in a country where sex between men opened you up to the possibility of blackmail, police harassment and jail, forcing you into furtive and secret liaisons and prompting you to rip pages from your own diary out of fear of exposure, the hypocrisy of a war for freedom cannot have been far from Fred's mind.

Fred had many reasons not to fight, but many of his friends signed up early in the war – even those who had shared his left-wing sentiments and anti-war attitudes. His publisher in London, Patrick Crichton-Stuart, had joined the army just before telling him that his new novel had been put in 'cold storage'.[41] Fred was initially advised by a friend to register as a conscientious objector, but he felt that he did 'not have the courage for that' as he risked being socially ostracised or even sent to prison if his application was refused.[42] Instead he had tried to get signed off by a doctor on the grounds that he had an 'enlarged heart', but was unsuccessful.[43] His next plan was to get a job with the Ministry of Food, but the ministry refused to take him as they were not employing anyone of military age. Fred then wrote to Crichton-Stuart to see if he could help, but was not hopeful, given that Crichton-Stuart was 'probably too busy wrangling a safe job for himself'.[44] If there was a degree of class-based bitterness in Fred's remarks, it was not entirely ill-placed. In the scramble to expand the armed forces, there was plenty of room for people to pull strings to get special treatment.

In English there are separate words for 'conscience' and 'consciousness', but in other languages, including French and German, they are one and the same. To have a conscience is to become conscious of something, and for many people like Fred their consciences emerged gradually, not appearing in a flash of light, nor shouted out clearly at a moment of crisis, but rather gaining shape in the middle of a host of otherwise inchoate experiences, creeping up slowly in fits and starts, retreating and coming forward at unpredictable moments. It is not clear from his diaries why Fred finally decided to register as a conscientious objector. He may simply have taken the decision having exhausted all other options, but the fact that it took him some time to decide does not mean that he did not object to taking up arms in a profound sense – his left-wing convictions and his sense of the pointlessness of violence ran deep – but registering as a conscientious objector did not initially appear as the best option for avoiding the call-up. Conscience – as a particular and effective way of opposing battle and conscription – slowly came into focus, and by the summer of 1940 his hatred of war was matched by an increasingly strong commitment to register. As he now put it in his diary, 'I think I'd prefer to go to jail' rather than join the army.[45] However, Mary Litchfield, having previously tried to talk him round into becoming a conscientious objector, now tried to persuade him that he would be better off in the army instead of being 'cooped up in jail without enough to eat and nothing to smoke'.[46] Mary was by now convinced that defeating Fascism was more important than anti-militarist principles. But Fred was determined to 'stick to my guns (funny phrase for a pacifist!). I hate war and I will not take part in any war, whether anti-Fascist or not.'[47]

What did conscience mean to the people who invoked it?

British law did not define conscience, and its form and content had been left deliberately vague and expansive. For some pacifists conscience was a deeply physical feeling linked to an abhorrence of violence. For John Middleton Murry, it was the 'name given to impulses'.[48] The First World War conscientious objector, poet and General Secretary of the PPU Max Plowman told Middleton

Murry that pacifism is 'nothing more than the instinctive feeling of the ordinary man made conscious'.[49] Plowman believed so strongly that pacifism must spring from an individual conscience that he insisted to a friend that he would not 'cross the road' to persuade someone to embrace the cause of peace.[50] This was conscience as an urge, an emotion, a physical and psychic response to wrongdoing. For others, in contrast, conscience was more rational. As a Mass Observation volunteer noted, most pacifists 'objected to war not simply due to a little voice of conscience, but [as a result of] thought'.[51] This was a way of understanding conscience as measured reflection, the weighing up of options, a deliberate and intellectual endeavour.

In theory, conscience could be secular or religious. There was nothing that said the pious had a monopoly on conviction. Socialist, anarchists, nationalists, libertarians and humanists all made claims in its name, but since the Reformation, if not earlier, it had often been taken for granted by many people that to talk about conscience was to talk about religion and a very particular type of religion at that; conscience seemed to walk most comfortably in Britain in the footsteps of Protestant forms of faith.

Conscience also moved between freedom and obligation. For some, conscience was about radical individual autonomy; it was a matter of liberty or it was nothing – freewheeling, untrammelled and unrestrained, capacious and unpredictable. For others conscience was all about obligation: we do not pick and choose the issues that activate our conscience, our conscience makes choices for us; it is a demand, wherever it comes from, that imposes burdens. In this sense, conscience is not entirely different from conscription: a duty, a calling, which operates whether we like it or not, a question of doing the right thing, not merely what you want to do. This is the conscience of absolute convictions, where people are urged to protect and respect it precisely because it is unwavering and unchanging, a matter of command not choice. Forcing someone to go against their conscience would somehow do them great damage, bending their sense of right and wrong to breaking point. Here I stand, I can do no other.

In short, conscience took many forms. As Middleton Murry saw it, just as 'humans are infinitely various, consciences are infinitely various'.[52]

However one approached it, conscience did not always have a

good name, even for those who opposed war. Throughout the first half of the twentieth century, there had been widespread criticism of the idea that individual scruples alone should guide action or determine our responsibilities to others. For many socialists in particular, the individualism of conscientious objection was a cause of unease, and there was an argument that because conscription represented a collectivised response to who should fight, it should be supported by those on the political left. The Fabian intellectual Beatrice Webb had written during the First World War that conscientious objectors seemed 'intent on thwarting the will of the majority of ordinary people'.[53] Arthur Creech Jones, himself a conscientious objector in the Great War, who later became a trade unionist and Labour MP, felt that pacifism tended to 'encourage individualism and weaken collective action'.[54] Tender moral scruples, it was argued, were a diversion from attempts to challenge systematic injustices.

Conscientious objectors were routinely criticised for the intensity of their belief in their own personal virtue, their apparent self-righteousness. Even Dick Sheppard was disparaging about the objectors of the First World War, describing them as 'fanatics and freaks who rush into every progressive cause'.[55] These were criticisms that returned with the approach of the Second World War. The Marxist critic Christopher Caudwell complained in 1938 that pacifists are 'So imbued ... with bourgeois notions of sin, that it never occurs to [them] that a preoccupation with one's own soul and one's own salvation is selfish'.[56] Cyril Joad, once a leading light of the pacifist movement in the early 1930s, criticised conscientious objection for being 'aimed at the preservation of individual integrity in the face of war, rather than the prevention of that war'.[57] Meanwhile, the *New Statesman*'s Kingsley Martin, accused pacifists of being 'intensely individualistic, supremely concerned with their own intellectual integrity, and continually haunted with a horror of pain and physical violence'.[58] All too often, this was a group of people seen as being too self-important for their own good, putting a concern for the protection of their own personal convictions above a concern for the fate of the world they shared with others.

To put it simply, the value of conscience was far from obvious.

It was among the tensions between reason and intuition, religion and secularism, freedom and obligation, virtue and vice, that

the conscientious objectors of the Second World War found themselves. In this space, pacifists had no monopoly on principle or
moral fervour. There was no self-evident connection between
opposing war and having a conscience; the link had to be forged
rather than found, and this was not always easy.

One month into the war Roy Ridgway had begun to question his
pacifist convictions, writing in his diary that 'some of the remarks
that slip from me in conversation are not the words of a pacifist . . .
I find myself saying things I ought not to say. It is hard to be an out
and out pacifist. The love of one's country is inherent in everyone.'[59]
Roy was worried that the general atmosphere in Britain during the
first months of the war was leading him off the pacifist path. He
was still convinced that war was wrong and that he could not kill
his 'fellow creatures', but he was less sure what that meant in practice. He was yet to make up his mind whether he would refuse any
and all types of conscripted service, disagreeing strongly with a
pacifist friend who declared that he would not even provide first
aid in the event of an air raid. The friend argued that any aid was
merely patching up men to send them back to fight. In contrast,
Roy wrote that he could not 'stand aloof in an attitude of sullen
superiority' and 'watch people writhing in agony'.[60] He could not
decide though how far he would go in giving help and if he would
allow anyone to tell him what to do.

At the start of October 1939, Derricke Ridgway had registered
as a conscientious objector at the Hendon Labour Exchange. He
was the youngest brother and, due to the way the system worked,
the first to be called up. Derricke wrote on his application that he
was a practitioner of yoga, with a deep interest in Indian philosophy, and therefore could not participate in violence.[61] This was
probably not a wise decision. By December 1939, Roy had been
sure he would be called up shortly, and the pressure to come to
some decision was mounting. Should he refuse any type of conscription, or should he agree to some kind of alternative service,
perhaps in the Royal Army Medical Corps? The thought of 'more
than a million German troops . . . massed on the Dutch and Belgium frontiers' terrified him.[62] He wrote that he was 'a bundle of
nerves . . . I can't talk to people in a normal way. Everyone seems
to avoid me. It is my own fault . . . I can't interest myself in the

things that most people are interested in.'[63] He was also feeling increasingly isolated, despite his close relationship with his brothers, confiding in his diary his fears that he would 'probably be branded a coward for the rest of my life . . . the pacifist ploughs a lonely furrow'.[64]

On New Year's Eve, Derricke collapsed in the family home, while waiting for the Ministry of Labour to decide whether to accept his application. Roy and his parents panicked, afraid that he had tried to poison himself with a bottle of potassium cyanide, only for the doctor to announce that he had simply drunk too much beer. Derricke had been spending most of his time in his room, getting ready to appear before the tribunal, and was determined not to compromise, refusing to do any type of work under compulsion – combatant or non-combatant. Roy wrote in his diary that he was afraid his brother would 'have to go to prison'.[65]

The uncertainties and loneliness of conscience could sometimes be too much to take, with its long dark nights of the soul and periods of intense introspection. Alone in their rooms at night, the pacifists' voices of conscience could act as uneasy reminders, asking uncomfortable questions, not necessarily telling them what to do, not providing answers but constantly querying. Many of those seemingly determined not to take up arms were full of doubt and anxiety as they faced up to the implications of their positions, both for themselves and for those around them. They were unsure what to do, what their consciences said and how to justify this to others, as well as how they could even begin to claim a position of moral purity in a world that had already fallen into war. Roy and Fred were filled with nerves, clearly divided over what was the best course of action. When a young boy asked Fred why he was not in uniform, much to his own disappointment Fred replied that he was medically unfit, in the moment unable to explain his own position.[66] Other conscientious objectors recall being deeply troubled by the decision not to fight. Doris Nicholls, who worked at the Fellowship of Reconciliation with Stella St John, recalled that 'many of us were torn in two. Any thinking person would be aware that the food you ate was being convoyed and that being able to live at all was because of the work the people in the services were doing.'[67] For her husband Bernard, 'real ethical life is a matter of dilemmas and paradoxes . . . And often there aren't answers that are wholly satisfactory at all.'[68] Vera Brittain, too old to be conscripted herself, wrote that the Second World War brought a 'succession of sharp anxieties ... a series of moral dilemmas ... Problems arose in which it was all too easy to make the wrong choice, and all too difficult to accept the consequences of decisions that seemed right.'[69]

Criticisms and remarks from friends, family and loved ones added to the hesitation. Ben Britten, the composer, experienced particular anxiety as he fretted over whether he should stay in the US or return to his family. A year into the war, he wrote that 'one feels bad about not suffering as well ... but one must try & be realistic, and that is what I am trying to work out now – where one is of most use & least bother.'[70] Some of his friends were beginning to question his prolonged sojourn, and he began to complain about 'preachy letters' and being told this was a 'just war'.[71] It was clearly an uncomfortable position to be in, and Ben complained that 'Americans are awfully inclined to treat the whole thing [the war] as an awfully interesting play.'[72] The longer he stayed in America, the more his musical reputation in the UK seemed to be under threat.[73] By the autumn of 1941 he had made up his mind to return to Britain, writing to a friend that 'I am not telling people because it sounds a little heroic, which it is far from being – it is really that I cannot be separated any longer from all my friends and family – going through all they are ...'[74] This was a conscience marked by mixed emotions and considerable personal uncertainty.

It could be difficult, if not impossible, to tell the difference between overlapping motivations, not least for the conscientious objectors themselves. One would-be conscientious objector remarked, 'I don't know whether I'm a coward. And, quite frankly, neither do you.'[75] Another wrote, 'Once I was a conchy. Why? For over twenty years I have been trying to find out if I could name some noble reasons; but even at the time, I was sure that there were some tares among the wheat.'[76] W. H. Auden felt similarly, writing that it was 'impossible to know whether it is prison or just cowardice that makes me think I wouldn't be of much military effectiveness'.[77] When and if conscience spoke to people, it could be hard to make out what it was saying. More often than not conscience did not shout loudly, but mumbled. It could be difficult even for conscientious objectors to tell the difference between conscience and fear. Roy Ridgway, Fred Urquhart, Ben Britten and others grappled with competing senses of obligation and duty – to themselves, to their families, to their country, to their class. Conscience could tell them to do more than one thing, and not fighting could seem as unconscionable as doing so.

Sometimes all these uncertainties and confusions could tip over into despair. Roy's brother Derricke was feared to have attempted suicide and Roy himself often felt isolated and unfulfilled, and would have his own psychic collapse later in the war. Ben Britten's biographer writes that he had a breakdown in 1940 brought on by agonising over whether to return to England, and Britten himself would later blame his ill-health on his 'mental perplexities' over the implications of his opposition to war and conscription.[78] The composer Michael Tippett's own absolute pacifism developed alongside considerable personal turmoil, as tensions over his own sexuality and relationships with those he loved combined with despair at a world seemingly gone mad to create mounting desperation as he confronted the dark sides of the human personality.

The story of Menlove Edwards seems to embody the tragedy of these tensions and turmoils. Menlove was one of the greatest rock climbers of 1930s Britain, an imaginative poet and a brilliant psychiatrist. He was also gay, a socialist and a deeply spiritual Christian. Throughout the 1930s, he constantly sought out adventure, trying to sail to Norway in a rickety dinghy and rowing across the hazardous waters of the Minch to the Outer Hebrides. He was convinced that homosexuality and Christianity were compatible, but he was also intensely lonely in a society that would not accept him for who he was. The onset of war had seen him writing to a friend in November 1939, 'I'm afraid a large part of me would like to be in on this war. Though not any part one would care to back up.'[79] Many of his friends were now in the army, and his pacifism was increasing his sense of isolation. The possibility of companionship and adventure in the army had its attractions for him: 'it would be grand to try and do some tough and cunning stuff . . . But one has chosen the other side of life.'[80] He eventually spent most of the war working as a child psychiatrist, but all the time his mental health was getting worse, and in the last year of the war he tried to commit suicide, his biographer writing that the act was 'surely an attempt to break not only an obsession, but also an inherited and developed moral imperative with which he no longer had the emotional strength to cope'.[81]

In the First World War, the military had sometimes tried to tie conscientious objection directly to mental health problems, and the tribunals that decided on conscientious and medical exemptions were one and the same. The poet Siegfried Sassoon's protests against the war were treated as mental breakdown, and he was sent to convalesce in a hospital on the outskirts of Edinburgh.[82] By the time the Second World War began, the processes for conscientious and medical exemptions were kept entirely apart. However, the Edinburgh-based psychiatrist Harry Stalker claimed that a link might remain between psychiatric conditions and opposition to war, arguing that conscientious objectors were marked by 'aggression' and 'pathological fear'.[83] Stalker seems to have been relatively unusual in making such direct arguments, and it would be oversimplistic to draw a line between conscientious doubts and mental health problems, but clearly the two could run alongside one another. It is impossible to tell how much of the despair was directly linked to conscientious objection and how much of it was part of a much broader pattern among young people in their twenties in a world apparently hellbent on destruction. It might well be that a particularly introspective type of young man and woman was drawn to conscientious objection, but only a very small number of conscientious objectors were driven to the edge of sanity.

Yet, despite all doubt and confusion, conscience does not have to result in immobilisation. It could also lead to action. To have doubts is not to be sceptical or cynical. W. H. Auden wrote that poetry was the 'clear expression of mixed feelings'. We might say the same for many pangs of conscience. Roy Ridgway finally decided that he would volunteer for humanitarian work 'to alleviate the suffering in this world' but would not accept any compulsion from the state.[84] Having convinced himself to register as a conscientious objector, he would now have to persuade others he was genuine.

CHAPTER 9

Conscience on Trial

After all the soul-searching of the preceding years, Roy Ridgway was finally having to put his convictions on the line. This meant standing in front of a tribunal that would pass judgement on his most deeply held beliefs, and Roy began to worry that he might not be able to get the words out when needed. He was still in his early twenties and often very shy. Talking about conscience with your brothers and in your diary was one thing, but making a persuasive case to a potentially hostile audience was quite another. If conscience was to be anything more than the lonesome introspection of an isolated individual, objectors had to find a way to make it both visible and persuasive to others. It is probably no coincidence that so many conscientious objectors were artists, writers and composers, as they grappled with what conscience meant to them. Ronald Duncan, Fred Urquhart and Ben Britten all tried to put their most personal convictions into their art, to give an otherwise enigmatic and intangible conscience a concrete presence. But now Roy was not facing poets and musicians. Now he had to convince not simply himself but a panel of grey and serious-looking men.

By the end of the war, over 62,000 people had appeared before the local tribunals, their numbers falling from around 2 per cent of all those conscripted in late 1939 to around 0.3 per cent by the end of 1942.[1] These people did not stand out just because they did not want to fight, as there were many people who did not wish to go to the front line and found other ways not to do so. Instead, what marked out conscientious objectors was their determination to stand in full public view and declare their deepest moral commitments. As Roy and others appeared before the tribunal, fighting against both their own uncertainty and the suspicions of those around them, they would find out things about themselves, as well as what other people really thought of them.

When Derricke Ridgway finally appeared before the tribunal in February 1940, the judge told him to take his hands out of his pockets. Derricke responded angrily that the tribunal was a 'farce', before the judge announced he was a 'very bad-mannered man' and removed him from the list of conscientious objectors. The written decision stated that Derricke was 'utterly insincere' and had 'no conscience in the matter at all'.[2] Things did not look good for Roy.

To prepare for his own tribunal, Roy had decided to go before a panel made up of other pacifists.[3] It was hoped that practice under pressure would help him put his convictions into words. The hearing took place in a suburban front room in north London, but to make it feel as authentic as possible the chair of the judges ensured that he came across as short-tempered and unsympathetic, asking Roy why he was willing to eat food imported by sailors who risked their lives, why he paid taxes when those taxes were spent on weapons and what he would do if Nazi troops occupied Britain. As he stood accused of hypocrisy and complicity, Roy became tongue-tied, stumbling over his words, hesitating and pausing before he spoke. The judges all agreed that they did not find him at all convincing. That evening, Roy decided that when it came to the real thing, his best option was to speak as little as possible, in case he said something he did not really mean.

It was clearly good to practise, but mock tribunals were also controversial. There was a pervasive feeling even among would-be conscientious objectors that preparing too much could be both morally and practically counterproductive. Some applicants were concerned that if they presented too polished a case, they might be exempted on the basis of their rhetorical skills rather than their beliefs. One man worried that if he had been granted an exemption after a persuasive performance, it would have been due to the skills of his advisers rather than his own 'merits'.[4] Another thought that preparing too much would be 'cheating in a way'.[5] The trick then was to become an expert in presenting a form of conscience that did not appear too prompted or trained. A coalition of like-minded groups known as the Central Board for Conscientious Objectors (CBCO) organised mock hearings, but studiously avoided telling people what to say, arguing they were not there to 'help you to outwit the Tribunals, and get a better exemption than you deserve'.[6] The best advice it gave was to 'look spontaneous' and to 'talk of your conscience without self-consciousness'. This was easier said than done. A conscious lack of self-consciousness is hard to pull off.

More worried than ever, Roy decided he would go and see a tribunal in action. At the west London court house, a portrait of George V dressed in the uniform of an admiral of the fleet loomed over the proceedings. For Roy it was 'more impressive than I had imagined it to be'.[7] The judge who had harangued his brother was absent this time, but the reception was just as hostile. One young man was told that he was a hypocrite because he was working as a stretcher-bearer for civil defence. Another applicant said that he could not kill a fellow Christian, at which one of the judges threw up his hands and said, 'So the only humans you won't kill are Christians!'

It took several months for Roy to be called to his own tribunal, and the long wait only added to his apprehension. He went for a walk with Derricke and a mutual friend, and as the other two young men discussed philosophy, Roy remained silent.[8] He wrote in his diary that 'not until the war is over will I be able to settle down'.

On 16 June, having appealed against the first decision, Derricke Ridgway appeared before the appellate tribunal, in the very week that German troops entered Paris. This time around he seems to have been more persuasive. Perhaps he was less antagonistic to the judge. Perhaps he was just lucky. Either way, he was given an exemption on condition that he carry out agricultural work.

The very next day Roy finally appeared before his own tribunal.[9] He had declared in his application that he was an 'ardent pacifist, and have always opposed the use of force ... I am firmly convinced that love and not force is the ultimate power in the universe ... I renounce war and absolutely refuse, on moral and religious grounds, to attach myself to any military organization.'[10] He backed up his claim by pointing to his vegetarianism and long-term membership of the PPU. But all that had been written several months before. Since then Roy and the wider world had changed significantly. It is hard not to feel for this young man, who spent his days as assistant to a credit manager in a bakery and his evenings at home with his parents. He was now out in front of a panel of intimidating men. To make matters worse, Roy faced one of the judges who had originally been so tough on his brother. Judge Hargreaves, bald and wearing a dark suit, sat behind a high wooden desk, his hectoring sarcasm not designed to put anyone at ease.

Things did not get off to a good start, with Hargreaves declaring that 'non-violence is a joke'.[11] Roy then told the tribunal that the early Christians were opposed to war, but on being asked to name some of those Christians, his mind went blank. He went on to say that in the event of a German invasion he would refuse to cooperate, but one of the other judges asked whether he meant that, for example, he would object to mending broken drains, even if people were dying of typhoid. It seemed that this was a rhetorical question, because before Roy could answer, a third judge enquired about his vegetarianism and whether he wore leather boots. Roy replied that it was impossible to be completely consistent in anything – only the dead were consistent – and he wore boots as he could hardly go about in his stockinged feet. The point about consistency might have been reasonable, but it was probably not a very sensible tactic.

The whole thing lasted for only ten minutes. That evening Roy reflected that it seemed the tribunal was trying to get through as many cases as possible, and he believed that 'they were convinced in their own minds that everyone who came before them was a shirker'.

The tribunal's decision was that Roy was to be given an exemption on condition that he take up duties in the Non-Combatant Corps. The Corps had been created especially for conscientious objectors, and although its members did not have to carry guns, they had to wear a uniform and were under formal military command. This was decidedly not the humanitarian work that Roy had hoped to carry out. He had wanted to relieve suffering, and instead he was being directed to a branch of the army which was famous for digging pit latrines. Equally importantly, Roy was after an unconditional exemption, one where his conscience was able to do as it demanded, to go in any direction, and not be placed under tight conditions by the British state. He wanted his conscience to be free.

Roy immediately appealed, giving himself a temporary breathing space. As he waited to be called back to the tribunal, he decided to visit his brothers, who had gone to live in South Wales and were both looking for agricultural work while staying with their grandmother in Capel-y-ffin – or, in English, the Chapel-at-the-End. It was a fitting name for a remote hamlet nestled in the shadow of the Black Mountains surrounded by moorland, heather and sheep farming.[12] Ten years previously the hamlet had been home to a cross between an artist's commune and a religious community, run by Eric Gill.[13] Gill's community had lasted only a few years and he had moved to a village near High Wycombe by the time Roy arrived.

As Roy stepped off the train, he saw that Alfred – who had also registered as a conscientious objector and was looking for agricultural work – had grown a beard and was looking decidedly bohemian. Before going to the cottage, the three young men, glad to be back together, stopped at the Skirrid Mountain Inn – reputed to be nearly a thousand years old – for a pint of 'potent' cider. The brothers then walked the rest of the way to Capel-y-ffin, singing as they went. Roy thought it was a 'beautiful little place' with a corrugated-metal roof and views over the countryside. Each day, the Ridgway siblings collected drinking water from a stream, and Roy cycled to the post office to pick up the post and buy cigarettes, noticing when RAF aircraft flew low over the hillsides. He was impressed by how Alfred and Derricke seemed to 'know everyone in the valley', especially many of the young women.[14] One afternoon, two policemen, huffing and puffing from the walk up the hill to the cottage, called by to ask what the three brothers were up to.[15] They were particularly keen to know if they were involved in politics of any sort. Over tea and cigarettes, with much laughter, Alfred showed them some short stories he was writing, before the officers went on their way, apparently satisfied that there was nothing untoward going on.

During the late summer of 1940, the bombing of British cities heated up. Although they were far from any urban area, at night the brothers watched the searchlights flickering across the sky, and heard the noise of bomber engines and anti-aircraft fire in the distance. Their parents were far closer to the action, and their mother wrote to them on 24 September describing the attacks on London, a bomb landing just yards from their granny's former home.[16] Two days later Roy woke in the night, thinking he could hear a plane about to crash into the cottage, 'the noise growing louder and louder and louder', until it passed over.[17] He tried to persuade their mother to come and join her sons, but she was very reluctant to leave their father.[18] On 14 October Roy's copy of Gandhi's weekly newspaper *Hajiran* arrived along with a letter from his mother reporting that 'People in the city are having a very trying time. Hundreds were machine gunned by German aeroplanes as they were crossing Waterloo Bridge on their way to work on Tuesday morning.'[19] As if to set his mind at ease, she added that she was very proud of her sons. The next month Roy added a small newspaper clipping to his diary, recording that there had been over 15,000 casualties and 6,000 civilians killed in mainland Britain in October.[20] Living in the quiet of rural South Wales, he began to get restless, telling himself this had been 'the worst year in human history' but that 'it was not my intention when I registered as a CO to bury myself in the countryside'.[21] His mood was made worse when he visited a doctor for an unspecified illness and was shouted at for not being in the army.[22]

Roy's mind slowly turned to his appeal. In his written submission he had rejected the claim by the judges that he had told the tribunal that 'any kind of peace was better than resisting', arguing that he had said that 'peace at any price is better than war at any price' and that 'we should overcome evil by active love'. Mr Priestley, a Quaker volunteer from Cardiff working with the Central Board for Conscientious Objectors, put himself forward to act on Roy's behalf, suggesting that he reconsider whether he would agree to some form of alternative service, as unconditional exemption was very rare. Roy turned down the advice, not wanting to be compelled in any way by a state at war.[23] He later recalled that although Priestley had a reputation for getting 'everyone off' he hoped to represent himself, believing that this would be more authentic and sincere.[24] The night before his appeal, Roy had the best night's sleep he had had all year.[25] But his sense of calm was misplaced. The appeal was rejected, and he now faced prison or joining the army in the shape of the Non-Combatant Corps.

*

Roy had been found wanting at his tribunal of conscience; the judges, having looked him up and down, found him insincere and ungenuine. Whereas in the US, almost all cases in both world wars were decided on the basis of the paper application, in Britain the cost of having such a wide definition was that a mechanism had to be put in place to decide where its edges lay and what fitted inside.[26] In the First World War, British MPs hostile to the conscience clause had insisted on the tribunals, fearing that otherwise exemption would be too easy. When it had set up exemptions from vaccinations at the end of the nineteenth century, the government had simply required a written declaration, but in 1916 a system of tribunals was established that sought to scrutinise the potential military conscripts, hear them speak a few words and then judge their moral virtue. This was a bureaucracy designed to delve into people's minds, if not their souls.

The government had very particular ideas about who was best placed to judge the conscience of others. In 1916–18, the tribunals were stuffed with army officers and local dignitaries, who saw their principal job as recruiting for the military and educating the public on their military responsibilities, and so were hostile to those seeking exemption. Conscription here was seen not simply as a method of labour recruitment, but also as a moral issue, and those who did not meet these obligations were punished. The First World War tribunals nearly always failed to give an unconditional exemption, generally refused to recognise any socialist as genuine and took the view that anyone under the age of twenty was too young to have a conscience of their own.[27]

In the Second World War, the tribunals were re-established, but in a new form, this time without a military officer and usually consisting of a lawyer, a trade union official and more often than not an academic – the people who by the standards of the time were thought most able to judge the conscience of another human being. They were also all, or nearly all, men. Roy and the others who appeared before them were soon to find out if they were as hostile as their predecessors. As in the First World War, those who came before the tribunals ranged from skilled labourers to white-collar workers.[28] Quakers and Methodists were particularly prominent, but there were also members of the Church of England and Catholics, as well as Jehovah's Witnesses, Christadelphians, socialists and secular humanitarians. Statistics taken from one tribunal for the period March 1940 to March 1942 show 662 Methodists, 531 Anglicans, 439 Brethren, 302 Quakers, 197 Baptists, 166 Christadelphians, 155 Jehovah's Witnesses, 18 Jews, 12 Buddhists and Hindus, 51 Socialists, 11 Communists and 8 National Socialists.[29] What these numbers hide is that many of the ostensibly religious applicants could also have been political too.

Initial applications for exemption were only a page long, and usually filled in with a few stock phrases: 'being a true lover of the Lord Jesus Christ . . . I could not with a clear conscience take life'; 'I cannot reconcile the taking of life with the principles which one desires to live up to'; 'as a member of the working class it has been my firm conviction . . . that war does not solve any of the difficulties of the countries of the world, but only increases the poverty, degradation and misery of the working class'.[30] Issues of the most personal and deepest convictions were reduced to a couple of sentences.

Repetition meant that such statements were in danger of sounding like insincere clichés. Judge G. C. Field, a philosopher at Bristol University specialising in Plato, who had served in the trenches in the First World War and spent time as a German prisoner before escaping to Switzerland, complained that the 'regularity with which the arguments, and even the phraseology, of the different groups are repeated by one applicant after another suggests . . . a ready-made set of ideas taken from other people [rather] than an individual and independent examination of the problem'.[31] Roy's statement might have been very personal and heartfelt to him, but it would have looked very familiar to a tribunal used to examining dozens of cases a day, using words and phrases found in hundreds of other applications. For the tribunal, it must have been hard not to let familiarity breed at least a measure of contempt.

The sense of what genuine conscience looked like was tied to notions of sincerity, the idea that what mattered was what people felt deep inside, and inner convictions had to match outward words and deeds.[32] But sincerity also raised the spectre of insincerity, that people were somehow dissimulating, or hiding behind claims of conscience that were only skin deep, virtuous words disguising malignant intentions.[33] The tribunal members seemed ever suspicious that applicants were seeking exemption out of cowardice or laziness; it was too easy to use conscience as a mask, hiding other motivations, or at least that is what they thought. One judge explained that they had to ask questions 'to plumb the depths of an applicant's convictions, and to see that conscience is not made a cloak'.[34] For G. C. Field there was 'a suspicion of various motives at work ... [such as] dislike of being disturbed in their accustomed way of life, dislike of being under discipline'.[35] Judges complained that many applicants were not being entirely honest, and they were therefore unwilling to take the evidence of conscience for granted, always looking behind the words of conscientious objectors for other desires and intentions. Common questions at the tribunal, often fired off in quick succession with little time to answer, included: 'What sacrifices have you made for your principles?'; 'What would you do if Hitler landed in England today?'; 'Aren't you forgetting you neighbour in "loving your enemies"?'; 'Would you use an air-raid shelter?'; and 'If you object to taking life are you a vegetarian?'[36] The most common theme in questioning concerned what an applicant would do if their wife, sister or daughter was being attacked, as if conscientious objectors were somehow failing in their masculine responsibilities. Real men, it was implied, did not refuse to fight.

If the words and deeds of conscientious objectors threatened to fail them on the stand, it was common to collect as many letters as possible, or to bring a witness to attest to the sincerity of their beliefs. The more formal the letterhead, and the more respectable-looking the witness, the better. Bank managers, vicars and head teachers seemed to go down best. The secretary of the Hendon PPU group wrote a letter on Roy's behalf noting that 'although he does not belong to any religious denomination' he was 'a genuine conscientious objector to war'.[37] When Ben Britten returned to Britain from the US and appeared before exactly the same tribunal as Roy, a BBC producer told the judge that ensuring Ben's availability for radio – rather than his sitting out the war in jail – was in the 'national interest'. He added, for good measure, that in his opinion Britten's 'whole outlook on life has been a living, genuine and conscientious protest against war'.[38] When Ben was given the exemption he sought, it probably did not hurt that the chair of the tribunal was the father of an old schoolfriend.

Although Roy had been worried about becoming tongue-tied when he appeared before the judges, it was hard to know whether being fluent and fluid would work entirely to your advantage. One judge complained to the *Birmingham Post* of 'organised' preparation – precisely the kind of work Roy had done – and said that it made their job harder to 'break through the veneer and varnish of artifice'.[39] Tone could be as important as content. Applicants were widely advised to be polite and courteous, above all not appearing quarrelsome, and that 'histrionics will do you no good'.[40] Keeping things cool and calm could be difficult, given how strongly people felt about the issues at stake. When Derricke Ridgway told the tribunal it was a 'farce' it had not helped. He was not the only person to behave in this way. One judge in Manchester had to take sick leave after being attacked by a man whose application he rejected. Presumably resorting to violence was not a very persuasive argument for a pacifist.

In many people's minds, the tribunals had been given an impossible task, asked to make profound judgements on the basis of a few pieces of paper and a handful of questions, a job that ranged between the futile and the absurd. If conscience rose up from deep inside a person, it risked remaining unknown, hidden in the depths, at best only guessed at and glimpsed fleetingly, through a glass darkly. In the parliamentary debates over the National Service Act in 1939, the Conservative MP Sir Arnold Wilson argued that the 'mind of man is not triable'.[41] Similarly T. Edmund Harvey, a Quaker, an independent MP and a First World War conscientious objector, stood up in parliament to say that 'there is no machinery ... for judging the conscience of men that would be satisfactory'.[42] One conscientious objector said that judges were 'in an impossible position' because you 'cannot really judge in human terms a person's conscience. You can listen to what a man says about his conscience ... but you can't really decide that the man's conscience tells him to do this or that ... the judge has to judge by externals.'[43] More digging and more questioning would not have produced more certainty, only more questions, more hesitation and more suspicion. The decisions of the tribunals could only end up being capricious.

On a damp day in July 1940, just two days after Roy had first appeared before his own tribunal in London, Fred Urquhart also stood before the panel of judges, this time on Edinburgh's Royal Mile.[44] Fred's hearing was being held in a recently refurbished neo-Georgian court building, standing on one of the most iconic streets in Scotland, just below Edinburgh Castle and next door to the austere splendour of St Giles' Cathedral, sometimes known as the 'mother church of world Presbyterianism'. This was a deeply serious place to have your conscience judged.

Fred later described his experiences for an American literary journal: 'there had been continuous heavy rain for over a week, and everything looked sodden ... Already the walls of the new Sheriff Court building were streaked with grime.'[45] The atmosphere was sombre as he walked through the 'high and gloomy' entrance hall; he had to wait an hour and a half before his case was called, during which he smoked incessantly and went to the bathroom every fifteen minutes. The small antechamber was full of the other men whose cases were being heard that day, and they chatted nervously about what might be in store, with one of them declaring, 'They've got a bad name in Edinburgh ... They hardly let anybody off.' Another man sat silently on a bench, contemplating the Bible on his knee. Fred had prepared his statement between writing novels and working in a market garden, and he had told his parents that he was confident his application would be a success.[46] His diary shows that privately he was much more worried.

The tribunal that day was headed by a senior Scottish lawyer, C. H. Brown, KC, who according to Fred had 'black and white hair parted down the centre, and a high white stiff collar'. The panel also included the Scottish philosopher and Kant translator Norman Kent Smith. Fred was clearly daunted, and thought that the judges seemed to be 'acting to the spectators in the gallery', adding that he was himself 'acutely conscious' of the members of the public and the journalists in the room, as the proceedings were often reported in the local press, usually in less than complimentary terms.

The long wait took its toll, exacerbating Fred's nerves, and he became flustered and inarticulate when finally asked to speak. He tried to argue that he had shown his pacifism throughout his published work but was repeatedly questioned over whether he was a member of a political party. Fred insisted that he was not – but the tribunal seems to have suspected, for reasons that are not clear, his

Communist sympathies. He was also asked if he would go to an air-raid shelter in the event of a raid, and he replied that he would not, but was too embarrassed to explain that this was because he 'had a horror of crowded places'. The tribunal then enquired whether he was willing to do anything for his country, and to his regret Fred said no, almost immediately thinking that he should have said he would help his country by continuing to be a writer. For some reason, he seemed unable to get the right words out at the right time.

The fifteen minutes in the courtroom had clearly not gone well. Towards the end, the chair, C. H. Brown, leaned forward and said ominously, 'You know, Urquhart, your answers make us doubt your honesty and sincerity. Are you sure you are not a member of a political party? . . . Are you sure this attitude of yours towards war isn't just a pose?' The possibility of insincerity had raised its head. Fred's application was duly rejected entirely and he was told that he appeared to recognise 'no sense of obligation'.

Fred appealed immediately. He was fortunate this time around to be represented by a young lawyer, Labour Party activist and fellow conscientious objector called Gordon Stott. In 1940 Gordon had been a practising lawyer for only a few years, but he was immensely talented and would go on to become one of the most influential Scottish legal figures of the second half of the twentieth century. On reading through the scrawled letters that Gordon sent to Fred, you get a sense of mild exasperation and worry about how his client will perform under cross-examination. Fred was clearly upset by his treatment first time around, but Gordon told him that 'the Appeal Tribunal does not like to hear a hard criticism of its colleagues in the local tribunal'.[47] On Gordon's advice, Fred barely spoke at his appeal, but took a friend – the playwright Alexander Reid, who specialised in writing in the Scottish vernacular – to testify that Fred objected to war on 'humanitarian' grounds.

The appeal tribunal was led by the aristocrat Sidney Buller-Fullerton-Elphinstone, the sixteenth in a long line of Lord Elphinstones. This particular Elphinstone was the former Lord High Commissioner of the Church of Scotland, the uncle by marriage to the future Queen Elizabeth II and the father of a prisoner of war. He was also noted for declaring publicly – and incorrectly – that unconditional exemption was not allowed by the National

Service Act.[48] Surprisingly, this time around Fred came away thinking that the tribunal had dealt with him in a courteous manner, 'although obviously unable to see my point of view'. The eventual decision was that he should undertake full-time agricultural work for the duration of the war. This was not the unconditional exemption he had asked for, and although Fred had hoped to be left alone to write, the relief at not being forced into the army was immense. That night he wrote in his diary, 'Behold we live again!'[49]

Fred was well advised not to mention his Communist sympathies. Political objectors, especially those from the left, had great difficulty before the tribunal, often accused by judges of picking and choosing the wars they wanted to fight. Although the law did not define conscience, it seemed clear to many judges that it was unlikely to look like a left-wing radical. The Ministry of Labour went so far as to appeal against any decision granting unconditional exemption to a political objector and G. C. Field argued that 'the only genuine and logical conscientious objection on political grounds would be that of a convinced Fascist'.[50] Given that the higher echelons of the British Union of Fascists had all been interned, there probably was not much chance of a leading Fascist openly appearing before the tribunal.

It was not just socialists who had difficulty convincing the tribunal about the sincerity of their consciences. Anarchists, as well as Scottish, Welsh and Indian nationalists, were routinely rejected.[51] The case of Suresh Vaidya, a thirty-three-year-old Indian journalist, trade unionist and activist in the Indian nationalist movement, who worked for *Time* magazine in London, briefly became a minor cause célèbre. While Indians did not face conscription in India, when in Britain, as subjects of the Empire, they were liable to be called up. In 1944 Vaidya was sentenced to ninety-three days in prison for refusing to serve in the British army. At his appeal Vaidya argued that he was opposed to Fascism and Nazism, but was not prepared to fight in an imperial army, telling the tribunal, 'I don't think there is anything immoral or unjust in wanting to be free.'[52]

As subjects of the British Empire were caught up in the process of conscription, the result could be occasional bafflement all round. Noor Mohammed appeared before a tribunal in Aberdeen and explained that he simply wanted to go home to India, could not stomach the army food and did not want to kill anyone.[53] Mr

Mohammed left very little behind in the archives, but he appears to have been a Punjabi-speaking itinerant merchant, selling silk door to door in the towns and villages of north-east Scotland. A local newspaper article from the time reports him as telling the tribunal, 'we come here as traders, and you are conscripting us to go and fight in a war that does not belong to us'.[54] The article observed that most of the others who appeared that day were Scottish fishermen belonging to various separatist Christian communities, such as the Open Brethren or Closed Brethren. The sitting judge was Sir William Hamilton Fyfe, a major in military intelligence during the First World War and the then Principal of Aberdeen University. It is hard to know what Mr Mohammed made of what happened to him that day and what he knew about the expectations of the tribunal and all the cultural baggage attached to what people thought conscience looked like at the time. This was almost certainly one of those moments when the very particular ways in which conscience has been defined in Britain were thrown into sharp relief. Noor Mohammed's application makes no mention of God or the Bible or tender scruples. Fyfe was clearly unsure what to do with him, and left lots of pencilled question marks down the side of the application, before writing: 'non-combatant duties, preferably with an Indian regiment'.

Women, once they faced conscription after 1941, also had difficulty having their consciences recognised.[55] In many ways they had the opposite problem from socialist or nationalist men, in that all too often the tribunal did not see them as a serious moral, political or social challenge to a country at war.[56] Despite the leading role that women played in the peace movement – Vera Brittain and Muriel Lester being two of the most obvious examples – the cultural association of women with the 'gentler virtues' meant that their pacifism was not usually seen as disruptive. Not only were they, unlike men, exempt from the call-up if they had children, but all too often the Labour Exchanges would simply turn them away when they tried to register their objection or direct them to other types of work away from the armed forces.[57] When Doris Nicholls, who worked at the Fellowship of Reconciliation, turned up to register as a conscientious objector, she was asked what she was prepared to do. As her aim was to be registered as a conscientious objector she responded, 'Nothing but what I am doing.'[58] To her disappointment, she never heard from the Ministry again. The

Central Board for Conscientious Objectors complained that women were being 'misled into thinking they could not' register.[59] As a result the official figure of just under 1,000 women conscientious objectors during the war grossly underestimates their number.

Of all convictions, religious beliefs were most persuasive at the tribunals. A CBCO observer wrote that 'the only objectors who will be recognized are those who base their objections on religious grounds'.[60] Given that many political objectors were religious in some way, they would try to articulate their claims in more explicitly religious terms. Roy's appeal documents certainly had more of a spiritual than a political bent to them. Ben Britten's application also argued that 'since I believe that there is in every man the spirit of God, I cannot destroy, and feel it my duty to avoid helping to destroy . . . The whole of my life has been devoted to acts of creation (being by profession a composer) and I cannot take part in acts of destruction . . .'[61] Ben's opposition to war was being framed in spiritual and artistic terms, his previous left-wing politics nowhere to be seen, but we should not necessarily regard this as an attempt at subterfuge; it was simply the emphasising of a particular aspect of what was always an overlapping and complex set of motivations and commitments.

Applicants were believed most easily when they could show that they had attended a particular pacifist church or group over a long period of time, and especially if their family had done so as well. Quakers represented the gold standard, as the group most readily associated with pacifism in the popular imagination. When the tribunals looked for conscience, they seemed to assume that it took a Quaker, or at least a Quaker-like, form. Indeed, when Ben Britten appeared before his tribunal, he was advised that he might find his 'spiritual home' with the Quakers, despite having no obvious link with the Society of Friends.[62] For some pacifists, an association with the Quakers was such persuasive evidence that they tried to downplay their own very real Quaker connections, lest it give them what they felt to be an unfair advantage. One later felt 'unworthy' for raising his Quaker history as he believed it made 'it somewhat easier. People understood the Quaker position and by saying you were a Quaker . . . you did not have to explain in very great detail anymore.'[63]

Not all religious belief was equally persuasive. Derricke Ridgway's

Indian mysticism was clearly too much for Judge Hargreaves to take. Catholics could also find it hard. The logic of the tribunal was often not only that the 'just war' tradition was a central part of Catholic thought, but also that a Catholic conscience meant following the teaching of the Church. It was not until 1965 and what became known as Vatican II that the Catholic Church supported the principle of individual freedom of conscience. Conscience was certainly important to Catholic doctrine in the 1940s, but it was seen as part of a duty to follow the true Church rather than an exercise in individual freedom.[64] The tribunals argued that the Catholic Church in Britain supported the war, therefore Catholics could not claim both to have a Catholic conscience and to be anti-war.

Following Fred into the Edinburgh tribunal was a twenty-eight-year-old elder of the Plymouth Brethren. Brethren communities were not pacifist in an absolute sense, but refused to fight in ungodly wars.[65] Jehovah's Witnesses took a similar position, arguing that they were neutral in the current war, and this could be difficult for tribunals to take.[66] Overall they seemed to represent a form of religiosity that the tribunal struggled to comprehend. G. C. Field described Jehovah's Witnesses as 'strange and even fantastic'.[67] A representative of the Ministry of Labour went so far as to call them 'a small band of canting, hypocritical humbugs' who 'earn an easy livelihood by playing on the gullibility of decent religious-minded people'.[68] More sympathetically, Denis Hayes from the CBCO thought that Jehovah's Witnesses found it most difficult of all applicants to persuade the tribunal judges of their case because they were 'more militant' than other applicants and seemed 'impervious to argument'.[69] For the tribunals at least, theirs was a radically different and peculiar conscience.

Far from being free and untrammelled, the forms of conscience that were accepted as genuine and sincere at the tribunals walked a very conventional path.

It is important to recognise that just as conscience was not the only game in town when it came to publicly refusing to fight, it was also not the only mode of refusal. Alongside the hundreds of thousands who, with a wide variety of motivations, found more low-key ways of avoiding military service – a desk job or a reserved occupation – there were some who sought other forms of public recognition for their objection. In 1942, Douglas Young, the wartime leader of the SNP and a friend of Mary Litchfield, refused conscription and became embroiled in a series of lengthy legal cases.[70] Young was no pacifist, and simply objected to being conscripted into a British rather than a Scottish army. There were certainly some Scottish and Welsh nationalists who contended that nationalism was a form of conscience, but conscience was not part of Young's claim – indeed he was effectively refusing the right of the British state to judge his conscience at all and did not even apply to appear before the tribunal.[71] Instead, he made an argument through the courts based on his interpretation of Scottish constitutional history and the claim of national self-determination. This was not a position that the British state recognised as a legitimate reason for refusing conscription, and Young spent much of the war going in and out of prison. It was tender moral scruples or nothing.

Despite all the difficulties in judging conscience, many applicants were, in the end, granted exemptions.[72] In the course of the war, of those who sought to register, fewer than 30 per cent were refused all and any exemptions. They then had to decide whether to sign up, face jail or find another way out. At this point some gave up, but a small minority, as many as 6,000, chose imprisonment or had it chosen for them. While less than 5 per cent of applicants were given unconditional exemption by local tribunals, the vast majority – around 65 per cent – were, like Roy and Fred, given an exemption conditional on taking up some kind of alternative service – agricultural or forestry work, ambulance driving, firewatching, civil defence, social work or a non-combatant role in the military. It seems that, in the face of the difficult task of judging another person's conscience, the judges reached for accommodation: we will take you at your word so long as you do something else for the country. Most conscientious objectors were more than happy to comply.

The contrast with the First World War is remarkable. Twenty-five years previously conscientious objectors had been widely branded as cowards or traitors and as many as a third ended up in jail.[73] This time around the treatment before the tribunal was much less harsh, despite being sceptical and hostile. Such was the general tolerance that the Fellowship of Reconciliation was worried: 'it is clear that instead of persecution every possible consideration is to be shown and that may be harder to resist than ill-treatment . . . We are concerned to maintain [that] the claim of the individual conscience follows what it sees to be the will of God' and 'resists its assimilation to the collectivity'.[74] The Fellowship was worried that it might be too easy to be a conscientious objector, that it did not stand as a test of faith and that it was now too difficult to provide witness, as conscientious objectors merged into the general population.

There are several possible reasons for this apparent shift in attitudes, both in the tribunals and in the responses of the British public. The first was, as previously noted, that very practical lessons had been learned from the First World War – it was simply a waste of time to force people to fight who did not want to, and as their numbers were never huge it did not matter so much. Equally important was a shift in the ways in which mutual sacrifice was understood, and the moral lens through which conscientious objectors were seen. Alongside the more 'tempered' forms of masculinity, the Second World War saw a marked change in what might be called the moral geography of sacrifice and destruction.[75] In the First World War nearly all of the violent death had been focused on the front lines. By the Second World War, bombing and rationing meant that it was not only soldiers who were suffering for the war effort, so violence and loss were much more dispersed. As Vera Brittain wrote in her memoir *England's Hour*, published in 1941, during the First World War 'England's first ordeal was mainly vicarious. Her suffering was the anguish of detached suspense . . . To-day both suffering and suspense are universal . . . The painful ache of anxiety is felt as often by husbands for wives as wives for husbands . . .'[76] Throughout 1939–45 there were more men who stayed at home – working in reserved occupations in the mines, on the docks or in hospitals – than were conscripted into the armed forces.[77] Churchill was fond of the phrase 'front-line civilians' to describe such work.[78] As Roy recalled, 'everybody was in the front line really', especially his family in London.[79] With much of the army still in barracks in Britain, during the early years of the war nearly as many British civilians were killed as soldiers.[80] Being a soldier was therefore not so heavily privileged, and there was some space for conscientious objectors to lay claim to the shared values of sacrifice and citizenship while not holding a weapon. As a result, those who took up arms did not have a monopoly on virtue and sacrifice. So long as they lived up to other forms of responsibility, conscientious objectors could still claim some public virtue for themselves.

There is a risk in overstating all these new forms of masculinity. There might have been more than one way of being a man, but ideas of bravery in battle were hard to shake, not least by conscientious objectors themselves. Militarised masculinities were still a powerful measure of manliness, and the tribunals still hung on to them in their questions. Roy in particular would be forced to confront this issue head on in the years to come.

Either way, the vast majority of conscientious objectors were happy to cooperate in the war effort. They did not want to carry arms or be told what to do, but they were still committed to their fellow citizens and wanted to participate in the wider culture and economy of mutual sacrifice. This was partly the result of the strongly patriotic seam that ran through many British pacifists. Although conscientious objectors could show a commitment to brotherly love or class solidarity that stretched across national boundaries, they were often keen to stress their national loyalty as well. Roy had written in his diary that 'The love of one's country is inherent in everyone', and his father had been keen to stress to the police officers who came to visit that his sons were all patriotic boys.[81] Vera Brittain wrote that she 'so dearly love my country and so sincerely admire its brave, imperturbable people', but only wished they had put all their efforts into a meaningful peace.[82] There was also the feeling that the British state was particularly hospitable to conscience. One conscientious objector later recalled, 'I rejoiced when I found out I could register as a CO. It was confirmation to me that this position was recognised by the state.'[83] As an evangelical Christian pacifist put it, 'There must be something right with a country who would allow people to take up this stand, because I know nowhere else in the world where it would have happened in this way.'[84] Many conscientious objectors felt there was something peculiarly British – or occasionally English – about the rights of conscience, and the CBCO spoke of the 'characteristic English humanity, characteristic English good sense' behind the 'respect for the right of individual judgement'.[85]

In claiming this link between what they saw as specifically

British political sentiments and conscience, pacifists were mirroring the things being said by politicians and religious leaders about the right to conscientious objection being proof of the particular British commitment to freedom. The patriotism of British conscientious objection was usually a quiet loyalty rather than a fervent jingoism. More often than not this patriotism was found in a willingness to help fellow citizens and in worries about being seen to 'reap the rewards of the sacrifices of other people'.[86] One conscientious objector who carried out social work in the East End recalled he did not see his pacifist stance as 'involving a break with society ... I saw it as a role to be played within society.'[87] As Roy later put it, 'we were not prepared to cut ourselves off completely from the war. Nobody could – you were involved' whether you liked it or not.[88] Vera Brittain wrote that 'We are not entitled to ... bury ourselves in an ivory tower; we are part of a community, and cannot escape the demands that citizenship lays upon us.'[89] She added, 'I shall state what I am prepared to do in the way of social service, first aid, or whatever form of activity is consistent with my beliefs. I should not refuse to obey the command of the state if the state asked me to undertake some form of work which was essential to the life of community, but not part of the war machine.'[90] This was a conscience that sought to make a positive and practical contribution. Easing suffering or carrying out other good works became a way – for the tribunals as much as for the conscientious objectors themselves – to bring to ground the otherwise inchoate and tangled ways of conscience. This was a way for many conscientious objectors to try and put their conscience into action, but it also meant having to confront the compromise and complicity of trying to live a very particular type of moral life in a time of war.

The tribunal might have been an ordeal, but the real tests of conscience were yet to come.

CHAPTER 10

On the Farm

As the war raged and the German military machine celebrated bloody victory after bloody victory, Ronald, Rose Marie and Bianca tended to the land, determined to show that it was possible to live at peace, and in a deeper sense than simply being in an out-of-the-way place. The worse the war became, the more important it was for them to demonstrate that another way was possible. Back in 1936, Ronald had written that 'Pacifism is a moral activity ... The pacifist, in desiring men to love each other, must wish for and work for an economic system in which men will not strive to gain, a thing which can only be done at the expense of others.'[1] The farm was Ronald's attempt to put these lofty aspirations into action.[2] For him, a community built on love 'should grow its own food, bake its own bread and weave its own clothes' as these activities 'contained some of the elements of a spiritual communion'.[3] This was not just a practical exercise. He saw the back-breaking work of turning Gooseham back into a viable farm as a form of penance for the sins of humanity, and 'cultivation of a kitchen garden' as the only alternative to militaristic jingoism.[4] A lot was riding on the oats growing on the Devon coast.

By now Ronald had long drifted away from socialism. Twenty-five years before, his father had experimented with farming in southern Africa; Ronald was now taking a similar path in rejecting industrial labour and revolutionary change, and seeking peace through a return to the land. There was a strongly romantic element that ran through his and wider British pacifism, a tradition that valued the supposedly lost virtues of rural life, in the tradition of William Blake or William Morris, built on a mystical and occasionally slightly patriotic vision of England (and sometimes Scotland

and Wales too) as a lost Eden, representing a simpler, more authentic way of life. The aim now was to show it was possible to live through love – in the very deepest sense – rather than war. The challenge was to stop 'loving your neighbour as you love yourself' from turning into heartbreak, both for yourself and for others.

Over the spring and summer of 1940, Ronald, Rose Marie and Bianca, aided by Nigel Spottiswoode, the German student Horst and a steady stream of new recruits, had planted vegetables, oats and barley. Ronald later recalled being 'half blind with hope and half deaf with enthusiasm'.[5] They had milk, butter and cheese from a cow, fuel from the woods, electricity generated by the newly refurbished mill, and pigs to be fattened and turned into bacon. Bianca boasted in her diary that the newly cultivated fields were, after much hard work, a 'great achievement'.[6] New life was everywhere. After cutting back some of the endlessly growing bracken, they discovered ten chicks previously thought lost.[7] Ronald spent weeks – sometimes wearing his best trousers covered in sacking – 'grappling with the young trees' growing around the farm boundary and 'trying to twist them into a live fence that would deter all beasts'.[8] A neighbouring farmer, known by everyone as Hancock, gave advice on harvesting techniques, and helped transport anything that was too heavy to carry or too messy to put in the car.

Food largely consisted of what they could grow, as well as their own chickens and the occasional pigeon which they found 'too tough to eat'.[9] Every day in her diary Rose Marie noted how many eggs had been laid that day; anything surplus was sold to neighbours. The set-up was that Nigel lived at Gooseham with the other new volunteers, whereas Ronald and Rose Marie stayed at West Mill, and Bianca in her own place with her mother just down the road, but most days were spent together. By the summer of 1940 the harvest was in full swing, and the new farmers learned to dry the hay in the fields before it was bundled up for winter.[10] Afternoons were filled with picking gooseberries and making jam. They were also busy with printing *Townsman*, Bianca typing out the articles and joining Rose Marie in setting out the pages and printing them off, while Ronald wrote by the hearth. The circulation of the magazine was always small, but it attracted contributions from leading literary figures, such as Ezra Pound – by then in exile in Fascist Italy – and T. S. Eliot. Evenings were spent gossiping, planning the future and listening to Berlioz and Ravel on the gramophone. Their diaries from the time reveal a great deal of affection for each other and joy in the hard work of cutting down trees and clearing away the weeds; the idea of the new community was clearly invigorating. Visitors included Ben Britten and Max Plowman, as well as the Anglo-Irish writer Gerald Brenan, who had fled his home outside Málaga after the town was overrun by Fascist troops.[11] Brenan had rented West Mill decades before and had now returned to the West Country to write an account of the lead-up to the Spanish Civil War. It must have been an exciting and fulfilling place to be. As Bianca admitted in her diary, 'I feel we shall look back to these days with much longing.'[12]

This was no utopia though. The fields were in the middle of two hills so steep that 'no average car could climb', and the cultivatable land was often waterlogged.[13] The farm was wind-swept, 'sour, derelict', and had been left to run wild for years, making it difficult to grow enough food for the increasing number of people who depended on Gooseham.[14] The neighbours predicted it would take ten years to return the fields fully to farming. Ronald, Rose Marie and Bianca were all affected by intermittent low moods, and money was in short supply. Ronald's energies and enthusiasms were almost entirely subsumed in the farm and in his writing, and Rose Marie sometimes felt that there was little room left for her, noting that she was 'envious of Nigel' because Ronald was 'only really animated' when he came over to West Mill to talk about the farm.[15] Still only in his mid-twenties, Ronald took the attempt to build a new community very seriously. After one argument, Bianca wrote that 'it is so silly our bickering . . . for we are really unanimous on most things and . . . get on well. Most people have nothing to live for with their families and homes depleted by bombs and we who are all together without bombs behave like spoilt children. I must try to be more aware of this.'[16]

Across the country, scores of pacifist community farms were established in the first years of the war. In many parts of Britain, as well as in the US, thousands of other pacifists turned to market gardens and smallholdings as a way to build communities based on love.[17] Many of them were influenced by John Middleton Murry, who had become an apostle of community farming and an occasional correspondent of Ronald Duncan. In 1940 Middleton Murry, by then nearing his fiftieth birthday, had become the editor of *Peace News* and added a supplement dedicated to the accounts of pacifist agricultural communities. For him, pacifist witness might not have prevented war, but it could demonstrate that a life which shunned violence in all its forms was just about possible, thereby building a 'fundamentally different society ... a society in which cooperation takes the place of competition, mutual trust takes the place of mutual mistrust'.[18] The internationalist commitments of many strands of pacifism receded into the background, because the neighbours to be loved were not, in the first instance, spread across the world but confined within Britain. Above all, for Middleton Murry community living was a matter of leading exemplary lives at the most personal level. Working on pacifist farms was important as a way to produce food for others, but also because of the love and cooperation it helped create. Kneeling in the mud, digging root vegetables or pruning apple trees helped put food on the table, but it also allowed people to develop self-discipline and learn the value of working with others.

A commitment to the transformative power of love was central, and in the hands of people like Ronald and Middleton Murry, love exploded out in all sorts of new directions, both secular and spiritual. Middleton Murry wrote in 1940 that 'our task is always to take the most creative and constructive action in the face of existing circumstances ... the way of justice and love'.[19] Love, for him, was not abstract but rooted in human relationships, and above all in his own relationships. He wrote to Mary Gamble, his mistress and future wife, 'I am convinced that love such as ours is the one complete and simple reply to the war: – that it is the only real pacifism.'[20] Others felt the same. Cyril Wright, a thirty-year-old clerk in the London office of the Canadian Pacific Steamship Company and former Labour Party activist, left his job and, along with his wife Nora and two small children, helped establish a new farm just to the north of London, hoping to 'share in common ... all that we possess in money, goods and ability'.[21] The Wrights tried to build 'a peaceful society in which the motive of love, fellowship and cooperation shall take the place of self-interest and competition'.[22] These sentiments were now being tested.

For a time, Middleton Murry, like Ronald Duncan, put his money where his mouth was. In the mid-1930s, with the support of other wealthy pacifists, he had purchased a rambling house in Essex – known as the Adelphi Centre – that he hoped would become a community settlement. The Centre was run by Max Plowman and the original idea was to set up a cultural centre and farm, with half the residents recruited from the unemployed working class. Vera Brittain stayed at the Adelphi on several occasions, although her own relationship with Middleton Murry was always strained; they were rivals in the world of pacifist journalism and Middleton Murry could also be deeply reactionary in his views on gender. Missing her children and feeling isolated from her husband, Vera even thought – very briefly – about moving permanently to the community.[23] However, when the original plans for the Adelphi Centre collapsed, the building was used to house groups of Basque orphans fleeing from Spain, and Middleton Murry bought Lodge Farm in Suffolk with his own funds and hoped to turn it into his very own pacifist paradise.

Pacifists such as Ronald Duncan and John Middleton Murry were taking part in a much wider and longer tradition of 'community experiments' that littered the British countryside, long predating the groups of the 1960s and 1970s.[24] In its own way Muriel Lester's Kingsley Hall was part of this tradition too. In the early twentieth century, Tolstoyan communes had been established around the country, and in the summer of 1939 Derricke Ridgway had cycled from the Adelphi Centre in Essex to a community in Elmsett in Suffolk, where a group of small children threw stones at him as he rode through the village. Derricke had stayed a few days, working from six in the morning until eight at night, before moving on.[25] It clearly was not for him. Elsewhere, just before the Second World War, the Bruderhof, a pious Protestant group formed in the aftermath of the Great War and devoted to pacifism and the renunciation of private property, bought a 300-acre farm in the rolling hills of the Cotswolds.[26] This small Christian movement had been expelled from Germany in 1937, and was made up of 200 mainly German-speaking members dressed in knee-breeches and homespun stockings. The community was deeply attractive to many pacifists, and many of them spent time in its fields. It was also one of the places that the German theologian Dietrich Bonhoeffer resorted to for inspiration when he was living in London. Douglas Turner, an English pacifist drawing back from left-wing sectarianism, recalled his time in the community as a decisive moment in his life, as it brought 'coherence' to his thinking, combining religion, politics and economics.[27] Turner thought he had seen the Kingdom of God on earth in this collection of yellow stone farm buildings in the west of England. Ultimately however he was alienated by the Bruderhof's austere way of life, rooted in sixteenth-century central European theology. By 1941 the Bruderhof were looking for a new home in Paraguay, as its German members faced the threat of internment by the British government.

Through early 1941 the farm at Gooseham was never short of volunteers, with at least ten adults working on the steep hillsides. Nigel and Horst were joined by Frank Smithson, a former collier whom Ronald had met during his brief time down a mine, as well as by John Connelly – a Communist from London, whose luggage consisted of a typewriter and the works of Lenin.[28] A Mr Wyles and two of his children moved in too. Wyles was a veteran of the First World War, stone deaf and with his 'nerves' badly damaged in the trenches. For years he had lived in the back of a lorry, working as a mason, but Ronald invited him to move into Gooseham, and he arrived with his two boys, 'a few blankets and trowel'.[29] Wyles was one of the few working-class residents at Gooseham, and one of the most 'practically minded'. Next came the Weston family: husband, wife and small baby. Ronald observed that Noel Weston was attracted by the possibility of a 'life as opposed to a mere living', but was a 'fragile looking person, almost twenty-five, with a degree in Classics and a live interest in the Chinese alphabet'.[30] Noel did not seem instantly suited to the hard life of manual labour. During the Weston family's first week on the farm, Bianca observed that Noel was 'an insignificant creature in appearance, but rather nice to talk to. We picked plums and apples solidly all afternoon ... A lovely day.'[31] Another couple joined shortly afterwards, and Ronald bought the nearby Rose Cottage with what was left of his father's inheritance to provide a roof over the heads of the growing group.

One of the reasons why recruits were turning up at Gooseham was that the tribunals were making applicants carry out farm work as a condition of exemption from military service – seemingly deciding that agricultural labour was both useful and suited to pacifist sentiments – and the countryside was therefore full of conscientious objectors searching for farm work, many of whom had no experience at all.[32] Fred Urquhart's own tribunal had declared that he must undertake agricultural labour for the duration of the war. He wrote letters, looking for a farmer who was willing to take him on, but soon received a reply from a Mr F. MacDonald in Perthshire who declared, 'You should count yourself lucky to be registered as a conscientious objector, and to be allowed to stay in this country. About here, fight for king and country is the rule . . . Germany is the place for you and all who profess the same thought.'[33] Similar letters followed.

Rural communities and farmers were often hostile to conscientious objectors. Farmhands sometimes refused to work alongside pacifists, who were largely unskilled when it came to farm labour. One agricultural official went so far as to insist that he would rather have one Land Army girl than a dozen conscientious objectors.[34] Farmers were not the only employers who could be hostile to conscientious objectors, and many other employers refused to give them pay rises; more often than not pay was reduced to that of private soldiers. Across the board, it was not easy for pacifists to find the work they were sometimes directed to.

In South Wales, Derricke and Alfred Ridgway, who had both been ordered by the tribunals to work on a farm, struggled to find suitable employment. Although they visited the Abergavenny Labour Exchange every week, the man behind the desk explained he had nothing for the young men from the city.[35] Early in the war, there were reports of more than 2,000 conscientious objectors looking for agricultural work, wandering the country and unable to find anyone to take them on.[36] The situation only eased from 1941, when there was a shortage of rural labour, as more and more agricultural workers entered the armed forces. One group of pacifists was sent to Jersey at the start of the war to help pick potatoes, and many were still there when the Germans occupied the islands. One infamous member of this group, Eric Pleasants, abandoned his colleagues, took up house burglary and was sent to prison in Germany, from where he joined the SS before being taken prisoner by the Soviets on the Eastern Front.[37] It is fair to say that Pleasants' case was very unusual.

Concerned that there were too many conscientious objectors with no place to go, a group of Christian pacifists joined together to establish the Christian Pacifist Forestry and Land Units, organised out of Donald Soper's Kingsway Hall.[38] More than fifty units, split equally between farms and forestry, were created all over Britain, with the aim of finding the 'practical expression in daily life' of Christian faith, and to 'plan a way forward in preparation for emergence from the present world-chaos'.[39]

Fred eventually persuaded a farmer in north-east Scotland to take him on. John 'Red' Mackie ran a 720-acre dairy and potato farm on the relatively fertile lowlands along the coast. Mackie, as his nickname suggested, was a socialist, and many years later became a Labour MP and junior government minister. His younger brother became a Liberal MP, but the family is probably most famous as owners of a well-known brand of Scottish ice cream. Yet, despite their apparently similar politics, Fred did not initially warm to John Mackie, writing in his diary a few weeks after arriving that 'his socialism is like most people's Christianity; a theory that you don like Sunday clothes'.[40]

The work on Mackie's farm, where Fred laboured alongside the volunteers and conscripts of the Women's Land Army, was hard. Looking after the cows and picking the crops from the sodden earth was very different from plodding away in an Edinburgh bookshop. Digging potato fields was gruelling, and he felt that he was underpaid and exploited by his employer. Above all, it was very cold. Several Polish officers were billeted in one of the houses on the farm, and Fred complained in his diary that they were Fascist, as he fell into frequent arguments with them about politics. Over the following years he published a series of short stories drawing on his experience among the potatoes and milk sheds, invariably focusing on the mud, cold and early starts.[41]

The reluctant agricultural labourer quickly became the farm's 'secretary', mainly checking and recording milk yields. John Mackie was also active in the Home Guard – a part-time local defence force designed to slow the German army in the event of an invasion – and Fred also began to work as a secretary for their meetings. Fred was criticised by Mary Litchfield for his apparent inconsistency in working so closely with the Home Guard, but responded angrily in his diary: 'To hell with her!'[42] There were more immediate problems with his new line of work: the Ministry of Labour wrote that he did not seem to be complying with his conditions of exemption, declaring that clerical work on a farm did not count as agricultural labour.[43] It took an intervention from John Mackie to straighten things out, with the tribunal finally ruling that Fred 'is not physically strong and is more use to his employer as a secretary'.[44]

Fred's diary entries became very intermittent while at the farm, but from the few brief paragraphs that he did write it is clear that his view of his employer shifted over the weeks and months, until he eventually declared that he was in love with John Mackie.[45] As far as can be inferred from the diary he told no one else at the time, least of all John himself. His ire was directed instead at John's wife: 'I have been here 13 months now. The first 6 months I hated him like hell, thinking him a selfish swine. I still think that, but now blame Jeannie for making him like that.'[46] He accused her of skimping on the food, of making John Mackie's life a misery and of being 'completely mental'.[47] Despite or perhaps even because of these romantic feelings, Fred stayed working at the Mackie farm until the last year of the war.

Further south, it was not always easy for the novice farmers at Gooseham. They had to learn fast and on the job. Ronald was determined to become more proficient, taking practical lessons from their neighbour Hancock and increasingly turning *Townsman* over to the discussion of new farming techniques. Mistakes were inevitable. In the spring of 1941 over twenty chickens died within two weeks and Rose Marie lamented in her diary that 'all profits are gone'.[48] One of the sows died too, as no one knew that it was dangerous for pigs to eat wet grass. Ronald wrote in his journal that by July 1941 it was 'difficult not to lose patience with ourselves because of our own incompetence'.[49] The idea was that the community at Gooseham would become self-sufficient, but money was often tight and the farm continually ran at a deficit.

The War Agricultural Executive Committee made frequent visits to Gooseham and seldom liked what it saw. The 'War Ag', as it was known, was all-powerful in the life of a farmer, charged by the government with increasing production and given the power to direct the work to be done, to determine which crops should be planted and, if it so decided, to take possession of the land.[50] Before the war, over 70 per cent of the food on British tables had been brought in from overseas, largely from the dominions and colonies. With so many borders now closed and the seas full of U-boats, there were worries that there simply would not be enough to go around. Every inch of farmable land had to be squeezed for all it was worth, and it was the War Ag's job to make sure this was done. At the local level, the War Ag was made up of 'committees of practical men' – local landowners in other words – who were not immediately welcoming to groups of young pacifists living in communes.[51] After one visit to Gooseham, the inspectors were clearly not happy with what was going on, and Rose Marie wrote in her diary that they had implied 'all sorts of things because there are 4 active bearded young men'.[52] After another visit they 'commanded' that a field should be ploughed again, complaining that it had not been done properly. Nigel was furious and threatened to have 'them up for libel' because they had criticised him in front of other people and were 'defaming' his character.[53] He challenged the inspectors to come back to show him how to set a plough correctly. They never did.

The problems at Gooseham were not unique. During their first full summer at the farm north of London, Cyril and Nora Wright got behind in the planting of crops, and the land was eventually requisitioned.[54] Middleton Murry had never farmed before he set up Lodge Farm and pretty soon 'everything was getting behind. Our potatoes, through insufficient cultivation, began to look a mess.'[55] He concluded that the 'average efficiency of our members was anything between half and two thirds that of the ordinary agricultural worker'.[56] The initial yields from the crops were disappointing and the community depended on donations from supporters. The War Agricultural Committee quickly decided there were too many people working on Middleton Murry's farm and redirected several of them to work in gangs clearing drainage ditches. Community farms did not find it easy to make the food for a new Jerusalem.

It was not just food that was hard to grow. Relationships could be fragile too. War throws people together unexpectedly, acting as what the novelist Patrick Hamilton called 'a sombre begetter of crowds', and although everyone working at Gooseham had, at least in principle, a broad set of pacifist commitments in common, they came from very different backgrounds and had very different aspirations, rubbing up alongside one another in sometimes awkward ways.[57] For those dedicated to the vision of building a new society from the ground up, there was a lingering suspicion that some of the conscientious objectors turning up on their doorstep were not properly committed to the cause of community living. The spectre of insincerity did not just haunt the tribunals. Ronald observed that it was 'difficult to know whether they were genuinely interested in farming or merely wished to escape into a reserved occupation and obtain a funk hole from the air-raids'.[58] In Cyril and Nora Wright's community there were accusations that a few members had joined as a 'matter of undisguised expediency'.[59] The community's newsletter remarked that residents seemed motivated by 'fulfilling their tribunal obligations ... [and] simply leading an easy life, free of responsibility'.[60] Conscientious objectors could doubt their own sincerity.

There were other issues too, as enthusiasm for the difficult work of growing food was not always sustained, and mutual cooperation suffered. The commitment at Gooseham declined over its first year, with the pigsty left uncleaned, the 'tools unsharpened' and everybody hoping 'that somebody would hang the gate'.[61] To Ronald's despair, people started getting up late. The question of how to organise everyone's time was particularly fraught, and it could be hard to rally pacifists to a common cause. Many of the residents at Gooseham were there precisely because they objected to the compulsion of conscription. More often than not they were determined, quite literally, to plough their own furrow. As Denis Hayes of the Central Board for Conscientious Objectors explained shortly after the war, it was 'only natural that the highly individual and libertarian COs should accept such a system with grave misgiving, misgivings that from time to time flared up into disobedience and revolt in an effort to secure greater personal freedom'.[62] Ronald reflected in his memoir that pacifists were at a 'considerable disadvantage, for among the current fallacies which many of us read into this dogma was the postulate that discipline was of no value unless it was self-imposed'.[63] For those determined to stand alone, it could be challenging to work together.

Arguments grew over the best way to run Gooseham. Should

the farm be a democracy or should Ronald, as the owner of the land, decide? For a while, they tried a weekly meeting to help clear the air, but in the end Ronald seems to have had the final say. Bianca became particularly exercised when one morning Ronald insisted they all work in the potato fields for a quarter of an hour before lunch and got angry when they disagreed. When everyone eventually made it to the table, they ate a meal of burned tapioca. That evening Bianca acknowledged in her diary, 'I felt I was obeying an order the same way that a private takes a stupid order from his superior officers.'[64]

Small disputes and annoyances simmered, occasionally boiling over. Nigel often visited Bianca's house for a bath – his own room 'littered with dead moths, dust, decayed socks and dirty clothes'.[65] He was a source of slightly amused affection for Bianca, but he was an increasing irritation for Rose Marie. One summer evening, after a long dinner with Nigel, she wrote: 'Heavens what a dull creature he is.'[66] Later, though, after a trip to the cinema on St Valentine's Day, she admitted that he looked nice: 'I don't know whether it is because he looks such a freak usually, but when he does dress up he looks really most presentable!'[67]

When the Westons were joined at their cottage by the Roche family, they argued over who should get the bigger of the two sitting rooms. Bianca turned up one afternoon in the pouring rain to find the house at the 'centre of another round of troubles'.[68] The Westons had initially been persuaded to switch to the smaller of the two rooms, as they had less furniture, but Noel Weston had complained to Ronald, who supported him in refusing to move. When Bianca arrived, much of the furniture was outside, getting wet; Mary Weston started to cry and Ronald 'screamed' at Bianca for 'interfering'. Bianca walked away through the mud, and reflected in her diary about the marked lack of manners among many pacifists. Ronald took his mood back to West Mill, and the next day Bianca observed that she was 'shocked by the suffering' on Rose Marie's face, feeling that it was 'better to bomb people into oblivion than to tramp on their feelings'.[69] Things were better the following day, despite the constant rain and cold, as Rose Marie and Ronald had 'made their peace' and Ronald seemed more amenable, helping to sharpen a knife so Bianca could feed scraps of meat to the dog. Even so, Bianca noted that unless

Ronald started 'thinking of other people's desires and less of his own' things would remain tense.[70]

Ronald and Rose Marie's relationship was often edgy, with Bianca usually siding with Rose Marie, and Rose Marie often doubting herself. Rose Marie particularly fretted that Ronald could 'scarcely contain his boredom' while in her company.[71] She worried too that she was being overwhelmed by the atmosphere at Gooseham and by Ronald's obsessions: 'I am having every sap of individuality taken away from me by a gradual superimposition of ideas – so that gradually I shan't be able to think for myself at all.'[72] Two weeks later, on Ronald's twenty-seventh birthday, she wrote in her diary: 'I hate, loathe, detest, despise myself for being a weak, maudlin, spineless, half-witted fool.'[73] She was now determined to stand up for herself.

If Gooseham was to be built on love, this love was often fraught, and not just between Rose Marie and Ronald. By February 1941 Rose Marie was fed up with the wider group of people living in the community, calling them 'Damned hypocrites!'[74] She was also increasingly lonely, and the mood at Gooseham was now heavy. She wrote that the community farm was as 'depressing as ever – though farm work is being got through somehow, but seemingly without pleasure to anyone except Nigel'.[75] Ronald was at his wits' end too, deciding he was going to ask several of the community to leave if 'they did not come around to working full time and damned hard at that'.[76]

It was hard to mould the residents of other pacifist communities together. John Middleton Murry faced particular problems. His daughter later observed that he saw communal living as a partial response to his fraught home life, and to his third marriage in particular.[77] His first two wives had died from tuberculosis, and his third marriage was a disaster. To his friends Betty Cockbayne seemed an unusual choice; the uneducated daughter of a farmer, she had previously worked as a housekeeper and was known for her violent and frequent rages. Their life together appears to have been miserable, and John wrote during this time that he 'died everyday'.[78] The home was full of arguments, if not violence, and John seems to have had some kind of nervous breakdown.[79] Shortly after setting up Lodge Farm, he started having an affair with the writer Mary Gamble, who would eventually become his fourth wife, but John did not leave Betty immediately because he was concerned that his inability to sustain his marriage reflected badly on his pacifism. Eventually the strain became too much, and after another breakdown Middleton Murry and Cockbayne separated.

Love was not just about cooperation. It was clearly also about sex. Sometimes pacifists could get along all too well, loving each other just a little too much, and Middleton Murry was not the only pacifist who had affairs. Horst appears to have had a relationship with one of the other residents at Gooseham, much to Rose Marie's disapproval. She described him in her diary as a 'snivelling cad'.[80] At the Wrights' community, two members became engaged, split up and shortly afterwards left the farm.[81] Before the war, *Peace News* reported that at Middleton Murry's and Max Plowman's Adelphi Centre 'the gregarious had their fill of human society in the bedrooms and bathrooms – the latter being responsible for the wholesale breaking down of inhibitions about taking one's bath in public'.[82] Heartbreak was not unusual either. One of the members of Lodge Farm, a former parson, tried to commit suicide after he unsuccessfully wooed another member.[83]

More sexually conservative Christian pacifists were often upset by the apparent erotic adventures of others. The PPU, with large numbers of clergymen in its leadership, decided to draw a line between 'irresponsible' and 'irregular' sexual behaviour among their staff; living together out of wedlock was just about okay, but they would put their foot down if a man 'went around from girl to girl'.[84] The fact that Mary Gamble and John Middleton Murry lived together while he was still married to Betty Cockbayne caused a minor scandal, and there was a campaign, led by the Anglican Pacifist Fellowship, to have him removed from the editorship of *Peace News*.

It is not easy to pin down exactly how Middleton Murry's pacifism related to his own home life. Perhaps his desire for communal living was the cause of the marital unhappiness. Perhaps communal life was a way to escape the tensions of his relationship with Betty. Perhaps communal living was a way for him to prove his ability to live at peace while both the world at large and his own family life were in turmoil. Perhaps it was a combination of all of these. Either way, although he preached the importance of love, he does not seem to have been much liked by the other residents of the community or by many other people. At one point the residents of Lodge Farm even suggested he leave completely.[85] Ronald Mallone, who lived on the farm for several years, later recalled that Middleton Murry was a 'very egocentric . . . cold person' who 'talked down to people'.[86] Another pacifist went further, describing him as 'slightly inhuman . . . you could almost see the horns coming out of his head'.[87] Even those who admired him could find him exasperating. Geoffrey Platt worked at Lodge Farm as the cowman, having previously served as an ambulance worker attached to the British army. He had been inspired to become a pacifist by Middleton Murry's writing, later concluding that his mentor was 'the only person I can remember . . . that I loved and hated'.[88]

From late 1941 and into early 1942, the people working at Gooseham would begin gradually drifting away, as a result of arguing with Ronald or each other, losing interest or simply deciding to move on. John Connelly, the Communist from London, had left for Dublin to avoid conscription, but signed up when the Soviets entered the war and was eventually killed at Tobruk.[89] Frank Smithson, the collier, went back to the mines, saying he preferred industrial labour. Horst was told by his guardians to go to university, but before he could do so was interned as an 'enemy alien'.[90] Mr Wyles dropped down dead with a blood clot. Mary Weston became pregnant, and there seemed to be no way to make the land feed the extra mouth, so she and her husband decided to leave and moved on to another farm.[91]

More babies were on the way. Early in 1941, Rose Marie had become pregnant and quickly married Ronald before the baby was born. It does not seem the day of the wedding was filled with romance. When Rose Marie went to bed that night Ronald stayed up writing letters, later regretfully reflecting that they 'ought to have been all addressed to myself, for the day had proved I was obsessed with myself, and in love with myself'.[92] Briony Duncan was born on 9 September 1941, weighing 8 pounds and, according to her mother, looking just like Ronald.[93] She cried throughout her christening, before being 'charmed by the bright tiles on the vestry floor'.[94] Over the coming years, Briony, and her brother Jeremy, who was born two years later, brought much joy and provided a welcome distraction for everyone.

By this time, it was just Ronald, Nigel, Rose Marie and Bianca left working at Gooseham. It was not long before Nigel left too and joined the RAF. Ronald later wrote in his memoir that it seemed by then 'the logical thing to do', all the pacifist energies of the early years seemingly dissipated.[95] The experiment of working together on the land had run out of steam, the war was still raging and, for Nigel at least, it no longer made sense to try and stand away from the crowd. For his part, Ronald's poetry was beginning to draw critical attention and he dissolved the community, continuing to farm but turning his attention to tobacco crops.

If love was to have been the basis of a new pacifist society, this was a love that was often difficult, painful and fickle, hard to divide from narcissism; it could also demand too much, or show too little consideration for others. In the end perhaps the problem was not that there was not enough love to go around, but that the love kept going off in new directions.

In the years to come, looking back on Gooseham, Ronald concluded that it had been a failure. He was taken aback by the 'depth of stupid childishness to which so many moderately intelligent people are brought when they are involved in any sort of community activity. It seems that the intelligence of a community is the lowest common denominator of its members; and, I think in our case, the cow must be included as a member.'[96] Abandoning the idea that humans contained within themselves the potential to live a better, more peaceful existence, he came away thinking that people were instead inherently marked by sin and self-interest, adding that all the 'rottenness which exists in the social elephant could be observed in our microscopic mouse of a community'.[97] Any optimism about human nature had gone.

To his credit, Ronald did not absolve himself from blame – he was too self-aware for that. Indeed, his writing, as well as Rose Marie's and Bianca's, is full of often very painful reflections on their own shortcomings. He wrote in his published journal that 'what annoys us most about our friends is not their failings but our own which we see parodied in them'.[98] Ronald knew he was hard work, titling the second volume of his memoirs *How to Make Enemies*. There is little hubris or pride here and a great deal of introspection. Other pacifists felt similarly about their experiments in community farms, and equally blamed themselves. Nora Wright wrote that 'living in the community has not lived up to expectations and the reason is that I was idealizing pacifists into saints, and expecting to shine in their reflected glory, expecting others to do what in my heart I am not prepared to do myself'.[99] After their farm had been dissolved – and following further disagreements over how to divide the movable property between the members – the Wrights went to work at a market garden. Lodge Farm struggled on, at one point employing a group of prisoners of war to get the work done, before John Middleton Murry decided to close down the farm shortly after the war ended.[100]

It is easy to dismiss the residents of community farms as naive, utopian and even self-important, and sometimes all those words do seem to fit. It is important to remember, though, that the Duncans and many others were in their mid-twenties, and that for a time they succeeded in bringing together a group of people from all walks of life to feed themselves and others. They were also setting themselves extremely high – even perfectionist – standards, and they were not the only people in the war to make mistakes. It is difficult to work out whether it was farming on tough land with little experience or community living itself that was the main problem. It might not be possible to separate out the two, but it is also difficult to draw simple conclusions about the possibilities of other ways of living. Ronald concluded in his memoir: 'As a community the experiment looked like a failure; but so were the social patterns around us failures too. At least we were not dropping bombs on each other.'[101] After failing to prevent the outbreak of war, pacifists like Ronald Duncan had turned inwards to try and build an island peace. Now, by their own admission, that too had faltered. But failures are not always an end; they can also be a new beginning. The question now was where this would lead them.

CHAPTER 11

Pacifist Service

There was more than one way to keep a commitment to peace. For Tom Burns, the former teacher from east London, it meant trying to heal the injured. In mid-April 1941 Tom drove an ambulance over the rain-soaked mountain roads of northern Greece, after being sent to the Balkans with a group of British volunteers known as the Friends Ambulance Unit (FAU). They were supposed to be helping at a hospital near the Yugoslav border, but when the men had arrived in the middle of a storm, the hospital was already deserted and the German army just over the horizon.[1] The Wehrmacht was ruthlessly completing its takeover of south-east Europe from the north, so Tom headed south, passing hungry and exhausted Greek soldiers on the roadside along the way.[2] It was a wretched time. In her semi-autobiographical account of the time, the novelist Olivia Manning describes seeing soldiers 'haggard with defeat. Their flesh had shrunk from want of food . . . it was as though their bones had become hollow like the bones of birds.'[3] As neutral ambulance crews, the laws of war said that Tom and the other volunteers were not supposed to help uninjured soldiers, no matter how desperate, but it seemed too much to leave them to their fate at the hands of the advancing and hostile Germans, so the men gave lifts on their running boards. The irony of a group of pacifists saving soldiers to fight another day would not have been lost on all those involved. Over 60,000 British and Commonwealth troops sent to support the Greeks were in retreat too, and the men of the FAU joined them, their destinies thrown together as they headed south, hoping for safety.[4]

Being opposed to war did not mean you could avoid it, and if war was terrible because it resulted in suffering, conscientious objectors could be single-minded in doing what they could to relieve the pain and injury that it caused. Pacifists like Tom Burns were determined to roll their sleeves up and get their hands dirty rather than simply sit the war out, comforted by their own moral purity. For them there was no neutral space beyond the fray to watch the battles go by; they were already implicated and therefore also had responsibilities to help those in need. The FAU's official policy was that while 'respecting the views of those pacifists who feel they cannot join an organization such as our own, we feel concerned . . . to build up a record of goodwill and positive service . . .'[5] War was here and there was no way to escape it, and so they responded by trying to relieve its effects. This could mean getting very close to where the guns were being fired. And while there might not have been redemption in bloodshed, solace was to be found in binding wounds. Throughout the war, volunteers from the Friends Ambulance Unit could be found not only in Greece but in China, Ethiopia, Syria, Finland and elsewhere. As they tried to help those in need, it was often very hard to draw a line between war and peace. This meant some painful compromises, and considerable danger and sacrifice as well. This was not actually the first time Tom had to retreat from an advancing and hostile army. Worse was to come.

The FAU had its roots in the First World War, when a group of Quakers had set up an ambulance service to help injured soldiers and civilians. In 1914–18 around 1,000 volunteers, many of them conscientious objectors, had ferried the sick and wounded for the British and French armies. Alongside medical work in Britain, it had run hospital ships and ambulance trains in France and Belgium, with many volunteers working close to the front lines. By the end of war, they had driven over two million miles, transporting more than 277,000 sick and injured, and twenty-one volunteers had died in action.[6]

On the eve of the Second World War, two prominent Quakers had got together to discuss what to do. Every summer, members of the Rowntree and Cadbury families holidayed on the north-west coast of Wales, and the summer of 1939 had been no different. Despite being rivals in the commercial world of chocolate making, both families knew each other well, and that August Paul Cadbury had called at the house of Arnold Rowntree to discuss what to do once war began.[7] As well as owning confectionery factories, the two men were steeped in the traditions of Quaker pacifism.[8] Paul was an energetic man, with a reputation for getting things done. As one acquaintance put it, he gave off the 'feeling that if a bomb dropped behind him he would just look over his shoulder gently to see what was interrupting the situation'.[9] These were not the qualities stereotypically associated with a pacifist, but they would stand him in good stead. Arnold Rowntree was a generation older, chairman of the family business and a former Liberal MP. Both men had been deeply involved in the first incarnation of the Friends Ambulance Unit during the First World War, Paul as a stretcher bearer and Arnold as Vice Chairman of the organisation. On the eve of the Second World War, they had decided to restart the old FAU.

On the same day that Chamberlain declared Britain to be at war with Germany, Paul Cadbury issued a call in the newsletter of the British Quakers asking for 'members of military age who wish to give positive proof that, although they register as conscientious objectors, they have no wish to be exempt from a period of constructive labour'.[10] He was determined that pacifists should not stand apart in this time of national emergency, but would instead throw themselves into working for their country and the greater good. He moved down to Cadbury's factory on the outskirts of Birmingham and set about recruiting the new FAU.[11] His aunt, Dame Elizabeth Cadbury, donated her former family home at Manor Farm as a training base, and the first wave of volunteers started to clean the barns and stables of mud and horse manure.

Tom Burns was a tall twenty-six-year-old with literary ambitions, a love of film and a touch of asthma. He was among the first recruits to the FAU, and had volunteered so fast that his age group had not been called up for military service and therefore he had not gone through the tribunal process. This young man came from a world very different from that of the Cadburys and Rowntrees. For one thing he was not a Quaker. For another, he was the youngest of fourteen children – only eight of whom survived past childhood – from a working-class family. After being taken under the wing of a teacher, Tom had lost his Cockney accent and had earned a general degree from Bristol University, with a scholarship from London County Council. He did not have a close relationship with much of his family, some of whom who had emigrated to North America, and one elder brother had become a Fascist, whereas Tom was both a socialist and a pacifist. Tom had written a series of short stories based on his East End childhood, full of pubs, petty criminals and children running the streets. One of these, 'Back Rent', describes a child whose parents are threatened with eviction and who has nightmares of 'standing by the furniture in the street and being watched by a giggling circle of neighbours ... and another of them sleeping under a railway arch'.[12] There is no evidence to suggest that Tom went through such experiences himself, but they must have been drawn from a world he was very familiar with. By the late 1930s he was working as a teacher in a small private school in Norfolk and indulging a new-found love of sailing. He had come a long way. Over the next few years he would go even further.

The volunteers arriving at the FAU training centre on the outskirts of Birmingham were, according to one member, 'nearer twenty than thirty', and 'a bourgeois group ... but not only so'.[13] An undated tally in the Unit's archives lists ten accountants, sixteen architects, three bakers, one blacksmith, twelve carpenters, ten solicitors, eighteen motor mechanics, two male nurses, thirty-two schoolmasters and twenty-four students, among others.[14] This was a particular, albeit fairly wide, slice of British life.

To join the FAU you had to be Christian and pacifist, and the Unit itself was part of a longer Quaker tradition. This relatively small Christian group had long played a disproportionately large role in British humanitarianism. This was a tradition that combined witness and service – witness against war and suffering, and service for those in need. Faith by itself was seen as empty. Salvation was instead to be found through human blood, sweat and witness. This was also a tradition that was firmly committed to the ideal of human perfection. Although war and violence might have their origins in human lust, these are vices that it is possible to overcome. In the words of one member, the FAU was to provide testimony for peace as part of a 'slender contribution to the welfare of humanity'.[15]

Crucially, however, although the FAU took the Quaker moniker 'Friends', and although many of the volunteers, but by no means all, were Quakers, it was not formally a Quaker organisation; it always remained loosely associated rather than tightly bound with the group from which it took its name. In 1939 the FAU planned to 'undertake ambulance and relief work in areas under both civilian and military control'.[16] It was the bit about 'military control' that official Quaker bodies did not like, worried that to bind the wounds of war it would have to get close to the front lines, and the volunteers would have to cooperate too much with the armed forces. Perfectionism sat awkwardly with the compromises of battle, when active witnessing against war could run into complicity.

Although humanitarian work was one possible condition given to conscientious objectors, the FAU was concerned not to get into too cosy a relationship with the tribunals. Applicants were often asked by the Unit's leadership not to use membership as evidence of conscience when they stood before a judge. It seems that they were worried that joining an ambulance team would be instrumentalised as a fast track to exemption.

Once accepted into the FAU, training took place in the landscaped grounds of Manor Farm and volunteers slept in the former servants' quarters or the barns. One remembered the 'gigantic bathroom' with three tubs in a row and the way rubber conveyor belts were brought from the nearby Cadbury factory and turned into bunks.[17] The first batch of sixty pacifists undertook a six-week crash course in first aid and mechanics. Days began with rising at dawn and running around the lake, with a parade and kit inspection after breakfast, then lectures and further exercises, often followed by singing.[18] One day a group of volunteers marched twenty-five miles to Stratford-upon-Avon, saw a play, then marched back again through the night.[19]

Near military-style discipline was a rather awkward part of this routine. It was assumed that when they went to the battlefield, the pacifists of the FAU would have to move around with the army and therefore understand martial methods. Indeed, the FAU could occasionally seem keen to mimic military life, partly and very controversially within pacifist circles due to admiration for some military virtues. Ronald Joynes, who was in Greece with Tom, later recalled that their training had taken on a martial tone, with drills and exercises.[20] When one volunteer first turned up at the FAU training camp outside Birmingham, he was immediately struck by the way so many of the other volunteers were 'inclined to be a little militaristic'.[21] Military hierarchy was a bit of a problem, though, as the Unit also tried to be egalitarian and cooperative, with all resources pooled. But there were concerns that not all the recruits had it in them to be leaders, so roles were created for commandants and quartermasters, despite considerable pushback.[22] The young men, usually wearing woollen suits, earnestly practised carrying stretchers and took part in exercises.

One volunteer recalled that by the end of the training they were a 'close knit community . . . of a very odd lot at the beginning, many of them who had never been away from home, from all backgrounds . . . a wonderful mixing'.[23] For many pacifists – who might well have been ridiculed or ostracised in the immediate run-up to the war – their early days with the FAU brought an immediate sense of common cause.

As important as a commitment to principles of service and witness might be, we should not discount other, perhaps less rarefied, motivations. A woman's section was formed only after intense opposition from some of the men, who feared that it 'would not be the first sign of softness creeping in'.[24] One of the reasons many of the male volunteers had joined the FAU was to show that they were just as brave as the next man, and they were anxious that having women in the Unit might somehow dilute this. Pacifists were not immune to a bit of machismo. A thirst for adventure could also be found in the volunteers, which could sometimes sit uncomfortably alongside a more restrained and modest Quaker ethos.[25] The young men at the FAU were particularly keen to travel beyond Britain, and as one put it in the Unit's newsletter what they needed was 'adventure into new paths of service'.[26] They were looking for excitement. The unofficial motto of the FAU was 'Go anywhere, do anything', and as ambulance workers who hoped to relieve suffering, getting close to the battlefield – into the thick of things – was essential. The trouble, at that stage, had been finding a 'thick of things' to get into.

The first few months of the Second World War were a source of frustration. The volunteers at Manor Farm had joined imagining that, as in the First World War, many of them would soon be serving at the front, but at that initial stage of the war British soldiers were still not in action on any scale. As there was no battlefield to go to yet, the pacifists at Manor Farm were sent to volunteer in London hospitals, cleaning the wards. It was worthy work, but not what they had signed up for. According to the official history of the Unit, scrubbing hospital floors and changing beds was seen as 'dull but useful'.[27] Michael Rowntree, one of Arnold Rowntree's sons, was one of the other early volunteers for the FAU and found it particularly frustrating. Before the war, as well as trying to help Jews escape from mainland Europe, he had been a student at Oxford University, a former head boy at his Quaker public school and a keen birdwatcher.[28] According to a friend from the time, he was also 'unruffled, realistic, practical'.[29] Michael later recalled that the young men were 'bursting to do something and getting progressively more disillusioned'.[30] The pacifists at the FAU were growing anxious that they had nothing much to do, little to witness and certainly no adventure.

Then, at the end of November 1939, hostilities had broken out between Finland and the Soviet Union. Throughout the nineteenth century Finland was a semi-autonomous part of the Russian Empire, but it had declared independence in the wake of the 1917 Russian Revolution. With the signing of the Nazi–Soviet Pact in August 1939, Finland came, far from willingly, back within the Soviet sphere of influence. This was not the end of the matter, however; Stalin was determined to move his international border still further westward to extend the buffer around St Petersburg, which was only twenty miles from Finnish territory. Soviet demands that the Finns concede land were rebuffed and the Red Army started to fight their way west. Fearing they would be overwhelmed, the Finns called for international help, and the Finnish Red Cross invited the FAU to send volunteers to tend wounded Finnish soldiers on the front line.

It was just the sort of work the Friends Ambulance Unit was looking for. As Michael Rowntree put it, 'the opportunity to serve in Finland, tragic as it was, was seized on with almost relief and glee'.[31] Ronald Joynes, an accountant and, alongside Tom Burns, one of the few FAU volunteers from a working-class background, similarly recalled that 'we wanted some action, just as some chaps in the army wanted some action'.[32] Money was raised, vehicles bought, uniforms fitted and permissions granted. Twenty-four two-ton Ford ambulances, a kitchen car and a repair vehicle were all set to go, and the Swedish railways company promised to look after the transport.

Tom Burns, Michael Rowntree, Ronald Joynes and twenty-one others were selected for this first mission of the new FAU.[33] The volunteers assembled at a youth hostel on the outskirts of London before heading north for the boat from Newcastle, only slowed down by a snowstorm. It was a small foretaste of what was to come. In late January 1940, the newly trained and inexperienced ambulance workers stood on the deck of a boat heading out across the cold North Sea, canvas and cork lifebelts close at hand. Others would follow in the coming weeks. The boat sailed north for Shetland and then east to Norway, passing a torpedoed Danish coaler and stopping to pick up the survivors. Tom wrote home to his close friend Cathy Bunting describing 'two long lines of oil covered with coal-dust on the water, debris and barrels, and two rafts, one with five, the other with four of the crew . . . They looked crooked and lumpy, their faces putty and purple coloured, and their expressions didn't change.'[34] Their grim looks were unsurprising. Half of this Danish crew had been lost at sea. As the FAU volunteers got closer to war, the atmosphere on board the ship became full of nervous energy, Tom writing that it all felt 'unnaturally exciting . . . the voyage was extraordinarily vivid . . . Every second counted heavily.'[35] A religious service was held one morning on the boat, with an elderly man – somewhere between a 'consular official and an African bishop' – declaring, much to Tom's annoyance, that the 'British Empire was held together by love'.[36] Everyone on board was bound for the Norwegian coastal town of Bergen, from where they would head further east.

The boat arrived in Bergen on 22 January. Michael Rowntree's first impression was 'seeing all the lights, because we had blackout' in Britain.[37] Tom was a little intimidated by the rugged landscape, noticing the 'extraordinarily bleak-looking hills around: it looked like the end of the world'.[38] He did not have to stay in Bergen for long, as they moved on to Oslo to wait for the ambulances, which were temporarily stuck in the winter ice further north. A photograph shows the eager young men collected together wearing their uniforms in the snow. They learned to ski, socialised with local students at the university, enjoyed the saunas and practised driving on snow-covered roads.[39] After a fortnight, the ambulances finally arrived. The party spent Michael Rowntree's twenty-first birthday in a Salvation Army hostel in Stockholm, before heading north along the long Swedish coast and around the frozen Gulf of Bothnia, finally arriving in Finland and travelling to the battle front near Lake Ladoga on the Soviet border. Tom wrote home that after the long journey it was 'very satisfactory to be at last able to do that which we came for. The Finns are extremely fine people ... I hope we prove an efficient help.'[40] It was a question members of the FAU would often ask themselves.

The Soviet advance was caught up in the forests and frozen lakes of south-east Finland, as snipers and machine-gunners picked off the Red Army from behind the trees.[41] The Finns' strategy aimed not to defeat the Soviets, but to delay them long enough for help from the British and French to arrive. They would be disappointed. Neville Chamberlain declared that the Soviet invasion had 'outraged the conscience of the whole world', but sent only a few small shipments of arms and a handful of firefighters.[42] For their part, the FAU volunteers were split into different teams. Tom headed to the main base at Savonlinna, helping at a casualty clearing station, and Michael Rowntree's group was sent to live in dugouts a couple of miles from the Russian front lines. They were now at the heart of the action, far closer to the battlefield at the time than the men who had joined the British army.

The ambulance drivers set to work in temperatures of minus 30 degrees Celsius. This was a brutally cold winter even by Finnish standards. Tom, at the wheel of one of the ambulances, experienced 'one of the worst blizzards for years, with snow driving horizontally, drifts every hundred yards that had to be charged and dug through' as they 'covered 16 miles in over five hours'.[43] A uniform of leftover First World War woollen battledress, thick socks, mitts and a fur hat was not enough to keep out the biting chill. It was so cold the ambulance engines had to be left running overnight so they did not freeze. The men on the front line slept in tents dug into the snow, with the central pole made from the chimney of a stove, and a rota had to be maintained through the night to keep the fire going. Tom and his colleagues were living off a standard Finnish army diet of porridge, black bread, tins of fish and potato stew. Communication with the Finnish soldiers was friendly but somewhat muted, as none of the FAU party spoke the language, and they had to rely on a series of interpreters. When a Finnish major asked the volunteers what they would do if a Russian parachutist attacked them with a machine gun, the men of the FAU could only reply that they did not know.[44]

The weather was not the only concern. As Tom drove the slow, heavy and gleaming ambulance past snow-covered trees, the Soviet army was advancing steadily westwards. Tom made his way by burned-out and abandoned villages, with bodies frozen in the snow, and Michael Rowntree got lost in the forest and ended right up against the Russian positions, before being called back by a Finnish guard.[45] They both feared coming face to face with a Russian ski patrol, and the ambulance drivers frequently abandoned their vehicles – smeared with the blood of Finnish casualties – to dive into the trees so as to avoid Soviet aircraft. If they were looking for excitement, they had found it. In letters home to Cathy Bunting, Tom recounted how 'we were machine-gunned out of bed by an aeroplane which had spotted the smoke ... We spent the morning ducking behind trees and under ambulances in the woods.'[46] He told the people back in England, however, that they were 'not to be concerned about my safety. I am with the Finns now, and cannot differentiate my lot from theirs. I am in comfortable circumstances, relatively, and suffer no hardship and fewer dangers than this people.'[47] He and the other volunteers were determined not to accept any privileges, but despite this stoicism he was also a little lonely, asking Cathy to write to him, because 'this is a very foreign country, and letters from home attain extreme significance in our lives'.[48]

The hoped-for Franco-British military intervention never materialised and the Finns capitulated on 13 March 1940. The FAU teams had been in Finland for barely three weeks when the territory where they were based was handed over to Moscow, Soviet troops rolled in and the roads filled with refugees pulling sledges laden with everything they could carry. The men of the FAU joined them heading north and west. At one point, as happened later in Greece, they were asked to transport uninjured soldiers, but this time they refused so that they could keep their Red Cross recognition as neutral ambulance workers.

As the war came to a halt in Finland, there was no time for Tom and his fellow pacifists to rest. In April the FAU was ordered to the emerging front line in Norway to support the British Expeditionary Force there. The ambulances headed north in the spring sunshine; but this time it was German rather than Soviet planes that shot at them. In the disaster of the Allied campaign in Norway, the decision was soon made to evacuate all British personnel, and the men of the FAU were ordered to meet before dawn at the North Sea port of Namsos, hoping to be picked up by British boats. In the rush to the coast Tom's vehicle suffered a split radiator and he had to abandon it at the roadside, walking through the night to reach the pick-up point.[49] Twenty-five men from the FAU made it on board the rescue convoy, but thirty-one, including Tom Burns, Michael Rowntree and Ronald Joynes, were left on the quay. The last rescue boat – with no FAU volunteers on board – was sunk by the Luftwaffe as it headed over the horizon.[50] On land, the German army would arrive at any moment, so Tom and his colleagues rushed off again, ditching more of their vehicles on the way, desperate to find shelter in neutral Sweden and fearing they would run into invading troops coming the other way.[51] If they had been worried about looking like cowards, the last few weeks had provided plenty of opportunities to test their resolve.

By the late spring of 1940, the men of the FAU were stranded in Stockholm. German troops blocked the routes to the north, west and south, controlling Norway and Denmark. To the east was Soviet-occupied territory. Ronald Joynes assumed that if they ever returned home 'it would be to an occupied country'.[52] A shop in the Swedish capital showed a map of Britain in its window, with London covered by a German flag. Ronald observed that the newsreels at the cinema were 'full of German successes'.[53] At the time, it must have felt as if they were nearing the end.

Cut off from the rest of the world, the FAU ambulance drivers changed back into civilian clothes and tried to find work.[54] Billeted in a pension outside the city, some of them took up agricultural work, a few found employment teaching English.[55] Others desperately sought a way to get home, but Tom decided against joining a plan to escape on a small fishing boat across the North Sea, fearing capture and 'internment camps for the rest of the war'.[56] As he waited in Sweden, there was a low-key coup in their Unit, as many of the volunteers felt, for reasons that are not entirely clear, that the leadership in Finland was not suited to the 'new reality'.

Ronald Joynes now found himself, as Quartermaster, in charge of the group's small funds.

Then in August 1940 a new window of opportunity opened up, as an agreement was reached to allow the evacuation of a small number of British troops stuck in Sweden, and the government chartered a boat that was to sail to Iceland and then on to Britain. The FAU was offered six places, so lots had to be drawn. Michael Rowntree was given a place on board, but Tom Burns and Ronald Joynes were not. Michael promised those left behind that he would visit their nearest and dearest as soon as he made it home, and Tom wrote to Cathy that 'he is very very likeable, and much more intelligent than his bouncing appearance shows him: he will be a very fine man'.[57] It looked as if they would have to see out the war far away from home.

The left-behind men did not have to stay in Sweden for long, as their help was needed again. The FAU had a new posting for them, this time thousands of miles away in Egypt. Tom was determined to go. Turning down a job teaching English in Helsinki, he decided that 'my first loyalty was to the Unit and my 1939 conscience', a conscience that drove him on to witness against war rather than teach English in a lecture hall.[58] This meant somehow getting all the way to north Africa. Between Sweden and Egypt was German-occupied Europe or the potentially hostile expanses of the Soviet Union. Eventually, the ambulance workers managed to obtain visas to travel through Russia, with the assistance of a Quaker serving in the British Embassy. After flying to Moscow, where it rained incessantly and which Tom thought a 'disappointing place', they stopped to have tea with the British Ambassador, and then travelled south, by train and boat, stopping in Odessa to enjoy an opera, and headed on to Istanbul, Beirut and Cairo, before finally arriving in Alexandria in November 1940.[59]

Alexandria was to be their home for the next few months. It was a cosmopolitan metropolis of Muslims and Copts, Arabs, Greeks, Armenians and Jews, and its wide tree-lined avenues were filling with British, Australian and Indian troops preparing for battle. A month before Tom and the others arrived, Italian forces had crossed the Egyptian frontier from Libya and encamped at Sidi Barrani – 260 miles west of Alexandria. Although nominally independent, Egypt was still dominated by the British Empire, which kept tight control over the Suez Canal. Strong nationalist and anti-imperial sentiments were running through north-east Africa, and although the Egyptian Prime Minister declared a state of emergency and broke off diplomatic relations with Berlin, he refused to declare war on Germany. For many Egyptians, this simply was not their war, although they would pay a heavy price in the violence it unleashed. When Tom arrived in town, Alexandria was under a blackout, and the residents were being evacuated in the face of bombing from the Axis powers. Rumours were also going around the city that British anti-aircraft guns were being stationed in the poorer districts in order to draw the bombs away from Allied troops based in other parts of town.

The plan was for the Friends Ambulance Unit to act as the transport section for two of the British army's hospitals, but when the Unit arrived no one seemed to know what to do with them. This was the first time in this war that the FAU had worked along-side British soldiers, and some of the volunteers, from more sheltered backgrounds, were taken aback by the language.[60] The nominally senior members of the party, including Ronald Joynes, were treated as officers, much to the annoyance of the others, and sent off to a 'good' hotel. They were not the types to kick up a fuss, though, at least in public, and some of the volunteers agreed to carry the Commandant's and Quartermaster's kit to 'save embarrassment'.[61] The other men were sent to a barracks, where they quickly caught fleas.[62]

The men settled into their new environment, so different from Finland, and eventually set up base in tents pitched in the grounds of a neo-classical building known as the Italian Hospital. They also found a small hotel on the waterfront, run by a large French-Syrian woman called Madame Haddad, and used it as a type of club house when they could find time to relax, playing ping pong and listening to the gramophone.[63] The pacifists were made members of the sergeants' mess too and were invited to evening dances. Local girls were asked to come, but there were not enough to go around, so Ronald found a regular partner in the shape of a soldier from Norfolk.[64] Tom and Ronald wrote a pantomime, performed for the troops on Boxing Day, that 'involved every cliché and melo-dramatic scene that any of us had ever seen or heard', but they both felt it to be a 'great success'.[65] The ambulance workers were being treated well by the soldiers, and were pleased to be known as the '25 conscies' as this meant that they were not assumed to be part of the regular army. This would not always be an easy line to draw.

There was work to do too. As the weather cooled and the rain seeped into the tents in Alexandria, the fighting in the desert heated up. The Italians were pushed back over the Libyan border, and the wounded started to arrive in Alexandria by boat, with the ambulance drivers transporting the maimed and injured to hospital. There were large numbers of burns from the tank battles, and on some days Tom and Ronald helped to carry more than 250 injured men.[66]

But then in early February 1941 Benghazi fell to the British; the speed of the British advance meant that the work soon slowed, and the pace of life went down several gears, so Tom and the others began to look for other things to do.

Very soon the doubts and anxieties of a guilty conscience began to set in. Things were suddenly a little too easy, a little too boring for the volunteers of the FAU. Tom told Cathy Bunting that 'Life is a great deal too undisturbed and workless: there is considerable restlessness about it among us – especially as much of the birthright pacifism and masked fear is wearing thin.'[67] The volunteers were starting to bicker among themselves. Two men left the Unit for the RAF, presumably feeling that what they were doing was not that different from life in the armed forces, where they might be put to better use. The semi-official *FAU Chronicle* expressed frustration at the nature of the work and noted that members were becoming depressed.[68] With all the dances and sitting around, there was a worry that the Unit was getting further and further away from its core mission.[69] One volunteer later wrote, 'we are getting into a mental and spiritual rut ... complacently jogging along without bothering to think about what our aims should be ... Only a radical advance in interpersonal, social and personal relationships can save the world.'[70] Playing bridge in a cheap hotel and waiting for the wounded to come in from a front line that was every day further away was not going to make a difference to a world at war.

As he sat on the Mediterranean coast, the new life that Tom and others in the FAU wanted to build seemed distant and he was getting more and more frustrated: 'This damned business of sitting here in these silly tents, a few casual hours of work here and there, no danger, no interest, nothing to make you feel you're doing a job worth doing . . . Stupid savage little bickerings start up very easily, people get mad about bits of inefficiency, cliquishness is coming back, and myself, I'm pretty much done up with the continued companionship of adolescents . . . I shall stick to my 1939 position, mostly because I'm too lazy, or too uncaring now to do anything about it. And I'm going bald.'[71] Pacifists might have been working for a new world, but they were not immune to petty vanities of the old world. Ronald Joynes felt somewhat similarly that 'we began to tire a little of it' and 'to pine for something more'.[72] The sentiment was widespread. Even the official history of the FAU conceded that the men fell into 'disappointment, boredom'.[73] Any dreams of human perfection they might have had had given way to more prosaic concerns.

But despite being bored and disappointed, the volunteers could also be very sanguine. Their letters, diaries and newsletters are full of jokes and light-hearted optimism, marked by a distinctive ironic sense of humour, quick to puncture any overdeveloped sense of pride and to point out the absurd and the ridiculous. Tom and Ronald's Alexandria pantomime was far from a one-off. Members of the Unit later self-published a collection of their poems and songs. After the war, one FAU volunteer, Donald Swann, went on to be one half of the popular comedy singing duo Flanders and Swann. Theirs was a very particular type of humour, familiar in other masculine middle-class environments of the mid-twentieth century, its mode slightly dry and droll rather than heroic.

There were rumours that the Unit might be broken up, and Tom used the time to reflect on his own stance. He wrote to Cathy, 'My own position, I think, is fairly clear, emotionally anyway, and I'm making something of an effort to work it out . . . Pacifism I'm not much concerned with. It is, after all, a wholly subordinate and contingent circumstance. What's going to happen after this occupies a great deal of our thoughts.'[74] It seemed for Tom that conscience was about much more than refusing to fight. Wars would come and go, but what was most important was the type of lives they might lead once all the fighting had stopped, and the pause in action allowed him to think at length about the possibilities. Pacifism was only one aspect of the world he hoped to help make, and it was hard to remake the world listening to old records in a rundown guest house.

War is often a strange and disturbing mix of peaks of intense fear and bloodshed and troughs of boredom and anxiety, waiting for the onslaught to begin again. There is more sitting around, taking shelter, looking for food and missing loved ones than there is dodging bullets and firing guns, even for soldiers. The experience of the FAU was no different. Troughs of inactivity can be as emotionally and personally difficult as the peaks of violence. Tom, Ronald and the other men of the FAU in Alexandria were deep in their own personal troughs, wishing for something more. They should have been careful what they wished for.

Greece was next.

A request came through from the Red Cross and once again the small group of FAU men set off, like pacifist guns for hire, this time for Athens. Delayed slightly by a bout of dysentery and a major sea battle off the coast of Crete, they arrived just as another spring was blossoming. It was a dangerous time to travel to the Balkans. An Italian invasion had been repulsed, but on 6 April 1941, the very day Tom, Ronald and their colleagues landed, German troops crossed into Greece. After being forced into reverse on reaching the northern border, Tom joined Greek and British soldiers as they tried to make their way south towards the sea and safety, until the land ran out and he reached the Peloponnese coastal town of Kalamata. In letters home, written several months later, Tom described hiding under trees from the Luftwaffe, surrounded by dry grass and white rocks, and peering out to sea for signs of a rescue, as he searched in his kit for the remnants of supplies. The 'accumulated fatigue of the last days and weeks sustained a parched fire in our skin, our head, our bones'.[75] Nursing sunburned skin and fatigued limbs, there was nothing much to do but sleep and wait. At night ships came to evacuate the British forces, and what seemed like thousands of men came down from the hills, queuing silently on the moonlit quayside, occasionally breaking into song. Just before dawn, those who were not lucky enough to board, went back into hiding. Having fled with another group along a different road, Ronald Joynes somehow managed to get on a barge that evacuated him on to a warship, tying the Unit's accounts around his waist as he waded through the water, eventually making it back to Egypt.[76]

As Tom stood on the shore surrounded by British and Commonwealth soldiers, he might well have reflected on how tightly woven his fate had become with that of the military men who stood next to him. Always opposed to war, he had now seen action on four different fields of battle – much more than many soldiers – and was standing in a khaki shirt looking out to sea for signs of rescue by the Royal Navy. Ronald Joynes later recalled that in Greece he slowly realised how dependent they had all become on the army.[77] It provided his food and rations, he wore what looked like, to all intents and purposes, a military uniform, he had travelled across Europe and north Africa effectively under military command, and now was fleeing from German troops and hoping to be picked up by the same warship as the soldiers that stood all around him.

The line between military and pacifist action was not always easy to draw, particularly when Tom and his colleagues were driven by a sense – probably greater than that among some soldiers – that they wanted to get close to the action. For one volunteer, ambulance work was a 'way of performing active service which isn't actually active military service but was as near as the pacifist could get to active service in the military sense'.[78] Quite how closely the FAU operated with the armed forces was the cause of considerable controversy, both within the Unit and among pacifists and Quakers more generally.[79] The question of just how far those who opposed war should go in relieving the suffering of others, not least when this meant patching them up to go and fight some more, troubled many pacifists. With much of the world mobilised to fight, it was increasingly difficult to find a space that was not in some way complicit in the waging of war; but standing apart could risk looking not only aloof and morally superior but also uncaring.

For some Quakers, the FAU 'compromised the Quaker witness against all war by its willingness to work with the military authorities', and it is for this reason that the FAU was never an official Quaker organisation.[80] As Michael Cadbury – another member of a Quaker family who served with the FAU in Finland and elsewhere – put it, 'in a sense we were letting the side down by being prepared to work with the army, because we had to *do* that. It was no good getting trained in ambulance work if you could not go out to an area where warfare was going on and there were people to heal, and to do that you had to work with the army . . . that was the compromise.'[81] But for some volunteers in the FAU, the compromises made by the Unit were too many. One wrote to the Unit's newsletter complaining that 'it seems as if we are . . . fitting in very nicely, oh so nicely, into the world that has been organised as one great war machine'.[82] For this volunteer, and not a few others, bearing witness against war was in danger of becoming little different from waging war.

For many in the FAU compromises were not a sign of moral impurity but an inevitable consequence of getting stuck in, of refusing to stand apart, of trying to live alongside others and to help them. The whole world was mobilising for war and the food on people's table and the clothes on their back were all produced through a war economy, and there was very little space outside of war in which you could operate. This meant either doing nothing or accepting some sort of compromise. As one volunteer later argued, 'It was quite impossible for anyone in 1939 to avoid being dependent on the services of a nation at war.'[83] The FAU tried to get this message out to its members, and a report to the Executive Committee noted that 'we must face up to the difficulties of co-operation with the army . . . it should also be pointed out to members that they have freedom of conscientious choice, but that they cannot have things all their own way, and that once they have made their decision, they are honour bound to abide by it'.[84] From this perspective, conscience was about a necessarily compromised obligation to others rather than an absolute personal freedom.

The pacifist principle 'thou shall not kill' can be seen as an absolute principle of moral purity, but it can also be seen as part of a general appreciation of the value of life rooted in constant and often difficult decisions. As FAU member John Wood later recalled, 'It's very important for the pacifist to recognise his dilemmas and face them. And a dilemma after all is a choice of action.'[85] To be against war when all around battles were being waged required constant adjustments and accommodation, but it also meant trying to do something to alleviate the suffering of that war. The question of whether it was actually possible to live with a commitment to peace in the midst of such widespread violence, and the linked question of just what compromises had to be made in order to relieve the suffering of others, would haunt the FAU throughout the six years of war.

In Greece, Tom Burns had long ago come to terms with the compromises he had to make to help those in need during war. He was now living with the consequences. Just as German soldiers reached the outskirts of Kalamata, the boat that he hoped to board off the coast of Greece was sunk.[86] Giving up hope of being rescued, the remaining men from FAU heard that casualties had been taken to the town hall, and they set off to see if they could help. They found 200 men crammed into a makeshift hospital, many lying on the floor, attended by two Greek doctors and three Greek nurses. Many of the casualties were in a pitiable state, and some had died in the night. Tom set to work dressing the wounds of those who were still alive. Twice before he had managed to escape advancing and hostile armies. This time he would not be so lucky. There was little drama, and the unarmed pacifists could put up little resistance when the German soldiers entered the hospital. Tom and the remaining FAU volunteers in Greece joined over 10,000 Allied troops who became prisoners of war as the Wehrmacht completed their occupation of the Balkans.

CHAPTER 12

Home Front

During the spring of 1941, as Tom Burns was taken prisoner in Greece, Stella St John served teas to vagrants under Charing Cross station. She was volunteering in the Hungerford Club, helping the homeless who had been refused entry to nearby bomb shelters – people deemed too dirty, too stigmatised, too 'down and out', to spend the night beside other residents of London sheltering from the bombs during the last weeks of the Blitz. The Club had been created by Westminster Council and was staffed by Christian pacifists as a 'public health' measure, after objections to the presence of long-term homeless men and women in the public shelters. As the bombs came down, Stella's nights were busy. Alongside working in the Hungerford Club, her veterinary work and the Fellowship of Reconciliation, she also volunteered as an ambulance driver in Marylebone, ferrying the maimed and wounded to hospital. There was hardly time to rest, let alone sleep, as the war came home.

The Battle of Britain of the summer of 1940 had given way over the following months to intense bombing. In early September, during an unusually warm late-summer night, the raids had been stepped up a gear, as 250 planes descended on the docks of east London and unleashed their bombs. This was merely the beginning. In September and October that year more than 20,000 bombs were dropped on the London area alone, with other cities across the country suffering similarly.[1] In the first month of the Blitz, just over 7,000 civilians – men, women and children – were killed in Britain, and 40,000 civilians would die between September 1940 and May 1941. Cities all over the country were smashed to pieces, houses and factories destroyed, their populations maimed and made homeless. If the 1930s had been marked by fear of total war from the air, that war had now arrived.

The British state, along with countless voluntary organisations and millions of individuals, responded on a scale seldom seen before or since, providing shelter, food and blankets to those who had no homes to go to, caring for those who had been injured and keeping a lookout for more German attacks. As Vera Brittain wrote after her own home had been damaged by bombing, 'the front line is part of our daily lives; its dugouts and first aid posts are in every street, its trenches and encampments occupy sections of every city park and every village green'.[2] This is the Blitz of popular memory, of being all in it together. But beneath the calls for mutual sacrifice there was a sea of inequality; not everyone was welcome in the shelters after all, and not everyone was 'in this together' in the same way. As Stella served up tea to the homeless she was standing at the uneven edges of collective solidarity, and it was along these edges that Stella and others opposed to war but committed to helping their fellow citizens tried to find their way.

As soon as the Blitz began, it became abundantly clear that the shelters built in Britain's parks and back gardens were inadequate. A poll taken in July 1940 had shown that 45 per cent of respondents had no access to domestic shelters.[3] When the Blitz started, the heaviest bombing was concentrated in the working-class East End of London, but the deepest and safest shelters were in the west of the city, and every night saw a mass trek across and out of the city as people searched for safety. The plush Savoy Hotel, just a few hundred yards from the Hungerford Club, had a particularly well-appointed shelter, leading to demonstrations from those denied entry and with nowhere secure to go. In the first weeks of the Blitz, the government had refused to open up the Underground stations, but the flood of people and their need were unstoppable, and officials soon gave in. At the peak over 120,000 people were using the deep shelters every night.[4]

By October 1940 nearly a quarter of a million Londoners were already homeless, and two months later, following three months of raids, over 30,000 London homes were uninhabitable.[5] Rest Centres were established by local councils under the Victorian-era

Poor Law for those with nowhere else to go, but there were not always enough blankets, toilets or food to go around. The public shelters were also far from salubrious. Conditions inside, particularly to begin with, were often unsanitary, with dirty bedding spread across floors, as thousands of people crowded in with not enough water, ventilation or toilets. Clementine Churchill, wife of the Prime Minister, visited one shelter and recoiled, describing the 'cold, wet, dirt, darkness and stench'.[6] There were bitter complaints that many of the people in them were drunk and ridden with lice. War had thrown people together in a bid for safety, and revealed an unpleasant underside.

Herbert Morrison, the Labour Party politician and wartime Cabinet minister, was brought in to sort it out. Morrison was born into a working-class south London family and had come of age politically in the ILP, becoming a conscientious objector in the First World War. In the years since, leaving the ILP behind, he had forged a reputation as a formidable and pragmatic politician with the ability to get things done, becoming Home Secretary in 1940. He was now determined to clean up the shelters.[7] On Morrison's watch, animals, smoking, musical instruments and cooking were all banned. So too were those whose 'person or clothing is offensively unclean or verminous'.[8] Hundreds of thousands of people were now homeless, but long-term vagrants, rather than becoming recognised as participating in a common experience, were further cast out. And this is where a small group of Christian pacifists stepped in.

Early in the Blitz, Bernard Nicholls was working in the crypt of St Martin-in-the-Fields, just off Trafalgar Square. The coffins had been cleared out to make a social club for soldiers, designed to keep them away from the other temptations of the West End. As the bombs fell, Bernard was approached for help by Fred Copeman, who ran the deep shelters for Westminster Council. Copeman was an unusual figure to occupy such a significant role in a Conservative-run borough. A 'great bull of a man' and a former heavyweight boxer, ten years previously he had been one of the leaders of the Invergordon Mutiny, when for two days the sailors of the Atlantic Fleet moored off the north coast of Scotland refused orders in protest over a pay cut.[9] A Communist Party activist, Copeman had then volunteered with the International Brigades during the Spanish Civil War and been wounded during the battle of Jarama, but his experiences left him disillusioned with the party and he converted to Roman Catholicism. Somehow, with the onset of war in Britain, Copeman was put in charge of providing shelter to the thousands of people who flocked to Westminster for refuge. It was his job to find the vagrants somewhere to bed down safely, but he could not persuade any of his own wardens to take them on. He turned to the Anglican Pacifist Service Unit for help, where Bernard Nicholls was working underneath St Martin-in-the-Fields.

The Blitz had re-energised the pacifist movement, as the suffering and rubble on the streets brought new opportunities for service close to home.[10] But Britain's cities were not the only places to be bombed. Winston Churchill declared that there was one thing that would defeat Hitler: 'an absolutely devastating, exterminating attack by very heavy bombers from this country upon the Nazi homeland'.[11] In the years to come, raids on the city of Hamburg set off a firestorm that killed around 37,000 people, the vast majority of them civilians. Dresden and Berlin, not to mention Tokyo, would suffer a similar fate. The PPU found a new lease of life in opposing the bombings, with Vera Brittain writing several pamphlets and addressing a regular *Letter to Peace Lovers*, setting out the case against the slaughter of civilians.[12] Night bombing was seen as particularly indiscriminate and became the focus of the campaign. Although Vera's publisher refused to take a longer book on the subject, she found a new press and in the US the book was distributed by the Fellowship of Reconciliation, gaining widespread, if often hostile, attention.[13]

As the campaign against bombing grew over the spring of 1941, it repeated controversies associated with the protests against the Allied blockade of occupied Europe, where the breaking of crucial supply chains exacerbated poor harvests, resulting in widespread hunger, especially in Belgium, Holland, Poland and Greece.[14] The PPU had established the Food Relief Campaign, with Vera Brittain among those in the lead. A non-pacifist Famine Relief Committee, led by George Bell, the Bishop of Chichester, had more direct access to government. For those behind the relief campaigns, the issue was fundamentally humanitarian, and it was the height of hypocrisy to condemn the Nazis but turn a blind eye to the starvation caused, directly or indirectly, by Allied policies.[15] The protests angered many pacifists as well as those who supported the Allied war effort. For some pacifists, the campaign sought not to oppose the war outright but merely to alleviate its effects. Middleton Murry refused to give it publicity in *Peace News*, seeing it as a distraction from the pacifist cause because it had little chance of success. For those behind the war, the campaign simply echoed Nazi propaganda, and seemed to ignore German responsibility for the suffering. Within government circles, the campaign fell largely on deaf ears, with the British Cabinet insisting that it was the occupying power's responsibility to look after civilians.[16]

The campaign to end night bombing was similarly bitterly criticised by both pacifists and non-pacifists.[17] For absolute pacifists, it simply tinkered at the edges of war. For non-pacifists, the campaign was either naive or complicit with Fascism; George Orwell wrote, characteristically, that 'all the talk of "limiting" or "humanising" war is humbug'.[18] For Orwell, and many others since, war is nasty and brutish, if not always short, and it was foolish and dangerous to think that violence could be made softer, gentler and more caring. In the US, the criticisms of Vera Brittain were particularly virulent, with President Roosevelt going out of his way to oppose her arguments, and the *New York Herald Tribune* accusing her of regurgitating Nazi propaganda.[19] It was Vera's call for compassion and forgiveness that seemed to draw the greatest ire. Hindsight would be, partly at least, more favourable, as controversy over the large scale of the bombing of German cities would rumble on, largely unresolved, for decades to come.[20]

In London, Bernard Nicholls and his friends jumped at the chance to help the down-and-outs. They also knew precisely where the shelter could be made. Hungerford Lane was a narrow alley made up of high brick arches reaching below Charing Cross station. The arches had once been used as stables and wine vaults, but by the late 1930s had already been appropriated by some of the homeless men and women of London, who lit fires at night, filling the vaults with smoke. Working with Nicholls, Westminster Council quickly requisitioned Arch 173, and made space for 120 men and women, installing bathrooms, a canteen and a medical aid post, and lining the walls with bunk beds stacked three tiers high. A partition divided the main part from a small women's section, and the internal walls were painted, with the occasional picture hanging on the wall. The Hungerford Club became the shelter for the people that no one else wanted.

Bernard turned to his wife Doris and the 'girls' at the Fellowship of Reconciliation to help with the food; pacifists were just as liable as the rest of the population to make assumptions about women's work. Stella St John was by then staying at Donald Soper's Kingsway Hall, where young residents ran a breakfast club for people emerging from the shelter of Holborn station before they headed to work or to see what was left of their homes.[21] At the Hungerford Club, Stella made sandwiches, tea and soup, as well as a kind of milk pudding and porridge for breakfast. Pathé News footage of the Hungerford Club shows groups of men shuffling down the alley, reading newspapers with a magnifying glass and occasionally grinning toothless smiles. For a brief moment there is a shot of a young woman in a patterned dress who looks like Stella, standing behind a rough wooden table surrounded by steaming urns.

Alongside Stella, Doris and Bernard Nicholls, other volunteers included Sydney Greaves, who was born into an Anglican family from Birmingham that had been very upset when he registered as a conscientious objector.[22] At his tribunal Greaves was given exemption on the condition that he continue with his job in local government, but he had asked for an unconditional exemption, and immediately quit in protest, objecting to being directed at all by the tribunal. For Greaves, conscience was always unconditional. When the bombing of Britain's cities started, he was in church and heard somebody over his left shoulder say, 'You will go to London.' He remembered these words, apparently coming from nowhere, as 'a remarkable experience, very distinct, and I was not frightened, I felt at peace'.[23] In all the letters, diaries and memoirs of conscientious objectors, it is extremely rare to find such an unequivocal voice of conscience – if that is what it was – as that heard by Sydney, speaking so clearly and directly. Sydney ended up at the Hungerford Club, where he was put in charge of the first-aid post, learning on the job from a volunteer nurse from Charing Cross Hospital. But Greaves was now breaking the conditions laid down by his tribunal – he was supposed to be back in the Midlands working in local government – and was sent to Wormwood Scrubs for a period of hard labour.[24]

The volunteers were completely immersed in the work in the shelter. As Sydney observed, 'it was totally absorbing. Time off really didn't exist ...'[25] Stella arrived at the Club straight from work, prepared dinner, stayed the night and made breakfast the next morning before heading back to work.[26] Although by now well into her thirties, Stella had never met people like this: people she described as 'dirty, drunk or objectionable ... cranks, neurotics'.[27] Sydney later recalled that the women – who made up around one in twenty of the people sleeping under the arches – were especially 'pitiable creatures'.[28] While the men played games and joked, many of the women would try and put up curtains around their bunks and close themselves off from the rest of the world.[29]

The pacifists at the Hungerford Club were confronted with a scale of poverty and desperation they had not come across before. Bernard recalled that he 'was astonishingly innocent' until he worked under the arches.[30] Many of the men and women who made their way there had been hit hard by the economic and social stresses of the 1930s. They included a Canadian deserter who later committed suicide, a woman known as 'Bundles' because she wore bags and sacks for clothes, and a self-proclaimed murderer.[31] There is a sketch from the time by an unknown artist, showing a former cobbler nicknamed 'Professor Joad' – after the well-known academic and radio presenter – because of his large vocabulary and love of long words. 'Joad' is sitting slumped in a chair with a walking stick between his knees, whiskers sprouting from his chin, a hat pulled down over his ears and coat dragging on the floor. Doris Nicholls later recalled another 'poor chap' who had contracted syphilis after 'going with a tart for two pence on Hampstead Heath when he was eleven' and ended up infecting his wife, who threw him out, from which point he drifted into alcoholism.[32]

The accounts of life in the shelter from the volunteers have a slightly romantic air at times, with the homeless men and women portrayed as tragic and otherworldly figures, reduced to stereotypes. There were almost certainly many deep and lasting interactions that went unrecorded, but the space between the volunteers and those in need seems wide, pity leading to separation rather than drawing people together. This was a pattern that could be seen repeatedly in pacifist humanitarian work throughout the war, and indeed in much humanitarian work elsewhere, the complex lives of those being helped turned into a one-dimensional need for food and shelter, as barriers of language, culture and prosperity, as well as the urgency of immediate demands, stand in the way of more open engagements.[33]

None of this is to say that the volunteers did not try to understand the lives of the people they helped, and there were some very notable exceptions to the general rule, as pity sometimes turned into compassion and even a kind of friendship. Doris Nicholls later recalled, 'I was terrified to start with ... But it turned out to be one of life's richest experiences.'[34] Most of her evenings at the Club were taken up with sitting on the men's and women's bunks, listening to them talk about the things they had seen and done. In her first months there, Doris had tried to wear the most rough-and-ready clothes she could find, but soon decided that this was dishonest, a form of 'make-believe'.[35] Some gaps remained.

It was hard to ease suffering that was so socially entrenched and long-term. Compassion had its limits as a form of practical action and could sometimes be dangerous. In an attempt to help, Bernard once gave an alcoholic with intense stomach problems a dose of medicine so strong that it would have killed him had the man not become violently sick immediately afterwards. Looking back, Bernard recalled that 'one had no cause to be proud of oneself in this sort of way'.[36] It was stressful work for everyone. Bernard's health began to suffer and he was eventually advised to take time off to recover, moving to a house in the country to convalesce.[37] There could also be trouble; many of the residents had severe mental-health or drink problems, and every now and again could become physically aggressive. This inevitably presented an issue for the pacifists. Bernard kept a blacklist of people who came in 'dead drunk' and created 'havoc', but this could not keep all troublemakers out, and if the point of the Club was to provide shelter to those most in need, it was hard to abandon anyone in distress.[38] Stella later recounted how when people did get violent, she learned to 'hang on to them'.[39] On one occasion they had to frogmarch a man out of the shelter, before slamming the door on him and shouting, 'No more tonight. Keep out!' Doris immediately felt guilty, as it was freezing cold outside. Forty years later, she looked back at this episode and concluded that 'even in love, choices have to be made ... I think until then it had all been fairly black and white. But the realities of the situation drove one's thinking deeper and deeper ... we learned fairly quickly not to be arrogant ...'[40] There was humility in working with the homeless.

It was lice not fights that presented the biggest challenge. Bed bugs, ticks and other insects were everywhere, burrowing, biting and infecting their hosts as they fed on their blood. Bernard Nicholls recalled taking off one man's clothes: when 'we got down to the man's naked skin, I was absolutely horrified . . . All the outside skin, on this man's back particularly, had gone and the whole of his back from his neck to his buttocks was just a wet, pussy mass.'[41] Many nights were spent picking through and fumigating infested clothes, hair and skin. Bugs were everywhere.

The government was particularly concerned that lice would spread typhus. In the trenches of the First World War lice had spread disease and discomfort on a massive scale, and the bodies tightly packed into often insanitary new overnight shelters were a public health disaster waiting to happen. A mile north of the Hungerford Club, Professor Patrick 'Buggy' Buxton, an entomologist who had learned his trade in Palestine and Samoa, was determined to find a solution, working at the London School of Hygiene and Tropical Medicine testing new ways to prevent infestations.[42] Looking for a regular source of insects on which he could run experiments, Buxton turned to the Hungerford Club; clothes were collected and sent to the labs up the road, where they 'meticulously went over every inch', picking out the lice. On one set of clothes they found a record 15,000 insects.[43]

The Hungerford Club became so good at delousing that the supply for the medical researchers dried up. Professor Buxton and his team then had an idea. Would the Christian pacifist volunteers like to breed lice on their own bodies? Bernard, Doris and Sydney – but not Stella, for reasons that are not clear – leaped at the opportunity. Small open pill boxes were tightly fastened to their legs and arms, allowing the lice to grow and feed on their skin but somehow staying confined within the container. When fat enough, the insects were sent to the lab. Sydney Greaves later estimated that he bred thousands of insects in this way, five or six boxes at a time.[44] The newly married Bernard and Doris shared a small flat off the Lambeth Road with two other volunteers, and when they first moved in the mattresses and carpets were, somewhat ironically, already infested with fleas. They soon made matters worse when Bernard dropped one of the pill boxes on their bedroom floor, lice running everywhere. Doris was asked to help test a new insecticide by infecting herself with lice, spraying on the chemicals and then not washing or changing her underwear for three days. She became 'itchier and itchier' and was amazed at how quickly the lice found their way to the damper parts of her body.[45]

The small-scale acts of sacrifice and mutual aid were part of a much wider picture. Through the Blitz and beyond, the British government was faced with the question of how to change a largely civilian society into one that was capable of withstanding wave after wave of bombing.[46] This required a mass mobilisation, not just on behalf of the state, but also by voluntary organisations, as the government promoted the idea that everyone was on the front line.[47] Over 1.4 million people were recruited into Civil Defence, working as air-raid wardens, fire watchers and in the Auxiliary Ambulance Service.[48] Volunteers, like those at the Hungerford Club, also provided shelter, food and rest for those in need. The Friends Ambulance Unit sent young men and women to run the Rest Centres across London, agreeing for the first time to allow women to join, and suffering their first casualty of the war when a volunteer called Norman Booth was killed by shrapnel from a falling bomb.[49]

Although some pacifists saw this work as indirectly contributing to the war effort, many more were happy, even eager, to volunteer. Stella, Doris and Bernard were among thousands of volunteers, conscientious objectors and otherwise, who came forward to help, trying in some way to be of service. Vera Brittain was convinced that pacifists had a responsibility to help the communities in which they lived 'rather than remain so self-righteously pure'.[50] She helped to set up a short-lived scheme to evacuate children to Canada and Australia, as well volunteering occasionally at Kingsley Hall and a shelter run by the FAU, serving soup from a van in the streets of the East End.[51] Other conscientious objectors set up social work units in Liverpool, Manchester and London.[52] In Sheffield, Dr Kenneth Mallenby, a former student of Professor Buxton, was conducting his own experiments with conscientious objectors, injecting scabies mites under their skin, placing them on starvation diets and asking them to go for months without calcium until their hair and nails fell out.[53] There were many ways to be of service.

*

While he was waiting to be called up to the Non-Combatant Corps, Roy Ridgway had joined the FAU. He was now betwixt and between: his claim of conscience denied but the army yet to send him his orders. In the meantime, he went to work as an orderly at Orpington Hospital, where Kent merges into London and not far from where Stella St John had grown up. Orpington had started life as a First World War military hospital for Canadian troops, and had since been requisitioned to look after the wounded of the Blitz. By the early spring of 1941 the wards were filling up. Roy later recalled that his days were taken up sorting 'out the living from the dead from the Blitz – young children, women, all sorts . . . I was more convinced than ever that war was a terrible evil.'[54] It was not just the wounded he had to deal with; even in suburban Kent, the sounds of the bombing through the night could be terrifying. Roy's colleagues tried to drown out the noise by playing the piano, and Roy noticed that as he lit his cigarettes, his hands were shaking.[55] When the first ambulance came in at 9.45 one evening, it carried a pregnant woman with one eye out, a crushed hand and her nose blown away. Her twelve-year-old daughter was already dead by the time she arrived at the hospital. 'I shall never forget this night. I didn't expect to be alive in the morning. The noise of the planes diving sent a cold shiver down my spine,' Roy wrote.[56]

Within a few weeks, Roy was physically and emotionally exhausted, and he fainted in an operating theatre.[57] He spent the next few days in bed, his temperature rising to 102 as he was wracked by hallucinations and the doctors tried to work out what was wrong with him. For a time they thought it was scarlet fever or meningitis, but it became clear that the problem was not entirely physical. This was the first time the young man had come face to face with death and injury on any scale, and Roy later recalled that he had 'cracked up', losing the will to live.[58] It took another young volunteer, sitting at his bedside, to help him come out the other side. In hindsight, Roy would see this period of 'going through hell' as a turning point in his ability to cope with a crisis.

After his recovery, Roy left Orpington and headed west, where he went to work with another FAU team at Gloucester City General Hospital, emptying bedpans, fetching meals and wheeling bodies to the morgue.[59] The hospital had cared for many of the wounded soldiers evacuated from Dunkirk, and to begin with the hospital staff had been slightly hostile to the conscientious objectors sweeping their floors.[60] There was a campaign from a local councillor to have them sacked, but that was quickly overruled by the city Mayor, who said the pacifists were both welcome and needed. Michael Cadbury who had been with Tom Burns in Finland and Norway, had also found his way to Gloucester, but the team was led by Stephen Verney, a deeply religious Anglican and great-nephew of Florence Nightingale. Roy clearly admired Verney and enjoyed his company, the two men often discussing philosophy and concluding that 'If you seek happiness it eludes you ... the joy of life is the joy of struggle ... the ultimate power in the universe is love.'[61] They also attended services together in the splendour of Gloucester Cathedral; by this time Roy had decided he was not a Christian, but thought the services beautiful and admired Christ as someone 'who came as near to perfection as anyone who has ever lived'.[62] As they sat and talked, Verney gently tried to persuade Roy to agree to the conditional decision of his tribunal, but Roy was determined to persevere with seeking an unconditional exemption, no matter where that took him.[63]

As important as Verney was, Roy's closest friend at the hospital was Bernard Llewellyn, a graduate of the London School of Economics. The two young men spent weekends hitchhiking around the country, often going to visit Roy's grandmother in not too distant Abergavenny. Roy's health had clearly improved, and he found time to take a local woman called Helen to the cinema.[64] Evenings were spent reading Huxley, Middleton Murry, Jung and Chinese philosophy. Roy and Bernard both read the theologian Reinhold Niebuhr, who had renounced his pacifism with the rise of Fascism, and Bernard told his friend that it left him in a confused state and made him realise that 'he admired the men who sincerely believed they were fighting for a just cause'.[65]

Volunteering for Civil Defence or other related work on the Home Front created conundrums for pacifists.[66] Civil Defence had started out as a civilian duty, separate and distinct from military conscription, and organised through local councils.[67] But if all citizens were expected to play their part in a total war, the line between military and civilian life, between protesting and participating in the war effort, could be hard to see. As the war impacted on the Home Front, it was not just ambulance workers on the battlefields of Europe and north Africa who had to find a way to make a distinction. Increasing levels of compulsion were also gradually introduced into the domestic labour market. The government already had sweeping powers to tell the population what to do under the Emergency Powers (Defence) Act 1940, and over the following months Herbert Morrison, as Home Secretary, introduced compulsory fire-watching and made refusing a Civil Defence order a criminal offence. By April 1941, nearly all conscientious objectors were liable to be called up to the full-time Civil Defence Force.[68] Importantly, there was no right of conscientious objection to such orders.

As they sought to help their fellow citizens on the Home Front, conscientious objectors were increasingly pulled into the war effort. For the Central Board for Conscientious Objectors 'the total requirements of a world war with only limited man-power have all contributed to decay the civil and humanitarian basis upon which the CD [Civil Defence] services were erected. More and more those services tended to become a military cog in the war machine.'[69] Early in the Blitz Bernard Nicholls had worked helping to rescue people from bomb-damaged buildings, but was then criticised at his tribunal for being a hypocrite for working so closely with the air-raid wardens.[70] He was already more than aware of the tensions. Occasionally when clearing the ruins he found household pets, some of them so badly injured 'we used to drown the poor things in a bucket of water if that was the kindest thing to do'.[71] One cat, determined to live, kept on jumping out of the bucket; Bernard put his foot on the cat's neck, and for him it was a sobering moment of self-realisation: 'one could easily be terribly sentimental about all this bringing out all the best in people and so on. It simultaneously brought near to the surface a lot of the worst.'[72] Forty years later, he reflected that 'Real life is a matter of dilemmas and paradoxes . . . and there are no simple answers.'[73] Acting conscientiously often did not bring a sense of moral clarity.

Fire-watching was particularly controversial.[74] Roy often spent the night on lookout duty on the roof of the Gloucester General Hospital, and Derricke Ridgway fire-watched in the City of London, while Alfred, to his unease, watched over an RAF arms depot.[75] On the one hand, this was work that prevented homes going up in flames and people burning to death. On the other hand, fire-watching was explicitly said by the government to be a valuable contribution to the war effort. The Fellowship of Reconciliation decided to take no position on whether members should fire-watch, but after equivocating the PPU gradually moved to support refusal.[76] Denis Hayes, the editor of the *CBCO Bulletin*, was jailed for refusing fire-watching duties in 1942.[77] By 1943, a total of 227 men and 35 women had been prosecuted for fire-watching offences linked to issues of conscience – some refusing to register on the grounds that they objected to compulsion, others because looking out for fires would be assisting the war machine.[78] In contrast, there were others who saw fire-watching as part of their pacifist duty to prevent suffering. As one conscientious objector put it, 'I mean, if a fire breaks out it has to be put out no matter who started it . . .'[79] Stella St John felt the same. She was determined to do her part: 'It is impossible to opt completely out of war work – by paying taxes, eating food brought in a convoy, you can't opt out. You can just do the best you can.'[80]

Roy argued bitterly with his brother Derricke over what compromises had to be made. Roy increasingly saw himself as necessarily complicit in the war, and although he chafed at the idea of conditions being set on his conscience, he still wanted to go out into the world and help people, whereas Derricke was determined to strike out alone. As far as Roy was concerned, there was a 'war on, whether we approve or not'.[81] One warm summer evening, while staying with their granny in Abergavenny, Derricke announced that he 'despised man' and was going to 'live on his own in the heart of the countryside' as it was no use trying to make the world a better place. Roy was tempted by his brother's pessimism, but argued 'nevertheless we must not run away from life – we must grapple with all the problems of life . . . we must live with people and we must try to understand people'.[82] If treading the pacifist path was difficult for Roy, he was determined to confront head-on the challenges he met on the way.

Through 1941 and 1942, after serving teas under Charing Cross during the day, Stella also worked as a voluntary ambulance driver during the night, wearing a peaked cap and dark-blue uniform. The ambulance work – helping those injured by falling buildings, exploding bombs or raging fires – was dangerous and exhausting, but Stella later downplayed it, noting, 'We had a lot of quiet nights when nothing happened and others when it did.'[83] But when it did happen, a lot happened. The nights were often bloody and gruesome, with the crew tying together broken limbs, using helmets to hold in gaping intestines or transporting rat-eaten bodies to the large refrigeration unit at Billingsgate Fish Market.[84] Ambulance Station 39, where Stella worked, was in the West End of London, just off Marylebone High Street. It might have escaped the extensive damage further east, but it saw plenty of bombs fall. One night the ambulance crew were called to the nearby BBC studio after a warden spotted a mine floating down slowly towards the roof. The crew arrived just in time to see the police officer on duty decapitated by the explosion.[85]

Stella's station was run for a time by 'Lady' Josephine Butler, who soon resigned in disgrace after being revealed as a fantasist and black marketeer, having invented a clandestine organisation called the 'Pimpernel' – supposedly working undercover in occupied Belgium – and used it to raise funds fraudulently from sympathisers.[86] After serving time in jail, Butler re-emerged after the war peddling a book in which she claimed to have been part of a top-secret spy ring run directly by Winston Churchill.[87] Also working alongside Stella were two male conscientious objectors – one of whom also attended Kingsway Hall – and the writer Rose Macaulay. Macaulay was a friend of Virginia Woolf and, although now largely forgotten, at the time was one of the most celebrated writers of her generation. During the war, she was technically too old to continue as an ambulance driver, but, pulling strings, somehow managed to stay on, enjoying the companionship of the other women and the exciting work, driving through the dark and rubble-strewn streets. Macaulay had been a leading pacifist writer of the 1930s and a sponsor of the PPU, but reluctantly came to see the war as the lesser of two evils, while remaining deeply opposed to violence. She wrote of the 'blind, maniac, primitive, stupid bestiality of war, into which human beings periodically leap, spitting in civilisation's face and putting her to confused rout'.[88] As it was for Stella, ambulance work was Rose's way of protesting against war without cutting herself off.

By early 1942 anyone performing ambulance duties was obliged to carry out at least forty-eight hours of work every four weeks. Stella objected – not to ambulance work itself, but being forced to do it. She wrote to the ambulance service arguing that for the past eighteen months she had done at least forty-eight hours every month, but also declaring, 'I am not prepared to accept the principle of compulsion for war purposes, but must retain the right at all times to act according to my conscience as a Christian pacifist.'[89] The London Ambulance Service disagreed.

Stella St John had drawn her line in the sand.

CHAPTER 13

Prisoners of Conscience

Roy Ridgway was in administrative limbo, between having his claim for unconditional exemption rejected and being called up into the Non-Combatant Corps. It would only ever be a temporary pause. When the order came he would have two options. He could quietly accept it and do as he was told. Or he could refuse. And refusing came at a cost: prison. Determined to stick to his unconditional position unless something changed, Roy was now heading to jail. The question was what the threat of punishment would do to him. While he did not want to go to war, he did not want to spend the next few years behind bars. He could remain absolutely committed to his principles and refuse to accept any conditions, but that could risk looking like a self-centred martyrdom wallowing in its own suffering. And, more importantly, shut away in jail he would be denied opportunities to fight for principles he thought important and to help those in need.

During the First World War, around a third of conscientious objectors, or about 6,000 people, had ended up in prison.[1] Their treatment was tough. While there, they were sentenced to hard labour, and the rule of silence – where speaking was forbidden – forced prisoners to communicate with each other by tapping on pipes.[2] The diet was bread and water, alternating with bread, porridge, peas and gruel. Some had been paraded naked, faced mock executions, dragged through ditches on the end of a rope, clad in irons so tight it cut off the circulation, or tied to barbed wire.[3] There had been hunger strikes and forced feedings. It is claimed that sixty-eight imprisoned conscientious objectors died and thirty-nine 'went mad as a direct or indirect result of their treatment'.[4] After the war, Fenner Brockway – who had spent eighteen months in prison for refusing to fight, the last eight months in solitary – helped to write a report using these experiences to reveal the more systematic brutality of British jails, a report which is now acknowledged as a major document in penal reform.[5] In the US, although the numbers were smaller, treatment could be equally harsh, with life sentences and even the death sentence a frequent occurrence, although these were later commuted.[6]

By the Second World War about one in ten conscientious objectors were sent to jail, but there were many different routes there. You could refuse to register at all; you could refuse to do as told by the tribunal; you could refuse to attend the military medical; or you could refuse to put on a military uniform. You could be sentenced by a civilian court or a court martial; and you could spend time in a civilian jail or in military detention. It was also possible to keep going in and out of prison indefinitely in a process known as 'cat and mouse'.[7] Stanley Hilton, a woodworker and French polisher who converted from Methodism to become a Jehovah's Witness just after the start of the war, appeared before five tribunals and courts martial and spent more than three years in prison.[8] Before his initial application was turned down Hilton told his first tribunal that 'my body is in your hands but my soul is my own'.[9] After being called up for military service, Hilton was arrested for going absent without leave. When his case returned to the tribunal it was rejected once more and he ended up in prison again. This happened time after time, with Hilton refusing to change his mind and the military and the Ministry of Labour equally determined not to compromise. Finally, he was granted exemption on condition he took up coal mining, the tribunal seemingly looking for the hardest job it could find. Hilton refused. This time, though, the Ministry seems either to have been too exhausted to carry on or simply to have lost interest, and it let Hilton be.

Roy was desperate to avoid Stanley Hilton's fate – going in and out of jail was not how he wanted to spend the war. Having lost his appeal, there seemed to be one remaining way out: to enter the army, refuse orders and then be sentenced to at least three months' imprisonment. He would then be entitled to return to the tribunal and make his case again, using his time behind bars as evidence of his commitment.[10] The three-month minimum sentence was key – without it there was no right to be reheard. This was a risky path to take where many things could go wrong in the maze of laws, regulations and punishments. Roy was putting himself at the mercy of the court martial, and his sentence would have to be finely calibrated: not so short that he would be forced to return again and again, and not so long that he would see out the rest of the war in prison.[11] Many courts martial passed sentences just below the threshold that allowed an appeal, or passed a sentence of detention, a lesser form of punishment that in practice could actually result in far harsher military discipline.[12] Courts martial were apparently reluctant to give three-month prison sentences, seeing them as an unwarranted ticket to exemption.[13] For Roy, getting just the right punishment would not be easy.

The medical was Roy's first encounter with military life. It was often a tense occasion, the first time when a conscientious objector was subjected to military control. Failure to turn up meant you were liable to up to two years' imprisonment in a civilian jail, and by the end of the war 3,000 conscientious objectors had been prosecuted in this way.[14] As the doctor placed his stethoscope on Roy's chest, the medic thought he could detect a slight murmur of the heart and, for a brief moment, it looked as if Roy would be rejected. But the doctor called on his colleagues and they decided it was not 'serious', passing Roy with an A1 grade, top marks. Roy was quietly pleased.[15] There were more tests to come.

Back at the Gloucester General Hospital, Stephen Verney suggested that Roy take the week off to prepare himself for military life and the seemingly inevitable time in prison that would follow. Roy wrote in his diary, 'I will not say I am not afraid at all ... The man who can say he has struck fear out of his heart is either a liar or a fool.'[16] The Ministry had a go at trying to accommodate Roy, and the man at the Labour Exchange asked him if he would consider joining the Auxiliary Fire Service.[17] He would not. Within days, Roy's enlistment papers arrived and he was ordered to present himself before the Commanding Officer at Number 3 Training Centre, Esplanade Hotel, Ilfracombe, Devon. The letter said, 'Welcome to His Majesty's Army ... You are about to become a soldier.' Roy wrote in his diary, 'I am not unduly worried. I shall probably spend Christmas in prison.'[18] The Non-Combatant Corps was calling.

The north Devon seaside resort of Ilfracombe, with its large

Victorian hotels, had been turned over to training the Non-Combatant and Pioneer Corps, made up of conscientious objectors, 'aliens' and those deemed not physically fit enough to take up combat duties.[19] For the first few years of the war the Pioneer Corps was the only branch of the British military that foreign citizens were allowed to join, while the Non-Combatant Corps was an unarmed unit designed especially for conscientious objectors and was perhaps unsurprisingly the lowest-status part of the military. In the course of the war just under 7,000 conscientious objectors joined its ranks.[20] Roy found Ilfracombe a strange and fascinating place, far removed from its normal life as a holiday town: 'Almost the whole of the Vienna Symphony Orchestra were there. I saw Arthur Koestler sweeping the NAAFI and looking utterly miserable.' Koestler, whose novel of totalitarian imprisonment, *Darkness at Noon*, was published in English that year, was a refugee from occupied Europe and had joined the Pioneer Corps.[21] For him, Ilfracombe meant being part of a 'motley crowd' doing foot drill on the promenade, a 'freakish assembly' of foreign doctors, lawyers and architects going through military exercises but kept separate from the British recruits. A conscientious objector who passed through at the same time described it as being full of 'university students, school masters, young dons from Oxford and Cambridge . . . Talk is mostly on the Big Subjects, art and life, literature, truth and philosophy.'[22]

Alongside the exiles and would-be intellectuals in Ilfracombe were 'Plymouth Brethren, Four Square Gospellers, Jehovah's Witnesses' who largely kept to themselves, having little contact even with other conscientious objectors.[23] The members of relatively inward-looking religious sects seemed to have little in common with the other conscientious objectors and exiles, who found them just as baffling as the judges at the tribunal. These people were usually not pacifists in any narrow sense. They simply wanted little to do with the ungodly wars and they also had no desire to change the world through human sweat and tears, but were waiting for God to intervene. Although making up a sizeable proportion of those applying for exemption, they moved in a very different moral and social world from other conscientious objectors.

When Roy arrived in Ilfracombe, he was immediately asked to put on a uniform, and when he declined was escorted to a room in the attic of a nearby hotel that had been taken over by the army as a military holding centre. In the neighbouring rooms were two other conscientious objectors, an actor and friend of John Gielgud called John Lindsay, who had been in and out of prison multiple times, and 'another fellow who was interested in Eastern religions'.[24] Roy's makeshift jail had views out over the open expanse of the Bristol Channel, and that night Roy wrote in his diary, 'I wonder what will happen tomorrow?'[25]

The next day Roy was charged with 'disobeying an order' and marched to the Commanding Officer, who gave him another day to think about his actions. Like the Ministry of Labour, the British army was giving Roy plenty of chances to back down. But when dawn came the next day, he again left the khakis sitting on the chair and was brought back before the Commanding Officer. This time, Roy refused to say anything but 'yes' or 'no'. Three more days passed, and a chaplain made a visit to Roy's room, trying gently to cajole him into changing his mind. Another week went by and not much happened, apart from Roy catching a cold and the FAU writing a letter to the army emphasising that if Roy was imprisoned for a minimum of three months, his case could go back before the tribunal.[26] They were essentially pleading for help. Finally, twelve days after first refusing to put on his uniform, Roy appeared before a court martial and was sentenced to three months in prison. This came as a considerable relief. The door had been left open just the right amount. Roy noted that all the other conscientious objectors in Ilfracombe had first been forced to serve an often difficult period of detention before receiving the three-month sentence.[27] As well as not providing the right to appear again before the tribunal, a shorter sentence was far tougher in practice and involved hard labour. Roy was made uncomfortable by the seemingly lenient treatment, later recalling that 'I felt a bit guilty, conscience stricken about this.'[28] The two other conscientious objectors with him 'really went through hell' coming back from detention 'after 20 or 28 days ... absolutely a shadow of themselves, worn out and weary and ill'. Roy could not help but think 'how lucky I was', later concluding that his sentence was probably because the officers approved of the work he had been doing with the FAU while he waited for his call up to the army.[29]

The first days of Roy's sentence were spent back in the

Esplanade Hotel as the army prepared to send him to Exeter jail, and he was set to work scrubbing the hotel floors. By now he had made his point and agreed to put on his military uniform in order to save his civilian clothes from the grime and dirt.[30] Other pacifists were rallying round him by this time, and someone from FAU headquarters wrote to Roy's mother, declaring that they were sure Roy would 'come through it stronger and better'.[31] Michael Cadbury wrote that he admired the 'stand' Roy was making.[32] Three weeks into his sentence Roy received a letter from his friend Bernard Llewellyn: 'I do hope, old man, your lot has not been too hard. I thought once I should have had to tread that path, but it seems I was lucky.'[33] Bernard was shortly to take the boat out to China, to serve with a new FAU group ferrying medicine and providing first aid. It was exactly the sort of work in faraway places that Roy was hoping to land when he was released from prison, but for now he had to wait.

Roy was soon diagnosed with a case of scabies caught in Gloucester and was transferred to a military hospital. This was not an entirely caring environment, and he got into trouble with the Sergeant Major after complaining about the food, and was called 'yellow' for refusing to take up arms.[34] The Anglican Chaplain also came to visit Roy's bedside, explaining that he would like to castrate all Germans without an anaesthetic.[35] Other visitors were more sympathetic, and Roy became slightly embarrassed when a Quaker came to sit next to him and read the Bible, feeling he did not deserve all the attention.

Then something surprising happened. Roy received a letter telling him that his sentence of ninety-three days' imprisonment had been turned into twenty-eight days of detention, time he had already served.[36] The formally lesser sentence also meant that he would not be able to go back to the tribunal after all, and instead could face years of going in and out of jails, just like Stanley Hilton. His plans in disarray, Roy immediately wrote to his Commanding Officer in protest, but was released from hospital and sent back to his attic room overlooking the sea, only this time he was free to leave. The Non-Combatant Corps seemed to be just as surprised as Roy by the early release, and for a week no one gave him any orders at all.[37] Ironically, this was the worst of all worlds. He was not in prison but was not absolved of his duties. Instead, he was ignored.

Without any orders, there was no way he could refuse to cooperate and therefore no way he could be sent back to prison on his path to freedom. Instead, his days were taken up walking along the sea front, worrying about why no one had written to him and wondering what to do next.[38]

Then Roy had an idea: to hitchhike to London and see his mum and dad, hoping to be arrested on the way for going absent without leave. He caught a lift with an army officer but did not have the nerve to reveal himself as going AWOL and sat terrified in the passenger seat all the way, making it to London without being stopped.[39] It is not clear what he expected, but he did not get a warm welcome when he entered the family home. His dad was furious with him, perhaps because he had endangered his case, and perhaps because he risked embarrassing the family if the military police turned up at the door. In the face of his father's anger, Roy quickly sent a letter to the Commanding Officer in Ilfracombe, apologising for what he had done and stating that he was 'anxious to serve my country and fellow man in a manner consistent with my conscience'.[40] He added that he did not wish to be any trouble, and the army should not bother to send an escort to bring him back, as he would return in a few days. The letter was signed 'Your obedient servant'. Roy's rebellion clearly had limits, and back in the family home his dissenting conscience had become much more compliant.

The AWOL conscientious objector arrived back in Ilfracombe in the late afternoon, stepping off the train and reporting to the Sergeant Major who asked, 'Well, what am I supposed to do with you?'[41] It was a good question. The Non-Combatant Corps seemed simply to want to get rid of him, and Roy was gently warned that his choices could have undermined his case.[42] He spent three more weeks on the Devon coast, including Christmas and New Year, before being sent north to Liverpool, reflecting in his diary that 'Although I have had some unpleasant experiences, on the whole I have been treated fairly well.'[43] His new home for the immediate future was Centre Number 5, Pioneer Corps, Huyton, a former housing estate that had been used as an overcrowded internment camp for 'enemy aliens' earlier in the war. Roy was allowed out to walk around Liverpool, where he visited the Cathedral for the first time since he was a child. The Pioneer Corps Centre was dirty and cramped, with the drains constantly blocked. Roy heard a rumour that during its time as an internment camp some of the internees had committed suicide. Conditions had not greatly improved since.

Roy's fears that his reduced sentence meant he would have to return to the army proved unfounded. The army took matters into its own hands and quietly discharged him on the grounds that he was 'unlikely to become an efficient soldier'.[44] Roy had not been granted an unconditional exemption, but he had the next best thing. The military had had enough of him. Although not formally registered as a conscientious objector, he was released from his obligations to the Non-Combatant Corps, out of jail and out of the army. Most importantly, he could now return to the FAU. Roy wrote a quotation in his diary from the writer Winifred Holtby, a great friend of Vera Brittain: 'In life we have to choose between barren ease and rich interest – or rather one does not choose. Life somehow chooses.'[45]

Just as there were many ways to end up in prison, there were many different types of conscientious objectors in jail. The pacifists who ended up behind bars were often described as absolutists – a term of both abuse and praise – but they were absolute about many different things and in very different ways. There were those who saw prison as a defeat, and those who saw it as a victory. There were those who wanted to prove a point, and those who had been backed into a corner. There were libertarians who objected to any type of compulsion, military or not, and just wanted to be free to do what they wanted to do. There were pacifists who objected to any type of compromise with the 'war machine'. There were devout Christians, committed revolutionaries and sensitive humanitarians. And there were many people in between.

Alongside anarchists, revolutionary socialists and nationalists of various stripes, Jehovah's Witnesses like Stanley Hilton were particularly common among the prison population. Ernest Beavor, a Jehovah's Witness from London, wrote in his statement for exemption, 'Having consecrated my life wholly to the service of Jehovah the most High God, it is quite impossible for me to take up service for any person or thing without violating my covenant which would mean my everlasting destruction.'[46] The tribunal was unmoved by the possibility of damnation and sent Beavor and hundreds like him to Wormwood Scrubs and other prisons across the country.

For some, it was not God that they owed a loyalty to but their vocation. Michael Tippett had refused any form of alternative service that was not teaching and composing, arguing that his music was 'so strongly . . . tied up with matters of conscience that I can't divorce them'.[47] For Michael art was a deeply moral issue, and he was determined to go to the Scrubs rather than work on the land. He shared with Fred Urquhart the sense that war and conscription were anathema to creativity. Writing a letter to his friend Francesca Allinson, he declared that 'Mere social work won't replace the music – only pacifist witness against the whole madness can do so.'[48] But unlike Fred he was willing to go to jail to prove his point.

For others, their first loyalty was to themselves and their own very individual conscience. The Edinburgh primary school teacher and poet Norman MacCaig, who like Roy, was sent to the Non-Combatant Corps in Ilfracombe and then sentenced to prison for refusing to put on a uniform, wrote a poem much later declaring, 'My only country / is six feet high / and whether I love it or not / I'll die / for its independence.'[49] This highly individualistic stance did not rule out doing something for your fellow citizens, or even making significant sacrifices, but it meant choosing for yourself how you would do so, and refusing any direction. There was an element of this in Roy, and it also ran through some of Fred Urquhart's thinking. As Roy later put it, 'I wanted it to be me making the choice and not somebody else ordering me. My choice was the FAU and I wanted to keep it that way . . . I was a bit stubborn that way . . .'[50] Sometimes this position could be taken to its logical end. One Quaker teacher from Kent had his application for exemption accepted on condition that he continued to work as a teacher.[51] He appealed, writing to the judge that he thought accepting conditional exemption would imply acquiescing in conscription.[52] He wanted to work as a teacher, but he did not want to be told to do this by someone else. There seems to be no record of what the judge made of this.

If the principle of absolute individual freedom was driven to its very limit, it could even mean refusing to apply for an exemption at all. Who was the state, after all, to make a judgement about so profound and personal an issue? This was the position taken by some Scottish nationalists as well as by a few Christians and anarchists. One PPU activist wrote to the Ministry of Labour from his home in the suburbs of south-west London, 'I refuse to register under the act ... I cannot admit to the moral right of competence of any tribunal to pass judgement upon my claim ...'[53] Against his wishes, someone in the Ministry decided to place him on the register, and even filled in the application form for him. The young man was clearly angry about this and refused to turn up at his tribunal, where he was taken off the register and told to attend a military medical. In an exceedingly rare move, someone in the Ministry then appealed on his behalf, apparently concluding that he was never going to make an efficient soldier either. The appeal tribunal agreed.

Life in detention could be hard for conscientious objectors, and Roy seems to have got off relatively lightly. Several of the other conscientious objectors detained in Ilfracombe were placed on a bread-and-water diet and put in solitary confinement.[54] As one conscientious objector sent to Leeds jail later recalled, 'Anyone who thinks prison is a home for holidaymakers is completely ignorant of the facts.'[55] Another observed that 'there were the usual appalling conditions, the bucket in the cell and slopping out in the morning was an appalling experience, faeces and urine everywhere'.[56] Sybil Morrison, who worked at the PPU and was sent to Holloway prison, wrote that living through the Blitz within the confines of a cell was particularly difficult: 'Physical fear under conditions of day and night bombing is natural under any circumstances; it is terribly enhanced by the helplessness of one's state in prison ... There was a consuming, nagging ... hysteria, ragged nerves ...'[57]

Roy was lucky that he reported to Ilfracombe when he did. Had he turned up six months earlier, he probably would not have been treated so well. When Dennis Waters, a student from Essex, arrived and refused to put on his uniform, he was beaten by a non-commissioned officer and sentenced to twenty-eight days in military detention.[58] Waters later recalled that Sergeant Moloney, 'an ex-wrestler from the dock area of London, with a broken nose ... exerted every kind of pressure, including physical violence, to make us change our minds'.[59] Moloney's techniques included ordering the prisoners to face a wall and hold their arms out at right angles for twenty minutes at a time, striking them if their arms fell to their sides – a method that might seem relatively innocuous but that over time can cause extreme pain, and one that was often used by the British army in the interrogation of prisoners of war. Waters managed to smuggle out a letter to the Central Board for Conscientious Objectors, and Moloney was later convicted at his own court martial, charged with thirteen charges of ill-treatment.[60]

The most systematic mistreatment of conscientious objectors took place at Dingle Vale on the outskirts of Liverpool in September and October 1940.[61] Over a period of weeks, a group of conscientious objectors who had been called up into the army and then refused to follow orders were subjected to a reign of terror, deprived of food, beaten, kicked, had their heads shaved, made to sleep on the floor of dark, cold cells and woken in the night to be forced to parade in bare feet and underclothes. At least one prisoner responded by going on hunger strike.[62] Another prisoner, in a letter to a friend, described the officers as 'the worst men I have ever met', with the Colonel in particular a 'swine who would stop at nothing'.[63] These imprisoned conscientious objectors were charged with mutiny and insubordination, put on bread-and-water rations and forced to clean the blood off the floor of a nearby butcher's.[64] One of the prisoners, a devout Christian, was worried that this treatment would persist for the duration of the war, and he could take it no more. After a fourteen-day period of solitary confinement, he agreed to put on the uniform of the Non-Combatants Corps, in a decision that caused him much regret. He wrote to Donald Soper that 'after the most miserable couple of days' he had ever known, he felt he had 'betrayed the whole cause'.[65] An officer and four sergeants were eventually charged with offences committed at the camp, but only one was found guilty of assault.

Dennis Waters and the prisoners at Dingle Vale were the victims of a particularly brutal group of officers and non-commissioned officers. These punishments might have been designed to force the conscientious objectors to repent, as a warning to others or somehow to compel them into being soldiers – an attempt to break them down, to make them surrender to the logic of military conscription. Or perhaps it was simply the result of a peculiar sadism. Probably it was a combination of all of these. But such incidents of direct violence against conscientious objectors were relatively isolated and were perhaps no worse than those meted out to other recalcitrant conscripts. The British army was worried that conscripts were somehow 'soft' – in the words of one commentator, 'a lot of quivering creatures who would never have gone to war of their own free will' – and therefore needed toughening up by military discipline.[66] And it was thought the best way to do this was through gruelling marches, drill and lots of rushing at sacks with bayonets, until the body was firm and obedient, even if the mind was not always enthusiastic. Army discipline was relentless, and the smallest infringements were cracked down upon in the harshest way as the military tried to turn civilian bodies into soldiers through a regime of physical control. Conscientious objectors might have got the sharp end of the stick, but it was a stick that was widely used.

In civilian jails conscientious objectors were on the whole treated just as badly as the other inmates in Britain's cold and damp Victorian prisons – give or take the particular sneering remarks of prison guards.[67] The overall sense is of a penal bureaucracy going through the motions, sometimes caught up in Kafkaesque absurdities or in the individual prejudices of an officer, but more often than not largely indifferent. There was seldom a sense of systematic and righteous anger in the infliction of punishment and this could be frustrating. There is almost nothing worse than being ignored.

On a cold late-winter day in 1943, prisoner 4766 entered the gates of Holloway prison. Stella St John had been found guilty at West London Police Court of a breach of the Defence Regulations and sentenced to six weeks' imprisonment.[68] She was taken into a small room, four foot by four, and given a slice of bread and a pint of cocoa. It was Stella's first experience of prison beverages and she could not drink it.[69] A nurse then went through Stella's hair looking for lice and she was asked about VD. Then she was told to take off her clothes and given a bath. It was the last soap she would see for a while.

Over the past year Stella had been in a dispute with the Ministry of Labour and National Service, whose officials – alongside the dispute over ambulance work – were now determined to direct her to what they saw as more useful employment at the British

Tabulating Machine Company. Volunteering at the Hungerford Club, driving an ambulance, working at the Fellowship of Reconciliation and running a veterinary clinic it seemed was not enough. Under sweeping wartime powers, the Ministry of Labour had the legal authority to select people for the work it thought would best serve the war effort. Stella was just too old for conscription into the armed forces, but she was still subject to other forms of compulsion for war service. Although the Ministry often quietly left women alone who refused to register for 'industrial conscription', more than 270 women were prosecuted for refusing directions under the Employment Orders. The British state, or at least a series of low-level officials in the Ministry of Labour, was determined that Stella should work as a clerk. Reading through the voluminous correspondence produced by her case, it is enough to make you think someone had a point to prove.

The British Tabulating Machine Company may have sounded innocuous, but it was one of the very first manufacturers of computers in Britain, producing the machine that broke the secret German Enigma code. Probably more significantly for Stella, it was also responsible for counting the war dead. She was being asked to help keep the tally of wartime destruction, and she had refused to do so, calmly and matter-of-factly writing to the Ministry, 'As I have previously stated I am unable to conscientiously accept any alternative to my present employment.'[70] She then tried to mount as strong a defence as possible. Donald Soper wrote to the Ministry testifying to the 'sincerity of her religious convictions', and Bernard Nicholls from the Hungerford Club argued that her work was 'difficult and dirty'.[71] In one sense, it was all a waste of time; there was no right to conscientious objection for the work Stella was being told to do. The magistrate, apparently sympathetic and reluctant to send her to jail, gave Stella an extra week to reconsider, but she held firm.[72]

You get a feeling from all the letters Stella sent and received around this time that 'winning' the case, in the narrow meaning of being found 'not guilty', was not what she was after. She had a point to prove and a witness to make. Her friends from Kingsway Hall, the Hungerford Club and the Fellowship of Reconciliation were right behind her. Bernard wrote to her apologising for not being able come to the court but observing that 'I know you will make a good witness to the faith ... and will face the issue calmly and courageously. As one who "got away with it" I envy you this opportunity of putting your convictions to the test.'[73] If prison had been a means to an end for Roy Ridgway, a way to get him back before the tribunal, for Stella St John Holloway prison was an end it itself, a way to make a statement.

For a time, Holloway was the largest women's prison in western Europe, built in the monumental Victorian style. Stella was just the latest in a long line of women jailed in north London for standing up for their convictions. Early in the twentieth century Holloway's inmates had included dozens of suffragettes – including Michael Tippett's mother – and it was the same prison where Muriel Lester had been held eighteen months previously. Coming from a very different politics, Oswald Mosley, leader of the British Union of Fascists, and his aristocratic wife Diana Mitford were still interned there. There were two other conscientious objectors in Holloway during Stella's time, a Quaker and a Jehovah's Witness, both sentenced for refusing to fire-watch. To begin with Stella could see them for only one hour a week, during Sunday-afternoon exercises in the yard, and although she tried to search them out she felt the Jehovah's Witness had 'little time' for her.[74]

Stella's first days in prison were spent down on her hands and knees scrubbing the stone floor with cold water. Subsequent weeks were slightly easier, as she graduated to the laundry or making underpants for male prisoners. She joked that she was making them for Sydney Greaves, her fellow volunteer from the Hungerford Club, who was in Wormwood Scrubs at the time.[75] Her cell contained a metal bed, a basin and a pail. The lavatories on each floor were hardly used, as they were covered with the slop from the emptied pails and were usually blocked. Breakfast was a slice of bread, a pat of margarine and a bowl of porridge, and Stella only made the mistake of eating the porridge on her first day, as it 'tasted of mould and decay'.[76] Dinner was served in a tin container, and could be bacon, or sometimes an 'indescribable' fish that had to be 'smelt and tasted to be believed'.[77] Stella's fellow prisoners included blackmailers, forgers, drunks and murderers, but only the 'tale-tellers' who informed on their companions, or the blackmailers, were despised. Stella wrote in an account she produced after her release that 'no one could have been kinder' than most of the prisoners she met. For someone with such a highly developed ethical sensibility, she was also taken aback though by what she saw as some of the inmates' complete 'lack of moral sense' and their celebration of 'outrageously immoral acts'.[78] She had seen another side of life at the Hungerford Club, but Stella still came away disturbed by the 'depths to which human nature can sink'.[79]

Halfway through her sentence, the monotonous scrubbing began to get to Stella. Accustomed as she was to being extremely busy, the constrictions of prison life must have been difficult. It was a cold winter too, and the stone walls of the prison held little heat. One evening she went to bed at 7.30 to keep warm and to ease the boredom, sleeping on a mattress that 'felt like flattened rocks', only to be woken by an air-raid siren.[80] The wardens unlocked the heavy cell doors, but Stella was unsure what to do or where to go and was too afraid to ask anyone, so stayed in bed. The central courtyard of the prison block had a glass ceiling, so all the lights had to be turned out, and some of the prisoners panicked, screaming into the night.[81] Stella was counting the days to her release.

Prisoners were allowed only one letter a fortnight, so Stella sent all her news to Doris Nicholls, who then passed it on. Doris also returned the good wishes of Stella's friends, many of them telling her that the 'test' of prison must be a 'tremendous experience'. One wrote that 'Your witness is not only to contemporary human beings who may or may not seem to be very greatly influenced by it, but it is primarily to God.'[82] An aunt wrote from Cornwall that although she disagreed with Stella's stance, she admired her fortitude, and invited her niece to come and visit after her release.[83] Doris's main worry in her letters to Stella was that someone in the office of the Fellowship of Reconciliation seemed to be stealing money from their postbag.[84] It also turned out that Bernard had written a letter to the magistrate who had sentenced Stella, thanking him for the way he dealt with the case.[85] The only visitor Stella was allowed was Donald Soper. Her brother did not visit or write to her at all during her time in Holloway. She later recalled that nearly everyone she met in prison was broadly 'sympathetic', and the warders did not single out the pacifists for special treatment.[86] Stella served one month of her six weeks' sentence, receiving remission for good behaviour, before Bernard picked her up from the gates and drove her to his flat, where Doris had cooked a fried breakfast. Stella later recalled, 'It was just wonderful.' She reflected many decades later on her prison experience, 'awful as it was, it was bearable'.

If the point of sending conscientious objectors to prison was a mixture of retribution, deterrence and rehabilitation, it had uneven results. Prison certainly inflicted a measure of suffering for going against the moral and legal order of a country at war. However, if the punishment was designed somehow to intimidate or make the perpetrators see the error of their ways, it was much less successful. Most became more convinced than ever. And if the punishment was designed to make conscientious objectors feel guilty, to do penance and come out reformed, it did so only in a very roundabout way.

For poets and philosophers, conscience is often associated with intense and very personal contemplation, with anxious reflection on what is right and wrong, good and bad, accompanied by a nagging and gnawing guilt that keeps you awake at night, what the pacifist writer Rose Macaulay called the 'flickering, guttering candles of conscience'.[87] Time in prison certainly gave Stella and Roy lots of time to think about what they had done, and why they had done it, but it did not produce a change of mind. Rather, it only increased their sense of righteousness. Sydney Greaves later recalled that his days and nights in Wormwood Scrubs were a 'period of very deep self-examination when one got to know oneself much more. And despite all the squalor and unpleasantness . . . one seemed to be living above it.'[88] For Stella, Roy, Sydney and other imprisoned conscientious objectors, the sacrifices of going to prison not only helped to prove – to themselves and others – that their convictions were sincere and genuine, but they also created a space for reflection, and in doing so the long cold nights in prison could bring their own solace.

The suffering of life behind bars was often embraced by conscientious objectors as a test of conviction and a witness to their faith. One conscientious objector who was imprisoned for twelve months in January 1942 wrote in his diary that as a result of his spell in jail he 'saw a glimpse of the spirit of Christ within', just as he had been drifting towards 'distractions'.[89] A much wider tradition of Christian witness saw moral value in the experience of degradation, as both producing and attesting to personal integrity. Although modelled on the figure of Christ on the cross, this is a tradition that can take on its own secular forms, as suffering is seen as a path to insight and knowledge. Stella's and Roy's friends expressed jealousy that they had been able to test their fortitude in prison. Although she never went to prison herself, Vera Brittain also perceived honour in the humiliations of peace activism – including the heartache of being separated from her children. In such losses, she argued, there was self-discipline and wisdom: 'the private lives of pacifists are often difficult just because their public witness makes perpetual nervous and emotional demands . . . The price must nevertheless be paid.'[90] As with some approaches to non-violence, there was supposed to be redemption in suffering.

Stella St John, though, was no martyr, and a quiet understatement and humility ran through her time in Holloway. This was not always the case with others. Reginald Bottini, a London socialist with Italian and Irish parents, wanted to make a show, determined that his arrest would be shocking and theatrical, forcing people to sit up and take notice. He recalled, 'I wanted to scandalise people who lived near me . . . I just wanted to make a stand and to be dealt with harshly and to be sent to prison to prove that this lot we were dealing with – forgive me for using the term – were a right lot of bastards and were just as bad as the people over there.'[91] By being sent to prison, Bottini hoped to reveal what he saw as the hypocritical brutality of the British state, which had such a long history of violence in Ireland. He later admitted he was slightly disappointed when he was not sent to jail, but rather directed to work on a farm. Michael Tippett was also determined to make something of being sent to prison, and to do so very publicly. Although he admitted to being physically afraid, he saw heroic virtue in the self-abnegation of jail.[92] He also wondered if his suffering would make the people who sent him to jail feel uncomfortable: 'Naturally the authorities hope I will compromise too, for there will be a certain moral difficulty in committing me . . . while there is hardly any difficulty in sentencing anonymous youngsters – poor kids.'[93] If he thought anyone other than pacifists would take any notice or sympathise, it was almost certainly wishful thinking. Tippett was sentenced in June 1943 and sent to Wormwood Scrubs, and after entering the prison gates he wrote, 'I thought I had come home.'[94] The logic that through non-violent protest you can make a violent state reveal its brutal hand and thereby gain support and sympathy would be taken up by civil rights movements in years to come.

Writing partly about absolutist pacifists just after the First World War, the German sociologist Max Weber famously described what he called an 'ethics of conviction', where even if the end result was tragic and painful, holding firm to a conviction was what was important; the integrity of the believer is all.[95] Outcomes are by the by. In the Second World War, Stella St John, Michael Tippett and others felt compelled to stand by their commitments, even if they led them through the gates of Holloway and Wormwood Scrubs prisons and took them away from the work and people they loved. They had commitments to particular principles that they would not, in the end, compromise. There is even a sense in which the refusal to compromise was the whole point. For Weber such a form of pacifism represented a particularly poignant, perhaps even tragic, example of the ethics of conviction, as pacifists are left finding it difficult to stand up for other values such as freedom, equality and justice which they might otherwise believe in. Time in prison left them unable to bind the wounds of war or be of service to those in need. This was a fate that Roy, for one, was determined to avoid. There were other ways of bearing witness that did not require going to jail. This would mean some difficult compromises.

CHAPTER 14

Stalag VIII-B

Conscientious objectors did not only end up behind bars in Britain. Back when he had been captured by the German army in the late spring of 1941, Tom Burns had sent a postcard back to England. It contained just nineteen words: 'Dear Cath, I am a prisoner of war. I am quite well. There is no need to worry. Tom'.[1] The understated postcard was similar to many others sent by over 100,000 British POWs during the war; for their recipients they must have produced a mixture of relief that their loved ones were alive and fear that they were in the hands of the enemy.

Soldiers often feel humiliated by the experience of capture, neither heroes nor dead, neither on the front line nor at home, but in a purgatory of confinement. For the pacifists of the FAU, the sense of defeat must have been very different, but life behind the wire still brought a mixture of loneliness, boredom and apprehension.[2] These were men whose conscience had told them to get out there into the world, to bear witness to suffering and serve others, but now, like Stella St John, Roy Ridgway and Michael Tippett back in Britain, they were being held prisoner, albeit for very different reasons and under very different circumstances. As they were marched to their POW camp at gunpoint, the captured men of the FAU must have imagined they would have lots of time to sit and think about their lives, how they had got there and whether they had done the right thing. They would do so living cheek by jowl in the most intimate manner with the soldiers of a war that they had so opposed. Fate, or at least the battlefield, had forced them together, and pacifists and soldiers would now have plenty of time to contemplate what, if anything, they had in common.

*

Life as a prisoner for the sixteen members of the FAU captured in Greece had started in a series of insanitary camps. Alongside Tom Burns was Alan Dickinson, who had been ousted as FAU Quartermaster after the retreat from Finland, and Oswald Dick, who had taken over as Commandant. Overlooking the waters of the Gulf of Corinth, the men were corralled in a facility filled with British, Dominion and Indian troops sheltering from the sun in holes dug into the sand, and where Tom thought 'the guards were an unpleasant crew at best'.[3] The German occupation of Greece had seen the largest number of Allied troops captured since Dunkirk, with 25,000 soldiers surrendering.[4] Many of the new prisoners were weak from the heat and lack of food, but they were soon forced to march on over rough terrain and then packed like sardines into the back of trains, eventually reaching the port city of Salonika. In this new camp, Tom received a tag and a number, FS 183/8171, that he would keep for the rest of the war.

The men stayed five months in Salonika, where the conditions were as bad as they had been in Corinth. They were set to work in an overcrowded camp hospital, where Tom quickly took on the role of medical dispenser.[5] Typhoid, malaria, TB, diphtheria and beriberi were common, and all the men lost significant amounts of weight due to hunger. The camp was a test of endurance and fortitude, with basic social bonds being put under immense strain. As one of the men captured with Tom wrote, 'To retain, when terribly hungry, the customary human decencies was difficult indeed . . . to divide the rations impartially; to resist the temptation to pick scraps of food from the rubbish bins.'[6] In the late summer, they were marched off through the countryside again and forced once more into the back of cattle trucks, alongside yet more captured soldiers. They were now headed towards central Europe.

The journey north took over a week. Many of the prisoners were suffering from dysentery, and Tom continued in his role as medical dispenser, passing opiates to those in need to help ease their pain.[7] While lying on the floor of the truck, he struck up a friendship with a young Lieutenant, John Phillips, of the Argyll and Sutherland Highlanders. John had been studying Classics at Oxford before enlisting, and had then served as an intelligence officer before being captured in Crete. Many years afterwards he became British Ambassador to Sudan. The two men bonded quickly. Reflecting back on his experiences John recalled that 'no praise could be too high' for Tom and his fellow pacifists.[8] By the end of the journey, the captured members of the Unit were scattered across several German camps; seven members, including Tom Burns and Oswald Dick, as well as Lieutenant John Phillips, found themselves in Stalag VIII-B.

Tom's new home stood in what is now southern Poland and at the time was one of the largest German-controlled prisoner-of-war camps, holding over 40,000 men between 1939 and 1945 – British, French, Polish, Russian, Canadian, Serb, Greek, Australian, Cypriot, Arab and others. Six months after his capture, Tom wrote, 'We are much better off here, in a regular, newly constructed place with . . . some regard to the continued existence & wellbeing of the prisoners.'[9] The relief was surely relative.

A photograph sent home to Britain through the Red Cross shows Tom in FAU khaki uniform, holding a pipe and looking thoughtful, as he stood near a high barbed-wire fence. He was one of thousands of men kept in row after row of whitewashed huts built of brick and wood, with rough concrete floors, each holding 300 men. In the winter, warmth was provided by the animal heat of closely packed bodies, as the single-brick walls failed to keep out the cold; in the summer there were flies, water shortages and constantly overflowing latrines.[10] The huts smelled of the odour of confinement – damp blankets and sweat – and the men slept in bunks three tiers high. They were constantly on the lookout for lice. The food was better than it had been on the march from Greece – the camp newsletter recommended a dish called *farcie* made by scooping out the contents of a potato and mixing it with meat paste.[11] There was also occasionally beer to wash it down, and the men made the most of the rations of margarine, tea, condensed milk and tins of vegetables.[12]

Just as the prisoners settled into a routine, adjusting to the particular idiosyncrasies and habits of the men sleeping, eating and playing just a few feet away, they were moved to a new hut and mixed up again, in a deliberate attempt by the guards to prevent escapes.[13] At night, the guard dogs barked incessantly. The days were punctuated by roll call, meal time and lights out, and in between Tom would have walked across the sandy ground, looking out beyond the double layers of barbed wire at the pine forests beyond. Thousands of the prisoners were sent out to work camps, labouring in factories, farms and forests, but Tom, for now, stayed behind. Desperate to get home, some of the soldiers tried to escape, over and over again, but were usually brought back within a few weeks, running out of energy, food, luck or all three. John Phillips had already made one failed attempt to escape in Crete, and would make several more, tunnelling under the sand. Tom, unlike the soldiers, was not under British military orders to try and escape, so presumably looked at the fence and decided the best way to get home was to wait it out.

No one seemed to know quite where to put Tom and the other pacifists of the FAU. They had been captured in Greece working with the Allied armies and wearing what looked like military uniforms, but they were under the impression that under the Geneva Conventions they should have been sent home as protected Red Cross personnel. Needless to say, the idea of conscientious objectors did not seem to resonate with the German camp commanders.[14] There was no legal right to conscientious objection under the Nazis, and people who refused to take up arms were routinely executed. The vast majority of such people were Jehovah's Witnesses, who also faced persecution for refusing to take an oath to Hitler and were the first religious organisation to be banned under the Nazis. A small number of Catholics and Protestants also publicly refused to take up arms, although many more either went into exile or sought other ways out.[15]

Dietrich Bonhoeffer had returned to Germany in 1939 and, with the help of his brother-in-law Hans von Dohnányi – an anti-Nazi lawyer who worked in Germany military intelligence – managed to avoid military service for three and a half years.[16] Many of the graduates from his underground seminary had gone into the army and large numbers had been killed, but Hans managed to get Dietrich registered as an agent of military intelligence and thereby avoid conscription. In April 1943 the arrangement was uncovered and both Dietrich and his brother-in law were arrested. What the authorities did not know at the time was that both men were also involved in a plan to blow up Hitler.

How had this man who had claimed to be pacifist become embroiled in an assassination attempt? Part of the answer has to do with family loyalty and connections. Alongside Hans von Dohnányi, Dietrich's brother Klaus and his other brother-in-law Rüdiger Schleicher were part of the plotting, and his sister Emmi had encouraged him to be more actively involved. More importantly, Dietrich's pacifism and conscientious objection were always far from straightforward; he had been developing a position which rejected all the usual ethical questions – 'what is right?', 'what is good?' – in favour of simply asking: what is God's will?[17] Being a Christian meant obedience to Christ and his example. Through Hans's role in military intelligence, Dietrich had become even more aware of Nazi atrocities, and felt God's call to act, having concluded that the evils of Fascism could not be defeated just by being a good person, but only by also taking on the responsibility to end them. Anything else was but a form of 'cheap grace'.[18] This meant avoiding the consolations of a clear conscience, and instead taking on the guilt of the world.[19] Discipleship had to come at a cost. While other Christian pacifists were trying to bring about peace, Dietrich had concluded that his duty was to remove Hitler altogether, and this could mean getting blood on his hands, even if only metaphorically. In being willing to embrace guilt, he had developed a position analogous – although coming from a very different theological position – to the humanitarian pacifists who recognised their complicity in war and suffering and then sought to do something about it, even if the choices faced by Dietrich – as a German citizen in Germany – were very different from those confronting young men and women from Britain, and his convictions took him into very different places.

To begin with Dietrich was treated relatively well in Tegel prison in the north of Berlin, and a guard even offered to help him escape, but Dietrich thought the risks of reprisals against his family were too great. Eighteen months after first being arrested, Hans's and Dietrich's involvement in the plan to kill Hitler was discovered. Dietrich was quickly moved to a high-security Gestapo prison, and eventually transferred, first to Buchenwald and then to Flossenbürg concentration camp. On 8 April 1945 he was sentenced to death by a court martial and executed by hanging early the next morning, just weeks before American troops liberated the camp. Dietrich's brother Klaus and his brothers-in-law Hans and Rüdiger were executed by the Nazis the same month.

*

Back in Stalag VIII-B the concerns, at least for now, were more mundane. It was also hard to place the largely middle-class but officerless men of the ambulance unit within the rigid hierarchies of Allied military life; they started out in the officers' hut, but were then moved to sleep alongside the batmen, the servants still retained by the British commanders in order to carry out domestic tasks, even in prison.[20] By February 1942, Tom was in cosmopolitan company, reflecting the vast diversity of the people pulled into and captured in the war, writing home of his fellow prisoners: 'Greeks, British sailors, Maltese, Arabs, Chinese . . .'[21]

Time stretched, slowly. There was little to look forward to apart from Red Cross parcels and intermittent letters, and Tom felt a 'fever of suspense' as he waited for a few words and tobacco from home.[22] Prisoners were allowed to send two postcards and two letters home a month. Tom wrote most of them to his friend Cathy, who was now teaching in Oxfordshire. It is these letters, often very personal, that give us a sense of what life was like behind the wire. The prisoners were limited in what they could say, because any negative comments about their treatment were quickly redacted by the German censors. The packages from Britain arrived in fits and starts, often wildly out of order, with parcels sent to Sweden finally, somehow, catching up with Tom in the camp years later.[23]

Apart from the distractions provided by letters and parcels, life must have seemed monotonous, especially after the excitement and fears of the previous months. Tom wrote to England asking for more books, khaki ties and a new pipe, while also worrying that the people he cared for back home might have forgotten him: 'I cannot help being repressed and stunted by this isolation from news, society and culture & by this experience of not so much imprisonment as bondage . . . Life will be very difficult until I hear from you, now that I can expect something. I have awful nightmares that this address won't find you.'[24] Growing plants from seeds sent from England was one of the few ways to lighten the mood.

The first winter was particularly difficult as the temperature in the central European forests became 'practically Finnish'.[25] Tom limited himself to scurrying outside to collect a bucket of coal or to visit the compound's latrines, and then huddled around the stove and played draughts with one of the sergeants. Far from having time to stop and think, he found the experience of camp life claustrophobic and cramped, and he regretted that 'the prevailing rhythms of the day are of noise'.[26] The other members of the Unit had been spread around the camp, but were getting on each other's nerves and bickering. Tom wrote that apart 'from Oswald who is as silent as I am most of the time, or sillily boisterous, I'm utterly browned off with the others of the Unit here'.[27] It is difficult to tell from the letters what they were arguing about, though one gets a sense that it was all low-key and slightly petty – the type of pettiness created by people living at close quarters with nothing to do. In the cold, with everyone staying inside as much as possible, the chatter was incessant and the atmosphere oppressive, especially when the camp band started to practise.[28] For Tom 'the temper of this life is such that a slight deterioration provokes nagging mental distress. It is all subjective & I know now temporary, but this thin life of narrow captivity, of crowd and noise has its bad days.'[29] The men in the camp talked about their misery with all the euphemism of mid-twentieth-century male life; they had 'barbed-wire fever', were 'going around the bend' or suffered from 'temporary lapses'.[30] However they described it, the discomfort, enforced intimacy and boredom clearly took their toll.

The weeks in Stalag VIII-B turned into months, and the months into years, as rumours of repatriation became a constant source of both optimism and disappointment. There seem to have been occasional visits from a Repatriation Commission – designed to swap injured and infirm soldiers – but FAU personnel did not appear to be on the agenda.[31] Tom was on tenterhooks, and frustrations grew because as far as the men in the camp could tell, the FAU back in London did not seem to be doing anything for them.[32] Discussions with the Stalag authorities about their return froze after an outbreak of typhus, but Oswald Dick was eventually granted an interview with a senior German officer, who seemed 'sympathetic' yet also pointed out all the difficulties.[33] A correspondence started up between the camp Commandant, Berlin and the Red Cross in Geneva, but never seemed to get anywhere.[34]

To take his mind off the discomfort of camp life, Tom tried to dedicate himself to reading and studying, asking Cathy to send him a rather high-minded collection of books on Kant, Locke, Old English grammar and the Saxon epic *Beowulf*. All this reading brought some consolation, Tom writing that 'I have been lowering myself deeper and deeper into books – history, criticism, poetry, philosophy, theology, mathematics – a range of course far too extensive to be any value as knowledge, but I am entering into a discipline even in this stuff, which I've never known before ... If only I hadn't wasted so many years!'[35]

The constantly thwarted possibility of home – flickering and dying down with incessant regularity – messed with various coping mechanisms that Tom and the others developed, so they tried to ignore the whispers, focusing on day-to-day life.[36] Tom wrote that the 'wildness of rumours has killed interest in the outside world, & we trot round in our little marked out circles with our eyes shut & with fold after fold of ... depression, small mindedness, bad temper, sheer ignorance and the inevitable humiliations of imprisonment ... You will find me very difficult to live with after this.'[37]

His studies seemed to help Tom develop what he described as a new sense of political and, he thought, perhaps even religious enthusiasm.[38] He also did a little work in the camp hospital, but soon took over as secretary of the Post-War Employment Bureau, finding satisfaction in helping the soldiers prepare for life back home.[39] He tried to start up a correspondence about Kant with one of his old professors from Bristol.[40] This was none other than G. C. Field. Tom probably did not know that he had become a member of the conscientious objector tribunal and would write a book that was extremely critical of pacifism.[41] Tom also set up a small study group in the camp with some of the officers and NCOs, including Lieutenant John Phillips, poring over Reinhold Niebuhr's classic anti-pacifist work of theology, *Moral Man and Immoral Society*.[42] Niebuhr's book describing the egoism and destructive pride of nations must have given the soldiers and the pacifists a lot to discuss.

As well as discussing Kant and Niebuhr, Tom enjoyed his time with Frank Parker, a Bostonian painter he found 'charming, awkward, difficult of speech but with a good flow of ideas'.[43] Frank was a Harvard drop-out, who had moved to Paris in the 1930s to paint, joined a French ambulance unit when the Germans invaded and fled to Spain as the French armed forces faced defeat, eventually managing to make his way to neutral Portugal. Although an

American citizen, Frank immediately volunteered for the Canadian army, at a time when the US was yet to enter the war, and was captured by the Germans during the ill-fated raid on the French port of Dieppe in 1942. During his time as a prisoner, Frank was horsewhipped at least once by his captors and thrown into a pit latrine, before managing to escape from the camp on his third attempt.[44] Despite their very different paths into the war, Tom and Frank clearly enjoyed their conversations about art, literature and life.

An early spring thaw in 1942 helped the mood. It meant that Tom could find more time to be by himself, without everyone being crowded into the huts for warmth. Remarkably, Tom wrote home to Cathy, 'I should like to get home, but I am not sure that I should, apart from being home, & seeing you and others ... I have still much to consider & try to order in myself, an activity which can be done here, I know, better than elsewhere.'[45] He was using his time in the camp, surrounded by all the fear of those defeated in war, to reflect deeply on his own character, on what following his conscience meant to him, trying to use the restrictions imposed by camp life to 'make myself into something better'.[46] He resolved to spend his new 'life carefully' and to treat the time in camp as a 'formative, disciplinary apprenticeship'.[47] He was by now well entrenched in the tradition that saw conscience as a matter of anxious, solitary and patient reflection. The seeds that he had planted earlier in the year also began to grow, producing radishes, spinach and turnips.

That first spring in captivity, Tom and the other medical personnel were allowed to walk beyond the high fence twice a week, and this was 'an immense boon'.[48] The first time they were allowed out, Tom and the other men walked for two hours through the flat sandy countryside, passing villages, farms and children, accompanied by only one English-speaking guard. Hot showers were also instituted once a week. But then there was bad news. Oswald Dick received information from Berlin that the FAU men had been classified as the equivalent of the Royal Army Medical Corps, not the Red Cross – apparently due to a clerical error back in London – and therefore under the Geneva Conventions were to be treated as part of the British army. Medics perhaps, but military medics nevertheless, and therefore not qualified for immediate repatriation.

The distinction between military and pacifist service was caus-
ing problems once again.

As the pacifists of the FAU lived with the captured soldiers of the
Allied and imperial armies, they reminisced together about home,
and complained about the food, played games and discussed
books, getting along better than one might have imagined. Just
after Christmas 1942, Tom wrote to Cathy, it 'would have done
your heart good to see what common humanity can make of a
dump like this when it really makes an effort'.[49] Over the previous
three years, the pacifists had developed close and intimate relationships with many soldiers, and in the camp these ties became even
more intense. Tom's letters home contain as much about his friendships with John Phillips and Frank Parker as they do about
his relations with other members of the FAU.[50] The differences
between those who had taken up arms and those who had refused
to do so seemed to have been partly forgotten in the common
experience of camp life. Even the soldiers who were not his friends
'proved quite understanding of the position we had taken'.[51] One
captured FAU volunteer, referring to the end of his time in a
prisoner-of-war camp, later remembered that 'the business of being
in the Army or FAU had by then disappeared completely'.[52]

It was not just the practicalities of humanitarian work near the
front line or the forced intimacy of camp life that drove conscientious objectors and soldiers together. Away from the German
prison camps, the memoirs, diaries and interviews of conscientious
objectors are full of claims about how well they got on with military people and how much they admired one another.[53] Roy
Ridgway recalled, 'Some of the officers I liked very much, they
were just normal people called up like myself.'[54] Michael Cadbury
observed that 'I was always received courteously and kindly.'[55]
There was a sense that soldiers and conscientious objectors – at
least those who had been directed to alternative forms of service –
had more in common with each other than with the rest of the
population. Michael Rowntree, who had been in Finland with
the FAU, thought that 'there was often less feeling against COs
among people in the forces than among civilians at home ... Most
of the time we were sharing the same kind of experiences, not
exactly in the front line but we were doing much the same thing as

parts of the forces were doing and weren't superficially any different.'[56] Even the *Bulletin* of the Central Board for Conscientious Objectors concluded that 'Perhaps there is some kind of kinship of spirit between men who, albeit in very different ways ... prepare the way for freedom and right. Both are crusaders though they fight with different weapons.'[57]

There was clearly some affinity between pacifists and soldiers, at least in the close confines created by war and imprisonment. In practice, for outside observers at least, the difference between pacifist volunteers in the Unit and servicemen was not obvious, and the khaki uniforms of the FAU could occasionally lead to them being saluted by soldiers. The FAU was part of a long pacifist tradition that hated war and violence but was attracted to many aspects of military discipline.[58] In 1906, the American psychologist, brother of the novelist Henry James and leading pacifist William James – whose books Tom also read in the POW camp – gave a famous speech in the halls of Stanford University where he called for the 'moral equivalent of war'.[59] The talk was somewhat unusual for a pacifist, as he was full of praise for militarism as 'the great preserver of our ideals of hardihood, and human life with no use for hardihood would be contemptible'. He particularly approved of military service, arguing that all 'the qualities of a man acquire dignity' when he works for the collectivity. James saw such service as a way to foster the personal qualities of 'toughness' and 'surrender of private interest', and called for a peaceful form of conscription. Such support for conscription ran through significant parts of the pacifist movement, and Richard Gregg, the great populariser of Gandhian non-violence to European and American audiences, often praised the courage characteristic of military life.[60] Gandhi himself approved of some aspects of military culture too. He had, after all, served in the Natal Indian Ambulance Corps during the South African War and strongly advocated enlistment during the First World War. He saw virtue in the discipline of military life, and hoped to raise a non-violent army whose members would lay their lives on the line. His speeches were full of military metaphors, calling on his followers to 'assimilate all the noble qualities of soldiery' or to become a 'body of civil resisters ... like an army subject to all the discipline of a soldier'.[61] While Gandhi might have been opposed to the imperialist chauvinism of militarism, he was certainly not opposed to what he saw as the heroism, self-sacrifice and unity of military life.

If pacifists were attracted to the camaraderie of military life, those who took up arms were also often reluctant warriors – there was perhaps a little bit of pacifism in them too. Not every soldier wanted to be a hero on the front line, killing the enemy at every opportunity.[62] Indeed, leaders of the Allied armies were worried that many soldiers were congenitally unfit for front-line service, either by temperament or by conviction; the army rated only 5 per cent of soldiers as 'highly suited' for combat in 1942, and feared that while most soldiers never fired a bullet in anger, when they did, they deliberately fired away from their human targets.[63]

In the POW camp, Tom and the men of the FAU would not have had a monopoly on hating violence. What is more, it was not as if only pacifists had a conscience, as many of those who took the fight to Fascism did so for reasons of strong conviction. We can only imagine that Frank Parker volunteered twice for military duty out of a strong sense of conviction. Passing night after night on the tightly packed bunks, Tom, his fellow ambulance drivers and the soldiers of the British army must have had a great deal in common. As one Second World War Quaker relief worker put it, 'I had a far deeper sense of spiritual unity with those of my friends in the fighting services, who, detesting war as deeply as I did, yet felt that there was no other way in which they could share in the agony of the world, than I had with those pacifists who talked as if the suffering of the world could be turned off like a water tap if only politicians would talk sensibly together.'[64] Pacifists like Tom and self-consciously heroic soldiers like John Phillips and Frank Parker were more alike in aspirations than one might think.

By the spring of 1943, rumours of repatriation became more and more intense; there was a possibility that disabled, unfit and medical personnel would be exchanged between Britain and Germany. Not all the medical men were to be returned, as 200 men had to stay behind to work in the camp hospitals. Tom wrote home that he would probably have to stay, as there were men who had been prisoners for much longer. There was part of him that wanted to remain, for the time to think and work on himself.

When Tom was eventually released in October 1943, he had been a prisoner for 733 days. Five other members of the Unit returned to Britain that same month, and three more the year after. The rest would not be free until the end of the war. One of them never came home. Alan Dickinson, who had been in the advance party from the Unit to Finland, died in hospital just before Christmas Day 1943, after falling from a window. Before his death he had written, 'I wanted to be in the section of the Unit that would have the best opportunities of proving its mettle. I wanted to live vividly for my ideal and if necessary die for it.'[65]

Tom and the others were lucky to leave Stalag VIII-B when they did. Towards the end of the war, with the Red Army rapidly advancing from the east, the German camp guards made the decision to force the prisoners west through the countryside, in what became known as the Long March. Many of the captured soldiers died of exhaustion in one of the coldest winters in memory.

On his journey home, Tom travelled through Germany by train, before being put on a boat to neutral Sweden and catching another boat across the North Sea to Britain. Arriving, he reflected on how familiar England seemed, the adventure and misery of the last three and a half years quickly taking on the quality of a vivid dream:

The spectacle would remain of course; the spectacle of Kalamata, the long silence, queues by the quayside at night, the air attack by the bridge, the herd of prisoners shuffling and trotting past the Town hall . . . the spectacle of Corinth Camp, the cooking fires in the dusk, the market at the gates, the crocodiles of men manoeuvring for position at the cookhouse, the ordure-smeared scraps of paper that fluttered everlastingly about the camp, the machine gun fire along the wire at night . . . the sleeping pits dug into the firm sand; the spectacle of Salonika Camps, the two-hour check parades on the centre square, the bed bugs and lice, Olympus across the bay, the dysentery patients walking naked with shreds of flesh between their skins and their bones . . . the fruit from the Greek Red Cross, the Serbs on parade, beriberi . . . for the rest I should take up where I had left off.[66]

It would not be so easy to recommence his old life, though. A Britain past the worst of the Blitz must have seemed very different from the one he had left almost four years before.

Many of the volunteers who had headed to Finland back in 1939 had done so at such speed that they had not had time to register as conscientious objectors, so they had to appear before a tribunal on their return, facing the infamous Judge Hargreaves in Fulham. On this occasion, Hargreaves shook their hands after they were formally classified as conscientious objectors and left the courtroom.[67]

Tom wanted to go abroad again immediately, as there were FAU groups in the Middle East, India and China who were right in the thick of it. He applied to go and provide relief during the Bengal famine, where an estimated two to three million people governed by the British Raj were being starved to death, as wartime policies led to a shortage of food.[68] But Tom's own health was suffering from all he had gone through, and he failed the medical. Forced to stay on the home front, he spent the rest of the war working at FAU headquarters in London. Adventures overseas would be for other people. People like Roy Ridgway.

CHAPTER 15

Take Courage

On 14 March 1943, Roy Ridgway finally left Britain and headed to the Middle East with the FAU. The converted troop carrier taking him across the sea was crowded with the uniforms of the Coldstream Guards and the Royal Army Medical Corps, as well as the Friends Ambulance Unit.[1] The journey to Egypt took six weeks, as the ship zigzagged through the Atlantic, the air becoming hotter and more humid the closer to the equator they sailed, passing the floating remains of torpedoed vessels on the way.[2] Roy rose early and ran laps of the deck before retiring to his cabin to read Aldous Huxley. He ate his meals with the warrant officers and got into an argument with a soldier who claimed that India would fall into chaos if Britain left. Roy pointed out that Europe was hardly a haven of order right now. After Cape Town, the ship headed north up the east coast of Africa, and finally docked near the Suez Canal in early May, where Roy caught a train to Cairo and reported to FAU headquarters.[3] He later recalled that it 'was marvellous to see Egypt, we were terribly excited about it all, young men and adventure'.[4] After years of anticipation he had arrived.

If Roy was looking for adventure, there would now be plenty of it to go around. Along with adventure comes fear and trepidation. Over the next two years Roy would confront what it meant to be both courageous and a pacifist in the middle of battle, forcing him and other members of his Unit to wonder if they were on the right side of the line between war and peace, and even if drawing this line made any sense at all.

The months at the Gloucester infirmary before being posted overseas had been frustrating for Roy. At one point he had contemplated leaving altogether, complaining that he was unable to live off his small allowance that did not even cover his cigarettes, while the independently wealthy volunteers were able to buy books and go to the theatre.[5] He was also still in limbo, discharged from the army but not yet given formal conscientious-objector status. He wrote, in typical style, to the Ministry of Labour: 'I do not wish to be awkward or stubborn, and I should be grateful if you allow me to continue to serve my country and my fellow man in a manner consistent with my conscience.'[6] To make matters worse, his friend Bernard Llewellyn was already out in China with the FAU, and Roy wrote to him, with a hint of jealousy, that 'you all seem to be having a very exciting time'.[7]

Since the retreat from Finland, Norway and Greece, the Friends Ambulance Unit had sent its volunteers across the world – to Ethiopia, India, Burma, Egypt and Syria, and then once more to Greece, as well as Italy, Austria and north-west Europe. But it was the mission to China that grabbed the most attention. As Roy was cleaning bedpans in Gloucester, Bernard was part of what became known as the China Convoy, driving a truck over the long and dangerous Burma Road and beyond.[8] The convoy ferried medical supplies and set up clinics, under the Chinese Red Cross, but was attached to the Kuomintang Nationalist Army of Chiang Kai-shek. Within the FAU it was known as the most glamorous posting of the whole operation. Part of this reputation had rubbed off from that of its leader, a doctor called Bob McClure. In the late 1930s, during his travels in China, the poet W. H. Auden had met McClure and described him as 'a stalwart, sandy, bullet-headed Canadian Scot with the energy of a whirlwind and the high spirits of a sixteen-year-old boy'.[9] McClure was an unusual man to lead a pacifist Unit – rumour had it that he carried a gun – but he added to the sense of adventure.

Bernard wrote regularly to Roy from China, describing the paddy fields, terraced hills and leper colonies. The roads were often too narrow for two trucks to pass and serious accidents were common, with 'crumbled steel memorials' lining the valley floors.[10] A shortage of fuel meant that the medical supply trucks were converted to work on charcoal burners that struggled up the steep hills, someone having to climb out and place a wooden chock under the rear wheel every time it lurched forward to stop the vehicle rolling back again, a task that could cause both amusement and frustration. It was definitely not all fun and games; there was considerable danger and suffering too. Bernard had arrived in China just as the Japanese army was making its brutal push across south-east Asia, occupying much of Indo-China and forcing the Chinese and Allied armies backwards in a desperate and often tragically savage rush for safety, where starvation, disease and death were all too common. Bernard later wrote, 'I cannot recall the details of that retreat ... only the atmosphere of terror remains – a terror that was for a time channelled along the road, the only road into China ...'[11] Back in England Bernard and Roy had dreamed of getting near to the front line. Bernard at least could not have got any closer.

Gloucester must have seemed a long way away from the battlefront in China. On his twenty-sixth birthday, Roy wrote in his diary, 'I have achieved absolutely nothing. As I grow older I am gradually losing my enthusiasm for many things ... I am no longer devoutly religious as I was ... I was happier in the army than I am now.'[12] Even his brothers were annoying him. Derricke came to visit, wearing a large black hat, his hair straggling down his neck and sporting a 'magnificent beard'.[13] Roy was not impressed, thinking his sibling a 'laughing stock' and writing to his mother that he thought it wrong for conscientious objectors to make themselves so 'conspicuous'. His other brother Alfred wrote back, telling Roy not to be so judgemental.

That autumn Roy took Ruth, a nurse from Hut 4 – the ward where he worked – to the cinema. After the film they bought fish and chips and walked through the park, hearing gunfire somewhere in the distance.[14] The heightened atmosphere of the time must have added to the romance. A couple of weeks later, he wrote in his diary, 'I believe I am falling in love with her. Whenever I see her I blush like a school boy. I cannot pass the ward where she is working without peering in to see if she is there.'[15] The turmoil of war raised the emotions of everyday life. When Roy received the news that he was to be shipped out to Syria, Ruth asked him not to go, their relationship still new and fragile, but he was pulled between what he thought might be love and the possibility of service overseas, and chose the Middle East.[16]

On New Year's Day 1943, as Roy waited to be shipped out, the potential danger of ambulance work was brought home. News came through that two senior members of the FAU had been lost at sea.[17] Tom Tanner and Peter Hume had been sent from London to investigate rumbles of discontent that seemed to be emerging from the China Convoy, only for their ship to be torpedoed.[18] Peter Hume had interviewed Roy when he first joined the Unit, and Roy remembered how Peter had put him at ease, endlessly smoking cigarettes and advising, 'When you join the FAU you must not talk too much about pacifism. We work quite a lot with soldiers, and it annoys them . . .'[19]

Despite being fearful about the voyage and what might come after, Roy had been given a new lease of life, telling Bernard, 'I think after the war I shall look back on these days as the happiest of my life. It is a grand thing to be young and healthy.'[20] Roy was going to work with part of the FAU attached to the Hadfield-Spears Mobile Hospital, which in turn worked alongside the Free French Forces. This was one of the many square pegs in a round hole with which the FAU operated. The hospital had been set up by two Anglo-American women: Lady Hadfield, whose family supplied the funds to get the hospital off the ground, and the writer Mary Borden, who was married to Major General Sir Edward Spears, the British government's head of mission to de Gaulle's Free French. The FAU agreed to provide orderlies and ambulance drivers to support the hospital, while Mary Borden, otherwise known as Lady Spears – recruited the nurses. Many of the other orderlies were from colonial French Equatorial Africa. All in all, it made for slightly awkward relationships. Spears was contemptuous of conscientious objectors, describing them as 'weak' and 'filled with half-baked ideas', although she grew to respect some of them greatly.[21] One Unit member recalled that 'she was not the easiest character to deal with' and would tell the conscientious objectors 'quite frankly' that they were shirking their responsibilities.[22]

De Gaulle's troops had particular difficulty understanding what it meant to be a conscientious objector. No such right existed in the French military, free or otherwise. The very Protestant-sounding conscience of the ambulance unit must have seemed somewhat alien to soldiers brought up in the republican and Catholic atmosphere of France, where the collective obligations of citizenship and military service had been tightly bound together since shortly after the Revolution at the end of the eighteenth century. The French peace movement had never been large, and had collapsed in disarray at the start of the Second World War. For those who had signed up for the Free French in particular, the call of peace was likely associated with defeatism and Vichy-style collaboration.[23] As Michael Rowntree, who had also joined the Hadfield-Spears and would eventually take over as leader, put it, 'most of the French had no clue what it was all about . . . they couldn't either rationally or emotionally understand or sympathise with our position'.[24] In the last few years, the choices faced by the people of France in the face of Vichy and the German occupation contrasted with those that confronted young men and women conscripted in Britain; the Free French were fighting for a freedom, but this was very different from the freedom of conscience so important to the members of the FAU. These were soldiers who had actively sought out military service after the surrender, imprisonment and demobilisation of the French armies in 1940. Conscientious objecting to military service could not have been further from their minds.

The first Commanding Officer of the Hospital, Colonel Fruchaud, was a veteran of the Spanish Civil War and a man of an 'uncertain temperament', who had little time for pacifist sensibilities, often ordering the FAU members – in defiance of the Geneva Conventions – to transport uninjured soldiers.[25] Things improved for the volunteers when Fruchaud was replaced by Colonel Vernier, who was more sympathetic to the FAU; he was the son of Protestant missionaries in Madagascar and his brother was a pacifist who had run a Quaker hospital in the First World War.[26] In the background were the increasingly strained relationships between the British and French militaries, and between de Gaulle and Spears in particular, as tensions over who should be the dominant power in the region rose to the surface and were occasionally echoed in fist fights between British and French troops.[27] What is more, the very name of the Hadfield-Spears Hospital meant it was increasingly associated with the policies of General Spears that were seen as undermining French influence in Syria and Lebanon.[28] Either way, the official history of the FAU remarked, 'it is doubtful whether the French ever fully understood them' as 'they worked and bantered and quarrelled together'.[29] Somehow, though, it worked. At the very least, the Free French respected the British volunteers for joining with them relatively early in the war, when many others were biding their time, waiting to see what would happen.

The FAU mission had originally left Britain in March 1941, headed, they thought, to join the Free French Forces in Eritrea and Sudan. The contingent was initially led by Raymond 'Nik' Alderson, a Cambridge University student with a French mother, described by Lady Spears as 'a very good-looking young man of twenty-one, tall, well built with a fair curly head, pleasant blue eyes and charming manners'.[30] Although Lady Spears disliked pacifists, she clearly had a soft spot for Nik Alderson. Before the hospital arrived in north-east Africa, the war took them in a new direction, as Allied troops – spearheaded by French colonial soldiers from north and west Africa – invaded Syria, which was then under the control of Vichy France. Along the way the Hadfield-Spears team was joined by another group of men from the FAU, who had originally been sent to join Tom Burns and the others in Greece but had been cut off by the German invasion.[31] The Unit followed the advancing Allied troops into the Levant in a short-lived but intense and confusing phase of the war, coming under fire from Vichy forces as they tended to the 'Frenchmen shot by other Frenchmen'.[32]

Once this round of fighting was over, Nik Alderson decided to set up a series of small remote clinics in the Syrian countryside, treating malaria, dysentery and eye disease. He saw this as exactly the sort of work pacifist volunteers should do, tending to the sick and needy. During the First World War, nearby Mount Lebanon had been subjected to a famine that killed an estimated 200,000 people, caused by a combination of an Entente blockade on the Mediterranean coast, a plague of locusts and the refusal of the Ottoman military to import enough food.[33] Thirty years later, there was no famine, but malnutrition and ill-health were widespread. Five clinics were established: high in the Beqaa Valley, near Damascus, on the edge of the Palmyra desert, in Latakia on the Mediterranean coast and at Tel Tamr in the far north-east of Syria. Lady Spears could not hide her exasperation at the speed with which Alderson seemed to want to get away from the fighting, telling him, 'Don't forget ... that if it weren't for the young men of your age who are holding the Syrian frontier, you would have no chance to do the village work.'[34] Alderson reputedly responded: 'I don't mind being killed . . . But I will not fight.' These were prophetic words.

After a brief stop in Egypt, Roy arrived in Beirut at six in the evening of a glorious spring day in May 1943, going immediately to a café and drinking two bottles of wine.[35] The bulk of the hospital had already left Syria and Lebanon to support the Allied pushback across north Africa as the battle ebbed and flowed. By the time Roy landed in the Middle East, Nik Alderson had been dead for over a year. As Rommel's tanks forced their way eastwards, the 1st Free French Brigade had been holding on to the oasis of Bir Hakeim, just south of Tobruk. German air raids were common, with one FAU volunteer writing in his diary that the 'din is terrific. At times the bombs land uncomfortably close but it is alright if you have a job to do, and exciting to watch from the cover of a doorway, which affords shelter against the flying shrapnel.'[36] In the middle of the desert, it was not always so easy to find shelter. Nik was working at a forward operating theatre, right on the front lines, and was lying in a slit trench dug into the sand when a German bomb landed right in the middle, killing him immediately.[37] Michael Rowntree had been on his way to visit Nik, stopping briefly to watch a rare bird on the way, and had arrived just half an hour after the bomb exploded.[38] Years afterwards he would say that ornithology had saved his life.

In the days before his death, Nik had been run down and exhausted, a large carbuncle developing on his neck, and Lady Spears had tried to persuade him to rest, but he had refused.[39] Nik wrote to FAU headquarters, 'we have had some busy and exciting hours but no casualties. The main Unit . . . has now started on some of the hardest and most satisfying work we have done since the Unit came out.'[40] There were supposed to be only a few weeks left for Nik in the Libyan desert before he headed back to the clinics in Syria and Lebanon, but he never made it. Instead, aged twenty-three, he was buried in a sandy grave on Valentine's Day 1942. A day after his death, Lady Spears wrote a letter to his parents back in England, declaring, 'I had grown so fond of him and had been so impressed with the way he was developing . . . stronger in every sense.'[41]

Nik Alderson's death was just one tragedy in a global war. In early 1942, Japanese troops had conquered much of south-east Asia, almost as quickly as the Germans had occupied most of Europe a few years previously. In the same week that Nik was killed, the Japanese took nearly 130,000 British, Commonwealth and Indian troops captive in Singapore. According to Churchill this was the 'worst disaster and largest capitulation in British history'.[42] Things would not improve quickly. In the summer of 1942 the Afrika Korps entered Egypt, and reached El Alamein, only sixty miles from Alexandria. Some 57,000 Allied troops were lost, nearly all of them made prisoners of war, as the Mediterranean Fleet set sail for safety and in Cairo the British started evacuating as many people as possible and burning their records.[43]

Things had not begun to turn the other way until the autumn of 1942, when the Eighth Army, newly under the command of General Montgomery, began to drive the German and Italian troops back across north Africa, capturing 30,000 Axis soldiers in the first significant British victory on the battlefield since the start of the war. One FAU volunteer with the Hadfield-Spears observed in his diary that 'the end of the war still appears a long way off', but there was some faint hope, as he noted, echoing Churchill's words, that this 'is not the beginning of the end, but only the end of the beginning'.[44] The sentiment was more true than he could have known.

Roy Ridgway went to work in the clinics set up by Nik Alderson in Syria and Lebanon, which had been left behind when the rest of the Hadfield-Spears Hospital had moved on to north Africa. For the first few days driving the heavy French-built ambulance was a little difficult, but he eventually got the hang of it and drove to the American University pharmacy to pick up some supplies. In May 1943 he was sent to work in the clinic in Latakia, a port on the Syrian coast near the border with Turkey. The city sat on a headland jutting out into the sea, with rugged hills behind. For a brief period in the chaos after the First World War and the fall of the Ottoman Empire, it had served as capital of the French-controlled Alawite Territory – established as a sectarian state for the small Muslim sect – before being incorporated into Mandate Syria. The surrounding countryside had a large Alawite population, but the city itself had significant numbers of Sunni Muslims and Christians, as well as Turkish-speakers and Armenians. This was a tempestuous time to be in Syria and Lebanon, where the conflict between the Vichy French and the Free French was only part of a larger picture. Anti-colonial agitation against France, Free or otherwise, was widespread and sometimes erupted into protests met with a ferocious and bloody response. Despite the Vichy troops being evicted from the region, it was not clear to many Syrians whether they had yet been liberated in any meaningful sense.

Roy lived in a flat on the top floor of an American missionary building, sleeping most evenings during the summer on the roof, as he tried to catch the breeze coming off the sea. His diet alternated between eggs and chips in a British army mess, and olives, fruit and rice he bought in the market. He made friends with a local family – the Awads – who had two sons around Roy's age, often visiting their large airy house to talk about pacifism and English literature, learn some Arabic, listen to the news on the radio, or sing, drink coffee and smoke a hookah. Roy was a long way from Hendon. At night when the electricity failed they sat in the dark and listened to Mozart on a wind-up gramophone.[45]

During the day Roy drove out to the countryside, helping with vaccinations and distributing anti-malarial drugs. The villages were often remote, reached along dusty tracks that snaked along the hillsides; he had to concentrate hard, his eyes fixed immediately on the road in front, as he passed cypress trees and caught flashes of the sea in the distance.[46] When it was particularly hot or, later in the year, particularly cold and wet, few villagers came out, but on a busy day, the ambulance could tend to well over 100 patients. Inspired, like so many Europeans before him, by what he saw as a biblical landscape, Roy resolved to read his Old Testament anew.[47]

At the back of his diary, Roy kept a tally of the letters he had received. Most were from his mother and sister Joy, and he usually copied them out word for word. That first summer in Lebanon, Ruth, the young nurse from the Gloucester hospital, sent seven letters, but Roy did not record what she wrote, the words perhaps too intimate and personal. He sent a note to Bernard reflecting on his experiences, and what he had learned about both conscience and pacifism:

you ask me whether I am happy in the pursuit of a single end which gives purpose to life . . . I think we should try, at all costs, to preserve our individuality. That does not mean we must cut ourselves off from the community, but we must try and remain detached, mentally balanced, in the midst of the crowd . . . [48]

Roy's own breakdown in Kent and his brother Alfred's difficulties were probably not far from his mind. As the temperature rose over the summer, he received a letter from his mother, telling him that Alfred had been sent to a mental hospital, but the news passed without comment in Roy's diary, again perhaps too personal or difficult to describe.[49] That year, Alan Ryan, who worked with Roy in the clinic in Syria, committed suicide, throwing himself off a cliff. He was not the first nor the last member of the FAU to do so.[50] Halfway across the world, Quentin Boyd, a doctor who worked with Bernard Llewellyn, died in Calcutta after suffering an acute period of depression.[51]

Over the radio in June 1943, Roy heard that Lampedusa, an island between Tunisia and Italy, had fallen 'after a terrific bombardment by the Allied Air Forces'.[52] He reflected that he was always pleased when he heard of an Allied success and wondered if other pacifists felt the same.[53] Many probably did. In England, John Middleton Murry was still writing editorials in Peace News as late as 1943 calling for a negotiated peace – ceding control of eastern Europe to the Nazis – but his position was controversial even within pacifist circles. Most pacifists had explicitly or implicitly decided not to obstruct Allied activities, and were instead focusing on witness and service.[54] This could still be a difficult position to hold, a delicate balance between opposing war and hoping for victory. At times Roy had considered leaving the Unit altogether, and when people asked him why he was a conscientious objector he could only recall the things he said at his tribunal, describing the 'voice inside' commanding that war was wrong. He told himself that if he abandoned his pacifism now he would be 'letting down' his brothers and sister. He had, after all, signed the pledge back in 1937 to renounce war.

Stephen Verney, who had run the Unit in Gloucester and had

travelled to the Middle East the year before Roy, did not feel entirely the same. Since arriving in Syria, Stephen had been working in a remote clinic, as well as running the Unit's choir, but in the summer of 1943 he announced that he was leaving the FAU to join the army.[55] He had been living in Tel Tamr, a village built for Assyrian Christian refugees from Turkey, where he worked under an Armenian doctor and treated Bedouin and Kurds from the nearby settlements.[56] Before Syria, the last time Roy and Stephen had met was just before going to Ilfracombe, but they saw each other several times that summer, bumping into one another during visits to Beirut for rest and relaxation. Back in Gloucester, the two young men had had long discussions about the limits of pacifism. Now, on the Mediterranean coast, Roy wrote in his diary that 'I don't think Stephen has been a convinced pacifist . . .'[57] He was right. When Stephen signed up as a conscientious objector back in 1939, he had admitted in his diary, 'the whole problem is very painful. I cannot sign cheerfully on either side . . . By refusing to fight I do feel I am betraying a lot of good people.'[58] The feeling evidently stayed with him over the next four years, before his conscience finally came down on the other side, in the Syrian desert.

It was not war but another human frailty that helped Stephen change his mind once and for all. After travelling to the nearest town to buy some firewood for the clinic, he found the Mayor demanding a bribe, and in this moment Stephen realised he had to resign from the FAU, having 'woken to the reality of human corruption'.[59] The FAU was driven by a Quaker vision of the human potential for perfection, but in the extortion of a small-town official the very Anglican Stephen Verney felt he had glimpsed the innate affliction of humanity. He wrote to his parents, 'I have been utterly wrong, and wrong for the wrong reasons.'[60] He later reflected that he had become a conscientious objector because he thought God was benign and the world had been created in that image, with no room for evil, but in the Middle East, his imagination formed by images from the Bible, he increasingly turned to the avenging God of the Old Testament, a God that seemed to leave little space for pacifism.

Other volunteers left the FAU too – not in large numbers, but there was a steady stream over the years who either changed their minds or concluded that their work was so close to being in the

Staff of the London office of the Fellowship of Reconciliation, *c.* 1940. Stella St John is being handed flowers by an unknown man. A Christian pacifist during the Second World War, Stella also worked as a vet, volunteered at the Hungerford Club and drove ambulances during the London Blitz.

A Fellowship of Reconciliation staff reunion, 1975. Stella St John is on the far right and her Pekingese dog is on the knee of an unknown woman in the front row. Doris Nicholls (née Steynor), who had been a source of great strength for Stella during the war, stands on the left in a white dress and glasses.

Tom Burns, probably taken sometime in the mid-1930s. He joined the Friends' Ambulance Unit at the outbreak of the Second World War.

The Friends' Ambulance Unit (FAU) vehicles in Norway (1939–40). The ambulances, known affectionately as 'Big Bertha', were notoriously difficult to drive.

The members of the FAU in their winter uniforms on the way to Finland in 1939. Tom is standing third from right.

Tom and other members of the FAU in the Stalag VIIIB camp after being taken as German prisoners of war in the spring of 1941. Tom is on the left in the back row, holding a pipe.

FAU volunteers training as mechanics at Manor Farm near Birmingham during the war.

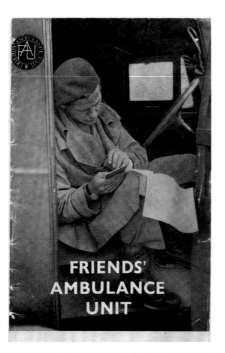

Cover of the FAU's fourth Annual Report, 1944, showing an unknown pacifist ambulance driver. The military appearance of the uniform worn by members of the FAU was controversial among some pacifists.

Cover of the FAU's Annual Report, 1946. After the end of the war, many FAU members undertook relief work with displaced persons.

FAU volunteers loading oil drums during the war at Hsiakwan depot in Nationalist-controlled Yunnan, south-west China. Fuel was in short supply and the FAU travelled as far as the Gobi Desert to find oil.

A Pacifist Service Unit leaflet published during the war. The PSU provided opportunities for conscientious objectors to carry out alternative service, particularly in social work.

WAR WILL CEASE WHEN MEN REFUSE TO FIGHT

What are YOU going to do about it?

THE PEACE PLEDGE UNION
DICK SHEPPARD HOUSE, 6 ENDSLEIGH STREET, LONDON, W.C.1

A late-1930s Peace Pledge Union poster calling on individuals to reject war.

Men of the Non-Combatant Corps undergoing training at a camp on the east coast of England, most probably Skegness. The Corps included men not physically fit for combatant service and conscientious objectors registered for non-combatant service.

Benjamin Britten and W. H. Auden, 1941. The pair were friends and both left for the US shortly before the war. Britten returned to England in 1942 and registered as a conscientious objector.

Muriel Lester (fifth from right) in Argentina, 1941, shortly before being interned in Trinidad. She had been touring the Americas as part of her campaign against the war.

The writer and critic John Middleton Murry who, in the 1930s and 1940s, moved between revolutionary socialism, pacifism and Christianity. During the war he was the controversial editor of *Peace News* and an advocate of community farms.

Portrait of Vera Brittain, 1936, taken at the height of her fame as a writer. Vera's pacifism was initially inspired by the death of both her brother and fiancé during the First World War, but during the Second World War her peace campaigning would attract much controversy, not least within her own family.

army as to make no practical or ethical difference. The reasons for disowning pacifism were just as varied as the reasons for becoming a conscientious objector in the first place. David Morris, a colleague of Bernard Llewellyn in the China Convoy, joined the army after refusing to give a Chinese soldier a lift, and the soldier had thrown stones at his truck. Enraged, David stopped the vehicle and hit his attacker. It was at this moment, he would later recall in his memoir, that he realised he was not a 'true pacifist'.[61] He concluded, 'I liked the life of a truck driver, but it certainly was not a Christian life . . . And since I was not prepared to live like a saint I did not see how I could continue to claim exemption . . .'[62] Within weeks of punching the soldier, David reported to a recruiting office in Calcutta and spent the rest of the war in British military intelligence.

Occasionally there was a conversion moment like David Morris's or almost literally on the road to Damascus in the case of Stephen Verney, but others slipped gradually away. Just as the reasons not to fight could be uncertain, so too could the motivations for joining the armed forces, formed out of a swirling mass of self-questioning and reflection that only occasionally provided resolution.[63] When one volunteer left the China Convoy, he wrote to the FAU, 'I doubt if I can make a coherent statement of all the things on my mind, indeed I am not sure that I know what I think or what I think I ought to think.'[64]

Others concluded that all their efforts were simply whistling in the wind, a futile gesture against impossible odds. The scale of the problem could be overwhelming. Hadley Laycock, one of the few surgeons in the FAU, observed that 'Anything we may do for suffering humanity . . . seems like a very small drop in a very large bucket.'[65] In the face of a possible cholera outbreak, Bill Brough – who went on to become a doctor and psychoanalyst – reflected that he 'felt shocked at my monumental inadequacy, which I always knew would sooner or later catch up with me'.[66] David Morris remarked that a 'general sense of uneasiness that all was not well was always in the background, haunting the minds of even the most complacent members of the Unit'.[67] Even the official history of the FAU concludes that in 'the welter of suffering amid the displaced and distressed millions . . . the efforts of a few voluntary workers over a year or two appeared puny and insignificant'.[68] Sometimes, the tools and commitments available to the FAU seemed inadequate to the task at hand, failing to match their aspirations.

It was often not so much that pacifists' consciences had shifted in content or detail as that the world had changed around them. Some former pacifists saw themselves as continuing to live by the same principles, but drawing different conclusions about how they should be applied, particularly as the war wore on and more and more information came out about the Nazi atrocities. Patrick Mayhew had worked as a pacifist ambulance worker with the Royal Army Medical Corps during the evacuation from Dunkirk back in 1940, but the sight of German troops forcing the British army into the sea helped to refocus his mind.[69] Faced with the prospect of a German invasion of Britain, and with his brothers already in the armed forces, he had felt he had no alternative but to 'join the damned', taking on the guilt of the world.[70] This is somewhat similar to how Dietrich Bonhoeffer apparently understood his experiences – not moving from pure pacifism to complicity with violence but always following God's will in relation to Fascism.

If the facts on the ground changed the direction that some people's conscience took, it is important to acknowledge what these facts were. In later life, Stephen Verney recalled that the news was coming through in 1943 about 'Hitler exterminating the Jews', and that helped shift his perspective.[71] In 1940 though, conscientious objectors like Mayhew who had renounced their exemptions and joined the military talked much more about an invasion of Britain and the general threat of Fascism than about the persecution of Jews. In doing so, they were merely reflecting a much wider pattern among the British population.[72] In was not until late 1942 that the British government formally acknowledged that the Nazis were trying to exterminate the Jews.[73] It is too simple to say there was a particular moment when people could have known about the Holocaust, as many were aware in different ways at a very early date, but more specific details begun to emerge into broader consciousness from early 1943, marked by the publication of Victor Gollancz's pamphlet *Let my People Go*, which sold over a quarter of a million copies in its first three months. The book reported that between one and two million Jews had already been murdered in German-occupied Europe.[74] Many British people were not particularly interested or failed to grasp the immensity of the horror, more concerned with making ends meet back in Britain or surviving the war in the armed forces. It was not until much later – perhaps even decades later – that the true abomination became understood by the wider British public.

When people left the Unit, there was seldom a sense of betrayal felt by the others, but rather one of regret and disappointment, a resigned recognition that it could not have been an easy decision, that people were doing it for the right reasons and that there was a very fine line between those who stayed and those who went. The last time Roy saw Stephen Verney, he thought that the future soldier looked 'very sad – It must be almost as difficult to leave the FAU as it was to sign on as a conscientious objector at the beginning of the war.'[75] Regret, not anger, was the dominant emotion.

A year after first arriving in the Middle East, Roy boarded yet another ship. This time, on 21 April 1944, he departed from the Tunisian port of Bizerte, headed for Naples, Italy. He had rejoined the rest of the Hadfield-Spears Hospital now attached to the Corps Expéditionnaire Français of Moroccans, Algerians, Senegalese and French settlers in north Africa, as they sailed to southern Europe to support the Allied armies making their way up Italy. After his time in northern Syria, Roy had been itching to move on, and summoned up the courage to ask for a transfer, apologising for being 'such a nuisance', but feeling that he was 'too remote from the war'.[76]

In one of the last battles of the north African campaign, almost a year previously, Bizerte had been the scene of an intense Allied bombardment, witnessed by the Scottish nationalist, associate of SNP leader Douglas Young and conscientious objector George Campbell Hay, who was serving with the British army in a non-combatant role. While working as a nightwatchman, Campbell Hay had a panoramic view of the bombing of German troops – so close that among the sound of explosions he could pick up the screams of the wounded and dying. Campbell Hay's mental health never recovered from what he saw and heard that night. A Gaelic speaker and poet, he wrote the poem *Bizerte* in response:

And who tonight are beseeching
Death to come quickly in all their tongues,
or are struggling among stones and beams,
crying in frenzy for help, and are not heard?
Who to-night is paying
the old accustomed tax of common blood?

Campbell Hay was one of the few British Second World War poets
to engage empathically with the experience of the enemy in war, a
fact that might perhaps have been linked to his status as a conscientious objector. When Roy arrived in Bizerte, only the physical
scars of the battle could be seen along the coast.

As they sailed for Italy, Roy and the men of the FAU were now
packed alongside thousands of soldiers in the sweltering hold of a
ship, stacked in bunks five tiers high, with only the length of a fore-
arm between them.[77] Disembarking in Naples, with the summit of
Vesuvius smouldering in the background, the FAU was sent north
to the mountain village of San Clemente. Southern Italy was suffering, not just from war, but from disease, hunger, poverty and the
corruption that came in its wake. One FAU volunteer observed
that 'sorrow and tragedy were the order of the day. Survivors
arrived in a terrible condition, malnourished. Children with sunken
eyes of despair ... One felt one might be swallowed up at any
moment.'[78] Mussolini was still propping up a puppet regime in the
north, but German troops were occupying the country and were
well dug in across the rugged terrain. After the euphoric victories
of north Africa, the advance through Italy was supposed to be
easy, but had instead turned into a hard grind, as the retreating
German army fought over every hill, laying waste to the countryside as it went. The eighteen months of fighting, across exposed
and treacherous terrain, was some of the most brutal the British
and Free French had seen, as they suffered more than 120,000
casualties.[79] Although the tide of the war had definitely turned, it
was still taking a bitter toll.

Roy and the Hadfield-Spears Hospital set off for the front, their
base just opposite the German lines and rather ominously in front
of the French artillery.[80] Michael Rowntree told the Unit it was
'going to be a tricky job'. Roy was put in charge of driving the
water truck, and as the Unit travelled through the night to avoid

German aircraft he thought back to something he had read by Arthur Koestler about the Spanish Civil War, that such situations were never as bad in reality as they were in the imagination.[81] This was wishful thinking. On the way to the battlefield, Michael Rowntree stopped the vehicles to listen to birdsong in a bombed-out landscape that was much greener than the deserts of north Africa and Syria but was littered with ruined villages. The men finally arrived in San Clemente, settling down for a few hours' rest in trenches dug into the rough fields. Roy immediately gave up on any idea of getting to sleep as the guns boomed and the shells screamed over their heads, jumping every time they fired.[82] The next morning he rose to see the mountain opposite occupied by German soldiers looking down on them. In the middle of it all, he heard a nightingale sing.

Following six days of bombardment, the noise suddenly stopped, and the ambulance workers knew that this meant the ground attack had begun. They sat and waited, assuming that many of the soldiers they had got to know well over the previous months would come back injured or not at all.[83] The largely colonial French troops had more success than the British or American soldiers, but the losses were still heavy. Over the next three weeks, Roy treated man after man with their 'insides hanging out and their legs blown off by mines'.[84] He took one soldier into the operating theatre to have his legs amputated and asked him how he felt; the man stoically replied, 'Well, I couldn't run a race, but I've got plenty of fight left in me,' before dying on the operating table. Michael Rowntree half-jokingly asked Roy if he wanted a transfer back to Syria.

And then it was over. Or over at least for now. Roy, Michael and the other men in the FAU woke up to find the soldiers had moved forward and everything was eerily quiet once more. Roy helped take down the tents and drove his water truck towards the new front line, passing roadside graves, the air filled with the stench of dead bodies. His truck broke down on a narrow road lined with mines, and in his panic he rather foolishly lit a match to see if there was anything in the petrol tank. Thankfully it was completely empty.[85] The hospital's Commanding Officer had chosen an even more exposed spot for the new hospital, just to the south of the fortified monastery of Monte Cassino, where Axis troops were thoroughly entrenched. The Germans had strung a series of fortifications across the mountains, rivers and valleys of central Italy to stop the Allied advance north, and the mountaintop monastery lay right at its heart, commanding a view over the surrounding countryside. The position had already been bombed by Allied aircraft in the belief that it was being used as a lookout post by German soldiers, but the resulting rubble simply made it easier for the Axis troops to dig themselves in. The bombardment was so heavy it attracted protests back in Britain from Vera Brittain as part of the campaign against bombing.[86] By the time Roy and the Hadfield-Spears arrived, American, Indian, French, Polish, British and New Zealand troops had attacked three times, throwing thousands of men and thousands of pounds of explosives at the mountain ridges, and three times they had been pushed back, resulting in thousands of dead and wounded.

At night Roy slept in a ditch that he shared with Michael Rowntree, as the hospital was frequently targeted by German shells. Roy wrote, 'I have never felt so scared in my life,' as explosions burst around them, and the sound of the bombardment echoed through the valley. It seemed the Germans could see the hospital tents, but ignored the Red Cross painted on them.[87] In contravention of the laws of war, the French had also placed two anti-tank guns in the middle of the clinic, and they became a frequent target.

On the mountain opposite, the volunteers could see the continuing slaughter as American aircraft pounded the German camp. Roy felt deeply torn, quietly celebrating as the Axis troops were driven back, but finding it difficult, once again, to reconcile such feelings with his pacifism, keeping alive a sense that the 'enemy is not an evil person . . . but a person feeling the same kind of things we feel'.[88] The Germans were finally driven off Monte Cassino, Moroccan soldiers serving with the French making one of the key breakthroughs over the high mountain terrain, but the cost in lives was high. After the Germans had retreated, some of the men from the FAU went up to what remained of the monastery: 'It was the most shocking scene of desolation and destruction imaginable . . . a vast pile of grey ruin.'[89] The hillsides were covered with burned-out fields and villages, as hungry Italian peasants climbed among the ashes.[90] This was what the aftermath of war looked like.

One of the few photographs that survive of Roy from the war shows him looking relieved, sitting in the back of a truck shortly after the battle. He looks happy even. His diary tells a different story. By 4 June, after a month of battle and bloodshed, exhaustion had set in and Roy was 'getting a bit tired of playing the hero'.[91] He had seen more than enough suffering, seen too many men with crushed limbs and gaping wounds and stayed awake through too many nights, unable to rest due to the sound of bombs and his own anxiety. He told his diary, 'I do not like having shells directed at me. I am anxious to live as long as possible. I am not prepared to die quite yet.'[92] He was also feeling nostalgic for home, wondering if in later life he would look back on this time with as much affection as his early days in London, hoping that 'things that are hard to bear are sweet to remember'.[93] Nine years before, he had been very afraid of the distant possibility of war, but when it actually came it was much worse, much more terrifying and much more horrific than he could possibly have imagined.

Fear was something Roy had come to live with, something he had learned to accept. In Gloucester, when challenged over whether he was simply too afraid to join the army, he had told his diary that 'The man who can say he has struck fear out of his heart is either a liar or a fool.'[94] Four years later in Syria, similar thoughts had returned, and he copied a quote into his diary from the Chinese writer Lin Yutang: 'All intelligent men are cowards, because intelligent men want to save their skins.'[95] Dread and terror had become a way of life, not something to be ashamed of.

Remarkably enough, the British army, or at least parts of it, had come to similar conclusions, accepting that soldiers were often afraid. The military had travelled a long way from the First World War, when it seemed to think that any hint of fear in battle was a sign of moral weakness and a failure of character.[96] By the Second World War, there was even occasional sympathy for the psychological casualties of war. Soldiers themselves talked about becoming 'bomb happy', and the official euphemism for psychological distress was 'exhaustion', as the army set up 'rest centres' a few miles behind the lines where troops could go to recuperate for a few days before being sent back to fight.[97] There was a recognition that war injured the mind as well as the body.

Fundamental attitudes had not shifted too much higher up in the army, however, and British generals were worried that in the face of ruthless Fascist soldiers the British were now somehow too gentle, too civil, to stand firm and fight.[98] All this tempered masculinity was all very well, but it had its limits if you were asking someone to kill another human being. Warrior virtues were still celebrated, even if in the twenty years since the First World War glory on the battlefield was no longer the only way of defining what it meant to be a British man. And this presented a problem for the British military. In an influential book on what it meant to be brave in war, Winston Churchill's personal doctor Lord Moran argued that soldiers of a previous generation had acted impulsively, innately, without thought, but the British soldier of the middle of the twentieth century was too likely to stop and think. Moran was a veteran of the First World War, and although *The Anatomy of Courage* was not published until 1945, the ideas it contained were widely in circulation before that.[99] For Moran, too much thinking led to fumbling and hesitation, and, most importantly, in the split second between thought and action, cowardice was liable to creep in. If too much of the wrong type of thoughtfulness was an issue for people like Moran, it was a particular problem for conscientious objectors, who seemed more liable than most to stop and reflect. This was a very personal issue for Roy, not least as he faced up to the shells and the injured on the battlefield. He found that when he stopped running around the field hospital, anxiety inched up on him, so he quickly looked for ways to get back to work. It was easier to clean the blood off the floor than to rest. The rush of immediate need took his mind off the carnage all around.[100]

For the British armed forces, cowardice was not the presence of fear but the failure to fulfil one's duty in the presence of fear. The Adjutant General Sir Ronald Forbes Adam wrote to senior officers in 1942 claiming that 'a man cannot be truly courageous unless he has felt and conquered fear. Conversely, cowardice is not the presence of fear, but the succumbing to it without a struggle or excuse.'[101] The army took it for granted that the duty to be fulfilled in the face of fear was a duty to King, Country and Commanding Officer, even if conscientious objectors could have a much wider sense of loyalty and obligation, not limited to a man in uniform.

Roy, like many other conscientious objectors, had been driven by a determination to show the world that he was not a coward, that he was not too afraid to go into battle or to make sacrifices for other people. This was a determination that had led him to Syria, Libya, Italy and (later) France, right up to the front line. The threat of being shamed in the minds of others was an important part of this. As they opposed war, many young pacifists felt the eyes of their friends, family, neighbours and lovers upon them, and were worried about their harsh judgements. Roy wrote in his diary in the summer of 1944, in the middle of the fighting in central Italy, that on the one hand he wanted to be as far away from the war as possible, but on the other hand he wanted to show the world that being a conscientious objector did not mean he was a coward. He concluded that perhaps he worried too much about what other people thought.[102]

Of course, you did not have to go to war to show you were brave. Conscience itself – in its varied forms – can demand bravery, and a commitment to principle can itself take courage in the face of criticism and stigma. Even Lady Spears admitted that pacifism 'demanded courage, the special courage of the individual outside the herd'.[103] Fred Urquhart had initially been worried that he did not have the bravery to become a conscientious objector, and Roy was worried that pacifists were too easily 'bullied' into taking up roles they did not want.[104] Tom Burns was offered a chance to sit out the war teaching English in Helsinki, but felt obliged to follow his conscience to north Africa and the Balkans. We can see a quiet courage in Stella St John's refusal to compromise, when it would have been far easier to go along with the demands of the Ministry of Labour. She faced prison with considerable apprehension, but felt she had a duty to follow through on her ideals, and friend after friend wrote praising her calm fortitude and bravery. And if pacifists looked to love as a guiding principle, loving one another, as Ronald and Rose Marie found, especially Rose Marie, could take a certain sort of bravery too.

For all the varieties of courage, though, there was still a strong feeling among volunteers of the FAU that combat was a paradigmatic test; even for pacifists, the front line still represented the ultimate measure of bravery. A desire to test themselves in the heat of battle, combined with a search for adventure and the commitment to service, drove conscientious objectors to volunteer not only for the FAU, but also for the Royal Army Medical Corps, Parachute Field Ambulance and bomb-disposal units.[105] For some,

dropping from an aircraft into battle or trying to defuse unex-
ploded ordnance was the greatest test of conscience. For all the
talk of tempered masculinity, there was still an anxiety at being
seen as effeminate and weak. On occasion, pacifists could be so
good at military-type bravery that they were awarded gallantry
medals, and were unsure how to respond. Michael Rowntree was
awarded a Croix de Guerre by the French for his work with the
Hadfield-Spears, sparking a debate over whether to accept. He
eventually decided to do so on the ground that it was given to him
as leader of the Unit, in recognition of all the work they had done,
later explaining that 'It would have been churlish to turn it
down . . . even if I have never used it since.'[106]

It is sometimes said that courage is the point between rashness
and cowardice, between rushing madly in and standing back too
afraid to act, but the space between these two poles is very large.
Most people, in war and elsewhere, are probably unwilling to take
extraordinary risks, but also unwilling to be seen as a coward, and
therefore hope to tread a middle ground, without calling too much
attention to themselves. This probably applies just as much to pacifists as to soldiers. In their own way, Roy Ridgway, Stella St John,
Fred Urquhart, Tom Burns, Ronald, Bianca and Rose Marie Duncan all confronted questions about what they were afraid of, and
what it meant to be brave in war, and came up with their own very
different responses.

But if courage is a virtue, like conscience, it can also be extremely
enigmatic. Courage can be in the moment, or long-term and enduring, it can be physical and moral, a matter of standing firm under
fire or standing firm in our convictions. The courage of conviction
can bleed into its own forms of cowardice, making us too afraid to
do what we really want, or what others demand of us, out of an
entrenched sense of right and wrong, good and bad. It can also be
hard to know both courage and cowardice when we see them,
even, or especially, within ourselves, as bravery merges into vanity,
recklessness and the fear of censure. Was Fred Urquhart afraid of
the army or revolted by war? Was Stella St John driven by principle or stubbornness? Were Ronald and Rose Marie moved by love
or a mixture of narcissism and masochism? They were not always
sure themselves, and the answer was probably a mixture of all of
these, as they moved between an anxious questioning of why they

were doing what they were doing and a resolute conviction that they were on the side of the good.

If the virtue of courage emerges between fear and conviction, shame and obligation, recklessness and duty, it is on this terrain of uncertain judgements that conscientious objectors, as well as soldiers and civilians, made their way. Courage is surely not a virtue that trumps all others, especially if it means fulfilling an obligation that is misplaced, or if the duty is misunderstood. It is not so simple that bravery means you have done the right thing. We can be brave defending a cause or a principle that takes us down the wrong track. Often an act appears brave, timid or foolhardy only in hindsight, as posteriority gives value to our efforts. After the war, conscientious objectors would have the rest of their lives to think this through.

Roy was working at a hospital on the French Mediterranean coast near Antibes when he heard the war was over, in Europe at least. He had spent almost a year moving around France, following the Free French Forces, as they flushed out the last pockets of occupying troops, and then stayed behind treating the wounded as Allied soldiers forced their way into Germany. Late in the war, the French had launched an attack eastwards from Provence on Italian lines near the Alps, and the wards of the hospital where Roy worked were full of casualties, tragically injured in this one last push. When Roy heard the first rumours on 7 May 1945 that Germany had surrendered, it was what he and millions of other people had been waiting for, hoping against hope, for the past six years.[107] But initially there was a sense of anticlimax. Roy wrote in his diary:

> when war broke out I was struck by the normality of everything. I expected the earth to suddenly change its appearance, but nothing very dramatic happened ... and now peace is upon us, one feels that it is a tremendous thing, but one stands at the window and looks out at the town, expecting to find that the sky is pink and the houses blue and that people are standing on their heads – but no, everything is the same.

As the news filtered through, the people on the street looked sad and weary, ground down by fear and lack of food. Somebody shouted 'The war is over' to a group of soldiers sitting in a truck, but they took no notice.

Victory had arrived, and it was a victory to be celebrated, but Roy felt bashful about being greeted as a liberator.[108] The battle was over, Fascism had been defeated and Roy was still alive, with his pacifist commitments still just about intact. Yet it was a bitter-sweet victory. Millions of people had died, and whole continents had been laid to waste. There was certainly relief that it was finished, but also a feeling of loss and melancholy. It was not until later that day that the celebrations and bonfires started. Roy and Colonel Vernier of the Hadfield-Spears Hospital drove to the Italian border, laughingly swapping each other's hats and drinking too much, as the Commanding Officer draped the French flag over lampposts.[109] When the Hadfield-Spears personnel went north to join the victory parade into Paris, Roy stayed behind on the wards.

A week after the Armistice, Roy received a letter from Ruth, declaring, 'Yes I shall marry you.'[110] More than two years of absence had brought them closer, and as the future opened up again they decided they wanted to spend it together. Two months later, Roy was in Hyde Park, walking with Bernard Llewellyn through the summer sunshine, the air fresh and clear after a storm. They wandered past the soapbox orators, listening briefly to an anarchist, and were unimpressed. Bernard had returned from China six months previously, but had been struck by the 'drab streets of England' and hoped to head off to newly liberated Europe to help with relief work.[111] That month Roy appeared before the conscientious objector tribunal, a mechanism that would continue for as long as conscription lasted – that is, until National Service came to an end when the last person was called up in 1960. When Roy stood up in Fulham once more, the ubiquitous Judge Hargreaves was there, sitting stone-faced on the bench, this time hardly saying a word before finally granting Roy an unconditional exemption.[112]

CHAPTER 16

After Lives

Within a year of the fall of Berlin, Hitler by now dead, Ronald Duncan was walking in the city's ruins. There was a smell of rotting flesh in the air and the streets were an apocalyptical vision of the worst that humanity could do to itself. Ronald was visiting as part of a British programme to support the deNazification of Germany, and was put up in a hotel amid the rubble on the previously fashionable Kurfürstendamm, a broad avenue that had once contained many Jewish-owned shops. The scars of nearly fifteen years of Fascism and war were still fresh, and if Berlin had once been at the vibrant heart of European civilisation, with British poets and politicians looking to it for inspiration, it now seemed to stand for everything that was base and pathological. Of the city's five million inhabitants before the war, two-fifths had gone: murdered in the concentration camps, killed by bombs and bullets or forced to flee by the war. Those that remained stood for hours in food queues or searched among the debris for anything to keep them alive. In the first winter after the war 60,000 Berliners perished, and in some parts of the city a quarter of all children under one year old died.[1] For many visitors, the German people had brought all this suffering on themselves, but the sense of just deserts was also often combined with sorrow and pity.[2] As Ronald wandered the streets, he also seems to have felt personal pangs of regret for the way he had spent the last six years, feeling overwhelmed by his 'secluded and selfish war years'.[3]

What, if anything, was left of the pacifist hope for a better world after so much death and destruction? Was it possible to remain optimistic once you knew about the charnel houses of Europe and beyond? Over seventy million people were dead, the large majority of them civilians – killed by gunfire and munitions, but also in death camps and by famine and disease, as hatred, persecution and disregard for human life rose to new heights. The end of the war in Europe did not bring simple respite. The Americans dropped atomic bombs on Hiroshima and Nagasaki in the summer of 1945, obliterating tens of thousands of people, and ushering in a terrifying new era. The Axis powers had been defeated, but elsewhere, smaller-scale conflicts continued to rumble on, and across the world people had to come to terms with the loss all around them. Millions were on the move, not only homeless, but also often stateless too.[4] New conflicts were breaking out, as the peoples of the world demanded their freedom in Palestine, Malaya, French Indo-China, India and elsewhere. In Europe, a Cold War was already leaving its mark, as the Iron Curtain was descending, and Britain, the US, France and the Soviets divided up Germany between them. The battles were over, but for many people peace seemed further away than ever, and if the recent past was drenched with blood, the future was frightening too.

In stark contrast, at a personal level at least, the years immediately after the war were very successful ones for Ronald. For a while he had one of the things he had always wanted: artistic recognition. In 1946, capping a period of remarkable creativity that had begun in the final years of the war, he had two plays running at the same time on the London stage. He was in Berlin to oversee a performance of *This Way to the Tomb*, his dramatisation of the life and death of St Anthony, which had opened at the Mercury Theatre in west London and been scored by Ben Britten. His translation of the French playwright Jean Cocteau's *The Eagle has Two Heads*, a tale of love and assassination, eventually transferred from London to New York where it starred a young Marlon Brando. Ronald also wrote the libretto for Ben Britten's opera *The Rape of Lucretia*, first performed at Glyndebourne in 1946 and featuring the singer Kathleen Ferrier, telling a story of brutal violence in the dying days of the Roman Empire. His themes were bloody, but Ronald's literary reputation was high.

Despite the critical acclaim, Ronald's view of the human condition was increasingly pessimistic, reflected in the morbid subjects that ran through much of his work. News of the deaths from the atomic bomb in Hiroshima plunged him into particular despair, and he suggested to Ben Britten that they write 'something as artistically painful as the burns we've inflicted on the Japanese'.[5] Ben never took him up on his offer, gradually moving away from collaborating with his friend after *The Rape of Lucretia* had been panned by the critics, but Ronald wrote the libretto *Mea Culpa* anyway, describing the 'fall of man' and ending with the dropping of the atomic bomb.[6] He dedicated the piece to 'an unknown child whose severed hand I had found like a glove on the floor' in a bombed-out house in Brixton in 1945. The title of the libretto implied both guilt and complicity, but whether personal or collective was not entirely clear.

Ronald still called himself a pacifist in some of his writings, but was largely resigned to a world of violence. He had come out of the war physically intact but despondent. All the hope of the pre-war years, and all the faith in the possibility of a better collective future, had evaporated in the losses and disappointments of the last six years. On a small scale, his community farm had been disbanded several years before as he had been unable to mould the volunteers to his vision of a common purpose. What he saw in Berlin and what he heard from Japan must have more dramatically confirmed his suspicions about human nature, as his sense of moral possibility turned inwards. By the end of the war, in a complete reversal of the pacifist line that there was something to be loved in all people, he came away concluding that 'There is a Hitler in everyone.'[7] Ronald now saw the capacity for evil as part of the human condition, and the inevitability of death came to be a dominant subject in his work. In 1950 he declared:

I cannot think of the wide world without becoming miserable from meditating on life's brevity ...

So do we all, day by day perish, fail, fall. It is that. That is it all.[8]

Humanity was corrupted and fallen, with little room for redemption. Ronald's politics had also moved steadily to the right since the late 1930s, and he was now resolutely conservative in his views, sometimes even giving up on democracy.[9]

Ronald, Rose Marie and Bianca continued to live on the Devon–Cornwall border, as Ronald's energies channelled into farming, journalism and literary work, and his moods fluctuated wildly.

Rose Marie seems to have borne the brunt of the ups and downs, and by Ronald's own admission their relationship remained tempestuous and volatile, with Ronald having more than one affair.[10] Bianca continued to live nearby, but died aged fifty-seven following a long period of ill-health, having dedicated her previous decades to supporting her brother's work. In some ways, the war years were the happiest times of the Duncan family's lives.

Across Britain, the hardships associated with the war did not simply end in 1945. Conscription would continue for another fifteen years, there were not enough houses for returning soldiers or for those who had stayed behind, and rationing lingered for everyone. But there was also hope and expectation. The election of a Labour government in the general election of 1945 was a sign that for many people there were new political possibilities. For those of a socialist persuasion at least, like Tom Burns and Stella St John, and for a while Fred Urquhart, this must have seemed an exciting time, their aspirations for once chiming with those of much of the rest of the population.

Although the end of the war is often seen as a great temporal dividing line, for many people – whether they fought or not – once they had picked up whatever pieces that remained of their lives, things went on much the same as they had before 1939. There were as many continuities as there were ruptures. Stella St John appears to have lived her life after the war much as she did before and during it: understated and determined. The day victory was declared in Europe, she was at a Fellowship of Reconciliation conference in Wales and later recalled that although she was 'delighted of course' the joy was mixed with new concerns as 'There was so much struggle around we didn't feel like celebrating much, with refugees and starving Europe.'[11] For the next two years she continued to work at the Hungerford Club, caring for the London homeless. She remained at Kingsley Hall as well, answering the letters sent to Donald Soper, but she dedicated most of her time to veterinary work, meeting up every now and again with the women she had worked with at the Fellowship of Reconciliation. Stella died just short of her ninetieth birthday. She never married and lived the rest of her life in north London, not far from where she spent much of the late 1930s and early 1940s.

For many others, their lives took off in completely new directions, the end of the war providing an opportunity to start again.
Tom Burns never returned to the life of a teacher in provincial
private schools. For a while he worked in the press office of the
FAU in central London, then he moved to the outskirts of Birmingham and took up a position with the Bourneville Village
Trust, looking after the estates built for Cadbury workers and living in a house owned by Paul Cadbury. He was once again offered
a job teaching English in Helsinki, but newly married to Elizabeth –
whom he had met at a Quaker hostel in 1944 – he was put off by
his memories of the cold Finnish winter.[12] He would go on to
become an eminent sociologist, famed for his study of the BBC,
and retiring from the University of Edinburgh in 1981. His obitu-
aries remember him as a cultured but shy and private person,
deeply loving and caring towards his wife and five children, morally serious, sometimes brusque and impatient, but also inspiring
great affection and loyalty. His family recall that, although he
remained a pacifist, like many people of his generation he rarely
spoke of his life during the war.

Once so all consuming, conscientious objection could slowly
melt away, disappearing into the background, not shaping lives in
any straightforward manner. Fred Urquhart spent the last year of
the war in England, first working in the grounds of Woburn Abbey,
then moving to London and hanging out on the edges of the London literary scene. Mary Litchfield died of TB shortly after the end
of the war. Fred had partly left Scotland as he felt it was too dominated by the Church and would never accept his sexuality. In the
following years, he did not come out to his family, but lived for
many years with the aristocratic ballet dancer Peter Wyndham
Allen, settling in the leafy gentility of the Ashdown Forest south of
London, and returning to the outskirts of Edinburgh only after
Peter's death. Fred continued to write and received favourable
reviews, although the sales were never high. His great talent lay in
his ear for Scottish working-class life and he kept his Edinburgh
accent throughout his life, continuing to think in the Scots vernacular. He made his living as a reader for literary agents and
publishing houses, for a short time working for the film-makers
Metro-Goldwyn-Mayer. Neither pacifism nor politics seemed to
play much of a part in Fred's life in the second half of the twentieth

century, and like Ronald Duncan he drifted slowly to the right politically.

For a while, Roy Ridgway had very little to do with public statements of pacifism either, as he tried to make a new life for himself. Forty years later, he looked back and reflected that by 1945 he and the other volunteers were no longer 'the young men who had started the war, wanting to show the world how they should behave. We had become involved in it as much as anybody and couldn't claim to be different . . .'[13] For Roy, the battlefield, and the sacrifices it demanded, had taught humility and he no longer yearned to stand apart. Although he still thought of himself as a pacifist, he wanted to dedicate his time to a career, first in journalism and then in public relations.[14] He also got married, not to Ruth after all, but to Dorothea, whom he met shortly after the war, and moved to Hampshire where they had three children. In an interview recorded in the 1980s Roy has only the very slightest hint of a Liverpool accent and sounds happy and contented, his voice quick to rise to gentle laughter.[15] Over the decades, his interests were drawn to holistic forms of health and psychology, and he wrote several books on childcare, although he eventually returned to journalism, becoming editor of a medical newspaper, the *BMA News Review*.[16] Roy and Dorothea's youngest son, Tony, was born with cystic fibrosis, and the couple spent twenty-nine years supporting their child, giving him a life filled with love.

Vera Brittain found it harder to move on from the war, as the stigma associated with her own form of opposition proved difficult to shake. She was one of the few to find wartime pacifism a major weight around her neck. It is not easy to say why. Perhaps it was because she was a generation older than the Second World War conscientious objectors who still had the rest of their lives in which to forge new reputations. Perhaps it was because she was a feminist who could be forthright in her views, and that made some people feel uncomfortable. Vera's public reputation, so high after she published *Testament of Youth* in the early 1930s, never really recovered, particularly in the US, and she entered the late 1940s feeling exhausted and isolated, finding some solace when it was revealed she had been on a Nazi 'blacklist' of people to be rounded up after an invasion of Britain. She remained a committed campaigner, becoming Vice President of the International League for

Peace and Freedom as well as the National Peace Council. Above all, it was the First World War that continued to dominate her life at the most personal level; she was never quite able to leave behind the horrors of the trenches. It would take a 1979 BBC dramatisation of her great book *Testament of Youth* to turn things around reputation-wise, nine years after her death, but as a result her role in the Second World War was largely erased from public memory.

Many others who opposed the war or refused to fight were able to hold prominent positions in public life, their stature relatively unaffected. Muriel Lester continued to travel the world, still collecting large fees in the US, which she used to fund the activities of the International Fellowship of Reconciliation. She moved between Belgium, Germany, China, India, Japan, Afghanistan, Kenya, South Africa and Burma, at a breathtaking pace. Her reputation as the 'mother of world peace' seemed to open doors wherever she went, and she met with Gandhi and the last Viceroy during the bloody final days of the Raj and shortly before the assassination of the leader of Indian independence. In the decades to come Muriel would be slowed down only by ill-health and old age.[17] Stephen Verney and Michael Rowntree, who had both volunteered in the FAU with Roy Ridgway, went on to become, respectively, a bishop in the Church of England and a newspaper editor. Ben Britten and Michael Tippett became eminent and controversial figures, but it was mainly their music rather than their politics that caused a stir, and they were eventually deemed respectable enough to be given knighthoods. Less than a month after VE Day in 1945, Ben's opera *Peter Grimes* was attracting rave reviews in the press, and he was being heralded as the future of English music.[18] Michael Tippett's *A Child of our Time* was being performed on the BBC even before the end of the war, and became increasingly popular across Europe, understood as a hymn for peace among the ashes of war.[19] In 1953 Donald Soper was elected to the most senior role in British Methodism, President of the Conference, and joined the House of Lords in 1965, supposedly describing it as 'proof of the reality of life after death'. Lord Soper always remained controversial, but he became a widely acknowledged and respected voice of a particular form of dissent.

There might have been a few professions and club houses where being a conscientious objector later caused a problem, but these seem to have been relatively rare. Non-combatant status created a barrier in some jobs – as regimental networks played an important role in forging connections – but this was a problem shared by all those who had worked in reserved occupations like teaching or agriculture.[20] A large number of conscientious objectors even became relatively establishment figures: a founder of the London Business School, the first woman to be elected as a Fellow to the Royal Society, a Vice President of the World Bank, the last British High Commissioner to the Federation of Rhodesia and Nyasaland, the most senior legal figure in Scotland, and several members of the House of Lords. All in all, after the war, conscientious objectors were very much part of the warp and weft of British social and cultural life.

The treatment of people like Fred, Stella, Tom, Ronald and Roy reveals a great deal about British traditions of freedom. During a period of national emergency the British state went further than any other at the time to accommodate those whose scruples would not allow them to fight. Those who refused to take up arms were on the whole treated with tolerance, condemned more by being forgotten than by being publicly vilified. But like all forms of tolerance this was a tolerance with limits. It implied a 'putting up with', a conditional acceptance, rather than a warm embrace. After all, you only tolerate things that you do not agree with or like. And often conscientious objectors were tolerated because it was a pragmatic thing to do, rather than from a fundamental sense that requiring someone to go against their conscience produced a deep moral harm. It was easier to grant exemptions to the relatively few who did not want to fight than it was to force them kicking and screaming into the armed services.

Above all, this was a freedom that had its boundaries and conventions. A quiet, understated and deeply personal conscience seemed easier to tolerate than those that were passionate, disruptive and collective. To be publicly accepted, conscience had to walk a narrow path – tempered, quiet and willing to accept the burdens associated with its position. This was freedom in a minor key. Not an effervescent and freewheeling liberty, but one that was restrained, respectable and loyal.

Not all consciences were tolerated equally. The commitments of women were systematically sidelined. Socialists and anarchists had more luck if they presented themselves as humanitarians. Scottish and Indian nationalists were given short truck. Religious minorities were met with bafflement and prejudice by everyone. Those who did not walk the narrow path risked being persecuted, ridiculed or ignored. Those who were successful before the tribunal can therefore be seen as practising an authorised form of dissent, a type of opposition that the British state felt comfortable in accommodating. In the decades since, as arguments about the limits and necessity of individual freedom have partially shifted to freedom of religion, speech and expression, this same path has continued to set the direction of travel. Freedom, British style, has more often than not been freedom for a very particular type of person.

As the years passed and conscientious objectors got on with their lives, they were inevitably asked by others and by themselves whether they had done the right thing, and whether they would do the same again. Had it all been worth it? The answers to these questions were inevitably formed in hindsight, as the moral lessons of the war, both personal and political, shifted in time. Above all, and increasingly so as the decades passed, the spectre of the Holocaust loomed unavoidably large – the ultimate challenge to pacifist optimism about human nature. In the decades since the Second World War, Nazism has become the great measure by which to judge evil and moral depravity, the key test of conscience. This is a standard that all those who failed to stand up to Nazism might be said to have failed. Conscientious objectors have therefore inevitably had to respond, both personally and publicly.

During the war many pacifists had simply refused to believe that anyone could be responsible for atrocities on the scale that were reported from occupied Europe. They saw Hitler as a passing phenomenon, a symptom of the underlying corruption of war. Middleton Murry's *Peace News*, in particular, tended to see reports of atrocities, massacres and other abuses as propaganda designed to stir up support for the war. But in the final years of the war he turned around abruptly and began advocating a 'defensive war' – something that did not go down very well in the Peace Pledge Union.[21] He was also beginning to question whether pacifists could have any answer to Fascism. A month after the war he wrote, 'I misjudged two things. First I misjudged the nature of the average decent man ... The second mistake was even more serious. I gravely underestimated the terrible power of scientific terrorism as developed by the totalitarian police-states ...'[22] For Middleton Murry, pacifism simply could not cope with Treblinka or, for that matter, with the gulag.

A handful of pacifists saw the direct aftermath of the camps head on. A group of FAU volunteers were among the first people to enter the newly liberated camp at Sandbostel in north-west Germany, where thousands of people had died during the war, and even after liberation hundreds perished from disease and starvation.[23] They were not the only conscientious objectors to witness such horrors. In the summer of 1945, Ben Britten visited Bergen-Belsen with the violinist Yehudi Menuhin. Across four days the two men gave recitals to the survivors of the concentration camps, many of whom were still extremely ill. The stench of death, disease and decay could be smelt for miles around, and the British authorities were struggling to cope. According to his biographer, Ben refused to talk about these experiences until much later in his life, eventually telling his partner Peter Pears that what he saw that week had shaped everything he had composed since.[24] As with his friend Ronald Duncan, Ben's creative energies were increasingly marked by themes of violence, but it was not until 1962 that he returned directly to the topic of war. *War Requiem* was commissioned to mark the reopening of Coventry Cathedral, itself a monument to reconciliation after having been bombed and rebuilt, and Ben saw this piece not simply as a protest against violence but also, like Tippett's *A Child of our Time*, as an attempt to repair its wounds.[25] It is notable, though, that Ben turned to the First World War rather than the Second for its central motifs, drawing on Wilfred Owen's poems of the trenches. On the title page of the score, he quoted Owen's lines: 'My subject is War, and the pity of War. The Poetry is in the pity ... All a poet can do today is warn.' At the first performance, Ben asked that there be no applause.

Ben remained a pacifist throughout his life, seeing Bergen-Belsen not as a unique event but as part of the wider logic of war and violence. He viewed what had been done in the camps as an abomination, not because it was somehow totally different from all other forms of killing, but because it represented a possible endpoint of the broader drive to war. An extreme horror certainly, but not fundamentally different from other horrors that had marked the twentieth century. Ben's friend Ronald came to similar conclusions, spending the last years of his life writing the epic poem *Man*, which features a section entitled 'Auschwitz'. He self-published a part of the poem in 1978, describing a train journey to the camp, where he imagines the genocide of the Jews as providing a looking glass for examining the human condition. Central to the poem are the lines: 'nothing terrifies us more than a mirror'.[26] He does not seem to have reflected at length, at least in his writing, about his own German family and their Jewish descent, and instead sought to draw more universal lessons.

If conscientious objectors looked back on their refusal to fight Fascism with regret and remorse, this did not necessarily mark a fundamental shift in the tone of their moral lives. Guilt had long marked the conscience of those who were opposed to war. Guilt over the consequences of their actions for friends, families, lovers and distant strangers. Guilt over whether they were just sending other people to die. Guilt over whether they were free-riding or taking the easy way out. Guilt over whether they had done enough to prevent suffering and heal the injured. Tom Burns spent many nights in his prisoner-of-war camp reflecting on what he had done and what he was going to do. Roy Ridgway was often a bundle of nerves, changing his mind several times and constantly looking for new directions. Ben Britten and Michael Tippett experienced the war as a period of emotional turmoil. Refusing to fight seldom brought certainty, but instead prompted a nagging and deep introspection.

What happened to their commitments to peace?

In October 1985 Roy Ridgway answered the phone in his family home. It was a man from the Reuters news agency. The voice down the line excitedly announced that 'there's a buzz going on in Oslo that you have won the Nobel Peace Prize'.[27] The rumours were correct. After retiring in the early 1980s, Roy had served as the European press officer for the International Physicians for the Prevention of Nuclear War (IPPNW), an organisation which brought together medical professionals from both sides of the Iron Curtain determined to stop nuclear annihilation. Much of the work had consisted in a detailed analysis of the burns from Nagasaki and Hiroshima and was designed to show the scale and cruelty of nuclear war. After several decades away from it, Roy had found his way back to the peace movement. Awarding the prize, the Nobel Committee declared that the IPPNW 'has performed a considerable service to mankind by spreading authoritative information and by creating an awareness of the catastrophic consequences of atomic warfare'.[28]

The search for peace in the second half of the twentieth century was not the concern only of anti-war activists. Many of their aspirations were once again mainstream. As governments and politicians looked at the debris all around them, they started to think once again about how another war like the last one could be avoided. In doing so, they returned to some of the tools advocated by the peace campaigners of the 1930s and gave them new forms. Despite the collapse of the League of Nations, great hopes were once again placed in the capacity for international cooperation to keep war at bay, so long as the right rules and procedures could be set in place. Within months of the end of the war, fifty countries met in San Francisco to found the United Nations, proudly declaring the goal to keep peace and end the 'scourge of war' throughout the world.[29] Conscience was seen as a central part of this mission. The Universal Declaration of Human Rights, adopted by the UN in 1948, declared that, as part of the aim for 'freedom, justice and peace', freedom of conscience was a fundamental human right.[30] The document, however, was no simple vindication of pacifism and conscientious objection to military service, supporting the right to 'rebellion against tyranny and oppression'. As the Declaration implied, conscience does not always lead to a refusal to fight.

For their part, once the fighting had stopped, the anti-war movements of the Second World War had to find their way again, direct their energies to new causes and new passions. This was not always easy. Wars might not have been over – far from it – but they were taking on new forms that demanded new responses. The Peace Pledge Union, once such a dominant force in British pacifism, was largely left behind, its membership plummeting, forced to move to much smaller headquarters further out from the centre of London. Vera Brittain became its chair in 1948 and Michael Tippett its President in the late 1950s, but by then the organisation was a shadow of its former self, losing influence to new types of peace campaign, as its particular brand of individual moral absolutism was increasingly felt to be out of step with events.

Conscription into the armed forces came to an end in Britain in 1960, with the last conscript discharged in 1962, meaning that a refusal to serve in the armed forces was no longer a significant issue for many. Indeed, the problem for the peace movement now was that it was far too easy for British citizens – with the notable exception of those in Northern Ireland – to have nothing to do with the armed forces at all, even as the government still sent soldiers to wars around the world. With an all-volunteer army, you could always send other people's sons and daughters to die on distant battlefields and not think about the consequences too much. Instead of opposing conscription and supporting conscientious objection, the British anti-war movement needed new tactics.

Away from Britain, in the second half of the twentieth century the right to conscientious objection was taken up in many places around the globe. As the number of countries with military conscription fell, those with formal rights to conscientious objection rose.[31] International human rights regimes also formally endorsed conscientious objection as a universal, albeit qualified, entitlement.[32] In many European countries, most notably West Germany, applications for exemption from military service as a conscientious objector become so straightforward as to be almost automatic, a predominantly formal and bureaucratic process, robbed of drama or moral torment. By the start of the twenty-first century, only in a very few states, most notably Russia, Korea, Turkey and Eritrea, would conscientious objection to military service remain a live and contentious issue.

In the US, opposition to the Vietnam War in the 1960s and 1970s played out on a much larger stage, as conscientious objection seemed somehow too restrained for what was at stake. After a landmark Supreme Court case, the legal right to exemption from military service on the grounds of conscience was at least partially secularised, so that it included those who could show that their individual beliefs about war were akin to religious commitments, even if religion still remained the measure against which conscience was judged.[33] For many American activists, though, an individualistic approach that emphasised tender scruples seemed far too restrictive for an anti-war movement mainly protesting on the collective basis of class, race and anti-imperialism.[34] Instead, it was demonstrations and to a lesser extent emigration that captured the imagination. The burning of draft cards also represented a more radical refusal than submitting to a tribunal and asking for exemption; a rejection of the very right of the state to demand that its citizens kill and be killed in its name, a rejection of the state's ability to ask people to fight and its claim to judge conscience.

In Britain, even if most young male citizens were not going to be sent off to war, the bombing of Hiroshima and Nagasaki and the start of the Cold War meant that the possible costs of armed conflict had risen considerably. If people thought in the 1930s that technological advances had made war more brutal and more deadly than ever before, nuclear weapons ratcheted up the possibility exponentially. In some ways, the anti-nuclear activism of the second half of the twentieth century seemed a natural fit for pacifists from the Second World War.[35] Roy was not the only one who found his way there. Donald Soper led some of the earliest anti-nuclear marches through London, and Michael Tippett and Ben Britten both supported the Campaign for Nuclear Disarmament. Yet the relationship between the pacifists of the Second World War and the new anti-nuclear activists was not always straightforward. Donald Soper and Stella St John both felt that CND was both too narrow in its concerns and too radical in its tactics.[36] Rather than focus on war in the round, it had chosen to emphasise one very particular but very destructive way of killing people. And chaining yourself to fences was very different from the more restrained approach of the anti-war activists of the previous generation.

The energies of peace activists from the Second World War perhaps made the biggest mark away from peace activism. As peace movements themselves rose and fell, waxed and waned over the course of the late twentieth and early twenty-first centuries, commitments were channelled into a wide range of causes, sometimes fracturing on the way. In an age that often seems cynical, tired and sceptical, the enthusiasms of the 1930s and 1940s did not disappear entirely, but took on new forms, drawing on new sources, seeking alternative forms of redemption and repair.

The art, music and writing of the second half of the twentieth century were particularly marked by the sentiments of conscientious objectors. Their numbers included some of the leading composers, writers and artists of their generation: the actors James Mason, Paul Eddington and Donald Pleasence; an early publisher of *Private Eye*; and Edwin Morgan – the first Scots Makar, or national poet.[37] The playwright Harold Pinter and the painter David Hockney became conscientious objectors in the last years of National Service. For these people, their work seldom, if ever – perhaps with the notable exceptions of Ben Britten and Michael Tippett – put the refusal to fight at centre stage, but there are clear parallels between the creative process and struggles of conscience, in the attempt to give form to the otherwise intangible.

Away from the arts, while Ronald Duncan and Fred Urquhart drifted to the political right, other conscientious objectors sought out new forms of protest. The passions and commitments of the British anti-war activists of the middle of the twentieth century might have been relatively restrained when compared to militants in other parts of the world at other times, but they had considerable and lasting presence. The former conscientious objector Eric Baker played a central role in the formation of Amnesty International, persuading the early movement to focus on prisoners of conscience and insisting that the organisation would only campaign on behalf of those who did not support violence.[38] This implicitly pacifist commitment would often be a source of unease when, for example, Amnesty could not adopt Nelson Mandela as a Prisoner of Conscience because he advocated a limited form of armed struggle against apartheid.[39] In the US, the American Civil Liberties Union initially grew out of the attempt to protect anti-war activists during the First World War, and the civil rights movement of the 1950s took up many of the ideas of non-violence.[40] In the struggle against racism and segregation Martin Luther King Jnr drew heavily on the ideas and experiences of American conscientious objectors.[41] But the wider human rights movement was decidedly not pacifist, and in the second part of the twentieth century would increasingly be caught up in advocating the use of force, as part of a declared 'responsibility to protect' those in need.

It is within humanitarianism that the most enduring legacy of British conscientious objectors can probably be found, and it was on such activities that conscientious objectors most often looked back with pride and fondness. It is here, in among all their doubts and disappointments, that there remained a strong sense that it had been worthwhile. Even so, humanitarianism was not an easy space for pacifists. Like human rights, humanitarianism is not an inherently pacifist movement, and could become thoroughly entangled with the use of force. Humanitarianism tries to tame war and alleviate its suffering rather than abolish violence, and humanitarians too have often espoused the use of force to prevent needless suffering. Despite this, many conscientious objectors and pacifists went on to have significant roles in the history of British humanitarian organisations. Muriel Lester played an important role in the Save Europe Now campaign which sought to bring food to the displaced and hungry of newly liberated Europe, and which later became War on Want. Oxfam grew out of the Oxford Committee for Famine Relief which had protested against starvation and blockade in occupied Europe, and many of the first generation of its leadership had cut their teeth working with the FAU.[42] Bernard Llewellyn, Roy Ridgway's great friend from the days in Gloucester, soon returned to China to work with the newly formed UN, and went on to play an important part in the history of Oxfam, becoming its first field director in Asia.[43] Michael Rowntree, who had been in Finland with Tom Burns and in Italy with Roy Ridgway, became Oxfam's Chair, working with the organisation for nearly sixty years.[44]

We can see the ethic of conscientious objection running like a thread through the moral imagination of British humanitarianism, with all its strengths and weakness. At times, this humanitarianism has been caught up admiring its own virtue, less concerned with whether it made any difference, but this humanitarian tradition has also been marked by a refusal to accept that suffering is inevitable and by a strong sense that we owe an obligation to others in whose misery we might be, in some way, complicit.

If in the middle of the twentieth century claims of conscience were widely associated with those who opposed war, this has not been the case in the early years of the twenty-first century. Conscience has been harnessed to new causes and conflicts. The issues we are commonly thought to have a conscience about have shifted their centre of gravity, and newspapers are more likely to write about conscientious objection to same-sex marriage or abortion than war.[45] In the UK, a baker famously refused to make cakes celebrating 2014's International Day Against Homophobia and Transphobia and claimed it is an issue of conscience. Marriage registrars have refused to officiate at same-sex weddings and civil ceremonies on similar grounds. Medical professionals have objected to direct or indirect involvement in abortions, saying it goes against their conscience. Similar cases can be found in the US, and in both countries the disputes have made it all the way to the Supreme Court. More widely, calls of conscience have also been linked to the treatment of displaced people, parliamentary votes on Brexit or the bombing of Syria, the impeachments of presidents, the growth of food poverty in Britain, the opening of pubs and schools in the face of the pandemic and the right to refuse vaccinations, among other things. There are a lot of things to have a conscience about.

In the midst of all this, the demand to protect conscience cuts across the political spectrum. Liberals have remained deeply committed to freedom of conscience as a foundational principle.[46] On the conservative right, freedom of conscience has come to be seen as the grounds for renewing a 'Christian civilisation', as a bulwark against atheism and secularism, and a practical way to defend a particular vision of moral life.[47] It can be hard to work out what unites the issues that are talked about as matters of conscience: what do war, abortion, marriage and vaccines have in common? In practice it is probably often most tempting to talk about conscience when we have no other way of talking about a difficult issue but to relegate it to deep personal moral beliefs and therefore seemingly to end the discussion. Conscience becomes an ethical black box for putting things into when we do not know how to talk about them in other terms. As we try and sort right from wrong, good from bad, virtue from necessity, sometimes it is as if the call of conscience – here I stand, I can do no other – is a trump card that closes down all discussion, turning complex issues into matters of unchallengeable individual moral scruples rather than difficult collective political conversations. Asking 'What does conscience say?' often provides only a very limited set of answers.

There are clear continuities, as well as differences, between some of the conscientious objectors of the middle of the twentieth century and those of the twenty-first. Refusing to bake a cake celebrating a same-sex marriage is part of a tradition of standing apart that could be found in some of those who refused to make any compromises and demanded unconditional exemption from military service. This is conscience as a deeply individual concern, focused on personal freedom, purity and objection to the world around you – not necessarily trying to change the world, but trying to keep your hands clean. It is a conscience that presents itself as absolute, uncompromising and self-assured. This is conscience as stepping back, wanting little to do with those with whom you disagree, but demanding accommodations, even privileges, from others for your own commitments.

Such claims of conscience stand in contrast to another strand: those who were willing to get their hands dirty, to accept the costs that their stances entailed – even if this meant going to jail – but who were also trying to make the world a better place, to help the sick and homeless or to travel the world to heal the wounded. This is a conscience that recognises compromise and complicity, but does not treat this as a source of paralysis or cynicism. People like Tom, Roy and Stella were determined not to stand aloof from a world with which they disagreed, but to get involved and make it better. They did not want to sit comfortably at home standing by their principles while sending others off to die. They recognised that there was no place from which they could stand back and watch the world go by, tut-tutting or proud in their own superiority. They recognised that living alongside others means that we are already implicated in the inequities of the world.[48]

This 'let's get our hands dirty' conscience constantly asks whether it is doing the right thing and did not settle into easy answers, wary of the dangers of hubris and pride, aware of where solipsistic convictions might take us. Conscience in a thoughtful, hesitant and slightly guilty mode can be paralysing. But it can also be the first step in moral and practical change. Ronald, Stella, Roy, Tom and Fred all thought long and hard about what they were doing, and experienced pangs of regret along the road, but sought to respond in the most practical way, constantly trying to make amends. We might say that a clean conscience was most obviously and commonly known by its absence. Indeed, even if an overly morbid sense of guilt has its own problems, it is probably not a good sign when someone says they have a clear conscience. It would seem to show they hold their own moral purity in too high a regard and have not thought long and hard enough about the complexity of their responsibilities.

This is also a conscience which recognises that its own privileges are built on the sacrifices of others. Tom, Roy and Stella understood that their own actions had an impact on the world. It is a conscience that is willing both to pay a price for what it believes in and to make amends for the costs borne by others.

In the particular combination of complicity, doubt and sacrifice, conscience is probably a contingent ingredient, a fleeting conjuncture that comes together in other forms in other times and places. We might find such elements, for example, in climate-change activism, grassroots human rights defenders or campaigns for racial and gender equality. We might find them too, and in unpredictable places, in our responses to the challenges posed by the long-term impact of Covid-19, with its tensions between individual liberty and collective solidarity.

It is often said that generals are always fighting the last war, and this is true for many others too. Anti-war activists of the late 1930s and 1940s all too often understood the threat of Fascism through the lens of the First World War, and thought that a repeat of the horrors of the trenches should be avoided at all costs, but in the years after the Second World War, as Fascism has become the frame through which we seem to assess all evils, the spectre of appeasement has also reared its head too often. As a result we have been quick to get carried away with the virtue of war when confronted with wrongdoing, and too ready to believe that a just measure of violence can solve the world's problems. The conscientious objectors of the Second World War could sometimes be blinkered and self-important. Yet they could also be compassionate and committed to the ideal that violence is not inevitable. We might be tempted to understand them in tragic terms, as being unable to come to terms with a cynical and brutal world. But at their best they confronted the world head on, taking it as it was, but not resigned to its fate, imagining in both hope and sorrow that things could be otherwise.

ACKNOWLEDGEMENTS

This book has been many years in the writing and would not have been possible without the support and inspiration of countless people. My friends and colleagues Harini Amarasuriya, Sidharthan Maunaguru, Galina Oustinova-Stjepanovic and Jonathan Spencer worked with me on the larger comparative project on conscience out of which this book has grown. Their always insightful thoughts, conversations and reflections have been invaluable and much cherished. The research for this book was made possible by the generous support of a European Research Council Horizon 2020 Consolidator Grant (648477 AnCon ERC-2014–CoG). In the very early days of the research Alice Forbes was a great source of assistance. More recently, Laura Major has been an always imaginative collaborator and I am grateful for her skill, perseverance and knowledge. Right at the end, Anita Klingler helped me get things in order. Colleagues in my school research office have been wonderful throughout, especially Juliet Craig, Anne Mourad, Eirini Souri and Jack Thorburn.

The research for this book was conducted in numerous archives, including the Archives and Special Collections at the University of Stirling, Bodleian Library, Bishopsgate Institute, Friends House, Centre for Research Collections at the University of Edinburgh, Harry Ransom Humanities Research Center at University of Texas – Austin, Imperial War Museum, Institute of International Social History, London School of Economics, Mass Observation Archives at the University of Sussex, Modern Records Centre at the University of Warwick, National Archives, Special Collection at the University of Aberdeen, Special Collections at the University of Exeter, Spirit of Revolt Archive at the Mitchell Library, Tate Library and Teesside Archives. The staff at these institutions have been uniformly helpful and generous. I would particularly like to thank Melissa Atkinson, Lisa McQuillan, Caroline Walter and Rachel Hosker. I have great admiration for Lyn Smith who conducted many of the original oral history interviews now in the Imperial War Museum.

Numerous individuals and families provided me with access to their private papers and I would like to thank them for their generosity, even where those accounts are not directly included in the final manuscript. Colin Affleck, the family of Tom Burns, the family of Ronald, Rose Marie and Briony Duncan and the family of Roy Ridgway have been particularly generous in allowing me access to their papers.

The ideas in this book have benefited from the feedback and expertise of numerous people. Jeremy Crang and Wendy Ugolini, great historians of Second World War Britain, were generous enough to read the whole manuscript and I have learned a great deal from them. Critique: Centre for Ethics and Critical Thought kindly organised a workshop on a draft of the manuscript. I am indebted to Lori Allen, Claire Duncanson and Maša Mrovlje for their characteristically smart readings. At the National Museums of Scotland, Maureen Barry, Dorothy Kidd and Henrie Lidchi taught me a great deal about how this story might be told. I am also grateful to my wonderful colleagues in Edinburgh for giving me the time to write this book. The following people in particular have been full of conversations and guidance: Christine Bell, Nehal Bhuta, Adam Budd, Janet Carsten, Jessica Cooper, Magnus Course, Alex Edmonds, Serra Hakyemez, Ian Harper, Naomi Haynes, Lotte Hoek, Delwar Hussain, Laura Jeffery, Maya Mayblin, Mihaela Mihai, Nicola Perugini, Lotte Segal, Mathias Thaler and Dimitri Tsintjilonis. The ideas in this book have benefited from audiences in Amsterdam, Baltimore, Belfast, Berlin, Cambridge, Colombo, Copenhagen, Durham, Edinburgh, Manchester, Oxford, Princeton, Singapore, St Andrews, Stanford, Stromboli, Sussex and Utrecht. Numerous people have given their thoughts on draft chapters or offered advice on the issues I was struggling with, sometimes without knowing, including Peter Agree, Jon Bialecki, Ruy Blanes, Rebecca Bryant, Matei Candea, Clare Collins, Jennifer Curtis, Julia Eckert, Matthew Engelke, Carlos Forment, Laure Humbert, Steffen Jensen, Webb Keane, akshay khanna, Lucy Noakes, Adam Reed, Linsey Robb, Alpa Shah, Sharika Thiranagama, Miriam Ticktin, Wendy Webster, Erica Weiss,

Richard Wilson and Fiona Wright. Colleagues at the journal *Humanity* have always been a critical inspiration: Ayça Çubukçu, Angela Naimou, Vasuki Nesiah, Tim Nunan and Jess Wright. Colin Affleck, Lucy Metcalfe, Michael Ridgway and Briony Lawson have all given invaluable and generous feedback on drafts.

At an early stage of turning this into a book Ed Lake gave me important advice. More recently, Sophie Scard has been a wonderful, patient and wise agent. Greg Clowes and Tom Atkins at Chatto & Windus deserve special thanks. Peter James was a meticulous and thoughtful copy-editor. Becky Hardie is the editor I always dreamed of – imaginative, careful and knowledgeable.

I would like to thank the following people and organisations for permission to quote or reproduce material for which they hold the copyright: Colin Affleck, the family of Tom Burns, British Yearly Meeting of the Society of Friends, Chetham's Library, Literacy Executor of Ronald Duncan, the family/estate of Ronald Duncan, the Fellowship of Reconciliation, Imperial War Museum, Kingsley Hall's Heritage Committee and Bishopsgate Institute, National Portrait Gallery, Pathé News, Peace Pledge Union, the family of Roy Ridgway, University of Exeter Special Collections and University of Stirling Archives. I have made every attempt to contact the copyright holders of other material quoted in this book, but would like to extend my apologies to any individual or organisation who has been inadvertently overlooked, and would ask them to please supply me with appropriate details, so I can endeavour to correct the information in any subsequent editions.

Acknowledgements have to end with a guilty conscience, and I am sure I have forgotten to mention by name numerous people to whom I am indebted. To them I offer thanks and apologies.

Above all, conscience is a personal debt, and this book would not have been possible without Faye, Matilda and Solomon. I starting writing this book before Solomon was born, wrote the last part under lockdown and finished it loving them more than ever.

LIST OF ILLUSTRATIONS

FIRST PLATE SECTION

p. 1: Illustrations from *Thy Kingdom Come* by Arthur Wragg, published by Selwyn & Blount (1939).

p. 2: (*Above*) Arthur Wragg's illustration for the cover of the Central Board of Conscientious Objectors Annual Report, April 1941–March 1942; (*below*) wartime sitting of the North Midlands tribunal for conscientious objectors (HU62359) (© Imperial War Museum, London).

p. 3: (*Above*) Conscientious objectors attending a mechanised agriculture course in Essex (HU36259) (© Imperial War Museum, London); (*below*) sketch of "Joad", resident of the Hungerford Club (by permission of Chetham's Library, Manchester).

p. 4: (*Above left*) Roy Ridgway in 1941; (*above right*) Roy Ridgway on the back of an army truck (both by permission of the family of Roy Ridgway); (*below*) Fred Urquhart (by permission of Colin Affleck).

p. 5: Pamphlet on James Maxton (© Tait and Watson Collection, University of Stirling Archives).

p. 6: Campaign leaflet for Douglas Young (© Tait and Watson Collection, University of Stirling Archives).

p. 7: (*Above left*) Ronald Duncan as a young man (EUL MS 397/10/8/95); (*above right*) Rose Marie Hansom, later Duncan (EUL MS 397/10/8/169); (*below*) Bianca Duncan (EUL MS 397/10/8/119) (all held at the University of Exeter and reproduced by permission of the Ronald Duncan Collection, University of Exeter Special Collections).

p. 8: (*Above left*) Rose Marie and an unknown boy at Gooseham Farm (by permission of the family of Ronald Duncan); (*above right*) view of West Mill and the surrounding valley (EUL MS 397/10/8/136); (*below*) the Duncan family at Welcombe

Beach (EUL MS 397/10/8/36/1) (both held at the University of Exeter and reproduced by permission of the Ronald Duncan Collection, University of Exeter Special Collections).

SECOND PLATE SECTION

p. 9: (*Above*) Staff of the London office of the Fellowship of Reconciliation, *c.* 1940 (FOR/19/5); (*below*) Fellowship of Reconciliation staff reunion, 1975 (FOR/19/5) (both held in the Fellowship of Reconciliation Papers at the LSE and reproduced by permission of the Fellowship of Reconciliation).

p. 10: (*Above left*) Tom Burns, late 1930s; (*above right*) FAU vehicles in Norway; (*below*) FAU members on the way to Finland in 1939 (all by kind permission of the family of Tom Burns).

p. 11: (*Above*) Members of the FAU in Stalag VIIB (by permission of the family of Tom Burns); (*below*) FAU volunteers training as mechanics at Manor Farm (held at Friends House, London © Britain Yearly Meeting).

p. 12: (*Above left*) Cover of the FAU's fourth Annual Report (1944); (*above right*) cover of the FAU's Annual Report (1946); (*below*) FAU volunteers loading oil drums at Hsiakwan depot (© Britain Yearly Meeting).

p. 13: (*Above*) PSU leaflet published during the Second World War (© Britain Yearly Meeting); (*below*) late-1930s Peace Pledge Union poster (by permission of the Peace Pledge Union).

p. 14: (*Above*) Men of the Non-Combatant Corps undergoing training (© Imperial War Museum, London); (*below*) portrait of Benjamin Britten and W. H. Auden, photographer unknown (© National Portrait Gallery, London).

p. 15: (*Above*) Muriel Lester in Argentina (by permission of Kingsley Halls Heritage Committee and Bishopsgate Institute); (*below*) portrait of John Middleton Murry by Howard Coster (1934) (© National Portrait Gallery, London).

p. 16: Portrait of Vera Brittain by Howard Coster (1936) (© National Portrait Gallery, London).

LIST OF ABBREVIATIONS

AI	Amnesty International
BEF	British Expeditionary Force
CBCO	Central Board for Conscientious Objectors
CBCOA	Central Board for Conscientious Objectors Archive, Friends House, London
CD	Civil Defence
CRC	Centre for Research Collections, Edinburgh University
FAU	Friends Ambulance Unit
FAUA	Friends Ambulance Unit Archive, Friends House, London
FoR	Fellowship of Reconciliation
HC	House of Commons
HL	House of Lords
ILP	Independent Labour Party
IPPNW	International Physicians for the Prevention of Nuclear War
IWM	Imperial War Museum, London
LSE	London School of Economics
MOA	Mass Observation Archives, University of Sussex
NA	National Archives, Kew
NAAFI	Navy, Army and Air Force Institutes
NCF	No-Conscription Fellowship

BIBLIOGRAPHY

Primary Sources

Archival Sources

Archives and Special Collections, University of Stirling
- Tait/Watson Archives (MS 41)

Bishopsgate Institute, London
- Butler Papers (Butler)
- Peter Hunot Papers (Hunot)
- Muriel Lester Papers (Lester)

Bodleian, Oxford University
- Oxfam Papers (MS Oxfam)

Centre for Research Collections, Edinburgh University
- John Middleton Murry Collection (Coll-62)
- Fred Urquhart Papers (Coll-49)

Friends House, London
- Central Board for Conscientious Objectors Archive (TEMP MSS 914)
- Friends Ambulance Unit Archive (MSS 876)

Harry Ransom Humanities Research Center, University of Texas at Austin
- Ronald Duncan Collection (MS-1252)

Imperial War Museum Collections, London
- Papers of E. E. Beavor (Documents.4536)
- Papers of F. B. Breakspear (Documents.1759)
- Papers of E. R. Harper (Documents.18959)
- Papers of R. J. Porcas (Documents.17303)
- Papers of Roy Ridgway (Documents.5997)
- Papers of C. Ruffoni (Documents.1024)
- Papers of C. Worrall (Documents.2126)
- Papers of Cyril Frederick Wright (Documents.4553)
- Ministry of Labour, January 1939 (LBY 17242)
- Notebook of Instructions for Conscientious Objectors in Answering Tribunal Questions, circa 1940 (Documents.87)

Oral History Interviews
- Interview with Stella St John, 7 August 1971 (4997)
- Interview with Ronald Mallone, 31 January 1980 (4581)
- Interview with Patrick Figgis, 5 February 1980 (4593)

- Interview with Jesse Hillman, 21 March 1980 (4612)
- Interview with Mervyn Taggart, 5 May 1980 (4657)
- Interview with Bernard Nicholls, 9 May 1980 (4631)
- Interview with Doris Nicholls, 13 May 1980 (4634)
- Interview with Frank Norman, 27 June 1980 (4652)
- Interview with Reginald Bottini, 15 July 1980 (4660)
- Interview with Alexander Bryan, 5 September 1980 (4746)
- Interview with Kenneth Wray, 9 September 1980 (4696)
- Interview with Kathleen Wigham, 17 September 1980 (4761)
- Interview with John Fleetwood Stewart Phillips, 22 October 1980 (4769)
- Interview with Cyril Wright, 17 November 1980 (4789)
- Interview with Denis Hayes, 26 February 1981 (4828)
- Interview with Leonard Bird, 12 June 1981 (5120)
- Interview with Arthur Koestler, 30 November 1981 (5393)
- Interview with Fenner Brockway, 16 March 1982 (4826)
- Interview with William Elliot, 1983 (7108)
- Interview with John Emburton, 1985 (10817)
- Interview with Sydney Greaves, 1985 (10850)
- Interview with Tony Parker, 17 February 1986 (9233)
- Interview with Michael Harris, 16 May 1986 (9325)
- Interview with Douglas Turner, 24 June 1986 (9338)
- Interview with John Wood, 8 July 1986 (9371)
- Interview with Victor Newcomb, 13 August 1986 (9400)
- Interview with John Petts, 2 March 1987 (9732)
- Interview with Stephen Verney, 9 June 1987 (9832)
- Interview with Roy Ridgway, 14 July 1987 (10350)
- Interview with Michael Cadbury, 27 November 1987 (10051)
- Interview with Harry Miller, 1988 (10449)
- Interview with Ronald Joynes, 22 March 1989 (10652)
- Interview with Michael Rowntree, 7 August 1989 (10883)
- Interview with Stephen Hubert Peet, 30 October 1990 (11736)
- Interview with Frederick Temple, 18 April 1991 (12035)
- Interview with Bernard Hicken, in *A Matter of Conscience*, BBC Radio 4, May 1992 (13166)
- Interview with Frank Chadwick, in *A Matter of Conscience*, BBC Radio 4, May 1992 (13193)
- Interview with Dennis Waters, in *A Matter of Conscience*, BBC Radio 4, May 1992 (13195)
- Interview with Ken Shaw, in *A Matter of Conscience*, BBC Radio 4, May 1992 (13197)
- Interview with Patrick Mayhew, 18 May 1992 (12589)
- Interview with Donald Soper, 1 September 1992 (12790)
- Interview with John Hunt, 6 April 1998 (18002)
- Interview with Alexander Bryan, 20 January 1999 (19956)
- Interview with Bryan Platt, 20 January 1999 (18273)
- Interview with Joyce Parkinson, unknown date (15615)

- Interview with John Miles, unknown date (20538)

Institute of International Social History, Amsterdam
- Amnesty International Secretariat Archives (AI)

London School of Economics
- Christian Pacifist Forestry and Land Units Committee (COLL MISC 0456/6/2)
- Fellowship of Reconciliation, London Union, Stella St John Papers (FOR 19/5)

Mass Observation Archives, University of Sussex
- The workers' week; what painters are painting and selling; repercussions of conscription, File Report 31 US 3 (SxMOA1/1/5/2/7)
- COs and Pacifists (SxMOA1/2/6: TC6)

National Archives, Kew
- ED 135/3/186, Employment of conscientious objectors; general circulation, 1943
- FD 1/6627, Typhus: proposal by conscientious objectors to work as vaccine typhus subjects, 1941
- FD 1/6673, Research on scabies, 1941–2
- HLG 51/568, Conscientious objectors: Suspension of pay during hostilities, 1940–3
- HO 45/25558, War: Conscientious objectors who refuse to undergo medical examination, 1940–55
- HO 45/23801, WAR: Arthur Donaldson, 1941
- HO 186/821, FIRE: Conscientious objectors, 1941–2
- HO 186/2835, PERSONNEL: Conscientious objectors, 1939–45
- HO 192/1298, Conscientious objectors: connection with air raids, 1942
- LAB 6/137, Conscientious Objectors Order to train with Civil Defence Service, 1939–41
- LAB 6/183, General procedure for dealing with women conscientious objectors, 1941–2
- LAB 6/414, Repeated prosecutions of conscientious objectors, 1942–56
- LCO 2/5315, Conscientious objectors, 1943–54
- MEPO 3/2122, Conscientious objectors, 1941
- PCOM 9/686, Conscientious objectors barred from promotion within Civil Service during the war, 1940–3

Modern Records Centre, University of Warwick
- Howard League for Penal Reform Papers (MSS.16)

Special Collections, University of Aberdeen
- Fyfe Papers, World War Two North-Eastern Scotland Local Tribunal for Conscientious Objectors (MS 2108)

Special Collections, University of Exeter
- Ronald Duncan Archive (EUL MS 397)

Spirit of Revolt Archive, Mitchell Library, Glasgow
- Alan Burnett Collection (GB243 T/SOR/1)

Tate Library, London

- Keith Vaughan Collection (TGA 200817)
Teesside Archives, Middlesbrough
- Pennyman Collection (U/PEN (4) Box 6)

Private Collections

Private Papers of Colin Affleck
Private Papers of the Burns family
Personal Papers of Ann Jacob
Private Papers of Gary Perkins

Newspapers

Aberdeen Press
Catholic Herald
Central Board for Conscientious Objectors Bulletin
Derby Evening Telegraph
Evening Telegraph and Post
The Friend
Glasgow Herald
Guardian
New York Review of Books
Peace News
Scotsman
The Times
West London Observer

Published Primary Materials

Auden, W. H., and Christopher Isherwood, 1939. *Journey to a War*. Random House.

Barnard, Clifford, 2010. *Binding the Wounds of War: A Young Relief Worker's Letters Home, 1943–47*. Pronoun Press.

Blishen, Edward, 1972. *A Cack-handed War*. Thames & Hudson.

Bonhoeffer, Dietrich, 2003 [1937]. *Dietrich Bonhoeffer Works*, Vol. 4: *Discipleship*, ed. John D. Dodsey and Geffrey B. Kelly, trans. Martin Kuske and Ilse Tödt. Fortress Press.

Bonhoeffer, Dietrich, 2005 [1949]. *Dietrich Bonhoeffer Works*, Vol. 6: *Ethics*, ed. Clifford Green, trans. Reinhard Krauss, Douglas W. Stott and Charles C. West. Fortress Press.

Borden, Mary, 1946. *Journey Down a Blind Alley*. Hutchinson.

Bowen, Elizabeth, 1938. *The Death of the Heart*. Knopf.

Brittain, Vera, 2005 [1941]. *England's Hour*. Continuum.

Brittain, Vera, 2005 [1943]. 'Humiliation with Honour', in *One Voice*. Continuum.

Brittain, Vera, 1944. *Massacre by Bombing: The Facts Behind the British–American Attack on Germany*. Fellowship.

Brittain, Vera, 1944. *Seed of Chaos: What Mass Bombing Really Means*. New Vision Publishing.

Brittain, Vera, 1957. *Testament of Experience: An Autobiographical Story of the Years 1925–1950*. Macmillan.

Brittain, Vera, 1986. *Chronicle of Friendship: Diaries of the Thirties, 1932–1939*, ed. A. G. Bishop. Victor Gollancz.

Brittain, Vera, 1988. *A Testament of a Peace Lover: Letters from Vera Brittain*, ed. Winifred and Alan Eden-Green. Virago.

Brockway, Fenner, 1941. *Stop War by Socialism: ILP Policy Statement*. ILP.

Brockway, Fenner, 1963. *Outside the Right*. George Allen & Unwin.

Brockway, Fenner, 1974. *Towards Tomorrow: The Autobiography of Fenner Brockway*. Rupert Hart-Davis.

Brough, Bill, 1995. *To Reason Why . . .* Hickory Tree Press.

Burns, Tom, 1995. 'Introduction', *Description, Explanation and Understanding: Selected Writings, 1944–1980*. Edinburgh University Press.

Butler, Josephine, 1991. *Cyanide in my Shoe*. This England Books.

Buxton, Patrick, 1947. *The Louse: An Account of the Lice Which Infest Man, their Medical Importance and Control*. Edward Arnold.

Caldwell, John Taylor, 1999. *With Fates Conspire: Memoirs of a Glasgow Seafarer and Anarchist*. Northern Herald Books.

Carter, Sydney, 1965. 'Voices of Conscience', in Clifford Simmons, Mark Holloway, Stuart Smith, Derek Savage and Sydney Carter, *The Objectors*. Times Press.

Catlin, George, 1972. *For God's Sake Go! An Autobiography*. Colin Smythe.

Catlin, John, 1987. *Family Quartet: Vera Brittain and her Family*. Hamish Hamilton.

Caudwell, Christopher, 1938. *Studies in a Dying Culture*. Bodley Head.

Chapman, Eddie, 1957. *I Killed to Live: The Story of Eric Pleasants*. Cassell.

Churchill, Winston S., 1957. *The Second World War*, Vol. II: *Their Finest Hour*. Cassell.

Crozier, F. P., 1930. *A Brass Hat in No Man's Land*. Jonathan Cape.

Dalton, Hugh, 1928. *Towards the Peace of Nations: A Study in International Politics*. George Routledge.

Day-Lewis, Cecil, 1960. *The Buried Day*. Chatto & Windus.

Duncan, Ronald, 1937. *The Complete Pacifist*. Peace Pledge Union.

Duncan, Ronald, 1944. *Journal of a Husbandman*. Faber & Faber.

Duncan, Ronald, 1950. *The Mongrel and Other Poems*. Faber & Faber.

Duncan, Ronald, 1964. *All Men are Islands*. Rupert Hart-Davis.

Duncan, Ronald, 1968. *How to Make Enemies*. Rupert Hart-Davis.

Duncan, Ronald, 1977. *Obsessed*. Michael Joseph.

Duncan, Ronald, 1978. *Auschwitz*. Rebel Press.

Duncan, Ronald, 1981. *Working with Britten: A Personal Memoir*. Rebel Press.

Eddington, Paul, 1995. *So Far, So Good: His Autobiography*. Coronet.

Field, G. C., 1945. *Pacifism and Conscientious Objection*. Cambridge University Press.

Gallacher, William, 2017 [1936]. *Revolt on the Clyde*. Lawrence & Wishart.

Gallup and Fortune Polls, 1940. *The Public Opinion Quarterly* 4(3): 533–53.

Gollancz, Victor, 1943. *Let my People Go: Some Practical Proposals for Dealing with Hitler's Massacre of the Jews and an Appeal to the British Public*. Victor Gollancz.

Gregg, Richard, 1935. *The Power of Non-Violence*. Greenleaf Books.

Gregg, Richard, 1937. *Training for Peace*. J. B. Lippincott.

Hamilton, Patrick, 2017 [1947]. *The Slaves of Solitude*. Abacus.

Heard, Gerald, 1949. *Prayers and Meditations: A Monthly Cycle Arranged for Daily Use*. Harper.

Huxley, Aldous, 1937. *Ends and Means*. Chatto & Windus.

ILP, 1939. *Why We Oppose Conscription*. ILP.

Isherwood, Christopher, 1966. *Exhumations*. Methuen.

Lester, Muriel, 1937. *It Occurred to Me*. Harper.

Lester, Muriel, 1947. *It So Happened*. Harper & Brothers.

Lester, Muriel, 2003. *Gandhi: A Wise Man*. Sumit.

Lidbetter, H. Martin, 1993. *Friends Ambulance Unit, 1939–1943: Experiences in Finland, Norway, Sweden, Egypt, Greece and Germany*. Sessions Book Trust.

Llewellyn, Bernard, 1953. *I Left my Roots in China*. George Allen & Unwin.

Lonsdale, Kathleen, 1943. *Some Account of Life in Holloway Prison for Women*. Prison Medical Reform Council, Bradford Peace Pamphlets.

Macaulay, Rose, 1940. 'Notes on the Way', *Time & Tide*, 5 October.

Macaulay, Rose, 1956. *The Towers of Trebizond*. Collins.

MacCaig, Norman, 2009. 'Patriot', in *The Poems of Norman MacCaig*, ed. Ewen McCaig. Polygon.

McClelland, Grigor, 1997. *Embers of War: Letters from a Quaker Relief Worker in War-Torn Germany*. I. B. Tauris.

McEwan, Ian, 2014. *The Children Act*. Jonathan Cape.

Macgregor, G. H. C., 1936. *The New Testament Basis of Pacifism*. James Clarke.

MacNeice, Louis, 1939. *Autumn Journal*. Faber & Faber.

MacNeice, Louis, 1965. *These Strings are False*. Faber & Faber.

Malleny, Kenneth, 1945. *Human Guinea Pigs*. Victor Gollancz.

Mandelstam, Nadezhda, 1999. *Hope against Hope*. Harvill.

Manning, Olivia, 1987. *The Balkan Trilogy*. Arrow Books.

Manson, John (ed.), 2011. *Dear Grieve: Letters to Hugh MacDiarmid (C. M. Grieve)*. Kennedy & Boyd.

Martin, Kingsley, 1938. 'The Pacifist's Dilemma To-day', *Political Quarterly* 9(2): 155–72.

Mayhew, Patrick (ed.), 1985. *One Family's War*. History Press.

Middleton Murry, John, 1930. 'The Creation of Conscience', *New Adelphi* 111(2), December: 107–19.

Middleton Murry, John, 1938. *The Pledge of Peace*. Peace Pledge Union.

Middleton Murry, John, 1939. 'Prepare the Peace', *Adelphi* 16(1), 16 October.

Middleton Murry, John, 1944. *Adam and Eve*. Andrew Dakers.

Middleton Murry, John, 1953. *Community Farm*. Country Book Club.

Mitchell, Donald, and Philip Reed (eds), 1991. *Letters from a Life: Selected Letters and Diaries of Benjamin Britten*, Vol. 1: *1923–1939*. Faber & Faber.

Mitchell, Donald, and Philip Reed (eds), 1998. *Letters from a Life: Selected Letters and Diaries of Benjamin Britten*, Vol. 2: *1939–1945*. Faber & Faber.

Moran, Lord, 1945. *Anatomy of Courage*. Constable.

Morris, David, 1948. *China Changed my Mind*. Houghton Mifflin.

Morrison, Sybil, 1962. *I Renounce War: The Story of the Peace Pledge Union*. PPU.

Muir, Edwin, 1935. *Scottish Journey*. Heinemann.

Nichols, Beverley, 1933. *Cry Havoc!* Doubleday.

[No author, no date]. 'The Standard of the Movement'. Christian Pacifist Forestry and Land, Friends House.

[No author], 1944. 'Stalag Recipes', *Clarion*, April, 13.

Orchard, W. E., 1933. *From Faith to Faith: An Autobiography of Religious Development*. M. A. Magnani and Sons.

Orwell, George, 2001 [1937]. *The Road to Wigan Pier*. Penguin.

Orwell, George, 2018 [1941]. *The Lion and the Unicorn: Socialism and the English Genius*. Penguin.

Orwell, George, 1942. 'London Letters', *Partisan Review*, March–April.

Orwell, George, 2001 [1943]. 'Looking Back on the Spanish Civil War', in *All Propaganda is Lies, 1941–1942*, ed. Peter Davidson. Secker & Warburg.

Orwell, George, 1944. 'As I Please', *Tribune*, 1 September, 12.

Orwell, George, 1949. 'Reflections on Gandhi', *Partisan Review*, January.

Plowman, Dorothy (ed.), 1944. *Bridge into the Future: Letters of Max Plowman*. Andrew Dakers.

Plowman, Max, 1942. *The Right to Live: Selected Essays*. Andrew Dakers.

Postgate, Oliver, 2009. *Seeing Things: A Memoir*. Canongate.

PPU, 1940. *Pacifists at Bow Street: A Full Report of Proceedings under the Defence Regulations against Officers and Members of the Peace Pledge Union, May–June, 1940*. PPU.

Royden, Maude, 1948. *A Threefold Cord*. Victor Gollancz.

St John, Stella, 1944. *A Prisoner's Log*. Howard League for Penal Reform.

Schuttenhelm, Thomas (ed.), 2005. *Selected Letters of Michael Tippett*. Faber & Faber.

Sheppard, Dick, and Laurence Housman, 1939. *What Can We Believe? Letters Exchanged between Dick Sheppard and Laurence Housman*. Jonathan Cape.

Simpson, John E., 2001. *Letters from China: Quaker Relief Work in Bandit Country, 1944–1946*. Ross-Evans.

Smith, Stevie, 1980 [1938]. *Over the Frontier*. Virago.

The Society of Brothers, 1952. *Ten Years of Community Living: The Wheathill Bruderhof*. The Plough Publishing House.

Spears, Edward, 1977. *Fulfilment of a Mission*. Leo Cooper.

Stalker, Harry, 1943. 'Conscientious Objectors with Psychiatric States', *Journal of Mental Science* 89(374): 52–8.

Tippett, Michael, 1991. *Those Twentieth Century Blues: An Autobiography.* Hutchinson.

Urquhart, Fred, 1938. *Time Will Knit.* Gerald Duckworth.

Urquhart, Fred, 1941. 'Let us Endure an Hour: A Conscientious Objector in England', *Southern Literary Journal* 3(3): 133–7.

Urquhart, Fred, 1946. *Selected Stories.* Maurice Fridberg.

Urquhart, Fred, 2011. *Jezebel's Dust,* with an Introduction by Colin Affleck. Kennedy & Boyd.

Verney, Stephen, 2016. *Snakes and Ladders.* Verney Books.

Wellock, Wilfred, 1922. *India's Awakening: Its National and World-Wide Significance.* Labour Publishing.

White, L. E., 1946. *Tenement Town.* Jason Press.

Wilson, Colin, 1974. 'The Genius of Ronald Duncan', in *A Tribute to Ronald Duncan.* The Harton Press.

Young, Douglas, 1944. *An Appeal to Scots Honour: A Vindication of the Right of the Scottish People to Freedom from Industrial Conscription and Bureaucratic Despotism under the Treaty of Union with England.* Scottish Secretariat Limited.

Court Cases

United States v. *Seeger,* 380 US 163 (1965), Supreme Court of the United States.

Television Programmes

Quintinshill: Britain's Deadliest Rail Disaster, BBC Two Scotland, 20 May 2015.

Speeches

James, William, 1906. 'The Moral Equivalent of War', speech given at Stanford University, https://www.laphamsquarterly.org/states-war/proposing-moral-equivalent-war, last accessed 2 March 2021.

Hansard

House of Commons
House of Lords

Secondary Sources

Books and Journal Articles

Addison, Paul, and Jeremy Crang (eds), 2010. *Listening to Britain: Home Intelligence Reports on Britain's Finest Hour – May to September 1940.* Bodley Head.

Allport, Alan, 2010. *Demobbed: Coming Home after the Second World War.* Yale University Press.

Allport, Alan, 2015. *Browned Off and Bloody-Minded: The British Soldier Goes off to War.* Yale University Press.

Al-Qattan, Najwa, 2014. 'When Mothers Ate their Children: Wartime Memory and the Language of Food in Syria and Lebanon', *International Journal of Middle East Studies* 46(4): 719–36.

Andrew, Edward, 2001. *Conscience and its Critics: Protestant Conscience, Enlightenment Reason and Modern Subjectivity.* University of Toronto Press.

Appelbaum, Patricia, 2009. *Kingdom to Commune: Protestant Pacifist Culture between World War I and the Vietnam Era.* University of North Carolina Press.

Arendt, Hannah, 1971. 'Thinking and Moral Considerations: A Lecture, for W. H. Auden', *Social Research* 38(3): 417–46.

Arendt, Hannah, 2003. *Responsibility and Judgment,* ed. Jerome Kohn. Schocken.

Armstrong-Reid, Susan, 2017. *China Gadabouts: New Frontiers of Humanitarian Nursing, 1941–51.* UBC Press.

Barker, Rachel, 1982. *Conscience, Government and War: Conscientious Objection in Britain, 1939–45.* Routledge.

Barnett, Victoria, 2019. 'Bonhoeffer and the Conspiracy', in *Oxford Handbook of Dietrich Bonhoeffer,* ed. Philip G. Ziegler and Michael Mawson. Oxford University Press.

Baylor, Michael, 1977. *Action and Person: Conscience in Late Scholasticism and the Young Luther.* Leiden: Brill.

Bayly, Christopher, and Tim Harper. 2004. *Forgotten Armies: Britain's Asian Empire and the War with Japan.* Penguin.

Beaumont, Joan, 2013. 'Starving for Democracy: Britain's Blockade of and Relief for Occupied Europe, 1939–1945', *War and Society* 8(2): 57–82.

Berry, Paul, and Mark Bostridge, 2001. *Vera Brittain: A Life.* Virago.

Bhuta, Nehal, 2014. 'Two Concepts of Religious Freedom in the European Court of Human Rights', *South Atlantic Quarterly* 113(1): 9–35.

Bibbings, Lois, 2010. *Telling Tales about Men: Conceptions of Conscientious Objectors to Military Service during the First World War.* University of Manchester Press.

Birkett, Jennifer, 2009. *Margaret Storm Jameson: A Life.* Oxford University Press.

Black, Maggie, 1992. *A Cause for our Times: Oxfam, the First Fifty Years.* Oxfam.

Bond, Brian, 2002. *The Unquiet Western Front: Britain's Role in Literature and History.* Cambridge University Press.

Bonham-Carter, Victor, 1958. *Dartington Hall: The History of an Experiment.* Phoenix House.

Boulton, David, 1967. *Objection Overruled.* MacGibbon & Kee.

Branford, David, 2008. 'From Pacifism to Just War: Changing Attitudes in the Church of England, 1930 to 1940', *Modern Believing* 49(2): 14–21.

Brewer, Susan A., 1997. *To Win the Peace: British Propaganda in the United States during World War II.* Cornell University Press.

Brock, Peter, 1999. 'Conscientious Objectors in Nazi Germany', in *Challenge to Mars: Pacifisms from 1918 to 1945*, ed. Peter Brock and Thomas Socknat. University of Toronto Press.

Brock, Peter, 2006. *Against the Draft: Essays on Conscientious Objection from the Radical Reformation to the Second World War*. University of Toronto Press.

Brock, Peter, and Nigel Young, 1999. *Pacifism in the Twentieth Century*. University of Toronto Press.

Brown, Callum, 2006. *Religion and Society in Twentieth-Century Britain*. Routledge.

Brown, Gordon, 1986. *Maxton*. Fontana.

Buchanan, Tom, 2002. "The Truth Will Set You Free': The Making of Amnesty International', *Journal of Contemporary History* 37(4): 575–97.

Burnham, Karyn, 2014. *The Courage of Cowards: The Untold Stories of First World War Conscientious Objectors*. Pen and Sword.

Bussey, Gertrude, and Margaret Tims, 1980. *Pioneers for Peace: Women's International League for Peace and Freedom, 1915–1965*. WILPF.

Byatt, Anthony, 2012. *Reminiscences towards a History of Jehovah's Witnesses in London, 1991–1977*. Golden Age Books.

Calder, Angus, 1993 [1969]. *The People's War: Britain, 1939–1945*. Pimlico.

Carpenter, Humphrey, 1981. *W. H Auden: A Biography*. George Allen & Unwin.

Carpenter, Humphrey, 1992. *Benjamin Britten: A Biography*. Faber & Faber.

Ceadel, Martin, 1979. 'The King and Country Debate, 1933: Student Politics, Pacifism and the Dictators', *Historical Journal* 22(2): 397–422.

Ceadel, Martin, 1980. *Pacifism in Britain, 1914–1945: The Defining of a Faith*. Clarendon.

Ceadel, Martin, 2000. *Semi-Detached Idealists: The British Peace Movement and International Relations, 1854–1945*. Oxford University Press.

Ceadel, Martin, 2003. 'The Quaker Peace Testimony and its Contribution to the British Peace Movement: An Overview', *Quaker Studies* 7(1): 9–29.

Churchwell, Sarah, 2018. *Behold America: A History of America First and the American Dream*. Bloomsbury.

Clark, Ann Marie, 2001. *Diplomacy of Conscience: Amnesty International and Changing Human Rights Norms*. Princeton University Press.

Couzin, John, 2005. *Radical Glasgow*. Voline Press.

Crang, Jeremy, 2000. *The British Army and the People's War, 1939–1945*. Manchester University Press.

Crang, Jeremy, 2020. *Sisters in Arms: Women in the British Armed Forces during the Second World War*. Cambridge University Press.

Cunningham, Valentine, 1988. *British Writers of the Thirties*. Oxford University Press.

Davies, A. Tegla, 1947. *Friends Ambulance Unit: The Story of the FAU in the Second World War, 1939–1946*. George Allen & Unwin.

Devji, Faisal, 2012. *The Impossible Indian: Gandhi and the Temptation of Violence.* Hurst.

Dietrich-Berryman, Eric, and Charlotte Hammond, 2010. *Passport Not Required: U.S. Volunteers in the Royal Navy, 1939–1941.* Naval Institute Press.

Duncan, Robert, 2015. *Objectors and Resisters: Opposition to Conscription and War in Scotland, 1914–1918.* Common Print.

Durbach, Nadja, 2001. 'Class, Gender and the Conscientious Objector to Vaccination, 1898–1907', *Journal of British Studies* 41(1): 58–83.

Dwarkadas, Kanji, 1966. *India's Fight for Freedom, 1913–1937.* Popular Prakashan.

Egremont, Max, 2014. *Siegfried Sassoon: A Biography.* Picador.

Evans, Malcolm, 1997. *Religious Liberty and International Law in Europe.* Cambridge University Press.

Evans, Richard J., 1987. *Comrades and Sisters: Feminism, Socialism and Pacifism in Europe, 1870–1945.* Wheatsheaf Books.

Evans, Richard, 2012. *The Third Reich in Power, 1933–1939: How the Nazis Won Over the Hearts and Minds of a Nation.* Penguin.

Feigel, Lara, 2016. *The Bitter Taste of Victory: Life, Love and Art in the Ruins of the Reich.* Bloomsbury.

Fernando, Mayanthi, 2010. 'Reconfiguring Freedom: Muslim Piety and the Limits of Secular Law and Public Discourse in France', *American Ethnologist* 37(1): 19–35.

Foley, Michael, 2003. *Confronting the War Machine: Draft Resistance during the Vietnam War.* University of North Carolina Press.

Foster, Catherine, 1989. *Women for All Seasons: The Story of the Women's International League for Peace and Freedom.* University of Georgia Press.

Freeberg, Ernest, 2008. *Democracy's Prisoner: Eugene V. Debs, the Great War, and the Right to Dissent.* Harvard University Press.

Freeman, Mark, 2010. 'Muscular Quakerism? The Society of Friends and Youth Organisations in Britain, c.1900–1950', *English Historical Review* 125(514): 642–69.

French, David, 1998. 'Discipline and the Death Penalty in the British Army in the War against Germany during the Second World War', *Journal of Contemporary History* 33(4): 531–45.

Frost, Brian, 1996. *Goodwill on Fire: Donald Soper's Life and Mission.* Hodder & Stoughton.

Fussell, Paul, 1975. *The Great War and Modern Memory.* Oxford University Press.

Gandhi, Leela, 1996. 'Concerning Violence: The Limits and Circulations of Gandhian "Ahisma" or Passive Resistance', *Cultural Critique* 35: 105–47.

Gardiner, Juliet, 2010. *The Thirties: An Intimate History.* Harper Press.

Gilbert, Mark, 1992. 'Pacifist Attitudes to Nazi Germany, 1936–1945', *Journal of Contemporary History* 27(3): 493–511.

Girard, Marion, 2008. *A Strange and Formidable Weapon: British Responses to World War I Poison Gas.* University of Nebraska Press.

Glass, Charles, 2012. *The Deserters: A Hidden History of World War II*. Penguin.

Gottlieb, Julie, 2014. '"The Women's Movement Took the Wrong Turning": British Feminists, Pacifism and the Politics of Appeasement', *Women's History Review* 23(3): 441–62.

Grass, Tim, 2006. *Gathering to His Name: The Story of the Brethren in Britain and Ireland*. Paternoster Press.

Green, Clifford, 2019. 'Bonhoeffer's Christian Peace Ethics, Conditional Pacifisms, and Resistance', in *Oxford Handbook of Dietrich Bonhoeffer*, ed. Philip G. Ziegler and Michael Mawson. Oxford University Press.

Guha, Ramachandra, 2018. *Gandhi: The Years that Changed the World, 1914–1928*. Allen Lane.

Gullace, Nicoletta, 2016. *The Blood of our Sons: Men, Women and the Renegotiation of British Citizenship during the Great War*. Palgrave.

Gurney, Jason, 1974. *Crusade in Spain*. Faber & Faber.

Hardy, Dennis, 2000. *Utopian England: Community Experiments, 1900–1945*. Routledge.

Hayes, Denis, 1949. *Challenge of Conscience: The Story of the Conscientious Objectors, 1939–1949*. George Allen & Unwin.

Hayes, Denis, 1949. *Conscription Conflict: The Conflict of Ideas in the Struggle for and against Military Conscription in Britain between 1901 and 1939*. Sheppard Press.

Heller, Richard, 1971. 'East Fulham Revisited', *Journal of Contemporary History* 6(4): 172–96.

Hinton, James, 1989. *Protests and Visions: Peace Politics in 20th Century Britain*. Hutchinson Radius.

Hochschild, Adam, 2011. *To End All Wars: A Story of Protest and Patriotism in the First World War*. Picador.

Holman, Brett, 2001. 'The Air Panic of 1935: British Press Opinion between Disarmament and Rearmament', *Journal of Contemporary History* 46(2): 288–307.

Hughes-Wilson, John, 2005. *Blindfold and Alone: British Military Execution in the Great War*. Weidenfeld & Nicolson.

Humbert, Laure. 2001. 'Gender, Humanitarianism and Soft Power', https://colonialandtransnationalintimacies.com/2021/03/05/gender-humanitarianism-and-soft-power/, last accessed 30 March 2021.

Ingram, Norman, 1991. *The Politics of Dissent: Pacifism in France, 1919–1939*. Oxford University Press.

Jenkins, Ray, 2009. *A Pacifist at War*. Arrow Books.

Kaufman, Edy, 1991. 'Prisoners of Conscience: The Shaping of a New Human Rights Concept', *Human Rights Quarterly* 13(3): 339–67.

Kaye, Elaine, 1968. *The History of the King's Weigh House Church*. George Allen & Unwin.

Kaye, Elaine, and Ross Mackenzie, 1990. *W. E. Orchard: A Study in Christian Exploration*. Education Series.

Kazin, Michael, 2017. *War against War: The American Fight for Peace, 1914–1918*. Simon & Schuster.

Keane, Webb, 2002. 'Sincerity, "Modernity" and the Protestant', *Cultural Anthropology* 17(1): 65–92.

Kelly, Tobias, 2018. 'A Divided Conscience: The Lost Convictions of Human Rights', *Public Culture* 30(3): 367–92.

Kessler, Jeremy, 2013. 'The Invention of a Human Right: Conscientious Objection at the United Nations, 1947–2011', *Columbia Human Rights Law Review* 44(3): 753–92.

Khan, Yasmin, 2015. *India at War: The Subcontinent and World War II*. Oxford University Press.

Kildea, Paul, 2014. *Benjamin Britten: A Life in the Twentieth Century*. Penguin.

Koonz, Claudia, 2003. *The Nazi Conscience*. Harvard University Press.

Kosek, Joseph Kip, 2005. 'Richard Gregg, Mohandas Gandhi, and the Strategy of Nonviolence', *Journal of American History* 91(4): 1318–48.

Kosek, Joseph Kip, 2009. *Acts of Conscience: Christian Nonviolence and Modern American Democracy*. Columbia University Press.

Kramer, Ann, 2014. *Conscientious Objectors of the First World War: A Determined Resistance*. Pen and Sword.

Lawrence, Jon, 2003. 'Forging a Peaceable Kingdom: War, Violence and Fear of Brutalization in Post-First World War Britain', *Journal of Modern History* 75(3): 557–89.

Lea, F. A., 1959. *The Life of John Middleton Murry*. Methuen.

Lukowitz, David, 1974. 'British Pacifists and Appeasement: The Peace Pledge Union', *Journal of Contemporary History* 9(1): 115–27.

MacCarthy, Fiona, 2011. *Eric Gill*. Faber & Faber.

McCarthy, Helen, 2011. *The British People and the League of Nations: Democracy, Citizenship and Internationalism, c.1918–1945*. Manchester University Press.

McGonigal, James, 2010. *Beyond the Last Dragon: A Life of Edwin Morgan*. Sandstone Press.

McKibbin, Ross, 1998. *Classes and Cultures: England, 1918–1951*. Oxford University Press.

Maclachlan, Lewis, 1952. *C.P.F.L.U.: A History of the Christian Pacifist Forestry and Land Units*. Fellowship of Reconciliation.

Maclure, Jocelyn, and Charles Taylor, 2012. *Secularism and Freedom of Conscience*. Harvard University Press.

McNeill, Marjory, 1996. *Norman MacCaig: A Study of his Life and Work*. Mercat Press.

Makepeace, Clare, 2017. *Captives of War: British Prisoners of War in Europe in the Second World War*. Cambridge University Press.

Martin, John, 2014. 'The State Directed Food Production Campaign and the Farming Community, 1939-45', *Family & Community History* 17(1): 47–63.

Marwick, Arthur, 1964. *Clifford Allen: The Open Conspirator*. Oliver & Boyd.

Maunaguru, Sidharthan. 2021. 'The Voice of Conscience amid the Populist Uproar: Politics and Popular Ideologies', Hot Spots, *Fieldsights*, 16 March. https://culanth.org/fieldsights/the-voice-of-conscience-amid-the-populist-uproar-politics-and-popular-ideologies, last accessed 6 April 2021.

Mendelsohn, Edward, 1999. *Early Auden*. Faber & Faber.

Metaxas, Eric, 2010. *Bonhoeffer: Pastor, Martyr, Prophet, Spy*. Thomas Nelson.

Middleton Murry, Katherine, 1986. *Beloved Quixote: The Unknown Life of John Middleton Murry*. Condor.

Middleton Murry, Mary, 1959. *To Keep Faith*. Constable.

Miles, Jonathan, 2018. *Try the Wilderness First: Eric Gill and David Jones at Capel-y-ffin*. Seren.

Misra, Maria, 2014. 'Sergeant-Major Gandhi: Indian Nationalism and Non-violent "Martiality"', *Journal of Asian Studies* 73(3): 689–709.

Moorehead, Caroline, 1987. *Troublesome People: Enemies of War, 1916–1986*. Hamish Hamilton.

Moses, Greg, 1997. *Revolution of Conscience: Martin Luther King, Jr., and the Philosophy of Nonviolence*. The Guildford Press.

Moskos, Charles, 1993. *The New Conscientious Objection: From Sacred to Secular Resistance*. Oxford University Press.

Mosse, George, 1996. *Image of Man*. Oxford University Press.

Moyn, Samuel, 2014. 'From Communist to Muslim: European Human Rights, the Cold War, and Religious Liberty', *South Atlantic Quarterly* 113(1): 63–86.

Nicholson, Hazel, 2007. 'A Disputed Identity: Women Conscientious Objectors in Second World War Britain', *Twentieth Century British History* 18(4): 409–28.

Noakes, Lucy, 2015. 'A Broken Silence? Mass Observation, Armistice Day and "Everyday Life" in Britain, 1937–1941', *Journal of European Studies* 45(4): 331–46.

Noakes, Lucy, and Juliette Pattinson (eds), 2014. *British Cultural Memory and the Second World War*. Bloomsbury.

Nussbaum, Martha, 2008. *Liberty of Conscience: In Defence of America's Tradition of Religious Equality*. Basic Books.

Oustinova-Stjepanovic, Galina. 2020. 'End of Organized Atheism: The Genealogy of the Law on Freedom of Conscience and its Conceptual Effects in Russia', *History and Anthropology* 31(5): 600–17.

Overy, Richard, 2010. *The Morbid Age: Britain and the Crisis of Civilization, 1919–1939*. Penguin.

Overy, Richard, 2013. *The Bombing War: Europe, 1939–1945*. Penguin.

Overy, Richard, 2013. 'Pacifism and the Blitz', *Past and Present* 219(1): 201–36.

Paris, Michael, 2006. *Warrior Nation: Images of War in Popular British Culture, 1850–2000*. Reaktion.

Pattinson, Juliette, 2006. '"Shirkers", "Scrimjacks" and "Scrimshanks"? British Civilian Masculinity and Reserved Occupations, 1914–1945', *Gender and History* 28(3): 709–27.

Pattinson, Juliette, Arthur McIvor and Linsey Robb, 2016. *Men in Reserve: British Civilian Masculinities in the Second World War*. Manchester University Press.

Pattinson, Juliette, Lucy Noakes and Wendy Ugolini, 2014. 'Incarcerated Masculinities: Male POWs and the Second World War', *Journal of War and Culture Studies* 7(3): 179–90.

Peel, Mark, 2008. *The Last Wesleyan: A Life of Donald Soper*. Scotforth Books.

Perrin, Jim, 1985. *Menlove: The Life of John Menlove Edwards*. Ernest Press.

Press, Eyal, 2014. *Beautiful Souls: The Courage and Conscience of Ordinary People in Extraordinary Times*. Farrar, Straus & Giroux.

Pugh, Martin, 2009. *We Danced All Night: A Social History of Britain between the Wars*. Vintage.

Purcell, William, 1983. *Odd Man Out: A Biography of Lord Soper of Kingsway*. Mowbray.

Raby, Angela, 1999. *The Forgotten Service: Auxiliary Ambulance Station 39, Weymouth Mews*. Battle of Britain International.

Rae, John, 1970. *Conscience and Politics: The British Government and the Conscientious Objector to Military Service*. Oxford University Press.

Redfield, Peter, 2013. *Life in Crisis: The Ethical Journey of Doctors without Borders*. University of California Press.

Rempel, Richard, 1978. 'The Dilemmas of British Pacifists during World War II', *Journal of Modern History* 50(4): 1213–29.

Robb, Linsey, 2018. 'The "Conchie Corps": Conflict, Compromise and Conscientious Objection in the British Army, 1940–1945', *Twentieth Century British History* 29(3): 411–34.

Robb, Linsey, and Juliette Pattinson (eds), 2018. *Men, Masculinities and Male Culture in the Second World War*. Palgrave.

Roper, Michael, 2017. 'Subjectivities in the Aftermath: Children of Disabled Soldiers in Britain after the Great War', in *Psychological Trauma and the Legacies of the First World War*. Springer International Publishing, 165–91.

Rose, Sonya, 2003. *Which People's War? National Identity and Citizenship in Britain, 1939–1945*. Oxford University Press.

Rothberg, Michael, 2019. *The Implicated Subject: Beyond Victims and Perpetrators*. Stanford University Press.

Royle, Trevor, 2011. *A Time of Tyrants: Scotland and the Second World War*. Berlinn.

Samuel, Raphael, 2006. *The Lost World of British Communism*. Verso.

Satia, Priya, 2020. *Time's Monster: History, Conscience and Britain's Empire*. Allen Lane.

Schwab, Gerald, 1990. *The Day the Holocaust Began: The Odyssey of Herschel Grynszpan*. Praeger.

Shepherd, John, 2002. *George Lansbury: At the Heart of Old Labour.* Oxford University Press.

Short, Brian, 2008. 'Death of a Farmer: The Fortunes of War and the Strange Case of Ray Walden', *Agricultural History Review* 56(2): 89–213.

Soden, Oliver, 2019. *Michael Tippett: The Biography.* Weidenfeld & Nicolson.

Stammers, Neil, 1983. *Civil Liberties in Britain during the 2nd World War.* St Martin's Press.

Starkey, Pat, 2000. *Families and Social Workers: The Work of the Family Service Units, 1940–1985.* Liverpool University Press.

Steinweis, Alan, 2009. *Kristallnacht 1938.* Harvard University Press.

Stockings, Craig, and Eleanor Hancock, 2013. *Swastika over the Acropolis: Re-interpreting the Nazi Invasion of Greece in World War II.* Brill.

Taylor, A. J. P., 1970. *English History, 1914–45.* Penguin Books.

Taylor, Charles, 1989. *Sources of the Self: The Making of the Modern Identity.* Harvard University Press.

Taylor, Frederik, 2019. *1939: A People's History.* Picador.

Taylor, Richard, and Colin Prichard, 1980. *The Protest Makers: The British Nuclear Disarmament Movement of 1958–1965.* Pergamon Press.

Terkel, Studs, 1997. *'The Good War': An Oral History of World War II.* New Press.

Todman, Daniel, 2017. *Britain's War: Into Battle, 1937–1941.* Penguin.

Todman, Daniel, 2020. *Britain's War: 1942–1947.* Allen Lane.

Tollefson, James W., 2000. *The Strength Not to Fight: Conscientious Objectors of the Vietnam War.* Brassey's.

Trotter, William R., 1991. *The Winter War: The Russo-Finnish War of 1939–1940.* Aurum.

Trout, Jessie, 1959. *Kagawa, Japanese Prophet.* World Christian Books.

Ugolini, Wendy, and Juliette Pattinson (eds), 2015. *Fighting for Britain? Negotiating Identities in Britain during the Second World War.* Peter Lang.

Wallis, Jill, 1991. *Valiant for Peace: A History of the Fellowship of Reconciliation, 1914–1989.* Fellowship of Reconciliation.

Wallis, Jill, 1993. *The Mother of World Peace: A Life of Muriel Lester.* Hisarlick Press.

Walzer, Michael, 1965. *The Revolution of the Saints: A Study of the Origins of Radical Politics.* Harvard University Press.

Weber, Max, 1946 [1919]. 'Politics as a Vocation', in *From Max Weber*, ed. and trans. H. H. Gerth and C. Wright Mills. Free Press.

Webster, Wendy, 2018. *Mixing It: Diversity in World War Two Britain.* Oxford University Press.

Weiss, Erica, 2014. *Conscientious Objectors in Israel: Citizenship, Sacrifice and Trials of Fealty.* Pennsylvania University Press.

Whitaker, Ben, 1983. *A Bridge of People: A Personal View of Oxfam's First Forty Years.* Heinemann.

Wilkinson, Alan, 1986. *Dissent or Conform: War, Peace and the English Churches, 1900-1945.* SCM Press.

Wilson, R. C., 1949. *Authority, Leadership and Concern: A Study in Motive and Administration in Quaker Relief Work.* George Allen & Unwin.

Wyckes, David, 1994. 'Friends, Parliament and the Toleration Act', *Journal of Ecclesiastical History* 45(1): 42–63.

Young, Michael, 1996. *The Elmhirsts of Dartington.* Routledge & Kegan Paul.

Zahn, Gordon C., 1964. *In Solitary Witness: The Life and Death of Franz Jägerstätter.* Henry Holt.

Newspaper and Magazine Articles

Barratt Brown, Michael, 'Michael Rowntree, Obituary', *Guardian*, 30 October 2007, https://www.theguardian.com/news/2007/oct/30/guardianobituaries. internationalaidanddevelopment, last accessed 3 March 2021.

Black, Maggie, 'Bernard Llewellyn, Obituary', *Guardian*, 24 June 2008, https://www.theguardian.com/theguardian/2008/jun/24/1, last accessed 2 March 2021.

House, Simon, 'Roy Ridgway, Obituary', *Guardian*, 16 December 2000, https://www.theguardian.com/news/2000/dec/16/guardianobituaries2, last accessed 2 March 2021.

Lewis, Michael, 'The Way They Live Now', *New York Review of Books*, 7 March 2013, https://www.nybooks.com/articles/2013/03/07/way-they-live-now/, last accessed 2 March 2021.

Mendelson, Edward, 'The Secret Auden', *New York Review of Books*, 20 March 2014, https://www.nybooks.com/articles/2014/03/20/secret-auden/, last accessed 2 March 2021.

[No author], 'Hugh MacDiarmid: Scots Would Have Been Better Off under the Nazis', *Scotsman*, 5 April 2010, https://www.scotsman.com/news-2-15012/hugh-macdiarmid-scots-would-have-been-better-off-under-the-nazis-1-797634, last accessed 4 April 2019.

Other Online Resources

Howell, David, 2011. 'Morrison, Herbert Stanley, Baron Morrison of Lambeth (1888–1965), Politician', *Oxford Dictionary of National Biography*, https://www.oxforddnb.com/view/10.1093/ref:odnb/9780198614128.001.0001/odnb-9780198614128-e-35121, last accessed 2 March 2021.

May, Alex, 2004. 'Kerry, Philip Henry, Eleventh Marquess of Lothian (1882–1940)', *Oxford Dictionary of National Biography*, https://www.oxforddnb.com/view/10.1093/ref:odnb/9780198614128.001.0001/odnb-9780198614128-e-34303, last accessed 2 March 2021.

[No author], 'The Hungerford Club', 12 July 2017, https://library.chethams.com/blog/the-hungerford-club/, last accessed 2 March 2021.

[No author], Friends Ambulance Unit in WWI, http://www.quakersintheworld.org/quakers-in-action/252/Friends-Ambulance-Unit-FAU-in-WWI, last accessed 2 March 2021.

The Nobel Peace Prize for 1985, https://www.nobelprize.org/prizes/peace/1985/press-release, last accessed 2 March 2021.

Riach, Alan, 'Hugh MacDiarmid', https://www.scottishpoetrylibrary.org.uk/poet/hugh-macdiarmid/, last accessed 28 September 2015.

United Nations, 1945. Charter of the United Nations, 24 October 1945, https://www.un.org/en/charter-united-nations/, last accessed 2 March 2021.

UN General Assembly, Universal Declaration of Human Rights, 10 December 1948, https://www.un.org/en/universal-declaration-human-rights/, last accessed 2 March 2021.

Theses

Trussler, Anna Claire, 2001. 'The Importance of Being: The Autobiographical Subject in the Drama and Memoirs of Ronald Duncan'. Unpublished PhD thesis, University of Plymouth.

NOTES

Introduction

1 Interview with Roy Ridgway, 14 July 1987, Imperial War Museum Collections (IWM).

2 Diary of Roy Ridgway, 2 September 1944, Papers of Roy Ridgway, IWM.

3 Ibid., 5 September 1944.

4 Ibid.

5 Studs Terkel, 1997. *'The Good War': An Oral History of World War II*. New Press.

6 Karyn Burnham, 2014. *The Courage of Cowards: The Untold Stories of First World War Conscientious Objectors*. Pen and Sword; Adam Hochschild, 2011. *To End All Wars: A Story of Protest and Patriotism in the First World War*. Picador; Michael Kazin, 2017. *War against War: The American Fight for Peace, 1914–1918*. Simon & Schuster; Ann Kramer, 2014. *Conscientious Objectors of the First World War: A Determined Resistance*. Pen and Sword.

7 Hochschild, 2011. *To End All Wars*, xvi.

8 Central Board of Conscientious Objectors. 'A Plea for Tolerance', Butler Papers, Bishopsgate Institute, London. See also Denis Hayes, 1949. *Challenge of Conscience: The Story of the Conscientious Objectors, 1939–1949*. George Allen & Unwin, 6.

9 For examples, see: Nadezhda Mandelstam, 1999. *Hope against Hope*. Harvill; Ian McEwan, 2014. *The Children Act*. Jonathan Cape; Eyal Press, 2014. *Beautiful Souls: The Courage and Conscience of Ordinary People in Extraordinary Times*. Farrar, Straus & Giroux.

10 For examples of the varied histories of conscience see: Edward Andrew, 2001. *Conscience and its Critics: Protestant Conscience, Enlightenment Reason and Modern Subjectivity*. University of Toronto Press; Michael Baylor, 1977. *Action and Person: Conscience in Late Scholasticism and the Young Luther*. Leiden: Brill; Charles Moskos, 1993. *The New Conscientious Objection: From Sacred to Secular Resistance*. Oxford University Press; Martha Nussbaum, 2008. *Liberty of Conscience: In Defence of America's Tradition of Religious Equality*. Basic Books; Charles Taylor, 1989. *Sources of the Self: The Making of the Modern Identity*. Harvard University Press; James W. Tollefson, 2000. *The*

Strength Not to Fight: Conscientious Objectors of the Vietnam War. Brassey's; Michael Walzer, 1982. *The Revolution of the Saints: A Study in the Origins of Radical Politics.* Harvard University Press; Erica Weiss, 2014. *Conscientious Objectors in Israel: Citizenship, Sacrifice and Trials of Fealty.* Pennsylvania University Press.

11 Claudia Koonz, 2003. *The Nazi Conscience.* Harvard University Press.

12 Jocelyn Maclure and Charles Taylor, 2012. *Secularism and Freedom of Conscience.* Harvard University Press; Nussbaum, 2008. *Liberty of Conscience.*

13 Interview with Stella St John, 7 August 1971, IWM.

14 Diary of Fred Urquhart, late June 1937, Fred Urquhart Papers, Centre for Research Collections (CRC), Edinburgh University.

15 Interview with Roy Ridgway, 14 July 1987, IWM.

16 Colin Affleck, 2011. 'Introduction' to Fred Urquhart, *Jezebel's Dust.* Kennedy & Boyd, v.

17 Lucy Noakes and Juliette Pattinson (eds), 2014. *British Cultural Memory and the Second World War.* Bloomsbury.

18 Angus Calder, 1992 [1969]. *The People's War: Britain, 1939–1945.* Pimlico; Wendy Ugolini and Juliette Pattinson (eds), 2015. *Fighting for Britain? Negotiating Identities in Britain during the Second World War.* Peter Lang; Wendy Webster, 2018. *Mixing It: Diversity in World War Two Britain.* Oxford University Press.

19 Sidharthan Maunaguru, 2021. 'The Voice of Conscience amid the Populist Uproar: Politics and Popular Ideologies', Hot Spots, *Fieldsights*, 16 March,https://culanth.org/fieldsights/the-voice-of-conscience-amid-the-populist-uproar-politics-and-popular-ideologies, last accessed 6 April 2021; Galina Oustinova-Stjepanovic, 2020. 'End of Organized Atheism: The Genealogy of the Law on Freedom of Conscience and its Conceptual Effects in Russia', *History and Anthropology* 31(5): 600–17; Weiss, 2014. *Conscientious Objectors in Israel.*

20 Priya Satia, 2020. *Time's Monster: History, Conscience and Britain's Empire.* Allen Lane.

21 See, for example, Andrew, 2001. *Conscience and its Critics.*

22 Ibid.; Baylor, 1977. *Action and Person*; Nehal Bhuta, 2014. 'Two Concepts of Religious Freedom in the European Court of Human Rights', *South Atlantic Quarterly* 113(1): 9–35; Webb Keane, 2002. 'Sincerity, "Modernity" and the Protestant', *Cultural Anthropology* 17(1): 65–92; Nussbaum, 2008. *Liberty of Conscience*; Taylor, 1989. *Sources of the Self*; Walzer, 1982. *The Revolution of the Saints.*

23 Walzer, 1965. *The Revolution of the Saints*, 124.

24 Michael Lewis, 'The Way They Live Now', *New York Review of Books*, 7 March 2013,https://www.nybooks.com/articles/2013/03/07/way-they-live-now/, last accessed 2 March 2021.

25 Peter Brock and Nigel Young, 1999. *Pacifism in the Twentieth Century.* University of Toronto Press; Jessie Trout, 1959. *Kagawa, Japanese Prophet.* World Christian Books.

26 Joseph Kip Kosek, 2009. *Acts of Conscience: Christian Nonviolence and Modern American Democracy.* Columbia University Press.
27 Richard J. Evans, 1987. *Comrades and Sisters: Feminism, Socialism and Pacifism in Europe 1870–1945.* Wheatsheaf Books.
28 Gertrude Bussey and Margaret Tims, 1980. *Pioneers for Peace: Women's International League for Peace and Freedom, 1915–1965.* WILPF; Martin Ceadel, 1980. *Pacifism in Britain, 1914–1945: The Defining of a Faith.* Clarendon; Catherine Foster, 1989. *Women for All Seasons: The Story of the Women's International League for Peace and Freedom.* University of Georgia Press; Jill Wallis, 1991. *Valiant for Peace: A History of the Fellowship of Reconciliation, 1914–1989.* Fellowship of Reconciliation.
29 Maggie Black, 1992. *A Cause for our Times: Oxfam, the First Fifty Years.* Oxfam; Tom Buchanan, 2002. '"The Truth Will Set You Free": The Making of Amnesty International', *Journal of Contemporary History* 37(4): 575–97; Ann Marie Clark, 2001. *Diplomacy of Conscience: Amnesty International and Changing Human Rights Norms.* Princeton University Press; Edy Kaufman, 1991. 'Prisoners of Conscience: The Shaping of a New Human Rights Concept', *Human Rights Quarterly* 13(3): 339–67.

Chapter 1: War, Fear and Hope

1 Diary of Fred Urquhart, 2 January 1938, Fred Urquhart Papers, CRC, Edinburgh University.
2 Martin Pugh, 2009. *We Danced All Night: A Social History of Britain between the Wars.* Vintage; Elizabeth Bowen, 1938. *The Death of the Heart.* Knopf.
3 Richard Overy, 2010. *The Morbid Age: Britain and the Crisis of Civilization, 1919–1939.* Penguin.
4 Diary of Fred Urquhart, 15 March 1938.
5 Stevie Smith, 1980 [1938]. *Over the Frontier.* Virago, 8.
6 Diary of Fred Urquhart, 6 October 1936.
7 Ibid., 20 February 1938.
8 Ibid., 13 September 1937.
9 Ibid., 4 January 1938.
10 Ibid., 20 February 1938.
11 Ibid., 24 May 1938.
12 Ibid., 18 January 1938.
13 Edwin Muir, 1935. *Scottish Journey.* Heinemann, 18.
14 Diary of Fred Urquhart, 14 October 1936.
15 Ibid., 15 September 1936.
16 Ibid., 28 October 1939.
17 Ibid., 2 April 1936.
18 Ibid., 2 March 1938.
19 Ibid., 16 May 1938.
20 Ibid., 23 October 1936.
21 Ibid., 17 March 1936.

22 Fred Urquhart, 1938. *Time Will Knit.* Gerald Duckworth, 115, 244.
23 Diary of Fred Urquhart, 27 November 1936.
24 Ross McKibbin, 1998. *Classes and Cultures: England, 1918–1951.* Oxford University Press, 155.
25 Diary of Fred Urquhart, 2 March 1938.
26 Valentine Cunningham, 1988. *British Writers of the Thirties.* Oxford University Press, 55.
27 Martin Ceadel, 1979. 'The King and Country Debate, 1933: Student Politics, Pacifism and the Dictators', *Historical Journal* 22(2): 397–422.
28 Brian Bond, 2002. *The Unquiet Western Front: Britain's Role in Literature and History.* Cambridge University Press; Michael Paris, 2006. *Warrior Nation: Images of War in Popular British Culture, 1850–2000.* Reaktion.
29 Paul Fussell, 1975. *The Great War and Modern Memory.* Oxford University Press.
30 George Mosse, 1996. *Image of Man.* Oxford University Press, 108.
31 Urquhart, 1938. *Time Will Knit,* 249.
32 Lucy Noakes, 2015. 'A Broken Silence? Mass Observation, Armistice Day and "Everyday Life" in Britain, 1937–1941', *Journal of European Studies* 45(4): 331–46.
33 Diary of Fred Urquhart, 12 November 1937.
34 *Quintinshill: Britain's Deadliest Rail Disaster,* BBC Two Scotland, 20 May 2015.
35 Juliet Gardiner, 2010. *The Thirties: An Intimate History.* Harper Press, 13.
36 Michael Roper, 2017. 'Subjectivities in the Aftermath: Children of Disabled Soldiers in Britain after the Great War', in *Psychological Trauma and the Legacies of the First World War.* Springer International Publishing, 165–91.
37 Cunningham, 1988. *British Writers in the Thirties,* 45.
38 Brett Holman, 2001. 'The Air Panic of 1935: British Press Opinion between Disarmament and Rearmament', *Journal of Contemporary History* 46(2): 288–301; Marion Girard, 2008. *A Strange and Formidable Weapon: British Responses to World War I Poison Gas.* University of Nebraska Press.
39 House of Commons (HC), 10 November 1932, vol. 270, col. 631.
40 Beverley Nichols, 1933. *Cry Havoc!* Doubleday, 16.
41 Paul Berry and Mark Bostridge, 2001. *Vera Brittain: A Life.* Virago, 364.
42 Diary of Fred Urquhart, 21 October 1939.
43 Ibid., 2 September 1939, 10 November 1940.
44 Ibid., 26 October 1936.
45 John Middleton Murry, 1939. 'Prepare the Peace', *Adelphi* 16(1), 16 October.
46 Ibid.
47 Overy, 2010. *The Morbid Age*; Jon Lawrence, 2003. 'Forging a Peaceable Kingdom: War, Violence and Fear of Brutalization in Post-First World War Britain', *Journal of Modern History* 75(3): 557–8.

48 Pugh, 2009. *We Danced All Night.*
49 Martin Ceadel, 1980. *Pacifism in Britain, 1914–1945: The Defining of a Faith.* Clarendon, 6.

Chapter 2: Pledging Peace

1 Diary of Roy Ridgway, 1 January 1938, Papers of Roy Ridgway, IWM.
2 Ibid., 1 September 1939.
3 Interview with Roy Ridgway, 14 July 1987, IWM.
4 Ibid.
5 Ibid.
6 Ibid.
7 Diary of Roy Ridgway, 6 April 1938.
8 Martin Ceadel, 2000. *Semi-Detached Idealists: The British Peace Movement and International Relations, 1854–1945.* Oxford University Press; Helen McCarthy, 2011. *The British People and the League of Nations: Democracy, Citizenship and Internationalism, c.1918–1945.* Manchester University Press, 11.
9 Hugh Dalton, 1928, *Towards the Peace of Nations: A Study in International Politics.* George Routledge, 89.
10 McCarthy, 2011. *The British People and the League of Nations,* 171.
11 Ibid., 172.
12 Ibid.
13 David Branford, 2008. 'From Pacifism to Just War: Changing Attitudes in the Church of England, 1930 to 1940', *Modern Believing* 49(2): 14–21.
14 Sybil Morrison, 1962. *I Renounce War: The Story of the Peace Pledge Union.* PPU, 1.
15 Martin Ceadel, 1980. *Pacifism in Britain, 1914–1945: Defining a Faith.* Clarendon; Morrison, 1962. *I Renounce War.*
16 Dick Sheppard and Laurence Housman, 1939. *What Can We Believe? Letters Exchanged between Dick Sheppard and Laurence Housman.* Jonathan Cape.
17 Julie Gottlieb, 2014. '"The Women's Movement Took the Wrong Turning": British Feminists, Pacifism and the Politics of Appeasement', *Women's History Review* 23(3): 441–62.
18 David Lukowitz, 1974. 'British Pacifists and Appeasement: The Peace Pledge Union', *Journal of Contemporary History* 9(1): 115–27.
19 Interview with Cyril Wright, 17 November 1980, IWM.
20 Clifford Worrall, 1989. 'A Soft Answer'. Unpublished Memoir. Papers of C. Worrall, IWM; interview with Victor Newcomb, 13 August 1986, IWM.
21 Morrison, 1962. *I Renounce War,* 17.
22 F. P. Crozier, 1930. *A Brass Hat in No Man's Land.* Jonathan Cape.
23 Interview with Ronald Mallone, 31 January 1980, IWM.
24 Diary of Roy Ridgway, 29 April 1938.

25 Ibid., 24 May 1938.
26 Ross McKibbin, 1998. *Classes and Cultures: England, 1918–1951.* Oxford University Press.
27 Diary of Roy Ridgway, 12 November 1938.

Chapter 3: Socialist Futures

1 Diary of Fred Urquhart, 13 September 1937, Fred Urquhart Papers, CRC, Edinburgh University.
2 Ibid., 4 March 1936.
3 See: Papers of the British Section of the International Socialist Labour Party 1912–1937, Papers of the Revolutionary Socialist Party 1936–1941, Independent Labour Party, Tait/Watson Archives (MS 41), Archives and Special Collections, University of Stirling.
4 Martin Pugh, 2009. *We Danced All Night: A Social History of Britain between the Wars.* Vintage, 88; Ross McKibbin, 1998. *Classes and Cultures: England, 1918–1951.* Oxford University Press, 145.
5 Adam Hochschild, 2011. *To End All Wars: A Story of Protest and Patriotism in the First World War.* Picador; David Boulton, 1967. *Objection Overruled.* MacGibbon & Kee.
6 Diary of Fred Urquhart, late June 1937.
7 Ibid., 19 January 1939.
8 Ibid., 31 March 1936.
9 Ibid., 22 October 1935.
10 Ibid., 13 December 1937.
11 Ibid., early December 1936.
12 Gordon Brown, 1986. *Maxton.* Fontana.
13 Ernest Freeberg, 2008. *Democracy's Prisoner: Eugene V. Debs, the Great War, and the Right to Dissent.* Harvard University Press.
14 Gertrude Bussey and Margaret Tims, 1980. *Pioneers for Peace: Women's International League for Peace and Freedom, 1915–1965.* WILPF; Martin Ceadel, 1980. *Pacifism in Britain, 1914–1945: Defining a Faith.* Clarendon, 46; Hochschild, 2011. *To End All Wars*; John Rae, 1970. *Conscience and Politics: The British Government and the Conscientious Objector to Military Service.* Oxford University Press.
15 Robert Duncan, 2015. *Objectors and Resisters: Opposition to Conscription and War in Scotland, 1914–1918.* Common Print, 91.
16 Ibid., 119.
17 Arthur Marwick, 1964. *Clifford Allen: The Open Conspirator.* Oliver & Boyd.
18 Boulton, 1967. *Objection Overruled*, 111.
19 Ibid., 114.
20 Michael Kazin, 2017. *War against War: The American Fight for Peace, 1914–1918.* Simon & Schuster.
21 Boulton, 1967. *Objection Overruled.*

22 Fenner Brockway, 1941. *Stop War by Socialism: ILP Policy Statement*. ILP, 3; Fenner Brockway, 1974. *Towards Tomorrow: The Autobiography of Fenner Brockway*. Rupert Hart-Davis, 34; Kazin, 2017. *War against War*.
23 Boulton, 1967. *Objection Overruled*, 99.
24 Ibid., 111.
25 Ceadel, 1980. *Pacifism in Britain*, 74.
26 Richard Heller, 1971. 'East Fulham Revisited', *Journal of Contemporary History* 6(4): 172–96.
27 A. J. P. Taylor, 1970. *English History, 1914–45*. Penguin, 191.
28 John Shepherd, 2002. *George Lansbury: At the Heart of Old Labour*. Oxford University Press, 341.
29 Diary of Fred Urquhart, 18 April 1938.
30 Letters to the Editor, *Glasgow Herald*, 16 July 1938.
31 Diary of Fred Urquhart, 18 April 1938.
32 Fenner Brockway, 1963. *Outside the Right*. George Allen & Unwin, 135.
33 Interview with Fenner Brockway, 16 March 1982, IWM.
34 Diary of Fred Urquhart, 5 February 1939.
35 Ibid., 16 March 1939.
36 Alan Riach, 'Hugh MacDiarmid', https://www.scottishpoetrylibrary. org.uk/poet/hugh-macdiarmid/, last accessed 28 September 2015; see also John Manson (ed.), 2011. *Dear Grieve: Letters to Hugh MacDiarmid (C. M. Grieve)*. Kennedy & Boyd.
37 'Hugh MacDiarmid: Scots Would Have Been Better Off under the Nazis', *Scotsman*, 5 April 2010, https://www.scotsman.com/news-2-15012/ hugh-macdiarmid-scots-would-have-been-better-off-under-the-nazis-1- 797634, last accessed 4 April 2019.
38 Raphael Samuel, 2006. *The Lost World of British Communism*. Verso.
39 William Gallacher, 2017 [1936]. *Revolt on the Clyde*. Lawrence & Wishart.
40 John Middleton Murry, 1936. 'Taking Bearings', John Middleton Murry Collection, MS 2508, CRC, Edinburgh University.
41 F. A. Lea, 1959. *The Life of John Middleton Murry*. Methuen, 200.
42 Ibid.
43 James Hinton, 1989. *Protests and Visions: Peace Politics in 20th Century Britain*. Hutchinson Radius, 81.
44 Ceadel, 1980. *Pacifism in Britain*, 48.
45 Cecil Day-Lewis, 1960. *The Buried Day*. Chatto & Windus, 209.
46 Lea, 1959. *The Life of John Middleton Murry*, 243.

Chapter 4: Christian Faith

1 Interview with Stella St John, 7 August 1971, IWM.
2 Elaine Kaye and Ross Mackenzie, 1990. *W. E. Orchard: A Study in Christian Exploration*. Education Series, 53.

3 Martin Pugh, 2009. *We Danced All Night: A Social History of Britain between the Wars*. Vintage, 7.

4 Callum Brown, 2006. *Religion and Society in Twentieth Century Britain*. Routledge.

5 George Orwell, 2018 [1941]. *The Lion and the Unicorn: Socialism and the English Genius*. Penguin, 113.

6 Juliet Gardiner, 2010. *The Thirties: An Intimate History*. HarperCollins, 507.

7 George Orwell, 2001 [1937]. *The Road to Wigan Pier*. Penguin.

8 Michael Young, 1996. *The Elmhirsts of Dartington*. Routledge & Kegan Paul; Victor Bonham-Carter, 1958. *Dartington Hall: The History of an Experiment*. Phoenix House.

9 Elaine Kaye, 1968. *The History of the King's Weigh House Church*. George Allen & Unwin; Kaye and Mackenzie, 1990. *W. E. Orchard*.

10 Kaye and Mackenzie, 1990. *W. E. Orchard*, 77.

11 W. E. Orchard, 1933. *From Faith to Faith: An Autobiography of Religious Development*. M. A. Magnani and Sons.

12 Interview with Stella St John, 7 August 1971, IWM.

13 Ibid.

14 Ibid.

15 Records of the Fellowship of Reconciliation, FOR 19/5, London School of Economics (LSE).

16 Jill Wallis, 1991. *Valiant for Peace: A History of the Fellowship of Reconciliation, 1914–1989*. Fellowship of Reconciliation, 7.

17 Maude Royden, 1948. *A Threefold Cord*. Victor Gollancz.

18 Alan Wilkinson, 1986. *Dissent or Conform: War, Peace and the English Churches, 1990–1945*. SCM Press, 88; David Branford, 2008. 'From Pacifism to Just War: Changing Attitudes in the Church of England, 1930 to 1940', *Modern Believing* 49(2): 14–21.

19 Joseph Kip Kosek, 2009. *Acts of Conscience: Christian Nonviolence and Modern American Democracy*. Columbia University Press, 4.

20 Ibid.

21 John Rae, 1970. *Conscience and Politics: The British Government and the Conscientious Objector to Military Service*. Oxford University Press, 74.

22 Interview with Doris Nicholls, 13 May 1980, IWM.

23 Interview with Bernard Nicholls, 9 May 1980, IWM.

24 Interview with Stella St John, 7 August 1971, IWM.

25 Interview with Doris Nicholls, 13 May 1980, IWM.

26 Ibid.

27 Ibid.

28 Brian Frost, 1996. *Goodwill on Fire: Donald Soper's Life and Mission*. Hodder & Stoughton.

29 Mark Peel, 2008. *The Last Wesleyan: A Life of Donald Soper*. Scotforth Books, 46.

30 Interview with Stella St John, 7 August 1971, IWM.

31 William Purcell, 1983. *Odd Man Out: A Biography of Lord Soper of Kingsway*. Mowbray, 133.
32 Paul Berry and Mark Bostridge, 2001. *Vera Brittain: A Life*. Virago, 356.
33 Ibid., 359.
34 Vera Brittain, 1957. *Testament of Experience: An Autobiographical Story of the Years 1925–1950*. Macmillan, 170.
35 *The Times*, 29 October 1935.
36 Alan Wilkinson, 1986. *Dissent or Conform: War, Peace and the English Churches, 1900–1945*. SCM Press, 264.
37 Fellowship of Reconciliation Minutes, March 1937, Papers of the Fellowship of Reconciliation, FOR 19/5, LSE; Wallis, 1991. *Valiant for Peace*.
38 Martin Ceadel, 2003. 'The Quaker Peace Testimony and its Contribution to the British Peace Movement: An Overview', *Quaker Studies* 7(1): 23.
39 Peter Brock, 1999. 'Conscientious Objectors in Nazi Germany', in *Challenge to Mars: Pacifisms from 1918 to 1945*, ed. Peter Brock and Thomas Socknat. University of Toronto Press; Peter Brock and Nigel Young, 1999. *Pacifism in the Twentieth Century*. University of Toronto Press, 97–9; Norman Ingram, 1991. *The Politics of Dissent: Pacifism in France, 1919–1939*. Oxford University Press.
40 Wilkinson, 1986. *Dissent or Conform*.
41 Ibid.
42 Kosek, 2009. *Acts of Conscience*, 138.
43 Richard Overy, 2010. *The Morbid Age: Britain and the Crisis of Civilization, 1919–1939*. Penguin.
44 Interview with Bernard Nicholls, 9 May 1980, IWM.
45 Interview with Jesse Hillman, 21 March 1980, IWM.
46 John Middleton Murry, 1944. *Adam and Eve*. Andrew Dakers.
47 Wilkinson, 1986. *Dissent or Conform*, 116.
48 See: G. H. C. Macgregor, 1936. *The New Testament Basis of Pacifism*. James Clarke.

Chapter 5: Non-Violence, Gandhi and Beyond

1 Ronald Duncan, 1964. *All Men are Islands*. Rupert Hart-Davis, 136.
2 Ramachandra Guha, 2018. *Gandhi: The Years that Changed the World, 1914–1928*. Allen Lane, 345.
3 Wilfred Wellock, 1922. *India's Awakening: Its National and World-Wide Significance*. Labour Publishing, 6.
4 Ronald Duncan, 1981. *Working with Britten: A Personal Memoir*. Rebel Press, 26.
5 Ronald Duncan, 1937. *The Complete Pacifist*. Peace Pledge Union, 7.
6 Duncan, 1964. *All Men are Islands*, 128.
7 Ronald Duncan, Holmewood diary, 31 June 1936, Ronald Duncan Collection, Harry Ransom Humanities Research Center, University of Texas at Austin.
8 Duncan, 1964. *All Men are Islands*, 128.

9 Ibid., 69.
10 Colin Wilson, 1974. 'The Genius of Ronald Duncan', in *A Tribute to Ronald Duncan*. The Harton Press, 77, 87.
11 Duncan, 1981. *Working with Britten*, 21.
12 Ibid., 11
13 Ibid., 19.
14 Duncan, 1964. *All Men are Islands*, 131.
15 Duncan, 1981. *Working with Britten*, 24.
16 Duncan, 1964. *All Men are Islands*, 133.
17 Ibid., 134.
18 Ronald Duncan, Journal of Visit to India, 1937, Ronald Duncan Archive, EUL MS 397/16/6/33, Special Collections, University of Exeter.
19 Ibid.
20 Ibid.
21 Guha, 2018. *Gandhi*, 22.
22 Duncan, 1964. *All Men are Islands*, 142.
23 Ibid., 144.
24 Duncan, Journal of Visit to India.
25 Joseph Kip Kosek, 2009. *Acts of Conscience: Christian Nonviolence and Modern American Democracy*. Columbia University Press.
26 Guha, 2018. *Gandhi*, 611–20.
27 Kanji Dwarkadas, 1966. *India's Fight for Freedom, 1913–1937*. Popular Prakashan, 458.
28 Fenner Brockway, 1963. *Outside the Right*. George Allen & Unwin; Fenner Brockway, 1977. *Towards Tomorrow: The Autobiography of Fenner Brockway*. Rupert Hart-Davis, 96.
29 Jill Wallis, 1993. *The Mother of World Peace: A Life of Muriel Lester*. Hisarlick Press; Muriel Lester, 1937. *It Occurred to Me*. Harper, 130.
30 Guha, 2018. *Gandhi*, 330.
31 Muriel Lester, 2003. *Gandhi: A Wise Man*. Sumit, 116.
32 Letter from Muriel Lester to Sir Samuel Hoare, 3 May 1933, Muriel Lester Papers, 2/7/6, Bishopsgate Institute, London.
33 Lester, 1937. *It Occurred to Me*, 60.
34 Muriel Lester, 1947. *It So Happened*. Harper & Brothers, 64, 100.
35 Lester, 2003. *Gandhi*, 2.
36 Lester, 1937. *It Occurred to Me*, 88–9.
37 Wallis, 1993. *The Mother of World Peace*, 69–72.
38 Lester, 1937. *It Occurred to Me*, 130.
39 Ibid., 134.
40 Lester, 1947. *It So Happened*, 64.
41 Lester, 1937. *It Occurred to Me*, 89.
42 Martin Ceadel, 1980. *Pacifism in Britain, 1914–1945: The Defining of a Faith*. Clarendon, 94.
43 Mark Peel, 2008. *The Last Wesleyan: A Life of Donald Soper*. Scotforth Books; Brian Frost, 1996. *Goodwill on Fire: Donald Soper's Life and Mission*. Hodder & Stoughton.

44 Lester, 1937. *It Occurred to Me*, 177.
45 Martin Ceadel, 2000. *Semi-Detached Idealists: The British Peace Movement and International Relations, 1854–1945*. Oxford University Press, 287.
46 Kosek, 2009. *Acts of Conscience*, 93.
47 Ibid., 89.
48 Richard Gregg, 1935. *The Power of Non-Violence*. Greenleaf Books; Richard Gregg, 1937. *Training for Peace*. J. B. Lippincott.
49 Aldous Huxley, 1937. *Ends and Means*. Chatto & Windus, 127.
50 Ibid., 141.
51 Joseph Kip Kosek, 2005. 'Richard Gregg, Mohandas Gandhi, and the Strategy of Nonviolence', *Journal of American History* 91(4): 1318–48.
52 Duncan, Journal of Visit to India.
53 Interview with Frederick Temple, 18 April 1991, IWM.
54 Ceadel, 1980. *Pacifism in Britain*, 89.
55 Faisal Devji, 2012. *The Impossible Indian: Gandhi and the Temptation of Violence*. Hurst.
56 Lester, 2003. *Gandhi*, 59.
57 Devji, 2012. *The Impossible Indian*.
58 Leela Gandhi, 1996. 'Concerning Violence: The Limits and Circulations of Gandhian "Ahisma" or Passive Resistance', *Cultural Critique* 35: 105–47, 106.
59 Duncan, 1964. *All Men are Islands*, 149.
60 Duncan, Journal of Visit to India.
61 Duncan, 1981. *Working with Britten*, 26
62 Duncan, Journal of Visit to India.
63 Ibid.
64 Lester, 2003. *Gandhi*, 119.
65 Lester, 1937. *It Occurred to Me*, 121.
66 Ibid., 209,
67 Gandhi, 1996. 'Concerning Violence: The Limits and Circulations of Gandhian "Ahisma" or Passive Resistance'.
68 Guha, 2018. *Gandhi*, 348.
69 George Orwell, 1949. 'Reflections on Gandhi', *Partisan Review* 16(1): 85–92, 89.
70 Letter from Max Plowman to Geoffrey West, 21 October 1936, in Dorothy Plowman (ed.), 1944. *Bridge into the Future: Letters of Max Plowman*. Andrew Dakers, 578–9.

Chapter 6: Confronting War

1 Ronald Duncan, 1964. *All Men are Islands*. Rupert Hart-Davis, 164.
2 Transcript of interview with Rose Marie Duncan, January 1991, Ronald Duncan Archive, EUL MS 397/16/5/1, Special Collections, University of Exeter.

3 Anna Claire Trussler, 2001. 'The Importance of Being: The Autobiographical Subject in the Drama and Memoirs of Ronald Duncan'. Unpublished PhD thesis, University of Plymouth, 66.
4 Transcript of interview with Rose Marie Duncan, January 1991, Ronald Duncan Archive.
5 Duncan, 1964. *All Men are Islands*, 173.
6 Letter from Benjamin Britten to Ronald Duncan, 3 January 1938, Ronald Duncan Archive, EUL MS 397/18/2/3, Special Collections, University of Exeter.
7 Diary of Bianca Duncan, 24 January 1939, Ronald Duncan Archive, EUL MS 397/15/1/32, Special Collections, University of Exeter.
8 Duncan, 1964. *All Men are Islands*, 179.
9 Ibid., 198.
10 Martin Ceadel, 1980. *Pacifism in Britain, 1914–1945: The Defining of a Faith*. Clarendon, 255.
11 Cited in ibid., 252.
12 Duncan, 1964. *All Men are Islands*, 199.
13 Ibid., 202.
14 Diary of Fred Urquhart, 19 May 1938, Fred Urquhart Papers, CRC, Edinburgh University.
15 Cited in Colin Affleck, 2011. 'Introduction' to Fred Urquhart, *Jezebel's Dust*. Kennedy & Boyd, v.
16 HC, 14 March 1938, vol. 333, col. 52.
17 Diary of Fred Urquhart, 15 March 1938.
18 Ibid., 20 October 1938.
19 David Lukowitz, 1974. 'British Pacifists and Appeasement: The Peace Pledge Union', *Journal of Contemporary History* 9(1): 115–27.
20 Humphrey Carpenter, 1992. *Benjamin Britten: A Biography*. Faber & Faber, 123.
21 Mark Peel, 2008. *The Last Wesleyan: A Life of Donald Soper*. Scotforth Books, 63.
22 Louis MacNeice, 1965. *These Strings are False*. Faber & Faber.
23 Daniel Todman, 2017. *Britain's War: Into Battle, 1937–1941*. Penguin, 147.
24 Ibid., 142.
25 Louis MacNeice, 1939. *Autumn Journal*. Faber & Faber, 28.
26 Muriel Lester, 1947. *It So Happened*. Harper Brothers, 33.
27 Ibid., 35.
28 Ibid., 48.
29 Ibid., 44.
30 Interview with Michael Cadbury, 27 November 1987, IWM.
31 Interview with Kenneth Wray, 9 September 1980, IWM.
32 Interview with Joyce Parkinson, unknown date, IWM.
33 Gerald Schwab, 1990. *The Day the Holocaust Began: The Odyssey of Herschel Grynszpan*. Praeger, 43.
34 Alan Steinweis, 2009. *Kristallnacht 1938*. Harvard University Press.

35 Michael Tippett, 1991. *Those Twentieth Century Blues: An Autobiography*. Hutchinson, 46.
36 Diary of Roy Ridgway, 26 September 1938, Papers of Roy Ridgway, IWM.
37 Ibid.
38 Ibid., 24 October 1938.
39 Ibid., 27 October 1938.
40 Ibid., 27 September 1938.
41 Ibid., 28 January 1939.
42 Ibid., 15 February 1939.
43 Ibid., 3 March 1939.
44 George Orwell, 2009 [1941]. *The Lion and the Unicorn: Socialism and the English Genius*. Penguin, 154.
45 Interview with Kathleen Wigham, 17 September 1980, IWM.
46 Interview with Cyril Wright, 17 November 1980, IWM.
47 Richard Evans, 2012. *The Third Reich in Power, 1933–1939: How the Nazis Won Over the Hearts and Minds of a Nation*. Penguin, 689.
48 Frederik Taylor, 2019. *1939: A People's History*. Picador, 110.
49 Ibid., 116.
50 Kingsley Martin, 1938. 'The Pacifist's Dilemma To-day', *Political Quarterly* 9(2): 155–72.
51 Julie Gottlieb, 2014. '"The Women's Movement Took the Wrong Turning": British Feminists, Pacifism and the Politics of Appeasement', *Women's History Review* 23(3): 441–62.
52 Vera Brittain, 1986. *Chronicle of Friendship: Diaries of the Thirties, 1932–1939*, ed. A. G. Bishop. Gollancz, 21 January 1939, 332.
53 Diary of Roy Ridgway, 26 April 1939.
54 Ibid., 5 May 1939.
55 Ibid.
56 Ibid., 28 April 1939.
57 Ibid., 18 May 1939.
58 Ibid., 24 May 1939.
59 Ibid., 26 May 1939.
60 Ibid., 1 June 1939.
61 Ibid., 3 June 1939.
62 Ibid., 14 July 1939.
63 Mark Gilbert, 1992. 'Pacifist Attitudes to Nazi Germany, 1936–1945', *Journal of Contemporary History* 27(3): 493–511.
64 Brittain, 1986. *Chronicle of Friendship*, 256, 16 March 1936.
65 '"You cannot have 'have nots' and have Peace": Mr. Spottiswoode Explains to Catholic Peace Organisation'. *Catholic Herald*, 3 December 1937.
66 Gilbert, 1992. 'Pacifist Attitudes to Nazi Germany, 1936–1945'; *Peace News*, 8 October 1938.
67 Gilbert, 1992. 'Pacifist Attitudes to Nazi Germany, 1936–1945'.
68 Brian Frost, 1996. *Goodwill on Fire: Donald Soper's Life and Mission*. Hodder & Stoughton, 48.

69 Gilbert, 1992. 'Pacifist Attitudes to Nazi Germany, 1936–1945'.
70 Paul Berry and Mark Bostridge, 2001. *Vera Brittain: A Life*. Virago, 279.
71 Vera Brittain, 2005 [1941]. *England's Hour*. Continuum, 51.
72 Berry and Bostridge, 2001. *Vera Brittain*, 399.
73 Ibid., 400.
74 John Catlin, 1987. *Family Quartet: Vera Brittain and her Family*. Hamish Hamilton.
75 Letter from Benjamin Britten to Enid Slater, 13 March 1939, in Donald Mitchell and Philip Reed (eds), 1991. *Letters from a Life: Selected Letters and Diaries of Benjamin Britten*, Vol. 1: *1923–1939*. Faber & Faber, 611.
76 Letter from Benjamin Britten to Peter Pears, 16 March 1939, in Mitchell and Reed (eds), 1991. *Letters from a Life*, Vol. 1: *1923–1939*, 615.
77 Letter from Benjamin Britten to Mary Behrend, 17 April 1939, in ibid., 618.
78 Interview with Lord Harewood, *People Today*, BBC Radio, 1960, cited in ibid., 6.
79 Christopher Isherwood, 1966. *Exhumations*. Methuen, 97.
80 Edward Mendelson, 'The Secret Auden', *New York Review of Books*, 20 March 2014, https://www.nybooks.com/articles/2014/03/20/secret-auden/, last accessed 2 March 2021.
81 Humphrey Carpenter, 1981. *W. H. Auden: A Biography*. George Allen & Unwin, 163.
82 Edward Mendelson, 1999. *Early Auden*. Faber & Faber, 326.
83 Eric Metaxas, 2010. *Bonhoeffer: Pastor, Martyr, Prophet, Spy*. Thomas Nelson, 238.
84 Ibid., 241.
85 Ibid., 285.
86 Ibid., 322.
87 Ibid., 330.
88 Duncan, 1964. *All Men are Islands*, 181.
89 Ibid., 199.
90 Diary of Rose Marie Duncan, 9 September to 12 October 1943, Ronald Duncan Archive, EUL MS 397/18/1, Special Collections, University of Exeter.
91 Duncan, 1964. *All Men are Islands*, 211.
92 Ibid., 214
93 Diary of Bianca Duncan, 13 July 1939, Ronald Duncan Archive, EUL MS 397/15/1/32, Special Collections, University of Exeter.
94 Ibid., 28 January 1939.
95 John Middleton Murry, 1936. 'Taking Bearings', John Middleton Murry Collection, MS 2508, CRC, Edinburgh University.
96 John Middleton Murry, 1938. *The Pledge of Peace*. Peace Pledge Union, 11–12.
97 *Peace News*, 15 December 1944.

98 Letter to Ruth and Jim Pennyman from Michael Tippett, 15–16 November 1939, Pennyman Collection, U/PEN (4) Box 6, Teesside Archives; see also Oliver Soden, 2019. *Michael Tippett: The Biography*. Weidenfeld & Nicolson.

99 Vera Brittain, 1957. *Testament of Experience: An Autobiographical Story of the Years 1925–1950*. Macmillan, 173.

100 Berry and Bostridge, 2001. *Vera Brittain*, 355.

101 F. A. Lea, 1959. *The Life of John Middleton Murry*. Methuen, 243.

102 Edward Blishen, 1972. *A Cack-handed War*. Thames & Hudson, 182.

103 Gerald Heard, 1949. *Prayers and Meditations: A Monthly Cycle Arranged for Daily Use*. Harper.

104 Diary of Roy Ridgway, 16 July 1939.

105 Diary of Fred Urquhart, 23 June 1939.

106 Ibid., 12 July 1939.

107 Ibid., 31 August 1939.

108 Diary of Roy Ridgway, 1 September 1939.

109 Ibid., 2 September 1939.

110 Mark Peel, 2008. *The Last Wesleyan: A Life of Donald Soper*. Scotforth Books, 67.

111 Vera Brittain, 2005 [1941]. *England's Hour*. Continuum, 9; John Catlin, 1987. *Family Quartet: Vera Brittain and her Family*. Hamish Hamilton.

112 Diary of Roy Ridgway, 3–4 September 1939.

113 Duncan, 1964. *All Men are Islands*, 217.

114 Letter to Barbara Britten from Benjamin Britten, 3 September 1939, in Donald Mitchell and Philip Reed (eds), 1998. *Letters from a Life: Selected Letters and Diaries of Benjamin Britten*, Vol. 2: *1939–1945*. Faber & Faber, 696.

Chapter 7: War Arrives

1 Diary of Roy Ridgway, 3–4 September 1939, Papers of Roy Ridgway, IWM.

2 Ibid., 11 November 1939.

3 Lois Bibbings, 2010. *Telling Tales about Men: Conceptions of Conscientious Objectors to Military Service during the First World War*. University of Manchester Press; David Boulton, 1967. *Objection Overruled*. MacGibbon & Kee, 213; Adam Hochschild, 2011. *To End All Wars: A Story of Protest and Patriotism in the First World War*. Picador, 189; John Hughes-Wilson, 2005. *Blindfold and Alone: British Military Execution in the Great War*. Weidenfeld & Nicholson; John Rae, 1970. *Conscience and Politics: The British Government and the Conscientious Objector to Military Service*. Oxford University Press.

4 Neil Stammers, 1983. *Civil Liberties in Britain during the 2nd World War*. St Martin's Press.

5 Ronald Duncan, 1964. *All Men are Islands*. Rupert Hart-Davis, 219
6 Diary of Rose Marie Duncan, 1 January 1940, Ronald Duncan Archive, EUL MS 397/18/1, Special Collections, University of Exeter.
7 Daniel Todman, 2017. *Britain's War: Into Battle, 1937–1941*. Penguin, 218.
8 Diary of Fred Urquhart, 30 September 1939, Fred Urquhart Papers, CRC, Edinburgh University.
9 Ibid., 21 October 1939.
10 Ibid., 19 September 1939.
11 Trevor Royle, 2011. *A Time of Tyrants: Scotland and the Second World War*. Birlinn.
12 Diary of Fred Urquhart, 21 October 1939.
13 Diary of Rose Marie Duncan, 2 January 1940.
14 Ibid., 1 February 1940.
15 Duncan, 1964. *All Men are Islands*, 219
16 Ibid., 222.
17 Diary of Bianca Duncan, 18 May 1940, Ronald Duncan Archive, EUL MS 397/15/1/32, Special Collections, University of Exeter.
18 John Kiszely, 2017. *Anatomy of a Campaign: The British Fiasco in Norway, 1940*. Cambridge University Press.
19 Diary of Bianca Duncan, 9 April 1940.
20 Ibid., 13 April 1940.
21 Ibid., 20 May 1940.
22 Diary of Rose Marie Duncan, 31 May 1940.
23 Ibid., 4 June 1940.
24 Ibid., 12 June 1940.
25 Ibid., 17 June 1940.
26 Ibid., 2 June 1940.
27 Diary of Bianca Duncan, 10 June 1940.
28 Ibid., 27 May 1940.
29 Ibid., 2 June 1940.
30 Diary of Rose Marie Duncan, 29 May 1940.
31 Ibid., 27–28 June 1940.
32 Ibid., 4 June 1940.
33 George Orwell, 2001 [1943]. 'Looking Back on the Spanish Civil War', in *All Propaganda is Lies, 1941–1942*, ed. Peter Davidson. Secker & Warburg, 496.
34 Alan Wilkinson, 1986. *Dissent or Conform: War, Peace and the English Churches, 1900–1945*. SCM Press, 264.
35 Ibid., 238.
36 Ibid., 255.
37 Ibid.
38 Travel Letter, September 1939, Trinidad Detention, Lester 2/5/9, Lester Collection, Bishopsgate Institute, London.
39 Vera Brittain, 1964. *The Rebel Passion: A Short History of Some Pioneer Peace Makers*. George Allen & Unwin, 151.
40 Muriel Lester, 1947. *It So Happened*. Harper & Brothers, 30.

41 Travel Letter, September 1939, Trinidad Detention, Lester 2/5/9.

42 Ibid.

43 Alex May, 2004. 'Kerry, Philip Henry, Eleventh Marquess of Lothian (1882–1940)', *Oxford Dictionary of National Biography*, https://www.oxforddnb.com/view/10.1093/ref:odnb/9780198614128.001.0001/odnb-9780198614128-e-34303, last accessed 2 March 2021.

44 Lester, 1947. *It So Happened*, 116.

45 Jill Wallis, 1993. *The Mother of World Peace: The Life of Muriel Lester*. Hisarlik Press, 184.

46 Gallup and Fortune Polls, 1940. *The Public Opinion Quarterly* 4(3), 533–53, 552.

47 George Catlin, 1972. *For God's Sake Go! An Autobiography*. Colin Smythe, 253.

48 Ibid., 286.

49 Susan A. Brewer, 1997. *To Win the Peace: British Propaganda in the United States during World War II*. Cornell University Press.

50 Travel Letter, September 1940, Trinidad Detention, Lester 2/5/9.

51 Sarah Churchwell, 2018. *Behold America: A History of America First and the American Dream*. Bloomsbury; Joseph Kip Kosek, 2009. *Acts of Conscience: Christian Nonviolence and Modern American Democracy*. Columbia University Press, 146.

52 Lester, 1947. *It So Happened*, 170.

53 Wallis, 1993. *The Mother of World Peace*, 201.

54 Letter to Doris Lester from Peggy Maughan, 27 August 1941, Lester 2/5/9, Lester Collection, Bishopsgate Institute, London.

55 Detention of Muriel Lester, Memorandum 2, From John Nevin Sayre, 29 August 1941; letter from Christopher Eastwood to Percy Bartlett, 23 September 1941, Lester 2/5/8, Lester Collection, Bishopsgate Institute, London.

56 Letter from British Embassy to Mr Sayre, 29 September 1941, Lester 2/5/8.

57 Letter from Colonial Office to Lord Lytton, 6 November 1941, Lester 2/5/8; Travel Letter, November 1941, Trinidad Detention, Lester 2/5/9.

58 Letter to Doris Lester from Muriel Lester, 31 July 1941, Trinidad Detention, Lester 2/5/8.

59 Diary of Roy Ridgway 25 January 1940.

60 Ibid., 6 July 1940.

61 George Orwell, 1942. 'London Letters', *Partisan Review*, March–April 1942.

62 Stammers, 1983. *Civil Liberties in Britain during the 2nd World War*, 39.

63 John Couzin, 2005. *Radical Glasgow*. Voline Press, 136; see also Alan Burnett, Letters from Prison, 1943–1944, Alan Burnett Collection (GB243 T/SOR/1), Spirit of Revolt Archive, Mitchell Library, Glasgow.

64 *Jehovah's Witness: The Position*, 1942. International Bible Students Association. Private papers of Gary Perkins.

65 PPU, 1940. *Pacifists at Bow Street: A Full Report of Proceedings under the Defence Regulations against Officers and Members of the Peace Pledge Union, May–June, 1940.* PPU.
66 Vera Brittain, 2005 [1941]. *England's Hour.* Continuum, 35.
67 Ibid., 39.
68 Fiona MacCarthy, 2011. *Eric Gill.* Faber & Faber.
69 Richard Rempel, 1978. 'The Dilemmas of British Pacifists during World War II', *Journal of Modern History* 50(4): 1213–29, 1214.
70 Paul Addison and Jeremy Crang (eds), 2010. *Listening to Britain: Hoe Intelligence Reports on Britain's Finest Hour – May to September 1940.* Bodley Head, 13.
71 Ibid., 86.
72 Report on COs, July 1940, 87, TC 6, Box 1 COs and Pacifists, Mass Observation Archives, University of Sussex (MOA).
73 Interview with Roy Ridgway, 14 July 1987, IWM.
74 Diary of Fred Urquhart, 25 October 1939.
75 Catlin, 1972. *For God's Sake Go!.*
76 Ibid., 326.
77 Paul Berry and Mark Bostridge, 2001. *Vera Brittain: A Life.* Virago, 356.
78 Jennifer Birkett, 2009. *Margaret Storm Jameson: A Life.* Oxford University Press, 196.
79 Berry and Bostridge, 2001. *Vera Brittain*, 415.
80 Ibid., 363.
81 Letter to C. Ruffoni from P. Moore, 10 August 1944, Papers of C. Ruffoni, IWM.
82 Letter to C. Ruffoni from P. Moore, 8 February 1944.
83 Letter to P. Moore from C. Ruffoni, 8 October 1944; letter to P. Moore from C. Ruffoni, 6 March 1944.
84 Interview with Tony Parker, 17 February 1986, IWM.
85 Interview with Ken Shaw, in *A Matter of Conscience*, BBC Radio 4, May 1992 (13187), IWM.
86 Interview with Ronald Mallone, 31 January 1980, IWM.
87 Interview with Leonard Bird, 12 June 1981, IWM.
88 Interview with Alexander Bryan, 5 September 1980, IWM.
89 Interview with Frank Norman, 27 June 1980, IWM.
90 Interview with Tony Parker, 17 February 1986, IWM.
91 Diary of Fred Urquhart, 19 September 1939.
92 Ibid., 24 October 1939.
93 Diary of Roy Ridgway, 1 November 1939.
94 Bibbings, 2010. *Telling Tales about Men.*
95 Diary of Roy Ridgway, 21 December 1939.
96 Ibid., 22 December 1939.
97 Ibid., 8 March 1940.
98 Ibid., 23 May 1940.
99 Brittain, 2005 [1941]. *England's Hour*, 36.

100 Report on COs, July 1940, 98, TC 6, Box 1, COs and Pacifists, MOA, University of Sussex.

Chapter 8: Conscription and Conscience

1 Diary of Rose Marie Duncan, 25 January 1940, Ronald Duncan Archive, EUL MS 397/18/1, Special Collections, University of Exeter.
2 Ibid., 14 March 1940.
3 Ibid., 29 April 1940.
4 Diary of Bianca Duncan, 23 May 1940, Ronald Duncan Archive, EUL MS 397/15/1/32, Special Collections, University of Exeter.
5 Denis Hayes, 1949. *Conscription Conflict: The Conflict of Ideas in the Struggle for and against Military Conscription in Britain between 1901 and 1939.* Sheppard Press.
6 Nicoletta Gullace, 2016. *The Blood of our Sons: Men, Women and the Renegotiation of British Citizenship during the Great War.* Palgrave, 104.
7 David Wyckes, 1994. 'Friends, Parliament and the Toleration Act', Journal of Ecclesiastical History 45(1): 42–63.
8 Nadja Durbach, 2001. 'Class, Gender and the Conscientious Objector to Vaccination, 1898–1907', *Journal of British Studies* 41(1): 58–83.
9 John Rae, 1970. *Conscience and Politics: The British Government and the Conscientious Objector to Military Service.* Oxford University Press, 26.
10 Ibid., 27.
11 Peter Brock, 2006. *Against the Draft: Essays on Conscientious Objection from the Radical Reformation to the Second World War.* University of Toronto Press; Charles Moskos, 1993. *The New Conscientious Objection: From Sacred to Secular Resistance.* Oxford University Press.
12 Peter Brock and Nigel Young, 1999. *Pacifism in the Twentieth Century.* University of Toronto Press, 171.
13 *United States* v. *Seeger*, 380 U.S. 163 (1965), Supreme Court of the United States.
14 Brock and Young, 1999. *Pacifism in the Twentieth Century,* 94–6.
15 Sonya Rose, 2003. *Which People's War? National Identity and Citizenship in Britain, 1939–1945.* Oxford University Press; Linsey Robb and Juliette Pattinson (eds), 2018. *Men, Masculinities and Male Culture in the Second World War.* Palgrave.
16 Alan Allport, 2015. *Browned Off and Bloody-Minded: The British Soldier Goes off to War.* Yale University Press, 41.
17 Daniel Todman, 2017. *Britain's War: Into Battle, 1937–1941,* Penguin, 155.
18 Allport, 2015. *Browned Off and Bloody-Minded,* 41.
19 Rachel Barker, 1982. *Conscience, Government and War: Conscientious Objection in Britain, 1939–45.* Routledge, 10.
20 ILP, 1939. *Why We Oppose Conscription.* ILP.

21 Jeremy Crang, 2020. *Sisters in Arms: Women in the British Armed Forces during the Second World War*. Cambridge University Press.

22 Denis Hayes, 1949. *Challenge of Conscience: The Story of the Conscientious Objectors, 1939–1949*. George Allen & Unwin, 21.

23 'Compulsory Service for Europeans in India', *The Times*, 27 June 1940; Christopher Bayly and Tim Harper. 2004. *Forgotten Armies: Britain's Asian Empire and the War with Japan*. Penguin; Yasmin Khan. 2015. *The Raj at War: A People's History of India's Second World War*. Penguin.

24 Jeremy Crang, 2000. *The British Army and the People's War, 1939–1945*. Manchester University Press; Todman, 2017. *Britain's War: Into Battle, 1937–1941*, 263.

25 'Repercussions of Conscription', 17 February 1940, File Report 31 US3, MOA, University of Sussex.

26 Allport, 2015. *Browned Off and Bloody-Minded*, 63.

27 Rose, 2003. *Which People's War?*.

28 Central Board of Conscientious Objectors. 'A Plea for Tolerance', Butler Papers, Bishopsgate Institute, London; see also Hayes, 1949. *Challenge of Conscience*, 6.

29 Hayes, 1949. *Challenge of Conscience*, 6

30 David Howell, 2011. 'Morrison, Herbert Stanley, Baron Morrison of Lambeth (1888–1965), Politician', *Oxford Dictionary of National Biography*, https://www.oxforddnb.com/view/10.1093/ref:odnb/9780198614128.001.0001/odnb-9780198614128-e-35121, last accessed 2 March 2021.

31 HC, 4 May 1939, vol. 346, col. 2097.

32 See for example: Schedule of Occupations (Provisional), Ministry of Labour, January 1939, LBY 17242, IWM.

33 Daniel Todman, 2020. *Britain's War: 1942–1947*. Allen Lane, 411.

34 Angus Calder, 1993 [1969]. *The People's War: Britain, 1939–1945*. Pimlico, 336.

35 Charles Glass, 2012. *The Deserters: A Hidden History of World War II*. Penguin.

36 Allport, 2015. *Browned Off and Bloody-Minded*, 93.

37 Diary of Fred Urquhart, 19 September 1939, Fred Urquhart Papers, CRC, Edinburgh University.

38 Ibid., 30 September 1939.

39 Humphrey Carpenter, 1992. *Benjamin Britten: A Biography*. Faber & Faber, 134

40 Donald Mitchell and Philip Reed (eds), 1998. *Letters from a Life: Selected Letters and Diaries of Benjamin Britten*, Vol. 2: 1939–1945. Faber & Faber, 872.

41 Diary of Fred Urquhart, 21 October 1939.

42 Ibid., 19 September 1939.

43 Ibid., 30 September 1939.

44 Ibid., 19 September 1939.

45 Ibid., 5 August 1940.

46 Ibid.

47 Ibid.
48 John Middleton Murry, 1930. 'The Creation of Conscience', *New Adelphi* 111(2), December: 107–19.
49 Letter from Max Plowman to the Adelphi, 2 February 1936, in Dorothy Plowman (ed.), 1944. *Bridge to the Future: Letters of Max Plowman.* Andrew Dakers, 555.
50 Letter from Max Plowman to Geoffrey West, 29 October 1935, in Plowman (ed.), 1944. *Bridge to the Future*, 539. See more generally: Max Plowman, 1942. *The Right to Live: Selected Essays.* Andrew Dakers.
51 Report on COs, July 1940. TC 6, Box 1, COs and Pacifists, MOA, University of Sussex.
52 Middleton Murry, 1930. 'The Creation of Conscience'.
53 Rae, 1970. *Conscience and Politics*, 85.
54 Ibid., 84.
55 Martin Ceadel. 1980. *Pacifism in Britain, 1914–1945: Defining a Faith.* Clarendon, 85.
56 Christopher Caudwell, 1938. *Studies in a Dying Culture.* Bodley Head, 117.
57 Jill Wallis, 1991. *Valiant for Peace: A History of the Fellowship of Reconciliation, 1914–1989.* Fellowship of Reconciliation, 26.
58 Kingsley Martin, 1938. 'The Pacifist's Dilemma To-day', *Political Quarterly* 9(2): 155–72, 155.
59 Diary of Roy Ridgway, 1 October 1939, Papers of Roy Ridgway, IWM.
60 Ibid., 6 December 1939.
61 Ibid., 1 November 1939.
62 Ibid., 5 January 1940.
63 Ibid., 1 November 1939.
64 Ibid., 22 December 1939.
65 Ibid., 17 February 1940.
66 Diary of Fred Urquhart, 26 July 1941.
67 Interview with Doris Nicholls, 13 May 1980, IWM.
68 Interview with Bernard Nicholls, 9 May 1980, IWM.
69 Vera Brittain, 1957. *Testament of Experience: An Autobiographical Story of the Years 1925–1950.* Macmillan, 14.
70 Letter from Benjamin Britten to Beth, Kit and Sebastian Welford, 18 September 1940, in Mitchell and Reed (eds), 1998. *Letters from a Life*, Vol. 2: *1939–1945*, 862.
71 Letter from Benjamin Britten to Beth Wilford, 19 October 1939, in ibid., 707.
72 Ibid.
73 Carpenter, 1992. *Benjamin Britten*, 142, 152.
74 Ibid., 159.
75 Interview with Michael Harris, 16 May 1986, IWM.
76 Sydney Carter, 1965. 'Voices of Conscience', in Clifford Simmons, Mark Holloway, Stuart Smith, Derek Savage and Sydney Cater, *The Objectors*. Times Press, 28.

77 Carpenter, 1992. *Benjamin Britten*, 293.

78 Ibid., 140.

79 Jim Perrin, 1985. *Menlove: The Life of John Menlove Edwards*. Ernest Press, 191.

80 Ibid., 192.

81 Ibid., 227.

82 Max Egremont, 2014. *Siegfried Sassoon: A Biography*. Picador.

83 Harry Stalker, 1943. 'Conscientious Objectors with Psychiatric States', *Journal of Mental Science* 89(374): 52–8.

84 Diary of Roy Ridgway, 31 January 1940.

Chapter 9: Conscience on Trial

1 Denis Hayes, 1949. *Challenge of Conscience: The Story of the Conscientious Objectors, 1939–1949*. George Allen & Unwin, 381–3.

2 Diary of Roy Ridgway, 26 February 1940, Papers of Roy Ridgway, IWM.

3 Ibid., 10 April 1940.

4 Interview with Alexander Bryan, 20 January 1999, IWM

5 Interview with Tony Parker, 17 February 1986, IWM.

6 Notebook of Instructions for Conscientious Objectors in Answering Tribunal Questions, circa 1940, IWM.

7 Diary of Roy Ridgway, 22 April 1940.

8 Ibid., 1 June 1940.

9 Ibid., 17 July 1940.

10 Ibid., 1 March 1940.

11 Ibid., 17 July 1940.

12 Ibid., 21 August 1941.

13 Jonathan Miles, 2018. *Try the Wilderness First: Eric Gill and David Jones at Capel-y-ffin*. Seren.

14 Diary of Roy Ridgway, 24 August 1941.

15 Ibid., 27 August 1940.

16 Ibid., 24 September 1940.

17 Ibid., 26 September 1940.

18 Ibid., 27 September 1940.

19 Ibid., 14 October 1940.

20 Ibid., 31 October 1940.

21 Ibid., 31 December 1940.

22 Ibid., 21 December 1940.

23 Ibid., 28 November 1940.

24 Interview with Roy Ridgway, 14 July 1987, IWM.

25 Diary of Roy Ridgway, 22 January 1941.

26 Peter Brock and Nigel Young, 1999. *Pacifism in the Twentieth Century*. University of Toronto Press, 172.

27 David Boulton, 1967. *Objection Overruled*. MacGibbon & Kee, 126.

28 Jobs of COs, 3 April 1940, TC 6, Box 1, file A, COs and Pacifists, MOA, University of Sussex.

29 Hayes, 1949. *Challenge of Conscience*, 26.
30 Fyfe Papers, World War Two North-Eastern Scotland Local Tribunal for Conscientious Objectors, MS 2108, Special Collections, University of Aberdeen.
31 G. C. Field, 1945. *Pacifism and Conscientious Objection*. Cambridge University Press, 6.
32 See for example: Edward Andrew, 2001. *Conscience and its Critics: Protestant Conscience, Enlightenment Reason and Modern Subjectivity*. University of Toronto Press.
33 Webb Keane, 2002. 'Sincerity, Modernity and the Protestants', *Cultural Anthropology* 17(1): 65–92.
34 Hayes, 1949. *Challenge of Conscience*, 42.
35 Field, 1945. *Pacifism and Conscientious Objection*, 107.
36 'The Workings of the Tribunal', 1941, MOA1/2/6/1/B, COs and Pacifists, MOA, University of Sussex.
37 Diary of Roy Ridgway, 12 December 1940.
38 Thomas Schuttenhelm (ed.), 2005. *Selected Letters of Michael Tippett*. Faber & Faber, 1049.
39 'The Workings of the Tribunal', 1941, MOA1/2/6/1/B, COs and Pacifists, MOA, University of Sussex.
40 Conscientious Objector Tribunals, 24 February 1940, TC 6, Box 2, file A, COs and Pacifists, MOA, University of Sussex.
41 HC, 8 May 1939, vol. 347, cols 45–167.
42 Ibid.
43 Interview with John Wood, 8 July 1986, IWM
44 Diary of Fred Urquhart, 19 July 1940, Fred Urquhart Papers, CRC, Edinburgh University.
45 Fred Urquhart, 1941. 'Let Us Endure an Hour: A Conscientious Objector in England', *Southern Literary Journal* 3(3): 133–7.
46 Letter from Fred Urquhart to parents, 17 May 1940, Fred Urquhart Papers, CRC, Edinburgh University.
47 Letter from Gordon Stott to Fred Urquhart, 2 August 1940, Private Papers of Colin Affleck.
48 House of Lords (HL), 2 March 1943, vol. 136, col. 349.
49 Diary of Fred Urquhart, 7 November 1940.
50 Field, 1945. *Pacifism and Conscientious Objection*, 15.
51 Alan Burnett, Letters from Prison, 1943–1944, Alan Burnett Collection (GB243 T/SOR/1), Spirit of Revolt Archive, Mitchell Library, Glasgow; WAR: Arthur Donaldson, Scottish nationalist extremist engaged in formation of United Scotland Party and Scottish Neutrality League: organiser of National Aid Society to assist conscientious objectors to evade military service by going into hiding; detention under Defence Regulation 18B, HO 45/23801, 1941, National Archives, Kew (NA).
52 *Derby Evening Telegraph*, 1 May 1944; *Evening Telegraph and Post*, 12 May 1944; 'Vaidya is Registered as a CO', *CBCO Bulletin*, May 1944, No. 51.

53 Fyfe Papers, World War Two North-Eastern Scotland Local Tribunal for Conscientious Objectors, MS 2108, Special Collections, University of Aberdeen.

54 'Mohammedan CO at Tribunal', *Aberdeen Weekly*, 19 June 1941.

55 General procedure for dealing with women conscientious objectors, LAB 6/183, 1941–1942, NA; John Taylor Caldwell, 1999. *With Fates Conspire: Memoirs of a Glasgow Seafarer and Anarchist*. Northern Herald Books, 156.

56 Hazel Nicholson, 2007. 'A Disputed Identity: Women Conscientious Objectors in Second World War Britain', *Twentieth Century British History* 18(4): 409–28.

57 Hayes, 1949. *Challenge of Conscience*, 17.

58 Interview with Doris Nicholls, 13 May 1980, IWM.

59 'The Position of Women C.O.s: An Anomaly and a Case for Redress', *CBCO Bulletin*, April 1942, No. 26, 1.

60 Memorandum. Political Objectors. n.d., Tribunal, box 6, Central Board for Conscientious Objectors Archive (CBCOA), Friends House, London.

61 Benjamin Britten, Statement to the Local Tribunal for the Registration of Conscientious Objectors, 4 May 1942; Schuttenhelm (ed.), 2005. *Selected Letters of Michael Tippett*, 1046.

62 Schuttenhelm (ed.), 2005. *Selected Letters of Michael Tippett*, 1034.

63 Interview with Mervyn Taggart, 5 May 1980, IWM.

64 Samuel Moyn, 2014. 'From Communist to Muslim: European Human Rights, the Cold War, and Religious Liberty', *South Atlantic Quarterly* 113(1): 63–86; Nehal Bhuta, 2014. 'Two Concepts of Religious Freedom in the European Court of Human Rights', *South Atlantic Quarterly* 113(1): 9–35.

65 Tim Grass, 2006. *Gathering to His Name: The Story of the Brethren in Britain and Ireland*. Paternoster Press, 337.

66 Tribunal Application 31/5/41, Papers of E. E. Beavor, IWM; Anthony Byatt, 2012. *Reminiscences towards a History of Jehovah's Witnesses in London, 1991–1977*. Golden Age Books, 67–102.

67 Field, 1945. *Pacifism and Conscientious Objection*, 17.

68 *Jehovah's Witness: The Position*, 1942. International Bible Students Association. Private papers of Gary Perkins.

69 Interview with Denis Hayes, 26 February 1981, IWM.

70 Douglas Young, 1944. *An Appeal to Scots Honour: A Vindication of the Right of the Scottish People to Freedom from Industrial Conscription and Bureaucratic Despotism under the Treaty of Union with England*. Scottish Secretariat Limited.

71 Hayes, 1949. *Challenge of Conscience*, 55–8.

72 Rachel Barker, 1982. *Conscience, Government and War: Conscientious Objection in Britain, 1939–1945*. Routledge, 145.

73 Lois Bibbings, 2010. *Telling Tales about Men: Conceptions of Conscientious Objectors to Military Service during the First World War*. University of Manchester Press.

74 Jill Wallis, 1991. *Valiant for Peace: A History of the Fellowship of Reconciliation, 1914–1989.* Fellowship of Reconciliation, 123.
75 Alan Allport, 2010. *Demobbed: Coming Home after the Second World War.* Yale University Press.
76 Vera Brittain, 2005 [1941]. *England's Hour.* Continuum, xiv.
77 Juliette Pattinson, 2006. '"Shirkers", "Scrimjacks" and "Scrimshanks"? British Civilian Masculinity and Reserved Occupations, 1914–1945', *Gender and History* 28(3): 709–27.
78 Juliette Pattinson, Arthur McIvor and Linsey Robb, 2016. *Men in Reserve: British Civilian Masculinities in the Second World War.* Manchester University Press, 13.
79 Interview with Roy Ridgway, 14 July 1987, IWM.
80 Daniel Todman, 2020. *Britain's War: 1942–1947.* Allen Lane, 13.
81 Diary of Roy Ridgway, 1 October 1939.
82 Vera Brittain, 1988. *A Testament of a Peace Lover: Letters from Vera Brittain,* ed. Winifred and Alan Eden-Green. Virago, 29 August 1940, 44.
83 Interview with Bernard Nicholls, 9 May 1980, IWM.
84 Interview with John Hunt, 6 April 1998, IWM.
85 Cyril Joad, 1944. 'The Strange Case of the Council for Civil Liberties', *CBCO Bulletin,* September 1944, No. 55, 3.
86 Interview with Harry Miller, 1988, IWM.
87 Interview with Bernard Nicholls, 9 May 1980, IWM.
88 Interview with Roy Ridgway, 14 July 1987, IWM.
89 Brittain, 1988. *A Testament of a Peace Lover,* 20 June 1940, 32.
90 Ibid., 8 May 1941, 64.

Chapter 10: On the Farm

1 Ronald Duncan, 1937. *The Complete Pacifist.* Peace Pledge Union, 10–11.
2 Ronald Duncan, 1964. *All Men are Islands.* Rupert Hart-Davis, 211, 223.
3 Ibid., 211.
4 Ibid., 223.
5 Ibid., 215.
6 Diary of Bianca Duncan, 24 June 1940, Ronald Duncan Archive, EUL MS 397/15/1/32, Special Collections, University of Exeter.
7 Ibid., 21 June 1940.
8 Ibid., 25 July 1940.
9 Ibid., 6 August 1940.
10 Ibid., 18 August 1940.
11 Duncan, 1964. *All Men are Islands,* 187; Diary of Bianca Duncan, 23 April 1939.
12 Diary of Bianca Duncan, 23 April 1939.
13 Duncan, 1964. *All Men are Islands,* 212.
14 Ibid., 222.

15 Diary of Rose Marie Duncan, 24 May 1941, Ronald Duncan Archive, EUL MS 397/18/1, Special Collections, University of Exeter.

16 Diary of Bianca Duncan, 5 November 1940.

17 Patricia Appelbaum, 2009. *Kingdom to Commune: Protestant Pacifist Culture between World War I and the Vietnam Era.* University of North Carolina Press.

18 John Middleton Murry, 1940. Case for a Negotiated Peace. Unpublished Manuscript. 8 March 1940, John Middleton Murry Collection, MS 2510, CRC, Edinburgh University.

19 Ronald Duncan, 1944. *Journal of a Husbandman.* Faber & Faber, 1; F. A. Lea, 1959. *The Life of John Middleton Murry.* Methuen, 175.

20 Lea, 1959. *The Life of John Middleton Murry,* 68.

21 Provisional Application for Registration as a Conscientious Objector, 17 July 1940, Papers of Cyril Frederick Wright, IWM.

22 Kingsland Community Newsletter, November 1941, Papers of Cyril Frederick Wright, IWM.

23 Paul Berry and Mark Bostridge, 2001. *Vera Brittain: A Life.* Virago, 412.

24 Dennis Hardy, 2000. *Utopian England: Community Experiments, 1900–1945.* Routledge.

25 Diary of Roy Ridgway, 5 June 1939, Papers of Roy Ridgway, IWM.

26 The Society of Brothers, 1952. *Ten Years of Community Living: The Wheathill Bruderhof.* The Plough Publishing House.

27 Interview with Douglas Turner, 24 June 1986, IWM.

28 Duncan, 1964. *All Men are Islands,* 223.

29 Ibid., 228.

30 Ibid., 239.

31 Diary of Bianca Duncan, 28 August 1940.

32 Rachel Barker, 1982. *Conscience, Government and War: Conscientious Objection in Britain, 1939–1945.* Routledge, 23.

33 Letter from F. MacDonald to Fred Urquhart, 16 November 1940, Private Papers of Colin Affleck.

34 Douglas Rogers, 1944. 'C.O.s on the Land – The Facts', *CBCO Bulletin,* June, No. 52, 13.

35 Diary of Roy Ridgway, 14 October 1940.

36 Barker, 1982. *Conscience, Government and War,* 45.

37 Eddie Chapman, 1957. *I Killed to Live: The Story of Eric Pleasants.* Cassell.

38 'The Standard of the Movement', no date. Christian Pacifist Forestry and Land, Friends House; Lewis Maclachlan, 1952. *C.P.F.L.U.: A History of the Christian Pacifist Forestry and Land Units.* Fellowship of Reconciliation; Christian Pacifist Forestry and Land Units Committee, COLL MISC 0456/6/2, Papers of the Fellowship of Reconciliation, LSE.

39 'The Standard of the Movement', no date. Christian Pacifist Forestry and Land, Friends House.

40 Diary of Fred Urquhart, 28 May 1941, Fred Urquhart Papers, CRC, Edinburgh University.
41 Fred Urquhart, 1946. *Selected Stories*. Maurice Fridberg.
42 Diary of Fred Urquhart, July 1941.
43 Ibid., 2 June 1942; letter from Ministry of Labour and National Service to Mr. F. B. Urquhart, 18 June 1942, Private Papers of Colin Affleck.
44 Letter from John Mackie to Aberdeen Local Tribunal, 1 July 1942; Findings of the Local Tribunal 29–30 September 1942, Private Papers of Colin Affleck.
45 Diary of Fred Urquhart, 11 February 1942.
46 Ibid.
47 Ibid., 17 February 1942, 24 May 1942.
48 Diary of Rose Marie Duncan, 23 May 1941.
49 Duncan, 1944. *Journal of a Husbandman*, 81.
50 John Martin, 2014. 'The State Directed Food Production Campaign and the Farming Community, 1939–45', *Family & Community History* 17(1): 47–63; Brian Short, 2008. 'Death of a Farmer: The Fortunes of War and the Strange Case of Ray Walden', *Agricultural History Review* 56(2): 89–213.
51 Martin, 2014. 'The State Directed Food Production Campaign and the Farming Community, 1939–45'.
52 Diary of Rose Marie Duncan, 18 February 1941.
53 Ibid., 22 January 1942.
54 *Kingsland Community Newsletter*, March 1942, Papers of Cyril Frederick Wright, IWM.
55 John Middleton Murry, 1953. *Community Farm*. Country Book Club, 82.
56 Ibid., 51.
57 Patrick Hamilton, 2017 [1947]. *The Slaves of Solitude*. Abacus, 2.
58 Duncan, 1964. *All Men are Islands*, 239.
59 *Kingsland Community Newsletter*, March 1942.
60 Ibid.
61 Duncan, 1964. *All Men are Islands*, 222.
62 Denis Hayes, 1949. *Challenge of Conscience: The Story of the Conscientious Objectors, 1939–1949*. George Allen & Unwin, 212.
63 Duncan, 1964. *All Men are Islands*, 245.
64 Diary of Bianca Duncan, 19 August 1940.
65 Ibid., 31 July 1940.
66 Diary of Rose Marie Duncan, 13 July 1940.
67 Ibid., 14 February 1941.
68 Diary of Bianca Duncan, 13 November 1940.
69 Ibid., 14 November 1940.
70 Ibid., 15 November 1940.
71 Diary of Rose Marie Duncan, 31 July 1941.
72 Ibid., 31 July 1941.
73 Ibid., 27 August 1941.

74 Ibid., 15 February 1941.
75 Ibid., 2 April 1941.
76 Ibid., 24 May 1941.
77 Katherine Middleton Murry, 1986. *Beloved Quixote: The Unknown Life of John Middleton Murry*. Condor, 153.
78 Lea, 1959. *The Life of John Middleton Murry*, 296.
79 Ibid., 238.
80 Diary of Rose Marie Duncan, 10 July 1940.
81 *Kingsland Community Newsletter*, November 1941.
82 *Peace News*, 6 August 1940.
83 Middleton Murry, 1953. *Community Farm*, 97.
84 Interview with Patrick Figgis, 5 February 1980, IWM.
85 Middleton Murry, 1953. *Community Farm*, 86.
86 Interview with Ronald Mallone, 31 January 1980, IWM.
87 Interview with Bryan Platt, 20 January 1999, IWM.
88 Ibid.
89 Duncan, 1964. *All Men are Islands*, 238.
90 Diary of Rose Marie Duncan, 15 July 1941.
91 Duncan, 1964. *All Men are Islands*, 257.
92 Ibid., 270.
93 Diary of Rose Marie Duncan, 9 September 1941.
94 Diary of Bianca Duncan, 13 January 1943.
95 Duncan, 1964. *All Men are Islands*, 280.
96 Duncan, 1944. *Journal of a Husbandman*, 30.
97 Duncan, 1964. *All Men are Islands*, 230.
98 Duncan, 1944. *Journal of a Husbandman*, 70.
99 *Kingsland Community Newsletter*, November 1941.
100 Middleton Murry, 1953. *Community Farm*, 113.
101 Duncan, 1964. *All Men are Islands*, 249.

Chapter 11: Pacifist Service

1 A. Tegla Davies, 1947. *Friends Ambulance Unit: The Story of the FAU in the Second World War, 1939–1946*. George Allen & Unwin, 84.
2 Interview with Ronald Joynes, 22 March 1989, IWM.
3 Olivia Manning, 1987. *The Balkan Trilogy*. Arrow Books, 1015.
4 Craig Stockings and Eleanor Hancock, 2013. *Swastika over the Acropolis: Re-interpreting the Nazi Invasion of Greece in World War II*. Brill.
5 Davies, 1947. *Friends Ambulance Unit*, 5.
6 Friends Ambulance Unit in WWI, http://www.quakersintheworld. org/quakers-in-action/252/Friends-Ambulance-Unit-FAU-in-WWI, last accessed 2 March 2021.
7 Interview with Michael Rowntree, 7 August 1989, IWM.
8 Ibid.
9 Interview with Bryan Platt, 20 January 1999, IWM; interview with Michael Rowntree, 7 August 1989, IWM.

10 *The Friend*, 1 September 1939.

11 Interview with Michael Rowntree, 7 August 1989, IWM.

12 Tom Burns, 'Back Rent', unpublished short story, May 1935, Private Papers of the Burns family.

13 Davies, 1947. *Friends Ambulance Unit*, 42; interview with John Wood, 8 July 1986, IWM

14 FAU Executive Report Files, Friends Ambulance Unit Archive (FAUA), Friends House, London.

15 Airgraph from Richard Wainwright to all members of the FAU from Staff meeting in London, June 1942, FAUA, Friends House, London.

16 Davies, 1947. *Friends Ambulance Unit*, 5–6.

17 Interview with Bryan Platt, 20 January 1999, IWM

18 Interview with Michael Cadbury, 27 November 1987, IWM.

19 Ibid.

20 Interview with Ronald Joynes, 22 March 1989, IWM.

21 Diary of Roy Ridgway, 4 January 1941, Papers of Roy Ridgway, IWM.

22 Executive Committee Report Book 2, 23 November 1943, FAUA, Friends House, London.

23 Interview with Michael Cadbury, 27 November 1987, IWM.

24 Davies, 1947. *Friends Ambulance Unit*, 42.

25 *China Convoy Newsletter* 29, October 1942, FAUA, Friends House, London.

26 Ibid.

27 Davies, 1947. *Friends Ambulance Unit*, 30–1.

28 H. Martin Lidbetter, 1993. *Friends Ambulance Unit, 1939–1943: Experiences in Finland, Norway, Sweden, Egypt, Greece and Germany.* Sessions Book Trust, 13.

29 Michael Barratt Brown, 'Michael Rowntree, Obituary', *Guardian*, 30 October 2007, https://www.theguardian.com/news/2007/oct/30/guardianobituaries.internationalaidanddevelopment, last accessed 3 March 2021.

30 Interview with Michael Rowntree, 7 August 1989, IWM.

31 Ibid.

32 Interview with Ronald Joynes, 22 March 1989, IWM.

33 Interview with Bryan Platt, 20 January 1999, IWM.

34 Letter from Tom Burns to Cathy Bunting, 22 January 1940, Private Papers of the Burns family.

35 Letter from Tom Burns to Helen, 22 January 1940, Private Papers of the Burns family.

36 Letter from Tom Burns to Cathy Bunting, 22 January 1940.

37 Interview with Michael Rowntree, 7 August 1989, IWM.

38 Letter from Tom Burns to Cathy Bunting, 22 January 1940.

39 Interview with Michael Rowntree, 7 August 1989, IWM.

40 Letter from Tom Burns to Cathy Bunting, 26 February 1940, Private Papers of the Burns family.

41 William R. Trotter, 1991. *The Winter War: The Russo-Finnish War of 1939–1940.* Aurum.

42 Daniel Todman, 2017. *Britain's War: Into Battle, 1937–1941*, Penguin, 291.

43 Letter from Tom Burns to Cathy Bunting, 26 February 1940.

44 Davies, 1947. *Friends Ambulance Unit*, 28.

45 Interview with Michael Rowntree, 7 August 1989, IWM.

46 Letter from Tom Burns to Cathy Bunting, 6 March 1940, Private Papers of the Burns family.

47 Letter from Tom Burns to Cathy Bunting, 26 February 1940.

48 Ibid.

49 Davies, 1947. *Friends Ambulance Unit*, 26.

50 Interview with Ronald Joynes, 22 March 1989, IWM.

51 Interview with Frederick Temple, 18 April 1991, IWM.

52 Interview with Ronald Joynes, 22 March 1989, IWM.

53 Ibid.

54 Ibid.

55 Interview with Michael Rowntree, 7 August 1989, IWM.

56 Letter from Tom Burns to Cathy Bunting, 10 November 1940, Private Papers of the Burns family.

57 Ibid.

58 Ibid.

59 Ibid.

60 Lidbetter, 1993. *Friends Ambulance Unit*, 65.

61 Interview with Ronald Joynes, 22 March 1989, IWM.

62 Ibid.

63 Lidbetter, 1993. *Friends Ambulance Unit*, 66.

64 Interview with Ronald Joynes, 22 March 1989, IWM.

65 Ibid.

66 Ibid.

67 Letter from Tom Burns to Cathy Bunting, 5 December 1940, Private Papers of the Burns family.

68 *FAU Chronicle*, 1940, FAUA, Friends House, London.

69 *Egyptian Newsletter* No. 13, 2 February 1942, FAU 1947/3/6/6, FAUA, Friends House, London.

70 Quentin Boyd, *China Convoy Newsletter* 38, 24 December 1942, FAUA, Friends House, London.

71 Letter from Tom Burns to Cathy Bunting, 1 January 1941, Private Papers of the Burns family.

72 Interview with Ronald Joynes, 22 March 1989, IWM.

73 Davies, 1947. *Friends Ambulance Unit*, 82.

74 Letter from Tom Burns to Cathy Bunting, 5 December 1940, Private Papers of the Burns family.

75 Tom Burns, 'The Lesson, April 26–29 1941 Greece', December 1943, 2, Private Papers of the Burns family.

76 Interview with Ronald Joynes, 22 March 1989, IWM.

77 Ibid.

78 Interview with John Wood, 8 July 1986, IWM.

79 *Egyptian Newsletter* No. 3, 24 November 1941; *Egyptian Newsletter* No. 6, 15 December 1941; *Middle East Newsletter* No. 28, 14 July 1942; *Middle East Newsletter*, No. 24, November 1941, FAU 1947/3/6/6, FAUA, Friends House, London.

80 Interview with Michael Rowntree, 7 August 1989, IWM.

81 Interview with Michael Cadbury, 27 November 1987, IWM.

82 *China Convoy Newsletter* 81, 30 October 1943, FAUA, Friends House, London.

83 Interview with Michael Rowntree, 7 August 1989, IWM.

84 Executive Committee Report Book 2, 23 November 1943, FAUA, Friends House, London.

85 Interview with John Wood, 8 July 1986, IWM.

86 Interview with Ronald Joynes, 22 March 1989, IWM.

Chapter 12: Home Front

1 Daniel Todman, 2017. *Britain's War: Into Battle, 1937–1941*. Penguin, 474.

2 Vera Brittain, 2005 [1941]. *England's Hour*. Continuum, 51.

3 Richard Overy, 2013. *The Bombing War: Europe, 1939–1945*. Penguin, 137.

4 Ibid., 148.

5 Todman, 2017. *Britain's War: Into Battle, 1937–1941*, 479.

6 Overy, 2013. *The Bombing War*, 149.

7 Ibid., 153.

8 Ibid., 152.

9 Jason Gurney, 1974. *Crusade in Spain*. Faber & Faber, 112.

10 Richard Overy, 2013. 'Pacifism and the Blitz', *Past and Present* 219(1): 201–36.

11 Winston Churchill, 1957. *The Second World War*, Vol. II: *Their Finest Hour*. Cassell, 567.

12 Vera Brittain, 1988. *Testament of a Peace Lover: Letters from Vera Brittain*, ed. Winifred and Alan Eden-Green. Virago.

13 Published in Britain as: Vera Brittain, 1944. *Seed of Chaos: What Mass Bombing Really Means*. New Vision Publishing; and in the US as: Vera Brittain, 1944. *Massacre by Bombing: The Facts behind the British–American Attack on Germany*. Fellowship.

14 Joan Beaumont, 2013. 'Starving for Democracy: Britain's Blockade of and Relief for Occupied Europe, 1939–1945', *War and Society* 8(2): 57–82, 58.

15 Vera Brittain, 2005 [1943]. 'Humiliation with Honour', in *One Voice*. Continuum, 52.

16 Todman, 2017. *Britain's War: Into Battle, 1937–1941*, 200.

17 Vera Brittain, 1957. *Testament of Experience: An Autobiographical Story of the Years 1925–1950*. Macmillan, 275.

18 George Orwell, 1944. 'As I Please', *Tribune*, 1 September 1944, 12.

19 Paul Berry and Mark Bostridge, 2001. *Vera Brittain: A Life*. Virago, 440.
20 Overy, 2013. *The Bombing War*, 609.
21 William Purcell, 1972. *Odd Man Out: A Biography of Lord Soper of Kingsway*. Mowbray, 84.
22 Interview with Sydney Greaves, 1985, IWM.
23 Ibid.
24 Ibid.
25 Ibid.
26 Interview with Doris Nicholls, 13 May 1980, IWM.
27 Interview with Stella St John, 7 August 1971, IWM.
28 Interview with Sydney Greaves, 1985, IWM.
29 Ibid.
30 Interview with Bernard Nicholls, 9 May 1980, IWM.
31 Interview with Stella St John, 7 August 1971, IWM; interview with John Emburton, 1985, IWM.
32 Interview with Doris Nicholls, 13 May 1980, IWM; 'The Hungerford Club', 12 July 2017, https://library.chethams.com/blog/the-hungerford-club/, last accessed 2 March 2021.
33 See, for example: Peter Redfield, 2013. *Life in Crisis: The Ethical Journey of Doctors without Borders*. University of California Press.
34 Interview with Doris Nicholls, 13 May 1980, IWM.
35 Ibid.
36 Interview with Bernard Nicholls, 9 May 1980, IWM.
37 Interview with Doris Nicholls, 13 May 1980, IWM.
38 Interview with Stella St John, 7 August 1971, IWM.
39 Ibid.
40 Interview with Doris Nicholls, 13 May 1980, IWM.
41 Interview with Bernard Nicholls, 9 May 1980, IWM.
42 Patrick Buxton, 1947. *The Louse: An Account of the Lice Which Infest Man, their Medical Importance and Control*. Edward Arnold.
43 Interview with Bernard Nicholls, 9 May 1980, IWM.
44 Interview with Sydney Greaves, 1985, IWM.
45 Interview with Doris Nicholls, 13 May 1980, IWM.
46 Overy, 2013. *The Bombing War*, 128.
47 Todman, 2017. *Britain's War: Into Battle, 1937–1941*, 453.
48 Ibid., 378.
49 A. Tegla Davies, 1947. *Friends Ambulance Unit: The Story of the FAU in the Second World War, 1939–1946*. George Allen & Unwin, 42, 46.
50 Berry and Bostridge, 2001. *Vera Brittain*, 389.
51 Brittain, 2005 [1943]. 'Humiliation with Honour', 65; Brittain, 1957. *Testament of Experience: An Autobiographical Story of the Years 1925–1950*, 273.
52 Pat Starkey, 2000. *Families and Social Workers: The Work of the Family Service Units, 1940–1985*. Liverpool University Press; L. E. White, 1946. *Tenement Town*. Jason Press.

53 Interview with Bernard Hicken, in *A Matter of Conscience*, BBC Radio 4, May 1992 (13166), IWM; Kenneth Malleny, 1945. *Human Guinea Pigs*. Gollancz; Research on scabies: proposed nutrition experiments, on conscientious objectors, Sheffield, FD 1/6673, 1941–1942, NA; Typhus: proposal by conscientious objectors to work as vaccine typhus subjects, FD 1/6627, 1941, NA.

54 Interview with Roy Ridgway, 14 July 1987, IWM.

55 Diary of Roy Ridgway, 16 April 1941, Papers of Roy Ridgway, IWM.

56 Ibid., 16 April 1941.

57 Ibid., 5 May 1941.

58 Interview with Roy Ridgway, 14 July 1987, IWM.

59 Diary of Roy Ridgway, 27 May 1941.

60 Stephen Verney, 2016. *Snakes and Ladders*. Verney Books, 42; Davies, 1947. *Friends Ambulance Unit*, 331.

61 Diary of Roy Ridgway, 25 June 1941.

62 Ibid., 12 June 1941.

63 Ibid., 13 June 1941.

64 Ibid., 2 September 1941.

65 Ibid., 28 August 1941.

66 Conscientious objectors: connection with air raids, HO 192/1298, 1942, NA; Conscientious Objectors Order to train with Civil Defence Service, 1939–1941, LAB 6/137, NA; PERSONNEL: Conscientious objectors: refusal to perform duties under National Services Acts involving civil defence, HO 186/2835, 1939–1945, NA.

67 Overy, 2013. *The Bombing War*, 129; Civil Defence publications, Papers of Peter Hunot, HUNOT 3/2, Bishopsgate Institute.

68 Denis Hayes, 1949. *Challenge of Conscience: The Story of the Conscientious Objectors, 1939–1949*. George Allen & Unwin, 190.

69 [No author], 1942. 'A Crisis in C.D. [Civil Defence]', *CBCO Bulletin*, April 1943, No. 38, 1.

70 Interview with Bernard Nicholls, 9 May 1980, IWM.

71 Ibid.

72 Ibid.

73 Ibid.

74 FIRE: Conscientious objectors: compulsory fire service duties, HO 186/821, 1941–1942, NA.

75 Diary of Roy Ridgway, 14 June 1941.

76 Hayes, 1949. *Challenge of Conscience*, 295.

77 *CBCO Bulletin*, December 1942, No. 34.

78 Fenner Brockway, 1943, 'Fire Watching and Conscience: A Claim for Recognition', *CBCO Bulletin*, June 1943, No. 40, 1.

79 Interview with William Elliot, 1983, IWM.

80 Interview with Stella St John, 7 August 1971, IWM.

81 Diary of Roy Ridgway, 10 April 1941.

82 Ibid., 5 July 1941.

83 Interview with Stella St John, 7 August 1971, IWM.

84 Angela Raby, 1999. *The Forgotten Service: Auxiliary Ambulance Station 39, Weymouth Mews*. Battle of Britain International, 28.
85 Ibid., 70.
86 Ibid.
87 Josephine Butler, 1991. *Cyanide in my Shoe*. This England Books.
88 Rose Macaulay, 1940. 'Notes on the Way', *Time & Tide*, 5 October 1940.
89 Letter to London Ambulance Service from Stella St John, 4 February 1942; letter to the London Ambulance Service from Stella St John, 27 April 1942, Papers of the Fellowship for Reconciliation, 19/1, LSE.

Chapter 13: Prisoners of Conscience

1 Lois Bibbings, 2010. *Telling Tales about Men: Conceptions of Conscientious Objectors to Military Service during the First World War*. University of Manchester Press.
2 Adam Hochschild, 2011. *To End All Wars: A Story of Protest and Patriotism in the First World War*. Picador, 190.
3 David Boulton, 1967. *Objection Overruled*. MacGibbon & Kee, 148, 152, 168.
4 Caroline Moorehead, 1987. *Troublesome People: Enemies of War, 1916–1986*. Hamish Hamilton, 10.
5 Peter Brock, 2016. *Against the Draft*. University of Toronto Press, 257–80.
6 Moorehead, 1987. *Troublesome People*, 70.
7 Repeated prosecutions of conscientious objectors: 'Cat and Mouse' pamphlet, LAB 6/414, 1942–1956, NA.
8 Denis Hayes, 1949. *Challenge of Conscience: The Story of the Conscientious Objectors, 1939–1949*. George Allen & Unwin, 111; CBCO, 1943. 'Hilton for Discharge at Last But Mining Conditions Imposed', *CBCO Bulletin*, December 1943, No. 46, 1.
9 CBCO, 1943. 'Two Years Detention for Hilton', *CBCO Bulletin*, August 1943, No. 42, 3.
10 Conscientious objectors. Complaint that the Croydon Justices are deliberately imposing sentences of less than 3 months' imprisonment, thus depriving persons of right of appeal to Appeal Tribunal under Sec. 5 of the National Service (No. 2) Act, 1941. Similar complaint against Salisbury City Magistrates, LCO 2/5315, 1943–1954, NA.
11 Stephen Thorne, 1942. 'Prosecution and Persecution: Bevin Affirms New "Medical" Policy', *CBCO Bulletin*, August 1942, No. 30, 1.
12 Jon Lindsay, 1942. 'I was in Detention Barracks', *CBCO Bulletin*, June 1942, No. 28, 3.
13 Hayes, 1949. *Challenge of Conscience*, 101.
14 Ibid., 389; Conscientious objectors: detention and medical examination, MEPO 3/2122, 1941, NA; War: Conscientious objectors who

refuse to undergo medical examination: power of courts to order detention; rights of appeal, HO 45/25558, 1940–1955, NA.

15 Diary of Roy Ridgway, 16 June 1941, Papers of Roy Ridgway, IWM.

16 Ibid., 19 May 1941.

17 Ibid., 8 August 1941.

18 Ibid., 8 October 1941.

19 Linsey Robb, 2018. 'The "Conchie Corps": Conflict, Compromise and Conscientious Objection in the British Army, 1940–1945', *Twentieth Century British History* 29(3): 411–34.

20 Hayes, 1949. *Challenge of Conscience*, 387.

21 Interview with Arthur Koestler, 30 November 1981, IWM.

22 Diary of Keith Vaughan, March 1941, Keith Vaughan Collection, Tate Library.

23 Ibid.

24 Interview with Roy Ridgway, 14 July 1987, IWM.

25 Diary of Roy Ridgway, 17 October 1941.

26 Ibid., 25 October 1941.

27 Ibid., 31 October 1941.

28 Interview with Roy Ridgway, 14 July 1987, IWM.

29 Ibid.

30 Diary of Roy Ridgway, 1 November 1941.

31 Letter from Edna Bailey to Mrs Ridgway, 19 November 1941, Papers of Roy Ridgway, IWM.

32 Diary of Roy Ridgway, 27 October 1941.

33 Ibid., 20 November 1941.

34 Ibid., 22 November 1941.

35 Interview with Roy Ridgway, 14 July 1987, IWM.

36 Diary of Roy Ridgway, 25 November 1941; letter from Roy Ridgway to Joy Ridgway, 7 November 1941, Papers of Roy Ridgway, IWM.

37 Letter from Roy Ridgway to Joy Ridgway, no date, Papers of Roy Ridgway, IWM.

38 Letter from Roy Ridgway to Joy Ridgway, 7 November 1941, Papers of Roy Ridgway, IWM.

39 Diary of Roy Ridgway, 9 December 1941.

40 Ibid., 11 December 1941.

41 Ibid., 15 December 1941.

42 Ibid., 16 December 1941.

43 Ibid., 16 January 1942.

44 Ibid., 25 February 1942.

45 Ibid., 27 February 1942.

46 E. E. Beavor, Statement in Support of Application, 31 May 1941, Papers of E. E. Beavor, IWM; CBCO, 1942. 'The "Medical" Mix-Up', *CBCO Bulletin*, September 1942, No. 21, 3.

47 Letter from Michael Tippett to Sir Adrian Boult, 21 April 1943, in Thomas Schuttenhelm (ed.), 2005. *Selected Letters of Michael Tippett*. Faber & Faber.

48 Letter from Michael Tippett to Francesca Allinson, 6 February 1942, in ibid.; Oliver Soden, 2019. *Michael Tippett: The Biography*. Weidenfeld & Nicolson, 259.

49 Norman MacCaig, 2009. 'Patriot', in *The Poems of Norman MacCaig*, ed. Ewen McCaig. Polygon.

50 Interview with Roy Ridgway, 14 July 1987, IWM.

51 Bernard Jacob, Application to Local Tribunal by a Person Provisionally Registered in the Register of Conscientious Objectors, 22 November 1940, personal collection of Ann Jacob.

52 Letter from Bernard Jacob to Judge Lawson Campbell, 5 March 1942, personal collection of Ann Jacob.

53 Letter from R. J. Porcas to Ministry of Labour and National Service, 3 June 1939, Papers of R. J. Porcas, IWM.

54 Letter from Roy Ridgway to Mother, 10 November 1941, Papers of Roy Ridgway, IWM.

55 Interview with Leonard Bird, 12 June 1981, IWM.

56 Interview with Sydney Greaves, 1985, IWM.

57 Kathleen Lonsdale, 1943. *Some Account of Life in Holloway Prison for Women*. Prison Medical Reform Council, Bradford Peace Pamphlets.

58 Interview with Dennis Waters, in *A Matter of Conscience*, BBC Radio 4, May 1992 (13195), IWM.

59 Ibid.

60 Hayes, 1949. *Challenge of Conscience*, 89.

61 Ibid., 81.

62 Interview with Frank Chadwick, in *A Matter of Conscience*.

63 Letter from John Radford to Miss Weaver, 27 September 1940, Papers of F. B. Breakspear, IWM.

64 Letter from John Radford to Dr Soper, 27 September 1940, Papers of F. B. Breakspear, IWM.

65 Letter from J. Radford to Dr Soper, 27 September 1940, Papers of F. B. Breakspear, IWM.

66 Alan Allport, 2015. *Browned Off and Bloody-Minded: The British Soldier Goes off to War*. Yale University Press, xxiii.

67 Fenner Brockway, 1941. 'Privilege for Conscience?', *CBCO Bulletin*, November 1941, No. 22, 4; Original completed questionnaires from prisoners [1943–1944], Howard League for Penal Reform Papers, MSS.16C/3/PC/3/1-109, University of Warwick Modern Records Centre.

68 'West London Police Court', *West London Observer*, 5 March 1943, p. 2.

69 Stella St John, 1944. *A Prisoner's Log*. Howard League for Penal Reform.

70 Letter from Stella St John to Ministry of Labour and National Service, 30 November 1942, Papers of the Fellowship of Reconciliation, LSE.

71 Note dated 10 June 1942, Papers of the Fellowship of Reconciliation, LSE.

72 Interview with Stella St John, 7 August 1971, IWM.

73 Letter from Bernard Nicholls to Stella St John, 23 March 1943, Papers of the Fellowship of Reconciliation, LSE.
74 Interview with Stella St John, 7 August 1971, IWM.
75 Letter from Stella St John to Doris Nicholls, 25 March 1943, Papers of the Fellowship of Reconciliation, LSE.
76 St John, 1944. *A Prisoner's Log*, 10.
77 Ibid., 11.
78 Ibid., 20.
79 Ibid., 21.
80 Ibid., 8.
81 Letter from Stella St John to Doris Nicholls, 10 March 1943, Papers of the Fellowship of Reconciliation, LSE.
82 Letter from George Price to Stella St John, 28 February 1943, Papers of the Fellowship of Reconciliation, LSE.
83 Letter from Stella St John to Doris Nicholls, 25 March 1943, Papers of the Fellowship of Reconciliation, LSE.
84 Ibid.
85 Letter from Doris Nicholls to Stella St John, no date, Papers of the Fellowship of Reconciliation, LSE.
86 Interview with Stella St John, 7 August 1971, IWM.
87 Rose Macaulay, 1956. *The Towers of Trebizond*. Collins.
88 Interview with Sydney Greaves, 1985, IWM.
89 Diary of F. B. Breakspear, 27 January 1942, Papers of F. B. Breakspear, IWM.
90 Vera Brittain, 2005 [1943]. 'Humiliation with Honour', in *One Voice*. Continuum, 68.
91 Interview with Reginald Bottini, 15 July 1980, IWM.
92 Letter from Michael Tippett to Francesca Allinson, 1942, in Schuttenhelm (ed.), 2005. *Selected Letters of Michael Tippett*, 96; Soden, 2019. *Michael Tippett*, 278.
93 Letter from Michael Tippett to Francesca Allinson, 1942, in Schuttenhelm (ed.), 2005. *Selected Letters of Michael Tippett*, 96.
94 Soden, 2019. *Michael Tippett*, 297.
95 Max Weber, 1946 [1919]. 'Politics as a Vocation', in *From Max Weber*, ed. and trans. H. H. Gerth and C. Wright Mills. Free Press.

Chapter 14: Stalag VIII-B

1 Postcard from Tom Burns to Cathy Bunting, 21 June 1941, Private Papers of the Burns family.
2 Clare Makepeace, 2017. *Captives of War: British Prisoners of War in Europe in the Second World War*. Cambridge University Press, 41; Juliet Pattinson, Lucy Noakes and Wendy Ugolini, 2014. 'Incarcerated Masculinities: Male POWs and the Second World War', *Journal of War and Culture Studies* 7(3): 179–90.

3 Tom Burns, 1943. 'A C.O. in Stalag VIIIB', *CBCO Bulletin*, 25 November 1943, No. 45, 1.
4 Makepeace, 2017. *Captives of War*, 33.
5 H. Martin Lidbetter, 1993. *Friends Ambulance Unit, 1939–1943: Experiences in Finland, Norway, Sweden, Egypt, Greece and Germany.* Sessions Book Trust, 81.
6 Ibid., 80.
7 Interview with John Fleetwood Stewart Phillips, 22 October 1980, IWM.
8 Ibid.
9 Letter from Tom Burns to Cathy Bunting, 13 October 1941, Private Papers of the Burns family.
10 Ibid., 29 March 1942.
11 'Stalag Recipes', *Clarion*, April 1944, 13.
12 Lidbetter, 1993. *Friends Ambulance Unit*, 86.
13 Burns, 1943. 'A C.O. in Stalag VIIIB', 1.
14 Letter from Tom Burns to Cathy Bunting, 1 December 1941, Private Papers of the Burns family.
15 Peter Brock, 1999. 'Conscientious Objectors in Nazi Germany', in *Challenge to Mars: Pacifisms from 1918 to 1945*, ed. Peter Brock and Thomas Socknat. University of Toronto Press; Peter Brock and Nigel Young, 1999. *Pacifism in the Twentieth Century*. University of Toronto Press, 206–7; Gordon C. Zahn, 1964. *In Solitary Witness: The Life and Death of Franz Jägerstätter*. Henry Holt.
16 Victoria J. Barnett, 2019. 'Bonhoeffer and the Conspiracy', in *Oxford Handbook of Dietrich Bonhoeffer*, ed. Philip G. Ziegler and Michael Mawson. Oxford University Press; Clifford Green, 2019. 'Bonhoeffer's Christian Peace Ethics, Conditional Pacifisms, and Resistance', in *Oxford Handbook of Dietrich Bonhoeffer*.
17 Eric Metaxas, 2010. *Bonhoeffer: Pastor, Martyr, Prophet, Spy*. Thomas Nelson, 468; Dietrich Bonhoeffer, 2003 [1937]. *Dietrich Bonhoeffer Works*, Vol. 4: *Discipleship*, ed. John D. Dodsey and Geffrey B. Kelly, trans. Martin Kuske and Ilse Tödt. Fortress Press; Dietrich Bonhoeffer, 2005 [1949]. *Dietrich Bonhoeffer Works*, Vol. 6: *Ethics*, ed. Clifford Green, trans. Reinhard Krauss, Douglas W. Stott and Charles C. West. Fortress Press.
18 Bonhoeffer, 2003 [1937]. *Dietrich Bonhoeffer Works*, Vol. 4: *Discipleship*.
19 Bonhoeffer, 2005 [1949]. *Dietrich Bonhoeffer Works*, Vol. 6: *Ethics*.
20 Letter from Tom Burns to Cathy Bunting, 13 October 1941; ibid., 28 December 1941, Private Papers of the Burns family.
21 Ibid., 14 February 1942.
22 Ibid., 30 October 1941.
23 Ibid., 14 November 1942.
24 Ibid., 22 September 1941.
25 Ibid., 20 January 1942.
26 Ibid., 14 February 1942.

27 Ibid., 20 January 1942.
28 Ibid., 22 May 1943.
29 Ibid., 8 March 1942.
30 Makepeace, 2017. *Captives of War*, 149.
31 Letter from Tom Burns to Cathy Bunting, 1 December 1941, Private Papers of the Burns family.
32 Ibid., 2 March 1942.
33 Ibid., 26 January 1942.
34 Ibid.
35 Ibid., 5 November 1941.
36 Ibid.
37 Ibid., 5 September 1941.
38 Ibid., 21 February 1942.
39 Ibid.
40 Ibid.
41 G. C. Field, 1945. *Pacifism and Conscientious Objection*. Cambridge University Press.
42 Letter from Tom Burns to Cathy Bunting, 21 February 1942, Private Papers of the Burns family.
43 Ibid.
44 Eric Dietrich-Berryman and Charlotte Hammond, 2010. *Passport Not Required: U.S. Volunteers in the Royal Navy, 1939–1941*. Naval Institute Press.
45 Letter from Tom Burns to Cathy Bunting, 21 February 1942, Private Papers of the Burns family.
46 Ibid.
47 Ibid.; ibid., 22 February 1942.
48 Ibid., 12 April 1942.
49 Ibid., 27 December 1942.
50 Ibid., 21 February 1942.
51 Burns, 1943. 'A C.O. in Stalag VIIIB', 1.
52 Interview with Stephen Hubert Peet, 30 October 1990, IWM.
53 Interview with Mervyn Taggart, 5 May 1980, IWM.
54 Interview with Roy Ridgway, 14 July 1987, IWM.
55 Interview with Michael Cadbury, 27 November 1987, IWM.
56 Interview with Michael Rowntree, 7 August 1989, IWM.
57 Lewis Maclachlan, 1942. 'The CO and the Second Front', *CBCO Bulletin*, June 1944, No. 52, 4.
58 Mark Freeman, 2010. 'Muscular Quakerism? The Society of Friends and Youth Organisations in Britain, *c.*1900–1950', *English Historical Review* 125(514): 642–69.
59 William James, 1906. 'The Moral Equivalent of War', speech given at Stanford University, available at https://www.laphamsquarterly.org/states-war/proposing-moral-equivalent-war, last accessed 2 March 2021.
60 Joseph Kip Kosek, 2009. *Acts of Conscience: Christian Nonviolence and Modern American Democracy*. Columbia University Press, 103.

61 Maria Misra, 2014. 'Sergeant-Major Gandhi: Indian Nationalism and Nonviolent "Martiality"', *Journal of Asian Studies* 73(3): 689–709.

62 Alan Allport, 2015. *Browned Off and Bloody-Minded: The British Soldier Goes off to War*. Yale University Press, 63.

63 Ibid., 95.

64 R. C. Wilson, 1949. *Authority, Leadership and Concern: A Study in Motive and Administration in Quaker Relief Work*. George Allen & Unwin, 9.

65 A. Tegla Davies, 1947. *Friends Ambulance Unit: The Story of the FAU in the Second World War, 1939–1946*. George Allen & Unwin.

66 Denis Hayes, 1949. *Challenge of Conscience: The Story of the Conscientious Objectors, 1939–1949*. George Allen & Unwin, 92.

67 Ibid., 234.

68 Yasmin Khan, 2015. *India at War: The Subcontinent and World War II*. Oxford University Press.

Chapter 15: Take Courage

1 Diary of Roy Ridgway, 14 March 1943, Papers of Roy Ridgway, IWM.

2 Ibid., 26 March 1943.

3 Ibid., 6 May 1943.

4 Interview with Roy Ridgway, 14 July 1987, IWM.

5 Diary of Roy Ridgway, 14 September 1942.

6 Ibid., 21 September 1942.

7 Ibid., 19 August 1942.

8 Bernard Llewellyn, 1953. *I Left my Roots in China*. George Allen & Unwin.

9 W. H. Auden and Christopher Isherwood, 1939. *Journey to a War*. Random House, 69. The literature on the China Convoy is extensive: Bill Brough, 1995. *To Reason Why* ... Hickory Tree Press; Susan Armstrong-Reid, 2017. *China Gadabouts: New Frontiers of Humanitarian Nursing, 1941–51*. UBC Press; David Morris, 1948. *China Changed my Mind*. Houghton Mifflin; John E. Simpson, 2001. *Letters from China: Quaker Relief Work in Bandit Country, 1944–1946*. Ross-Evans. For the FAU in Europe see: Grigor McClelland, 1997. *Embers of War: Letters from a Quaker Relief Worker in War-Torn Germany*. I. B. Tauris.

10 Llewellyn, 1953. *I Left my Roots in China*, 25.

11 Ibid., 36, 37.

12 Diary of Roy Ridgway, 16 April 1942.

13 Ibid., 4 November 1942.

14 Ibid., 1 October 1942.

15 Ibid., 24 October 1942.

16 Ibid., 14 December 1942.

17 *FAU Weekly Newsletters*, 30 December 1942, FAUA, Friends House, London.

18 Minutes of the Executive Committee 1940–1942, 31 August 1942, FAU 1947/2/2/4, FAUA, Friends House, London.

19 Diary of Roy Ridgway, 1 January 1943.

20 Ibid., 6 February 1943.

21 Mary Borden, 1946. *Journey Down a Blind Alley*. Hutchinson, 132.

22 Interview with Michael Rowntree, 7 August 1989, IWM.

23 Norman Ingram, 1991. *The Politics of Dissent: Pacifism in France, 1919–1939*. Oxford University Press, 6.

24 Interview with Michael Rowntree, 7 August 1989, IWM.

25 Diary of E. R. Harper, 21 February 1944, Papers of E. R. Harper, IWM; A. Tegla Davies, 1947. *Friends Ambulance Unit: The Story of the FAU in the Second World War, 1939–1946*. George Allen & Unwin, 119.

26 Interview with Michael Rowntree, 7 August 1989, IWM.

27 Edward Spears, 1977. *Fulfilment of a Mission*. Leo Cooper.

28 Laure Humbert, 2001. 'Gender, Humanitarianism and Soft Power', https://colonialandtransnationalintimacies.com/2021/03/05/gender-humanitarianism-and-soft-power/, last accessed 30 March 2021.

29 Davies, 1947. *Friends Ambulance Unit*, 109.

30 Ibid., 119; Borden, 1946. *Journey Down a Blind Alley*, 132.

31 Interview with Michael Rowntree, 7 August 1989, IWM.

32 Borden, 1946. *Journey Down a Blind Alley*, 129.

33 Najwa Al-Qattan, 2014. 'When Mothers Ate their Children: Wartime Memory and the Language of Food in Syria and Lebanon', *International Journal of Middle East Studies* 46(4): 719–36; Report from Hadfield-Spears Unit, *Middle East Newsletter*, 1 January 1942, FAUA, Friends House, London; J.S.G., 1946. 'The Work of the Spears Mobile Clinics in Syria and Lebanon 1941–1945', Syrian Clinics – Miscellaneous Reports, FAU 1947 3/5, FAUA, Friends House, London.

34 Borden, 1946. *Journey Down a Blind Alley*, 151.

35 Diary of Roy Ridgway, 13 May 1943.

36 Diary of E. R. Harper, 18 February 1942, Papers of E. R. Harper, IWM.

37 Davies, 1947. *Friends Ambulance Unit*, 118.

38 Interview with Michael Rowntree, 7 August 1989, IWM.

39 Borden, 1946. *Journey Down a Blind Alley*, 162.

40 Davies, 1947. *Friends Ambulance Unit*, 188.

41 Letter from Mary Borden to Mrs Alderson, 15 February 1942, Papers of Nik Alderson, FAUA, Friends House, London.

42 Daniel Todman, 2020. *Britain's War: 1942–1947*. Allen Lane, 82.

43 Ibid., 210.

44 Diary of E. R. Harper, 14 January 1943, Papers of E. R. Harper, IWM.

45 Diary of Roy Ridgway, 14 January 1944.

46 Ibid., 1 June 1943.

47 Ibid., 2 June 1943.

48 Ibid., 11 June 1943.

49 Ibid., 11 July 1943.

50 Interview with Roy Ridgway, 14 July 1987, IWM.

51 Quentin Boyd, *China Convoy Newsletter* 38, 24 December 1942, FAUA, Friends House, London.
52 Diary of Roy Ridgway, 13 June 1943.
53 Ibid., 18 June 1943.
54 Martin Ceadel, 1980. *Pacifism in Britain, 1914–1945: Defining a Faith*. Clarendon, 299.
55 Diary of Roy Ridgway, 18 June 1943.
56 Borden, 1946. *Journey Down a Blind Alley*, 202.
57 Diary of Roy Ridgway, 3 July 1943.
58 Stephen Verney, 2016. *Snakes and Ladders*. Verney Books, 20.
59 Ibid., 53.
60 Ibid., 54.
61 Morris, 1948. *China Changed my Mind*, 200.
62 Ibid., 199–200.
63 Ray Jenkins, 2009. *A Pacifist at War*. Arrow Books.
64 Letter from Stanley Macintosh to Duncan Wood, 13 February 1944, Temp Mss 876 Boxes FAU 9–10, FAUA, Friends House, London.
65 Hadley Laycock, *China Convoy Newsletter* 39, 9 January 1943, FAUA, Friends House, London.
66 Brough, 1995. *To Reason Why . . .* , 37.
67 Morris, 1948. *China Changed my Mind*, 130.
68 Davies, 1947. *Friends Ambulance Unit*, 367.
69 Patrick Mayhew (ed.), 1985. *One Family's War*. History Press; interview with Patrick Mayhew, 18 May 1992, IWM.
70 Interview with Patrick Mayhew, 18 May 1992, IWM.
71 Verney, 2016. *Snakes and Ladders*, 54; interview with Stephen Verney, 9 June 1987, IWM.
72 Alan Allport, 2015. *Browned Off and Bloody-Minded: The British Soldier Goes off to War*. Yale University Press, 63.
73 Todman, 2020. *Britain's War: 1942–1947*, 405.
74 Victor Gollancz, 1943. *Let my People Go: Some Practical Proposals for Dealing with Hitler's Massacre of the Jews and an Appeal to the British Public*. Victor Gollancz.
75 Diary of Roy Ridgway, 3 July 1943.
76 Ibid., 12 February 1944.
77 Diary of E. R. Harper, 27 April 1944, Papers of E. R. Harper, IWM.
78 Interview with John Miles, unknown date, IWM.
79 Allport, 2015. *Browned Off and Bloody-Minded*, 154–65.
80 Diary of Roy Ridgway, 5 May 1944.
81 Ibid., 6 May 1944.
82 Ibid.
83 Davies, 1947. *Friends Ambulance Unit*, 125.
84 Diary of Roy Ridgway, 1 June 1944.
85 Interview with Roy Ridgway, 14 July 1987, IWM.
86 Vera Brittain, 1944. *Seed of Chaos: What Mass Bombing Really Means*. New Vision Publishing.

87 Diary of E. R. Harper, 23 May 1944, Papers of E. R. Harper, IWM.
88 Interview with Roy Ridgway, 14 July 1987, IWM.
89 Diary of E. R. Harper, 31 May 1944, Papers of E. R. Harper, IWM.
90 Diary of Roy Ridgway, 2 June 1944.
91 Ibid., 4 June 1944.
92 Ibid.
93 Ibid., 26 June 1944.
94 Ibid., 19 May 1941.
95 Ibid., 25 January 1944.
96 Paul Fussell, 1975. *The Great War and Modern Memory*. Oxford University Press; Sonya Rose, 2003. *Which People's War? National Identity and Citizenship in Wartime Britain, 1939–1945*. Oxford University Press.
97 Todman, 2020. *Britain's War: 1942–1947*, 643–7.
98 Allport, 2015. *Browned Off and Bloody-Minded*, 277.
99 Lord Moran, 1945. *Anatomy of Courage*. Constable.
100 Interview with Roy Ridgway, 14 July 1987, IWM.
101 David French, 1998. 'Discipline and the Death Penalty in the British Army in the War against Germany during the Second World War', *Journal of Contemporary History* 33(4): 531–45.
102 Diary of Roy Ridgway, 4 June 1944.
103 Borden, 1946. *Journey Down a Blind Alley*, 132.
104 Diary of Roy Ridgway, 4 June 1944.
105 Interview with John Petts, 2 March 1987, IWM.
106 Interview with Michael Rowntree, 7 August 1989, IWM.
107 Diary of Roy Ridgway, 7 May 1945.
108 Ibid., 4 September 1944.
109 Interview with Roy Ridgway, 14 July 1987, IWM.
110 Diary of Roy Ridgway, 15 May 1945.
111 Ibid., 31 January 1945.
112 Interview with Roy Ridgway, 14 July 1987, IWM.

Chapter 16: After Lives

1 Lara Feigel, 2016. *The Bitter Taste of Victory: Life, Love and Art in the Ruins of the Reich*. Bloomsbury, 122.
2 Ronald Duncan, 1968. *How to Make Enemies*. Rupert Hart-Davis, 101.
3 Ibid.
4 Daniel Todman, 2020. *Britain's War: 1942–1947*. Allen Lane, 778.
5 Duncan, 1968. *How to Make Enemies*, 57.
6 *Mea Culpa*, 82, Ronald Duncan Archive, EUL MS 997/2/11/7, Special Collections, University of Exeter.
7 Duncan, 1968. *How to Make Enemies*, 104.
8 Ronald Duncan, 1950. *The Mongrel and Other Poems*. Faber & Faber, 87.
9 Duncan, 1968. *How to Make Enemies*, 304.
10 Ronald Duncan, 1977. *Obsessed*. Michael Joseph.

11 Interview with Stella St John, 7 August 1971, IWM.
12 Tom Burns, 1995. 'Introduction', *Description, Explanation and Understanding: Selected Writings, 1944–1980*. Edinburgh University Press.
13 Interview with Roy Ridgway, 14 July 1987, IWM.
14 Ibid.
15 Ibid.
16 Simon House, 'Roy Ridgway, Obituary', *Guardian*, 16 December 2000, https://www.theguardian.com/news/2000/dec/16/guardianobituaries2, last accessed 2 March 2021.
17 Jill Wallis, 1991. *Valiant for Peace: A History of the Fellowship of Reconciliation, 1914–1989*. Fellowship of Reconciliation, 231.
18 Paul Kildea, 2014. *Benjamin Britten: A Life in the Twentieth Century*. Penguin, 248.
19 Oliver Soden, 2019. *Michael Tippett: The Biography*. Weidenfeld & Nicolson, 371.
20 Juliette Pattinson, Arthur McIvor and Linsey Robb, 2016. *Men in Reserve: British Civilian Masculinities in the Second World War*. Manchester University Press.
21 F. A. Lea, 1959. *The Life of John Middleton Murry*. Methuen, 311; Mary Middleton Murry, 1959. *To Keep Faith*. Constable; Katherine Middleton Murry, 1986. *Beloved Quixote: The Unknown Life of John Middleton Murry*. Condor.
22 Mark Gilbert, 1992. 'Pacifist Attitudes to Nazi Germany, 1936–1945', *Journal of Contemporary History* 27(3): 493–511, 506; Lea, 1959. *The Life of John Middleton Murry*, 273.
23 Clifford Barnard, 2010. *Binding the Wounds of War: A Young Relief Worker's Letters Home, 1943–47*. Pronoun Press.
24 Kildea, 2014. *Benjamin Britten*, 254.
25 Ibid., 453.
26 Ronald Duncan, 1978. *Auschwitz*. Rebel Press.
27 Interview with Roy Ridgway, 14 July 1987, IWM.
28 The Nobel Peace Prize for 1985, https://www.nobelprize.org/prizes/peace/1985/press-release, last accessed 2 March 2021.
29 United Nations, 1945. Charter of the United Nations, 24 October 1945, https://www.un.org/en/charter-united-nations/, last accessed 2 March 2021.
30 UN General Assembly, Universal Declaration of Human Rights, 10 December 1948, https://www.un.org/en/universal-declaration-human-rights/, last accessed 2 March 2021.
31 Peter Brock and Nigel Young, 1999. *Pacifism in the Twentieth Century*. University of Toronto Press; Charles Moskos, 1993. *The New Conscientious Objection: From Sacred to Secular Resistance*. Oxford University Press.
32 Malcolm Evans, 1997. *Religious Liberty and International Law in Europe*. Cambridge University Press; Edy Kaufman, 1991. 'Prisoners of Conscience: The Shaping of a New Human Rights Concept', *Human*

Rights Quarterly 13(3): 339–67; Jeremy Kessler, 2013. 'The Invention of a Human Right: Conscientious Objection at the United Nations, 1947–2011', *Columbia Human Rights Law Review* 44(3): 753–92.

33 *United States* v. *Seeger*, 380 U.S. 163 (1965), Supreme Court of the United States.

34 Michael Foley, 2003. *Confronting the War Machine: Draft Resistance during the Vietnam War*. University of North Carolina Press; James W. Tollefson, 2000. *The Strength Not to Fight: Conscientious Objectors of the Vietnam War*. Brassey's.

35 Caroline Moorhead, 1987. *Troublesome People: Enemies of War, 1916–1986*. Hamish Hamilton; Richard Taylor and Colin Prichard, 1980. *The Protest Makers: The British Nuclear Disarmament Movement of 1958–1965*. Pergamon Press.

36 Interview with Donald Soper, 1 September 1992, IWM; interview with Stella St John, 7 August 1971, IWM.

37 See, for example: Paul Eddington, 1995. *So Far, So Good: His Autobiography*. Coronet; James McGonigal, 2010. *Beyond the Last Dragon: A Life of Edwin Morgan*. Sandstone Press; Marjory McNeill, 1996. *Norman MacCaig: A Study of his Life and Work*. Mercat Press; Oliver Postgate, 2009. *Seeing Things: A Memoir*. Canongate.

38 Interview with Joyce Baker, Amnesty International Origins: Oral History Project, Amnesty International Secretariat Archives (AI) (AI 980), Institute of International Social History, Amsterdam; interview with Peter Benenson, AI (AI 982); Tobias Kelly, 2018. 'A Divided Conscience: The Lost Convictions of Human Rights', *Public Culture* 30(3): 367–92;

39 3rd International Assembly, 26–27 September 1964, Canterbury, Great Britain, AI (AI 5); interview with Peter Benenson, AI (AI 982).

40 Joseph Kip Kosek, 2009. *Acts of Conscience: Christian Nonviolence and Modern American Democracy*. Columbia University Press.

41 Ibid.; Greg Moses, 1997. *Revolution of Conscience: Martin Luther King, Jr., and the Philosophy of Nonviolence*. The Guildford Press.

42 Maggie Black, 1992. *A Cause for our Times: Oxfam, the First Fifty Years*. Oxfam; Ben Whitaker, 1983. *A Bridge of People: A Personal View of Oxfam's First Forty Years*. Heinemann; See also: Help in Hard Times: A Conversation between Sir Leslie Kirkley and Malcolm Harper, 29 June 1982, MS. Oxfam COM/5/4/75, Oxfam Papers, Bodleian, Oxford University; Minutes of meetings of the Oxford Committee for Famine Relief and related papers, October 1942–November 1948 and n.d., MS. Oxfam GOV/1/1/1, Oxfam Papers, Bodleian, Oxford University.

43 Maggie Black, 'Bernard Llewellyn, Obituary', *Guardian*, 24 June 2008, https://www.theguardian.com/theguardian/2008/jun/24/1, last accessed 2 March 2021.

44 Interview with Michael Rowntree, 7 August 1989, IWM.

45 Kelly, 2018. 'A Divided Conscience: The Lost Convictions of Human Rights'.

46 Jocelyn Maclure and Charles Taylor, 2012. *Secularism and Freedom of Conscience*. Harvard University Press; Martha Nussbaum, 2008. *Liberty of Conscience: In Defence of America's Tradition of Religious Equality*. Basic Books.
47 Nehal Bhuta, 2014. 'Two Concepts of Religious Freedom in the European Court of Human Rights', *South Atlantic Quarterly* 113(1): 9–35; Samuel Moyn, 2014. 'From Communist to Muslim: European Human Rights, the Cold War, and Religious Liberty', *South Atlantic Quarterly* 113(1): 63–86.
48 Hannah Arendt, 2003. *Responsibility and Judgment*, ed. Jerome Kohn. Schocken; Michael Rothberg, 2019. *The Implicated Subject: Beyond Victims and Perpetrators*. Stanford University Press.

INDEX